CAPITAL ALLOWANCES ACT 2001 (UK)

Updated as of March 26, 2018

THE LAW LIBRARY

TABLE OF CONTENTS

Introductory Text   4

Part 1. Introduction   4

No double relief through pooling under Part 2. (plant and machinery allowances)   10

Part 2. Plant and machinery allowances   10

Application of Part to thermal insulation, safety measures, etc.   150

Part 3. Industrial buildings allowances   151

Part of expenditure within time limit for qualifying enterprise zone expenditure 179

Part 3A Business Premises Renovation Allowances   181

Part 4. Agricultural buildings allowances   190

Part 4A FLAT CONVERSION ALLOWANCES   200

Part 5. Mineral extraction allowances   209

Part 6. Research and development allowances   225

Part 7. Know-how allowances   231

Part 8. Patent allowances   234

Part 9. Dredging allowances   239

Part 10. Assured tenancy allowances   242

Part 11. Contributions   253

Contribution allowances under Part 9   256

Contribution allowances under Part 9   256

Part 12. Supplementary provisions   257

Schedules   274

Schedule 1. Abbreviations and defined expressions   274

Schedule 2. Consequential amendments   279

Schedule 3. Transitionals and savings   310

Schedule 4. Repeals   333

Open Government Licence v3.0   336

Introductory Text

Capital Allowances Act 2001

2001 CHAPTER 2

An Act to restate, with minor changes, certain enactments relating to capital allowances.
22nd March 2001
Be it enacted by the Queen's most Excellent Majesty, by and with the advice and consent of the Lords Spiritual and Temporal, and Commons, in this present Parliament assembled, and by the authority of the same, as follows:—Be it enacted by the Queen's most Excellent Majesty, by and with the advice and consent of the Lords Spiritual and Temporal, and Commons, in this present Parliament assembled, and by the authority of the same, as follows:—Be it enacted by the Queen's most Excellent Majesty, by and with the advice and consent of the Lords Spiritual and Temporal, and Commons, in this present Parliament assembled, and by the authority of the same, as follows:—Be it enacted by the Queen's most Excellent Majesty, by and with the advice and consent of the Lords Spiritual and Temporal, and Commons, in this present Parliament assembled, and by the authority of the same, as follows:—Be it enacted by the Queen's most Excellent Majesty, by and with the advice and consent of the Lords Spiritual and Temporal, and Commons, in this present Parliament assembled, and by the authority of the same, as follows:—Be it enacted by the Queen's most Excellent Majesty, by and with the advice and consent of the Lords Spiritual and Temporal, and Commons, in this present Parliament assembled, and by the authority of the same, as follows:—Be it enacted by the Queen's most Excellent Majesty, by and with the advice and consent of the Lords Spiritual and Temporal, and Commons, in this present Parliament assembled, and by the authority of the same, as follows:—Be it enacted by the Queen's most Excellent Majesty, by and with the advice and consent of the Lords Spiritual and Temporal, and Commons, in this present Parliament assembled, and by the authority of the same, as follows:—
Modifications etc. (not altering text)
C1. Act construed as one with Capital Allowances Act 2001 (c. 2) (5.10.2004) by Energy Act 2004 (c. 20), s. 198. (2), Sch. 9 para. 37. (4) (with s. 38. (2)); S.I. 2004/2575, art. 2. (1), Sch. 1
C2. Act applied (5.10.2004) by Energy Act 2004 (c. 20), s. 198. (2), Sch. 9 para. 7 (with s. 38. (2)); S.I. 2004/2575, art. 2. (1), Sch. 1
C3. Act 2005 c. 14, Sch. 10 construed as one with 2001 c. 2 (E.W.S.) (8.6.2005 for specified purposes, 24.7.2005 in so far as not already in force) by Railways Act 2005 (c. 14), s. 60. (2), Sch. 10 para. 34. (3); S.I. 2005/1444, art. 2. (1), Sch. 1; S.I. 2005/1909, art. 2, Sch.
C4. Act modified (E.W.S.) (8.6.2005) by Railways Act 2005 (c. 14), s. 60. (2), Sch. 10 paras. 12-14; S.I. 2005/1444, art. 2. (1), Sch. 1
C5. Act modified by SI 2006/964 reg. 69. V(6)(7) (as inserted (6.4.2008) by The Authorised Investment Funds (Tax) (Amendment) Regulations 2008 (S.I. 2008/705), regs. 1, 5)
C6. Act modified by SI 2006/964 reg. 69. Z41. (5)(6) (as inserted (6.4.2008) by The Authorised Investment Funds (Tax) (Amendment) Regulations 2008 (S.I. 2008/705), regs. 1, 5)

Part 1. Introduction

Part 1. Introduction

Chapter 1. Capital allowances: general

1 Capital allowances

(1) This Act provides for allowances in respect of capital expenditure (and for charges in connection with those allowances).
(2) The allowances for which this Act provides are those under—
    (a) Part 2 (plant and machinery allowances);
    (b) Part 3 (industrial buildings allowances);
    [F1. (ba)Part 3. A (business premises renovation allowances)]
    (c) Part 4 (agricultural buildings allowances);
    [F2. (ca)Part 4. A (flat conversion allowances);]
    (d) Part 5 (mineral extraction allowances);
    (e) Part 6 (research and development allowances);
    (f) Part 7 (know-how allowances);
    (g) Part 8 (patent allowances);
    (h) Part 9 (dredging allowances);
    (i) Part 10 (assured tenancy allowances).
(3) This Act also provides for allowances in respect of contributions to expenditure incurred on plant or machinery, industrial buildings or agricultural buildings, for the purposes of a mineral extraction trade or on dredging (see Part 11).
Amendments (Textual)
F1. S. 1. (2)(ba) inserted (with effect in accordance with s. 92 of the amending Act) by Finance Act 2005 (c. 7), Sch. 6 para. 2; S.I. 2007/949, art. 2
F2. S. 1. (2)(ca) inserted (with effect as mentioned in s. 67 of the amending Act) by Finance Act 2001 (c. 9), s. 67, Sch. 19 Pt. 2 para. 1

2 General means of giving effect to capital allowances

(1) Allowances and charges are to be given effect—
    (a) for income tax purposes, in calculating income for a chargeable period, and
    (b) for corporation tax purposes, in calculating profits for a chargeable period.
(2) For the meaning of "chargeable period", see section 6.
(3) Subsection (1) needs to be read with the following provisions about giving effect to allowances and charges—
sections 247 to 262 (plant and machinery allowances);
sections 352 to 355 (industrial buildings allowances);
[F3sections 360. Z and 360. Z1 (business premises renovation allowances)]
sections 391 and 392 (agricultural buildings allowances);
[F4section 393. T (flat conversion allowances);]
section 432 (mineral extraction allowances);
section 450 (research and development allowances);
section 463 (know-how allowances);
sections 478 to 480 (patent allowances);
section 489 (dredging allowances);
section 529 (assured tenancy allowances).

(4) In subsection (1)(b) "profits" has the same meaning as in section 6 of ICTA.

Amendments (Textual)

F3. Words in s. 2. (3) inserted (with effect in accordance with s. 92 of the amending Act) by Finance Act 2005 (c. 7), Sch. 6 para. 3; S.I. 2007/949, art. 2

F4. S. 2. (3): entry inserted (with effect as mentioned in s. 67 of the amending Act) by Finance Act 2001. (c. 9), s. 67, Sch. 19 Pt. 2 para. 2

3 Claims for capital allowances

(1) No allowance is to be made under this Act unless a claim for it is made.

(2) The claim must be included in a tax return.

[F5. (2. A)Any claim for an allowance under Part 3. A (business premises renovation allowances) must be separately identified as such in the return.]

(3) In this Act "tax return" means—

    (a) for income tax purposes, a return required to be made under TMA 1970, and

    (b) for corporation tax purposes, a company tax return required to be made under Schedule 18 to FA 1998 (company tax returns, assessments and related matters).

(4) Subsection (2) does not apply for income tax purposes to a claim for an allowance under—

    (a) section 258 (claim for allowance in respect of special leasing of plant or machinery),

    (b) section 355 (claim to carry back balance of allowance in respect of buildings for miners etc.), or

    (c) section 479 (claim for patent allowance in respect of non-trading expenditure),

which is instead subject to section 42 of TMA 1970 (procedure for making claims and claims not included in returns).

(5) Subsection (2) does not apply for corporation tax purposes to a claim for an allowance under—

    (a) section 260. (3)(b) (claim to carry back allowance in respect of special leasing of plant or machinery), or

    (b) section 355 (claim to carry back balance of allowance in respect of buildings for miners etc.),

which is instead subject to paragraphs 54 to 60 of Schedule 18 to FA 1998 (general provisions as to claims).

(6) This section is subject to section 42. (6) and (7) of TMA 1970 (special provisions relating to partnerships).

Amendments (Textual)

F5. S. 3. (2. A) inserted (with effect in accordance with s. 92 of the amending Act) by Finance Act 2005 (c. 7), Sch. 6 para. 4; S.I. 2007/949, art. 2

Modifications etc. (not altering text)

C1. S. 3. (1) excluded (19.7.2006) by Finance Act 2006 (c. 25), s. 120. (7)

C2. S. 3. (1) excluded by SI 2006/964 reg. 69. Z1. (8) (as inserted (6.4.2008) by The Authorised Investment Funds (Tax) (Amendment) Regulations 2008 (S.I. 2008/705), regs. 1, 5)

4 Capital expenditure

(1) In this Act "capital expenditure" and "capital sums" are used in the sense given in this section.

(2) "Capital expenditure" and "capital sums" do not include, in relation to a person incurring the expenditure or paying the sums—

    (a) any expenditure or sum that may be deducted in calculating the profits or gains of a trade, profession or vocation or property business carried on by the person, or

    [F6. (b)any expenditure or sum that may be allowed as a deduction under a relevant provision from the taxable earnings from an employment or office held by the person.]

[F7. (2. A)In subsection (2)—

"relevant provision" means any of the following—

6

(a) section 262;

(b) section 232 of ITEPA 2003 (giving effect to mileage allowance relief);

(c) Chapters 2 to 6 of Part 5 of that Act (general deductions allowed from earnings); and

[F8. (d) sections 188 to 194of FA 2004 (contributions under registered pension schemes), and]

"taxable earnings" has the meaning given by section 10 of ITEPA 2003.]

(3) "Capital expenditure" and "capital sums" do not include, in relation to a recipient of the expenditure or sums—

(a) any amounts that are to be added in calculating the profits or gains of a trade, profession or vocation or property business carried on by the recipient, or

(b) any amounts that are [F9earnings] of an employment or office held by the recipient.

(4) "Capital expenditure" and "capital sums" do not include, in relation to—

(a) a person incurring the expenditure or paying the sums, or

(b) a recipient of the expenditure or sums,

any expenditure or sum in the case of which a deduction of income tax falls or may fall to be made under [F10. Chapter 6 of Part 15 of ITA 2007 (deduction from annual payments or patent royalties) or under section 906 of that Act (certain royalties etc where usual place of abode of owner is abroad)].

F11. (5). . . . .

Amendments (Textual)

F6. S. 4. (2)(b) substituted (with effect in accordance with s. 723. (1)(a)(b) of the amending Act) by Income Tax (Earnings and Pensions) Act 2003 (c. 1), s. 723, Sch. 6 para. 247. (2) (with Sch. 7)

F7. S. 4. (2. A) inserted (with effect in accordance with s. 723. (1)(a)(b) of the amending Act) by Income Tax (Earnings and Pensions) Act 2003 (c. 1), s. 723, Sch. 6 para. 247. (3) (with Sch. 7)

F8. Words in s. 4. (2. A) substituted (6.4.2006) by Finance Act 2004 (c. 12), s. 284. (1), Sch. 35 para. 48 (with Sch. 36)

F9. Word in s. 4. (3) substituted (with effect in accordance with s. 723. (1)(a)(b) of the amending Act) by Income Tax (Earnings and Pensions) Act 2003 (c. 1), s. 723, Sch. 6 para. 247. (4) (with Sch. 7)

F10. Words in s. 4. (4) substituted (6.4.2007) by Income Tax Act 2007 (c. 3), s. 1034. (1), Sch. 1 para. 397. (2) (with Sch. 2)

F11. S. 4. (5) repealed (6.4.2007) by Income Tax Act 2007 (c. 3), s. 1034. (1), Sch. 1 para. 397. (3), Sch. 3 Pt. 1 (with Sch. 2)

Modifications etc. (not altering text)

C3. S. 4 applied (with effect in accordance with s. 883. (1) of the amending Act) by Income Tax (Trading and Other Income) Act 2005 (c. 5), ss. 608, (with Sch. 2)

C4. S. 4 applied by 1988 c. 1, s. 349. ZA(5) (as inserted (with effect in accordance with s. 883. (1) of the amending Act) by Income Tax (Trading and Other Income) Act 2005 (c. 5), Sch. 1 para. 149 (with Sch. 2))

C5. S. 4 applied (6.4.2007) by Income Tax Act 2007 (c. 3), ss. 910. (5), 1034. (1) (with Sch. 2)

5 When capital expenditure is incurred

(1) For the purposes of this Act, the general rule is that an amount of capital expenditure is to be treated as incurred as soon as there is an unconditional obligation to pay it.

(2) The general rule applies even if the whole or a part of the expenditure is not required to be paid until a later date.

(3) There are the following exceptions to the general rule.

(4) If under an agreement—

(a) the capital expenditure is expenditure on the provision of an asset,

(b) an unconditional obligation to pay an amount of the expenditure comes into being as a result of the giving of a certificate or any other event,

(c) the giving of the certificate, or other event, occurs within the period of one month after the end of a chargeable period, and

(d) at or before the end of that chargeable period, the asset has become the property of, or is otherwise under the agreement attributed to, the person subject to the unconditional obligation to pay,

the expenditure is to be treated as incurred immediately before the end of that chargeable period.

(5) If under an agreement an amount of capital expenditure is not required to be paid until a date more than 4 months after the unconditional obligation to pay has come into being, the amount is to be treated as incurred on that date.

(6) If under an agreement—

(a) there is an unconditional obligation to pay an amount of capital expenditure on a date earlier than accords with normal commercial usage, and

(b) the sole or main benefit which might have been expected to be obtained thereby is that the amount would be treated, under the general rule, as incurred in an earlier chargeable period,

the amount is to be treated as incurred on the date on or before which it is required to be paid.

(7) This section—

(a) is subject to any provision of this Act which has the effect that expenditure is to be treated as incurred on a date later than would result from the application of this section, and

(b) does not apply to expenditure treated as incurred as a result of a person incurring an additional VAT liability.

Modifications etc. (not altering text)

C6 S. 5. (1)-(5) applied (with modifications) by 1998 c. 48, s. 42. (8. B) (as inserted (2.12.2004 retrospective) by Finance Act 2005 (c. 7) , Sch. 3 para. 9. (4) (5) (with Sch. 3 para. 9. (6) (8) (9)))

6 Meaning of "chargeable period"

(1) In this Act "chargeable period" means—

(a) for income tax purposes, a period of account, or

(b) for corporation tax purposes, an accounting period of a company.

(2) "Period of account" means—

(a) in the case of a person entitled to an allowance or liable to a charge in calculating the profits of his trade, profession or vocation, a period for which accounts are drawn up for the purposes of the trade, profession or vocation, and

(b) in the case of any other person entitled to an allowance or liable to a charge, a tax year.

(3) Subsection (2)(a) is subject to subsections (4) to (6).

(4) If—

(a) two periods of account overlap, or

(b) one period of account includes another,

the period common to both is to be treated as part of the first period of account only.

(5) If there is a gap between two periods of account, the gap is to be treated as part of the first period of account.

(6) If a period of account would (apart from this subsection) be longer than 18 months, that period must be treated as divided into separate periods of account—

(a) the first beginning with the start date of the original period, and

(b) each subsequent one beginning with an anniversary of that date,

so as to ensure that none of the periods of account is longer than 12 months.

Chapter 2. Exclusion of double relief

7 No double allowances

(1) If an allowance is made under any Part of this Act to a person in respect of capital expenditure, no allowance is to be made to him under any other Part in respect of—
  (a) that expenditure, or
  (b) the provision of any asset to which that expenditure related.
(2) This section does not apply in relation to Parts 7 and 8 (know-how and patent allowances).

8 No double relief through pooling under Part 2 (plant and machinery allowances)

(1) Subsection (2) applies if, under Part 2—
  (a) any capital expenditure has been allocated to a pool, and
  (b) an allowance or charge has been made to or on any person in respect of the pool.
(2) The person to or on whom the allowance or charge has been made is not entitled to an allowance under any Part other than Part 2 in respect of—
  (a) the expenditure allocated to the pool, or
  (b) the provision of any asset to which the allocated expenditure related.
(3) Subsection (4) applies if under any Part other than Part 2 an allowance has been made to a person in respect of any capital expenditure.
(4) The person to whom the allowance has been made is not entitled to allocate to any pool—
  (a) that expenditure, or
  (b) any expenditure on the provision of any asset to which the expenditure mentioned in paragraph (a) related.
(5) This section does not apply in relation to Parts 7 and 8 (know-how and patent allowances).

9 Interaction between fixtures claims and other claims

(1) A person is not entitled to make a fixtures claim in respect of any capital expenditure relating to an asset if—
  (a) any person entitled to do so has at any previous time claimed an allowance under any Part other than Part 2, and
  (b) the claim was for an allowance in respect of capital expenditure relating, in whole or part, to the asset.
(2) Subsection (1) does not prevent a person making a fixtures claim in respect of capital expenditure if—
  (a) the only previous claim was under Part 3 or 6 (industrial buildings and research and development allowances), and
  (b) section 186. (2) or 187. (2) (limit on amount of expenditure that may be taken into account) applies to that expenditure.
(3) If a person entitled to do so has made a fixtures claim in respect of capital expenditure relating to an asset, no one is entitled to an allowance on a later claim under any Part other than Part 2 in respect of any capital expenditure relating to the asset.
(4) A person makes a fixtures claim in respect of expenditure if he makes a claim (in the sense given in section 202. (3)) under Chapter 14 of Part 2 in respect of the expenditure as expenditure on the provision of a fixture.

10 Interpretation

(1) In this Chapter "capital expenditure" includes any contribution to capital expenditure.
(2) For the purposes of this Chapter—
  (a) expenditure relates to an asset only if it relates to its provision, and
  (b) the provision of an asset includes its construction or acquisition.

No double relief through pooling under Part 2. (plant and machinery allowances)

8 No double relief through pooling under Part 2 (plant and machinery allowances)

(1) Subsection (2) applies if, under Part 2—
    (a) any capital expenditure has been allocated to a pool, and
    (b) an allowance or charge has been made to or on any person in respect of the pool.
(2) The person to or on whom the allowance or charge has been made is not entitled to an allowance under any Part other than Part 2 in respect of—
    (a) the expenditure allocated to the pool, or
    (b) the provision of any asset to which the allocated expenditure related.
(3) Subsection (4) applies if under any Part other than Part 2 an allowance has been made to a person in respect of any capital expenditure.
(4) The person to whom the allowance has been made is not entitled to allocate to any pool—
    (a) that expenditure, or
    (b) any expenditure on the provision of any asset to which the expenditure mentioned in paragraph (a) related.
(5) This section does not apply in relation to Parts 7 and 8 (know-how and patent allowances).

Part 2. Plant and machinery allowances

Part 2. Plant and machinery allowances

Modifications etc. (not altering text)
C2. Pt. 2 modified (24.2.2003) by Proceeds of Crime Act 2002 (c. 29), s. 458. (1), Sch. 10 para. 12 (with Sch. 10 para. 17. (1)); S.I. 2003/120, art. 2, Sch. (with arts. 3 4) (as amended (20.2.2003) by S.I. 2003/333, art. 14)
C3 Pt. 2 restricted (5.10.2004) by Energy Act 2004 (c. 20) , s. 198. (2) , Sch. 9 paras. 10, 22 (with s. 38. (2)); S.I. 2004/2575 , art. 2. (1) , Sch. 1
C4 Pt. 2 modified (5.10.2004) by Energy Act 2004 (c. 20) , s. 198. (2) , Sch. 9 paras. 9. (2), 21. (2) (with s. 38. (2)); S.I. 2004/2575, art. 2. (1) , Sch. 1
C5 Pt. 2 restricted (5.10.2004) by Energy Act 2004 (c. 20) , s. 198. (2) , Sch. 4 para. 4 ; S.I. 2004/2575 , art. 2. (1) , Sch. 1

Chapter 1. Introduction

11 General conditions as to availability of plant and machinery allowances

(1) Allowances are available under this Part if a person carries on a qualifying activity and incurs qualifying expenditure.
(2) "Qualifying activity" has the meaning given by Chapter 2.

(3) Allowances under this Part must be calculated separately for each qualifying activity which a person carries on.

(4) The general rule is that expenditure is qualifying expenditure if—

(a) it is capital expenditure on the provision of plant or machinery wholly or partly for the purposes of the qualifying activity carried on by the person incurring the expenditure, and

(b) the person incurring the expenditure owns the plant or machinery as a result of incurring it.

(5) But the general rule is affected by other provisions of this Act, and in particular by Chapter 3.

12 Expenditure incurred before qualifying activity carried on

For the purposes of this Part, expenditure incurred for the purposes of a qualifying activity by a person about to carry on the activity is to be treated as if it had been incurred by him on the first day on which he carries on the activity.

13 Use for qualifying activity of plant or machinery provided for other purposes

(1) This section applies if a person—

(a) brings plant or machinery into use for the purposes of a qualifying activity carried on by him, and

(b) on the date when he does so, owns the plant or machinery as a result of having incurred capital expenditure ("actual expenditure") on its provision for purposes other than those of that qualifying activity.

(2) The person is to be treated—

(a) as having incurred capital expenditure ("notional expenditure") on the provision of the plant or machinery for the purposes of the qualifying activity on the date on which it is brought into use for those purposes, and

(b) as owning the plant or machinery as a result as having incurred that expenditure.

(3) Subject to subsection (4), the amount of the notional expenditure is the market value of the plant or machinery on the date when it is brought into use for the purposes of the qualifying activity.

(4) If the market value is greater than the actual expenditure, the amount of the notional expenditure is the amount of the actual expenditure, less any amount required to be deducted under subsection (5).

(5) The amount to be deducted is any amount that under section 218 or 224 would have been left out of account in determining the person's available qualifying expenditure if the actual expenditure had been incurred on the provision of the plant or machinery for the purposes of the qualifying activity.

(6) The question whether the provision of the plant or machinery is to be treated as wholly or only partly for the purposes of the qualifying activity is to be determined according to whether the use referred to in subsection (1)(a) is wholly or only partly for those purposes.

(7) This section is subject to section 161 (pre-trading expenditure on mineral exploration and access).

Modifications etc. (not altering text)

C6. S. 13 applied (with effect in accordance with s. 883. (1) of the amending Act) by Income Tax (Trading and Other Income) Act 2005 (c. 5), ss. 827, (with s. 828. (2), Sch. 2)

[F113. AUse for other purposes of plant or machinery previously used for long funding leasing

(1) This section applies if a person who has been using plant or machinery for the purpose of

leasing it under a long funding lease (see Chapter 6. A)—

(a) ceases to use the plant or machinery for that purpose without ceasing to use it for the purposes of a qualifying activity carried on by him, and

(b) on the date of the cessation, owns the plant or machinery as a result of having incurred capital expenditure on its provision for the purposes of the qualifying activity.

(2) The person is to be treated—

(a) as having incurred capital expenditure ("notional expenditure") on the provision of the plant or machinery for the purposes of the qualifying activity on the day after the cessation,

(b) as owning the plant or machinery as a result of having incurred that expenditure, and

(c) as if the plant or machinery on and after that day were different plant or machinery from the plant or machinery before that day.

(3) The amount of the notional expenditure is an amount equal to the termination amount, determined in accordance with section 70. YG, in the case of the long funding lease under which the plant or machinery was last leased before the cessation.]

Amendments (Textual)

F1. S. 13. A inserted (with effect in accordance with Sch. 8 para. 15 of the amending Act) by Finance Act 2006 (c. 25), Sch. 8 para. 2

14 Use for qualifying activity of plant or machinery which is a gift

(1) This section applies if a person—

(a) is the owner of plant or machinery as a result of a gift, and

(b) brings the plant or machinery into use for the purposes of a qualifying activity carried on by him.

(2) The person is to be treated—

(a) as having incurred capital expenditure on the provision of the plant or machinery for the purposes of the qualifying activity on the date on which it is brought into use for those purposes, and

(b) as owning the plant or machinery as a result of having incurred that expenditure.

(3) The amount of that capital expenditure is to be treated as being the market value of the plant or machinery on the date when it was brought into use for the purposes of the qualifying activity.

(4) The question whether the provision of the plant or machinery is to be treated as wholly or only partly for the purposes of the qualifying activity is to be determined according to whether the use referred to in subsection (1)(b) is wholly or only partly for those purposes.

(5) This section is subject to section 161 (pre-trading expenditure on mineral exploration and access).

Chapter 2. Qualifying activities

15 Qualifying activities

(1) Each of the following is a qualifying activity for the purposes of this Part—

(a) a trade,

(b) an ordinary [F2property] business,

(c) a furnished holiday lettings business,

(d) an overseas property business,

(e) a profession or vocation,

(f) a concern listed in [F3section 12. (4) of ITTOIA 2005 or] section 55. (2) of ICTA (mines, transport undertakings etc.),

[F4. (g)managing the investments of a company with investment business,]

(h) special leasing of plant or machinery, and

(i) an employment or office,

but to the extent only that the profits or gains from the activity are, or (if there were any) would be, chargeable to tax.

(2) Subsection (1) is subject to the following provisions of this Part.

(3) This section, in so far as it provides for—

(a) an ordinary [F5property] business,

(b) an overseas property business, or

(c) special leasing of plant or machinery,

to be a qualifying activity, needs to be read with section 35 (expenditure on plant or machinery for use in a dwelling-house not qualifying expenditure in certain cases).

(4) Also, subsection (1)(i) needs to be read with sections 36 (restriction on qualifying expenditure in case of employment or office) and 80 (vehicles provided for purposes of employment or office).

Amendments (Textual)

F2 Word in s. 15. (1)(b) substituted (6.4.2005) by Income Tax (Trading and Other Income) Act 2005 (c. 5) , s. 883. (1) , Sch. 1 para. 526. (2)(a) (with Sch. 2)

F3 Words in s. 15. (1)(f) inserted (6.4.2005) by Income Tax (Trading and Other Income) Act 2005 (c. 5) , s. 883. (1) , Sch. 1 para. 526. (2)(b) (with Sch. 2)

F4 S. 15. (1)(g) substituted (with effect in accordance with art. 1. (2) of the commencing S.I.) by Finance Act 2004, Sections 38 to 40 and 45 and Schedule 6 (Consequential Amendments of Enactments) Order 2004 (S.I. 2004/2310) , art. 1. (2) , Sch. para. 52. (2)

F5 Word in s. 15. (3)(a) substituted (6.4.2005) by Income Tax (Trading and Other Income) Act 2005 (c. 5) , s. 883. (1) , Sch. 1 para. 526. (3) (with Sch. 2)

16 Ordinary [F6property] businesses

In this Part "[F7ordinary property] business" [F8means a UK property business, or a Schedule A business,] except in so far as it is a furnished holiday lettings business.

Amendments (Textual)

F6 Word in s. 16 substituted (6.4.2005) by Income Tax (Trading and Other Income) Act 2005 (c. 5) , s. 883. (1) , Sch. 1 para. 527. (4) (with Sch. 2)

F7 Words in s. 16 substituted (6.4.2005) by Income Tax (Trading and Other Income) Act 2005 (c. 5) , s. 883. (1) , Sch. 1 para. 527. (2) (with Sch. 2)

F8 Words in s. 16 substituted (6.4.2005) by Income Tax (Trading and Other Income) Act 2005 (c. 5) , s. 883. (1) , Sch. 1 para. 527. (3) (with Sch. 2)

17 Furnished holiday lettings businesses

(1) In this Part "furnished holiday lettings business" means [F9a UK property business, or a Schedule A business, which consists in, or so far as it consists in, the commercial letting of furnished holiday accommodation] as it consists of the commercial letting of furnished holiday accommodation in the United Kingdom.

(2) All commercial lettings of furnished holiday accommodation made by a particular person or partnership or body of persons are to be treated as one qualifying activity.

[F10. (3) For the purposes of income tax the " commercial letting of furnished holiday accommodation " has the same meaning as it has for the purposes of Chapter 6 of Part 3 of ITTOIA 2005.

For the purposes of corporation tax the " commercial letting of furnished holiday accommodation " has the meaning given by section 504 of ICTA.]

(4) If there is a letting of accommodation only part of which is holiday accommodation, such apportionments are to be made for the purposes of this section as are just and reasonable.

Amendments (Textual)

F9. Words in s. 17. (1) substituted (with effect in accordance with s. 883. (1) of the amending Act) by Income Tax (Trading and Other Income) Act 2005 (c. 5), s. 883. (1), Sch. 1 para. 528. (2) (with Sch. 2)

F10. S. 17. (3) substituted (with effect in accordance with s. 883. (1) of the amending Act) by Income Tax (Trading and Other Income) Act 2005 (c. 5), s. 883. (1), Sch. 1 para. 528. (3) (with Sch. 2)

[F1118.Managing the investments of a company with investment business

(1) For the purposes of this Part, managing the investments of a company with investment business consists of pursuing those purposes expenditure on which would be treated as expenses of management within section 75 of ICTA .

(2) In this Part "company with investment business" has the meaning given by section 130 of ICTA .]

Amendments (Textual)

F11. S. 18 substituted (with effect in accordance with art. 1. (2) of the amending S.I.) by Finance Act 2004, Sections 38 to 40 and 45 and Schedule 6 (Consequential Amendments of Enactments) Order 2004 (S.I. 2004/2310), art. 1. (2), Sch. para. 53

19 Special leasing of plant or machinery

(1) In this Part "special leasing", in relation to plant or machinery, means hiring out the plant or machinery otherwise than in the course of any other qualifying activity (and references to a lessor or lessee in the context of special leasing are to be read accordingly).

(2) A qualifying activity consisting of special leasing of plant or machinery begins when the plant or machinery is first hired out in the circumstances given in subsection (1).

(3) A qualifying activity consisting of special leasing of plant or machinery is permanently discontinued if the lessor permanently ceases to hire out the plant or machinery otherwise than in the course of any other qualifying activity.

(4) A person who has more than one item of plant or machinery that is the subject of special leasing has a separate qualifying activity in relation to each item.

(5) If a company carrying on any life assurance business—

(a) hires out plant or machinery which is an investment asset (as defined by section 545. (2)), and

(b) does not do so in the course of a property business,

the company is to be treated for the purposes of subsection (1) as hiring out the plant or machinery otherwise than in the course of a qualifying activity.

20 Employments and offices

(1) In section 15. (1)(i) "employment" does not include an employment the performance of the duties of which is treated as the carrying on of a trade under [F12section 15 of ITTOIA 2005] (divers and diving supervisors in the North Sea etc.).

(2) Subsection (3) applies if the [F13earnings] for any duties of an employment or office [F14fall within section 22 or 26 of ITEPA 2003].

(3) This Part applies in relation to—

(a) [F15those earnings] , or

(b) any [F16other taxable earnings (as defined by section 10 of ITEPA 2003)] of the employment or office,

as if the performance of the duties did not belong to that employment or office.

Amendments (Textual)

F12 Words in s. 20. (1) substituted (6.4.2005) by Income Tax (Trading and Other Income) Act 2005 (c. 5) , s. 883. (1) , Sch. 1 para. 529 (with Sch. 2)

F13 Word in s. 20. (2) substituted (with effect in accordance with s. 723. (1)(a)(b) of the amending Act) by Income Tax (Earnings and Pensions) Act 2003 (c. 1) , s. 723 , Sch. 6 para. 248. (2)(a) (with Sch. 7)

F14 Words in s. 20. (2) substituted (with effect in accordance with s. 723. (1)(a)(b) of the amending Act) by Income Tax (Earnings and Pensions) Act 2003 (c. 1) , s. 723 , Sch. 6 para. 248. (2)(b) (with Sch. 7)

F15 Words in s. 20. (3) substituted (with effect in accordance with s. 723. (1)(a)(b) of the amending Act) by Income Tax (Earnings and Pensions) Act 2003 (c. 1) , s. 723 , Sch. 6 para. 248. (3)(a) (with Sch. 7)

F16 Words in s. 20. (3) substituted (with effect in accordance with s. 723. (1)(a)(b) of the amending Act) by Income Tax (Earnings and Pensions) Act 2003 (c. 1) , s. 723 , Sch. 6 para. 248. (3)(b) (with Sch. 7)

Chapter 3. Qualifying expenditure

21 Buildings

(1) For the purposes of this Act, expenditure on the provision of plant or machinery does not include expenditure on the provision of a building.

(2) The provision of a building includes its construction or acquisition.

(3) In this section, "building" includes an asset which—

(a) is incorporated in the building,

(b) although not incorporated in the building (whether because the asset is moveable or for any other reason), is in the building and is of a kind normally incorporated in a building, or

(c) is in, or connected with, the building and is in list A.

List A

 Assets treated as buildings

1. | Walls, floors, ceilings, doors, gates, shutters, windows and stairs. |

2. | Mains services, and systems, for water, electricity and gas. |

3. | Waste disposal systems. |

4. | Sewerage and drainage systems. |

5. | Shafts or other structures in which lifts, hoists, escalators and moving walkways are installed. |

6. | Fire safety systems. |

(4) This section is subject to section 23.

22 Structures, assets and works

(1) For the purposes of this Act, expenditure on the provision of plant or machinery does not include expenditure on—

(a) the provision of a structure or other asset in list B, or

(b) any works involving the alteration of land.

List B

 Excluded structures and other assets

1. | A tunnel, bridge, viaduct, aqueduct, embankment or cutting. |

2. | A way, hard standing (such as a pavement), road, railway, tramway, a park for vehicles or containers, or an airstrip or runway. |

3. | An inland navigation, including a canal or basin or a navigable river. |

4. | A dam, reservoir or barrage, including any sluices, gates, generators and other equipment associated with the dam, reservoir or barrage. |

5. | A dock, harbour, wharf, pier, marina or jetty or any other structure in or at which vessels may be kept, or merchandise or passengers may be shipped or unshipped. |

6. | A dike, sea wall, weir or drainage ditch. |

Any structure not within items 1 to 6 other than—

(a) a structure (but not a building) within Chapter 2 of Part 3 (meaning of "industrial building"),

(b) a structure in use for the purposes of an undertaking for the extraction, production, processing or distribution of gas, and

(c) a structure in use for the purposes of a trade which consists in the provision of telecommunication, television or radio services.

(2) The provision of a structure or other asset includes its construction or acquisition.

(3) In this section—

(a) "structure" means a fixed structure of any kind, other than a building (as defined by section 21. (3)), and

(b) "land" does not include buildings or other structures, but otherwise has the meaning given in Schedule 1 to the Interpretation Act 1978 (c. 30).

(4) This section is subject to section 23.

23 Expenditure unaffected by sections 21 and 22.

(1) Sections 21 and 22 do not apply to any expenditure to which any of the provisions listed in subsection (2) applies.

(2) The provisions are—

section 28 (thermal insulation of industrial buildings);

section 29 (fire safety);

section 30 (safety at designated sports grounds);

section 31 (safety at regulated stands at sports grounds);

section 32 (safety at other sports grounds);

section 33 (personal security);

section 71 (software and rights to software);

section [F17143 of ITTOIA 2005 or section] 40. D of F(No.2)A 1992 (election relating to tax treatment of films expenditure).

(3) Sections 21 and 22 also do not affect the question whether expenditure on any item described in list C is, for the purposes of this Act, expenditure on the provision of plant or machinery.

(4) But items 1 to 16 of list C do not include any asset whose principal purpose is to insulate or enclose the interior of a building or to provide an interior wall, floor or ceiling which (in each case) is intended to remain permanently in place.

List C

Expenditure unaffected by sections 21 and 22

1. | Machinery (including devices for providing motive power) not within any other item in this list. |

Electrical systems (including lighting systems) and cold water, gas and sewerage systems provided mainly—

(a) to meet the particular requirements of the qualifying activity, or

(b) to serve particular plant or machinery used for the purposes of the qualifying activity.

3. | Space or water heating systems; powered systems of ventilation, air cooling or air purification; and any floor or ceiling comprised in such systems. |

4. | Manufacturing or processing equipment; storage equipment (including cold rooms); display equipment; and counters, checkouts and similar equipment. |

5. | Cookers, washing machines, dishwashers, refrigerators and similar equipment; washbasins, sinks, baths, showers, sanitary ware and similar equipment; and furniture and furnishings. |

6. | Lifts, hoists, escalators and moving walkways. |

7. | Sound insulation provided mainly to meet the particular requirements of the qualifying activity. |

8. | Computer, telecommunication and surveillance systems (including their wiring or other links). |

9. | Refrigeration or cooling equipment. |

10. | Fire alarm systems; sprinkler and other equipment for extinguishing or containing fires. |

11. | Burglar alarm systems. |

12. | Strong rooms in bank or building society premises; safes. |

13. | Partition walls, where moveable and intended to be moved in the course of the qualifying activity. |

14. | Decorative assets provided for the enjoyment of the public in hotel, restaurant or similar trades. |

15. | Advertising hoardings; signs, displays and similar assets. |

16. | Swimming pools (including diving boards, slides and structures on which such boards or slides are mounted). |

17. | Any glasshouse constructed so that the required environment (namely, air, heat, light, irrigation and temperature) for the growing of plants is provided automatically by means of devices forming an integral part of its structure. |

18. | Cold stores. |

19. | Caravans provided mainly for holiday lettings. |

20. | Buildings provided for testing aircraft engines run within the buildings. |

21. | Moveable buildings intended to be moved in the course of the qualifying activity. |

22. | The alteration of land for the purpose only of installing plant or machinery. |

23. | The provision of dry docks. |

24. | The provision of any jetty or similar structure provided mainly to carry plant or machinery. |

25. | The provision of pipelines or underground ducts or tunnels with a primary purpose of carrying utility conduits. |

26. | The provision of towers to support floodlights. |

The provision of—

(a) any reservoir incorporated into a water treatment works, or

(b) any service reservoir of treated water for supply within any housing estate or other particular locality.

The provision of—

(a) silos provided for temporary storage, or

(b) storage tanks.

29. | The provision of slurry pits or silage clamps. |

30. | The provision of fish tanks or fish ponds. |

31. | The provision of rails, sleepers and ballast for a railway or tramway. |

32. | The provision of structures and other assets for providing the setting for any ride at an amusement park or exhibition. |

33. | The provision of fixed zoo cages. |

(5) In item 19 of list C, "caravan" includes, in relation to a holiday caravan site, anything that is treated as a caravan for the purposes of—

    (a) the Caravan Sites and Control of Development Act 1960 (c. 62), or

    (b) the Caravans Act (Northern Ireland) 1963 (c. 17 (N.I.)).

Amendments (Textual)

F17 Words in s. 23. (2) inserted (6.4.2005) by Income Tax (Trading and Other Income) Act 2005 (c. 5) , s. 883. (1) , Sch. 1 para. 530 (with Sch. 2)

24 Interests in land

(1) For the purposes of this Act, expenditure on the provision of plant or machinery does not include expenditure on the acquisition of an interest in land.

(2) In this section "land" does not include—

    (a) buildings or other structures, or

    (b) any asset which is so installed or otherwise fixed to any description of land as to become, in law, part of the land,

but otherwise has the meaning given in Schedule 1 to the Interpretation Act 1978 (c. 30).

(3) Subject to subsection (2), "interest in land" has the meaning given by section 175 (definitions in connection with provisions about fixtures).

25 Building alterations connected with installation of plant or machinery

If a person carrying on a qualifying activity incurs capital expenditure on alterations to an existing building incidental to the installation of plant or machinery for the purposes of the qualifying activity, this Part applies as if—

(a) the expenditure were expenditure on the provision of the plant or machinery, and

(b) the works representing the expenditure formed part of the plant or machinery.

Demolition costs

26 Demolition costs

(1) This section applies if—

(a) plant or machinery is demolished, and

(b) the last use of the plant or machinery was for the purposes of a qualifying activity.

(2) If the person carrying on the qualifying activity replaces the plant or machinery with other plant or machinery then, for the purposes of this Part, the net cost of the demolition to that person is treated as expenditure incurred on the provision of the other plant or machinery.

(3) If the person carrying on the qualifying activity does not replace the plant or machinery, the net cost of the demolition to that person is allocated to the appropriate pool for the chargeable period in which the demolition takes place.

(4) In subsection (3)—

"the appropriate pool" means the pool to which the expenditure on the demolished plant or machinery has been or would be allocated in accordance with this Part, and

"the net cost of the demolition" means the amount, if any, by which the cost of the demolition exceeds any money received for the remains of the plant or machinery.

(5) Subsection (3) is subject to section 164. (4) (abandonment expenditure before cessation of ring fence trade: election for special allowance).

Expenditure on thermal insulation, safety measures, etc.

27 Application of Part to thermal insulation, safety measures, etc.

(1) Subsection (2) has effect in relation to expenditure if—

(a) it is expenditure to which any of sections 28 to 33 applies, and

(b) an allowance under Part 2 or a deduction in respect of the expenditure could not, in the absence of this section, be made in calculating the income from the qualifying activity in question.

(2) This Part (including in particular section 11. (4)) applies as if—

(a) the expenditure were capital expenditure on the provision of plant or machinery for the purposes of the qualifying activity in question, and

(b) the person who incurred the expenditure owned plant or machinery as a result of incurring it.

28 Thermal insulation of industrial buildings

(1) This section applies to expenditure if a person carrying on a qualifying activity consisting of a trade has incurred it in adding insulation against loss of heat to an industrial building occupied by him for the purposes of the trade.

(2) This section also applies to expenditure if a person carrying on a qualifying activity consisting of an ordinary [F18property] business [F19or an overseas property business] has incurred it in adding insulation against loss of heat to an industrial building let by him in the course of the business.

(3) "Industrial building" means a building or structure which is in use for the purposes of a qualifying trade (within the meaning of Chapter 2 of Part 3).

Amendments (Textual)

F18. Word in s. 28. (2) substituted (with effect in accordance with s. 883. (1) of the amending Act) by Income Tax (Trading and Other Income) Act 2005 (c. 5), , Sch. 1 para. 531 (with Sch. 2)

F19. Words in s. 28. (2) inserted (with effect as mentioned in s. 69. (2) of the amending Act) by Finance Act 2001 (c. 9), s. 69. (1), Sch. 21 para. 1

29 Fire safety

(1) This section applies to expenditure if a person carrying on a qualifying activity has incurred it in taking required fire precautions in respect of premises which he uses for the purposes of the qualifying activity.

[F20. (2)A person takes required fire precautions in respect of premises if—

(a) he has been served with a notice under section 5. (4) of the Fire Precautions Act 1971 (c. 40) specifying steps to be taken in respect of the premises, and

(b) he takes the steps specified in the notice.

(3) A person also takes required fire precautions in respect of premises if—

(a) he has not been served with a notice by the fire authority under section 5. (4) of the 1971 Act, but has been sent or given a document by or on behalf of the fire authority that specifies steps that might have been specified in respect of the premises in such a notice, and

(b) he takes the steps specified in the document.

(4) A person also takes required fire precautions in respect of premises if—

(a) he has been served with a prohibition notice under section 10 of the 1971 Act in respect of the premises specifying matters giving rise to a risk of a kind mentioned in subsection (2) of that section, and

(b) he takes steps to remedy the matters specified in the prohibition notice.]

[F21. (4. A)A person takes required fire precautions in respect of premises if—

(a) he has been served with a notice under article 31 of the Regulatory Reform (Fire Safety) Order 2005 (prohibition notices) in respect of the premises specifying matters giving rise to a risk of a kind mentioned in paragraph (1) of that article, and

(b) he takes steps to remedy the matters specified in the prohibition notice.]

[F22. (4. A)A person takes required fire precautions in respect of premises if–

(a) he has been served with a notice under section 63 of the Fire (Scotland) Act 2005 (asp 5) (prohibition notices) in respect of the premises specifying matters giving rise to a risk of a kind mentioned in subsection (2) of that section, and

(b) he takes steps to remedy the matters specified in the prohibition notice.]

(5) This section has effect in relation to Northern Ireland subject to the modifications in subsection (6).

(6) The modifications are—

(a) for the references to section 5. (4) of the 1971 Act substitute references to Article 26. (4) of the Fire Services (Northern Ireland) Order 1984 (S.I.1984/1821 (N.I.11)),

(b) for the reference to section 10 of the 1971 Act substitute a reference to Article 33 of the 1984 Order, and

(c) for the references to a fire authority substitute references to the Fire Authority for Northern Ireland.

Amendments (Textual)

F20. S. 29. (2)-(4) repealed (E.W.) (1.4.2006) by The Regulatory Reform (Fire Safety) Order 2005 (S.I. 2005/1541), art. 1. (3), Sch. 2 para. 49. (a), Sch. 4 (with art. 49); and repealed (S.) (1.10.2006) by The Fire (Scotland) Act 2005 (Consequential Modifications and Savings) Order 2006 (S.S.I. 2006/475), art. 1, Sch. 2

F21. S. 29. (4. A) inserted (E.W.) (1.4.2006) by The Regulatory Reform (Fire Safety) Order 2005 (S.I. 2005/1541), art. 1. (3), Sch. 2 para. 49. (b) (with art. 49)

F22. S. 29. (4. A) inserted (S.) (1.10.2006) by The Fire (Scotland) Act 2005 (Consequential Modifications and Savings) Order 2006 (S.S.I. 2006/475), art. 1, Sch. 1 para. 15

30 Safety at designated sports grounds

(1) This section applies to expenditure if a person carrying on a qualifying activity has incurred it in taking required safety precautions in respect of a sports ground which is—

(a) designated under section 1 of the Safety of Sports Grounds Act 1975 (c. 52) as requiring a safety certificate, and

(b) used by him for the purposes of the qualifying activity.

(2) A person takes required safety precautions in respect of the sports ground if—

(a) a safety certificate has been issued under the 1975 Act for the sports ground, and

(b) he takes steps necessary for compliance with the terms and conditions of the safety certificate.

(3) A person also takes required safety precautions in respect of the sports ground if—

(a) he has been sent or given a document by or on behalf of the local authority for the area in which the sports ground is situated,

(b) the document specifies steps which, if taken, would—

(i) be taken into account by the local authority in deciding what terms and conditions to include in a safety certificate to be issued under the 1975 Act for the sports ground, or

(ii) lead to the amendment or replacement of a safety certificate issued or to be issued under the 1975 Act for the sports ground, and

(c) he takes the steps specified in the document.

31 Safety at regulated stands at sports grounds

(1) This section applies to expenditure if a person carrying on a qualifying activity has incurred it in taking required safety precautions in respect of a stand at a sports ground—

(a) the use of which requires a safety certificate under Part III of the Fire Safety and Safety of Places of Sport Act 1987 (c. 27), and

(b) which he uses for the purposes of the qualifying activity.

(2) A person takes required safety precautions in respect of the stand at the sports ground if—

(a) a safety certificate has been issued under the 1987 Act for the stand, and

(b) he takes steps necessary for compliance with the terms and conditions of the safety certificate.

(3) A person also takes required safety precautions in respect of the stand at the sports ground if—

(a) he has been sent or given a document by or on behalf of the local authority for the area in which the sports ground is situated,

(b) the document specifies steps which, if taken, would—

(i) be taken into account by the local authority in deciding what terms and conditions to include in a safety certificate to be issued under the 1987 Act for the stand, or

(ii) lead to the amendment or replacement of a safety certificate issued or to be issued under the 1987 Act for the stand, and

(c) he takes the steps specified in the document.

32 Safety at other sports grounds

(1) This section applies to expenditure if a person carrying on a qualifying activity has incurred it in taking required safety precautions in respect of a sports ground—

(a) which is of a kind described in section 1. (1) of the Safety of Sports Grounds Act 1975 (c. 52) but in respect of which no designation order under that section is in force at the time when he takes those precautions, and

(b) which he uses for the purposes of the qualifying activity,

and the expenditure is not incurred in respect of a sports ground stand which is within section 31. (1)(a).

(2) A person takes required safety precautions in respect of the sports ground if he takes steps which the relevant local authority certify would have fallen within section 30. (2) or (3) if—

(a) a designation order under section 1 of the 1975 Act had then been in force, and

(b) a safety certificate had then been issued or applied for under the 1975 Act.

(3) Any provision of regulations made under section 6. (1)(b) of the 1975 Act (power of local authorities to charge fees) applies, with the necessary modifications, to the issue of a certificate for the purposes of subsection (2) as it applies to the issue of a safety certificate.

(4) In subsection (2)—

(a) "the relevant local authority" means the local authority for the area in which the sports ground is situated, and

(b) "local authority" has the same meaning as in the 1975 Act.

33 Personal security

(1) This section applies to expenditure if—

(a) it is incurred by an individual or partnership of individuals in connection with the provision for, or for use by, the individual, or any of the individuals, of a security asset,

    (b) the individual or partnership is carrying on a relevant qualifying activity, and

    (c) the special threat conditions are met.

(2) The special threat conditions are that—

    (a) the asset is provided or used to meet a threat which—

(i) is a special threat to the individual's personal physical security, and

(ii) arises wholly or mainly because of the relevant qualifying activity, and

    (b) the person incurring the expenditure—

(i) has the sole object of meeting that threat in incurring that expenditure, and

(ii) intends the asset to be used solely to improve personal physical security.

(3) If—

    (a) the person incurring the expenditure intends the asset to be used solely to improve personal physical security, but

    (b) there is another use which is incidental to improving personal physical security,

that other use is ignored for the purposes of this section.

(4) The fact that an asset improves the personal physical security of any member of the family or household of the individual concerned, as well as that of the individual, does not prevent this section from applying.

(5) If—

    (a) the asset is not intended to be used solely to improve personal physical security, but the expenditure incurred on it would otherwise be expenditure to which this section applies, and

    (b) the person incurring the expenditure intends the asset to be used partly to improve personal physical security,

this section applies only to the proportion of the expenditure attributable to the intended use to improve personal physical security.

(6) In this section "security asset" means an asset which improves personal security; and here "asset"—

    (a) does not include—

(i) a car, ship or aircraft, or

(ii) a dwelling or grounds appurtenant to a dwelling, but

    (b) subject to paragraph (a), includes equipment, a structure (such as a wall) and an asset which becomes fixed to land.

(7) Section 81 (extended meaning of "car") does not apply in relation to subsection (6)(a).

(8) In this section "relevant qualifying activity" means a qualifying activity consisting of—

    (a) a trade,

    (b) an ordinary [F23property] business,

    (c) a furnished holiday lettings business,

    (d) an overseas property business, or

    (e) a profession or vocation.

Amendments (Textual)

F23 Word in s. 33. (8)(b) substituted (6.4.2005) by Income Tax (Trading and Other Income) Act 2005 (c. 5) , s. 883. (1) , Sch. 1 para. 532 (with Sch. 2)

Exclusion of certain types of expenditure

34 Expenditure by MPs and others on accommodation

(1) Expenditure is not qualifying expenditure if it is incurred by—

    (a) a member of the House of Commons,

    (b) a member of the Scottish Parliament,

    (c) a member of the National Assembly for Wales, or

    (d) a member of the Northern Ireland Assembly,

in or in connection with the provision or use of residential or overnight accommodation for the purpose given in subsection (2).

(2) The purpose is enabling the member to perform the duties of a member of the body in or about—

(a) the place where the body sits, or

(b) the constituency or region for which the member has been returned.

[F2434. AExpenditure on plant or machinery for long funding leasing not qualifying expenditure Expenditure is not qualifying expenditure if it is incurred on the provision of plant or machinery for leasing under a long funding lease (see Chapter 6. A).]

Amendments (Textual)

F24. S. 34. A inserted (with effect in accordance with Sch. 8 para. 15 of the amending Act) by Finance Act 2006 (c. 25), Sch. 8 para. 3

35 Expenditure on plant or machinery for use in dwelling-house not qualifying expenditure in certain cases

(1) This section applies if a person is carrying on a qualifying activity consisting of—

(a) an ordinary [F25property] business,

(b) an overseas property business, or

(c) special leasing of plant or machinery.

(2) The person's expenditure is not qualifying expenditure if it is incurred in providing plant or machinery for use in a dwelling-house.

(3) If plant or machinery is provided partly for use in a dwelling-house and partly for other purposes, such apportionment of the expenditure incurred in providing that plant or machinery is to be made for the purposes of subsection (2) as is just and reasonable.

Amendments (Textual)

F25. Word in s. 35. (1)(a) substituted (with effect in accordance with s. 883. (1) of the amending Act) by Income Tax (Trading and Other Income) Act 2005 (c. 5), , Sch. 1 para. 533 (with Sch. 2)

[F2636 Restriction on qualifying expenditure in case of employment or office

(1) Where the qualifying activity consists of an employment or office—

(a) expenditure on the provision of a mechanically propelled road vehicle, or a cycle, is not qualifying expenditure, and

(b) other expenditure is qualifying expenditure only if the plant or machinery is necessarily provided for use in the performance of the duties of the employment or office.

(2) In this section " cycle " has the meaning given by section 192. (1) of the Road Traffic Act 1988.]

Amendments (Textual)

F26. S. 36 substituted (with effect as mentioned in s. 59. (3)(4) of the amending Act) by Finance Act 2001 (c. 9), s. 59. (1)(3)(4)

37 Exclusion where sums payable in respect of depreciation

(1) Expenditure incurred by a person in providing plant or machinery for the purposes of a qualifying activity is not qualifying expenditure if it appears—

(a) that during the period during which the plant or machinery will be used for the purposes of the qualifying activity sums are, or are to be, payable to that person directly or indirectly, and

(b) that those sums are in respect of, or take account of, the whole of the depreciation of the plant or machinery resulting from its use for those purposes.

(2) Subsection (1) does not apply if the sums fall to be taken into account as income of the person or in calculating the profits of a qualifying activity carried on by him.

38 Production animals etc.

Expenditure is not qualifying expenditure if it is incurred on—

(a) animals or other creatures to which [F27section 30 or Chapter 8 of Part 2 of ITTOIA 2005 or] Schedule 5 to ICTA (treatment of farm animals etc. for purposes of [F28. Part 2 of ITTOIA 2005 or] Case I of Schedule D) applies, or

(b) shares in such animals or creatures.

Amendments (Textual)

F27. Words in s. 38. (a) inserted (with effect in accordance with s. 883. (1) of the amending Act)

by Income Tax (Trading and Other Income) Act 2005 (c. 5), , Sch. 1 para. 534. (a) (with Sch. 2)
F28. Words in s. 38. (a) inserted (with effect in accordance with s. 883. (1) of the amending Act))
by Income Tax (Trading and Other Income) Act 2005 (c. 5), , Sch. 1 para. 534. (b) (with Sch. 2)

Chapter 4. First-year qualifying expenditure

39 First-year allowances available for certain types of qualifying expenditure only
A first-year allowance is not available unless the qualifying expenditure is first-year qualifying
expenditure under [F29any of the following provisions]—
section 40 | expenditure incurred for Northern Ireland purposes by small or medium-sized
enterprises, |
section 44 | expenditure incurred by small or medium-sized enterprises, F30... |
section 45 | ICT expenditure incurred by small enterprises , F31... |
[F32section 45A | expenditure on energy-saving plant or machinery] |
[F33section 45D | expenditure on cars with low CO2 emissions,] |
[F34section 45E | expenditure on plant or machinery for gas refuelling station] F35... |
[F36section 45F | expenditure on plant and machinery for use wholly in a ring fence trade.] |
[F37section 45H | expenditure on environmentally beneficial plant or machinery.] |
Amendments (Textual)
F29. Words in s. 39 inserted (with effect in accordance with s. 167 of the amending Act) by
Finance Act 2003 (c. 14), Sch. 30 para. 2. (a)
F30. Word in s. 39 repealed (with effect in accordance with s. 65 of the amending Act) by Finance
Act 2001 (c. 9), s. 110, Sch. 33 Pt. 2. (4) Note
F31. Word in s. 39 repealed (with effect as mentioned in s. 59 of the amending Act) by Finance
Act 2002 (c. 23), s. 141, (Sch. 40 Pt. 3. (7) Note)
F32. Words in s. 39 inserted (with effect as mentioned in s. 65 of the amending Act) by Finance
Act 2001 (c. 9), s. 65, Sch. 17 para. 1
F33. Words in s. 39 inserted (with effect as mentioned in s. 59 of the amending Act) by Finance
Act 2002 (c. 23), s. 59, Sch. 19 para. 2
F34. Words in s. 39 inserted (with effect as mentioned in s. 61 of the amending Act) by Finance
Act 2002 (c. 23), s. 61, Sch. 20 para. 2
F35. Word in s. 39 repealed (with effect in accordance with s. 167 of the amending Act) by
Finance Act 2003 (c. 14), Sch. 30 para. 2. (b), Sch. 43 Pt. 3. (9)
F36. Words in s. 39 inserted (with effect as mentioned in s. 63 of the amending Act) by Finance
Act 2002 (c. 23), s. 63, Sch. 21 para. 2
F37. Words in s. 39 added (with effect in accordance with s. 167 of the amending Act) by Finance
Act 2003 (c. 14), Sch. 30 para. 2. (c)

Types of expenditure which may qualify for first-year allowances

40 Expenditure incurred for Northern Ireland purposes by small or medium-sized enterprises
(1) Expenditure is first-year qualifying expenditure if—
    (a) it is incurred on or before 11th May 2002,
    (b) it is incurred by a small or medium-sized enterprise,
    (c) it is incurred on the provision of plant or machinery for use primarily in Northern Ireland,
and
    (d) it is not excluded by—
(i) section 41 (miscellaneous exclusions from this section),
(ii) section 42 (plant or machinery partly for use outside Northern Ireland), or
(iii) section 46 (general exclusions).
(2) This section is subject to section 43 (effect of plant or machinery subsequently being primarily
for use outside Northern Ireland).

41 Miscellaneous exclusions from section 40 (expenditure for Northern Ireland purposes etc.)
(1) Expenditure is not first-year qualifying expenditure under section 40 if—
    (a) it is long-life asset expenditure,
    (b) it is expenditure on the provision of an aircraft or hovercraft, or
    (c) it is expenditure on the provision of a goods vehicle for the purposes of a trade which consists primarily of the conveyance of goods.
(2) Expenditure is not first-year qualifying expenditure under section 40 if it is incurred on the provision of plant or machinery for use primarily in—
    (a) agriculture, fishing or fish farming, or
    (b) any relevant activity carried out in relation to agricultural produce, fish or any fish product for the purpose of bringing it to market,
unless it is authorised for the purposes of this section by the Department of Agriculture and Rural Development in Northern Ireland.
(3) An authorisation given by the Department—
    (a) may be given either generally or specially, and
    (b) may in any case be absolute or conditional;
and, if the authorisation is given generally, it may be modified by the Department.
(4) An authorisation is given specially if it is given so as to apply only to a specified item of expenditure or a specified person; otherwise, it is given generally.
(5) In this section—
[F38 " agricultural produce " has the same meaning as in section 6 of the European Communities Act 1972 (c. 68),
" agriculture " has the same meaning as in the Agriculture Act 1947 (c. 48),]
"fish" includes shellfish,
"fish farming" means the intensive rearing, on a commercial basis, of fish intended for human consumption,
"fishing" means a trade, or part of a trade, which consists of the catching or taking of fish,
"goods vehicle" has the same meaning as in the Road Traffic (Northern Ireland) Order 1995 (S.I.1995/2994 (N.I.18)),
"hovercraft" has the same meaning as in the Hovercraft Act 1968 (c. 59), and
"relevant activity" means transportation, storage, preparation, processing or packaging.
Amendments (Textual)
F38 Words in s. 41. (5) substituted (15.11.2001) by The Intervention Board for Agricultural Produce (Abolition) Regulations 2001 (S.I. 2001/3686) , reg. 6. (20)
42 Exclusion of plant or machinery partly for use outside Northern Ireland
(1) Expenditure on plant or machinery is not first-year qualifying expenditure under section 40 if—
    (a) at the time when it is incurred, the person incurring it intends the plant or machinery to be used partly outside Northern Ireland, and
    (b) the main benefit, or one of the main benefits, which could reasonably be expected to arise from the relevant arrangements is the obtaining of a first-year allowance, or a greater first-year allowance, in respect of the part of the expenditure that is attributable to that intended use outside Northern Ireland.
(2) For the purposes of subsection (1)—
    (a) "the relevant arrangements" means—
(i) the transaction under which the expenditure is incurred, and
(ii) any scheme or arrangements of which that transaction forms part, and
    (b) the part of the expenditure that is attributable under subsection (1)(b) is to be determined on a just and reasonable basis.
43 Effect of plant or machinery subsequently being primarily for use outside Northern Ireland
(1) Expenditure on the provision of plant or machinery is to be treated as never having been first-year qualifying expenditure under section 40 if, at any relevant time—
    (a) the primary use to which the plant or machinery is put is a use outside Northern Ireland, or

(b) the plant or machinery is held for use otherwise than primarily in Northern Ireland.

(2) In subsection (1) "relevant time" means a time which—

(a) falls within the relevant period, and

(b) is a time when the plant or machinery is owned by—

(i) the person who incurred the expenditure, or

(ii) a person who is, or at any time in that period has been, connected with that person.

(3) "The relevant period" means—

(a) if the expenditure concerned exceeds £3.5 million, the period of 5 years beginning with the date of the incurring of that expenditure;

(b) in any other case, the period of 2 years beginning with that date.

(4) All such assessments and adjustments of assessments are to be made as are necessary to give effect to subsection (1).

(5) If a person who has made a return becomes aware that, after making it, anything in it has become incorrect because of the operation of this section, he must give notice to the [F39an officer of Revenue and Customs] specifying how the return needs to be amended.

(6) The notice must be given within 3 months beginning with the day on which the person first became aware that anything in the return had become incorrect because of the operation of this section.

Amendments (Textual)

F39. Words in Act substituted (18.4.2005) by Commissioners for Revenue and Customs Act 2005 (c. 11), s. 53. (1), Sch. 4 para. 83. (1); S.I. 2005/1126, art. 2. (2)(h)

Modifications etc. (not altering text)

C7. S. 43. (3) modified by 1993 c. 34, s. 93. A(6) (as inserted (with effect as mentioned in s. 80. (2) of the inserting Act) by Finance Act 2002 (c. 23), s. 80, Sch. 24 para. 4 (with Sch. 23 para. 25))

44 Expenditure incurred by small or medium-sized enterprises

(1) Expenditure is first-year qualifying expenditure if—

(a) it is incurred by a small or medium-sized enterprise, and

(b) it is not excluded by subsection (2) or section 46 (general exclusions).

(2) Long-life asset expenditure is not first-year qualifying expenditure under subsection (1).

Modifications etc. (not altering text)

C8 S. 44 modified (22.7.2004) by Finance Act 2004 (c. 12) , s. 142. (1) (2)

C9. S. 44 modified (19.7.2007) by Finance Act 2007 (c. 11), s. 37. (1) (with s. 37. (2))

45 ICT expenditure incurred by small enterprises

(1) Expenditure is first-year qualifying expenditure if—

(a) it is incurred on or before [F4031st March 2004],

(b) it is incurred by a small enterprise,

(c) it is expenditure on information and communications technology, and

(d) it is not excluded by section 46 (general exclusions) [F41or subsection (4) below].

(2) "Expenditure on information and communications technology" means expenditure on items within any of the following classes.

Class A. Computers and associated equipment

This class covers—

(a) computers,

(b) peripheral devices designed to be used by being connected to or inserted in a computer,

(c) equipment (including cabling) for use primarily to provide a data connection between—

(i) one computer and another, or

(ii) a computer and a data communications network, and

(d) dedicated electrical systems for computers.

For this purpose "computer" does not include computerised control or management systems or other systems that are part of a larger system whose principal function is not processing or storing information.

Class B. Other qualifying equipment

This class covers—

(a) wireless application protocol telephones,

(b) third generation mobile telephones,

(c) devices designed to be used by being connected to a television set and capable of receiving and transmitting information from and to data networks, and

(d) other devices—

(i) substantially similar to those within paragraphs (a), (b) and (c), and

(ii) capable of receiving and transmitting information from and to data networks.

This is subject to any order under subsection (3).

Class C. Software

This class covers the right to use or otherwise deal with software for the purposes of any equipment within Class A or B.

(3) The Treasury may make provision by order—

(a) further defining the kinds of equipment within Class B, or

(b) adding further kinds of equipment to that class.

[F42. (4)Expenditure on an item within Class C is not first-year qualifying expenditure under this section if the person incurring it does so with a view to granting to another person a right to use or otherwise deal with any of the software in question.]

Amendments (Textual)

F40 Words in s. 45. (1)(a) substituted (10.7.2003) by Finance Act 2003 (c. 14) , s. 165

F41 Words in s. 45. (1)(d) inserted (10.7.2003) by Finance Act 2003 (c. 14) , s. 166. (2) (with s. 166. (4))

F42 S. 45. (4) inserted (10.7.2003) by Finance Act 2003 (c. 14) , s. 166. (3) (with s. 166. (4))

[F4345. A Expenditure on energy-saving plant or machinery

(1) Expenditure is first-year qualifying expenditure if—

(a) it is expenditure on energy-saving plant or machinery that is unused and not second-hand,

(b) it is incurred on or after 1st April 2001, and

(c) it is not excluded by section 46 (general exclusions).

(2) Energy-saving plant or machinery means plant or machinery in relation to which the following conditions are met—

(a) when the expenditure is incurred, or

(b) when the contract for the provision of the plant or machinery is entered into.

(3) The conditions are that the plant or machinery—

(a) is of a description specified by Treasury order, and

(b) meets the energy-saving criteria specified by Treasury order for plant or machinery of that description.

(4) Any such order may make provision by reference to any technology list, or product list, issued by the Secretary of State (whether before or after the coming into force of this section).

Amendments (Textual)

F43. Ss. 45. A-45. C inserted (with effect as mentioned in s. 65 of the amending Act) by Finance Act 2001 (c. 9), s. 65, Sch. 17 para. 2 (with Sch. 17 para. 6)

45. B Certification of energy-saving plant and machinery

(1) The Treasury may by order provide that, in such cases as may be specified in the order, no section 45. A allowance may be made unless a relevant certificate of energy efficiency is in force. A " section 45. A allowance " means a first-year allowance in respect of expenditure that is first-year qualifying expenditure under section 45. A.

(2) A certificate of energy efficiency is one certifying that—

(a) particular plant or machinery, or

(b) plant or machinery constructed to a particular design,

meets the energy-saving criteria specified in relation to that description of plant or machinery by order under section 45. A.

(3) A relevant certificate of energy efficiency means one issued—

(a) by the Secretary of State or a person authorised by the Secretary of State;

(b) in the case of plant or machinery used or for use in Scotland, by the Scottish Ministers or a person authorised by them;

(c) in the case of plant or machinery used or for use in Wales, by the National Assembly for Wales or a person authorised by it;

(d) in the case of plant or machinery used or for use in Northern Ireland, by the Department of Enterprise, Trade and Investment in Northern Ireland or a person authorised by it.

(4) If a certificate of energy efficiency is revoked—

(a) the certificate is to be treated for the purposes of this section as if it had never been issued, and

(b) all such assessments and adjustments of assessments are to be made as are necessary as a result of the revocation.

(5) If a person who has made a tax return becomes aware that, as a result of the revocation of a certificate of energy efficiency after the return was made, the return has become incorrect, he must give notice to [F39an officer of Revenue and Customs] specifying how the return needs to be amended.

(6) The notice must be given within 3 months beginning with the day on which the person first became aware that anything in the tax return had become incorrect because of the revocation of the certificate.

Amendments (Textual)

F39. Words in Act substituted (18.4.2005) by Commissioners for Revenue and Customs Act 2005 (c. 11), s. 53. (1), Sch. 4 para. 83. (1); S.I. 2005/1126, art. 2. (2)(h)

F43. Ss. 45. A-45. C inserted (with effect as mentioned in s. 65 of the amending Act) by Finance Act 2001 (c. 9), s. 65, Sch. 17 para. 2 (with Sch. 17 para. 6)

45. C Energy-saving components of plant or machinery

(1) This section applies for the purpose of apportioning expenditure incurred on plant or machinery if one or more components of the plant or machinery (but not all of it) is of a description specified by Treasury order under section 45. A(3).

(2) If—

(a) only one of the components is of such a description, and

(b) an amount is specified by the order in respect of that component,

the part of the expenditure that is section 45. A expenditure must not exceed that amount.

(3) If—

(a) more than one of the components are of such a description, and

(b) an amount is specified by the order in respect of each of those components,

the part of the expenditure that is section 45. A expenditure must not exceed the total of those amounts.

(4) If the expenditure is treated under this Act as incurred in instalments, the proportion of each instalment that is section 45. A expenditure is the same as the proportion of the whole of the expenditure that is section 45. A expenditure.

(5) If this section applies, the expenditure is not apportioned under section 562. (3) (apportionment where property sold with other property).

(6) In this section " section 45. A expenditure " means expenditure that is first-year qualifying expenditure under section 45. A.]

Amendments (Textual)

F43. Ss. 45. A-45. C inserted (with effect as mentioned in s. 65 of the amending Act) by Finance Act 2001 (c. 9), s. 65, Sch. 17 para. 2 (with Sch. 17 para. 6)

[F4445. D Expenditure on cars with low carbon dioxide emissions

(1) Expenditure is first-year qualifying expenditure if—

(a) it is incurred in the period beginning with 17th April 2002 and ending with 31st March 2008,

(b) it is expenditure on a car which is first registered on or after 17th April 2002 and which is unused and not second-hand,

(c) the car—

(i) is an electrically-propelled car, or

(ii) is a car with low CO_2 emissions, and

(d) the expenditure is not excluded by section 46 (general exclusions).

(2) For the purposes of this section a car with low CO_2 emissions is a car which satisfies the conditions in subsections (3) and (4).

(3) The first condition is that, when the car is first registered, it is so registered on the basis of an EC certificate of conformity, or a UK approval certificate, that specifies—

(a) in the case of a car other than a bi-fuel car, a CO_2 emissions figure in terms of grams per kilometre driven, or

(b) in the case of a bi-fuel car, separate CO_2 emissions figures in terms of grams per kilometre driven for different fuels.

(4) The second condition is that the applicable CO_2 emissions figure in the case of the car does not exceed 120 grams per kilometre driven.

(5) For the purposes of subsection (4) the applicable CO_2 emissions figure in the case of a car other than a bi-fuel car is—

(a) where the EC certificate of conformity or UK approval certificate specifies only one CO_2 emissions figure, that figure, and

(b) where the certificate specifies more than one CO_2 emissions figure, the figure specified as the CO_2 emissions (combined) figure.

(6) For the purposes of subsection (4) the applicable CO_2 emissions figure in the case of a bi-fuel car is—

(a) where the EC certificate of conformity or UK approval certificate specifies more than one CO_2 emissions figure in relation to each fuel, the lowest CO_2 emissions (combined) figure specified, and

(b) in any other case, the lowest CO_2 figure specified by the certificate.

(7) The Treasury may by order amend the amount from time to time specified in subsection (4).

(8) In this section any reference to a car—

(a) includes a reference to a mechanically propelled road vehicle of a type commonly used as a hackney carriage, but

(b) does not include a reference to a motorcycle.

(9) For the purposes of this section, a car is an electrically-propelled car only if—

(a) it is propelled solely by electrical power, and

(b) that power is derived from—

(i) a source external to the vehicle, or

(ii) an electrical storage battery which is not connected to any source of power when the vehicle is in motion.

(10) In this section—

" bi-fuel car " means a car which is capable of being propelled by—

- petrol and road fuel gas, or

- diesel and road fuel gas;

" car " has the meaning given by section 81 (extended meaning of "car");

" diesel " means any diesel fuel within the definition in Article 2 of Directive 98/70/ EC of the European Parliament and of the Council;

" EC certificate of conformity " means a certificate of conformity issued by a manufacturer under any provision of the law of a member State implementing Article 6 of Council Directive 70/156/ EEC , as amended;

" petrol " has the meaning given by Article 2 of Directive 98/70/ EC of the European Parliament and of the Council;

" road fuel gas " has the same meaning as in section 168. AB of ICTA ;

" UK approval certificate " means a certificate issued under—

- section 58. (1) or (4) of the Road Traffic Act 1988, or

- Article 31. A(4) or (5) of the Road Traffic (Northern Ireland) Order 1981.]

Amendments (Textual)

F44. S. 45. D inserted (with effect as mentioned in s. 59 of the amending Act) by Finance Act

2002 (c. 23), s. 59, Sch. 19 para. 3

[F4545. E Expenditure on plant or machinery for gas refuelling station

(1) Expenditure is first-year qualifying expenditure if—

(a) it is incurred in the period beginning with 17th April 2002 and ending with 31st March 2008,

(b) it is expenditure on plant or machinery for a gas refuelling station where the plant or machinery is unused and not second-hand, and

(c) it is not excluded by section 46 (general exclusions).

(2) For the purposes of this section expenditure on plant or machinery for a gas refuelling station is expenditure on plant or machinery installed at a gas refuelling station for use solely for or in connection with refuelling vehicles with natural gas or hydrogen fuel.

(3) For the purposes of subsection (2) the plant or machinery which is for use for or in connection with refuelling vehicles with natural gas or hydrogen fuel includes—

(a) any storage tank for natural gas or hydrogen fuel,

(b) any compressor, pump, control or meter used for or in connection with refuelling vehicles with natural gas or hydrogen fuel, and

(c) any equipment for dispensing natural gas or hydrogen fuel to the fuel tank of a vehicle.

(4) For the purposes of this section—

" gas refuelling station " means any premises, or that part of any premises, where vehicles are refuelled with natural gas or hydrogen fuel;

" hydrogen fuel " means a fuel consisting of gaseous or cryogenic liquid hydrogen which is used for propelling vehicles;

" vehicle " means a mechanically propelled road vehicle.]

Amendments (Textual)

F45. S. 45. E inserted (with effect as mentioned in s. 61 of the amending Act) by Finance Act 2002 (c. 23), s. 61, Sch. 20 para. 3

[F4645. F Expenditure on plant and machinery for use wholly in a ring fence trade

(1) Expenditure is first-year qualifying expenditure if—

(a) it is incurred on or after 17th April 2002,

(b) it is incurred by a company,

(c) it is incurred on the provision of plant or machinery for use wholly for the purposes of a ring fence trade, and

(d) it is not excluded by section 46 (general exclusions).

(2) This section is subject to section 45. G (plant or machinery used for less than five years in a ring fence trade).

(3) In this section " ring fence trade " means a ring fence trade in respect of which tax is chargeable under section 501. A of the Taxes Act 1988 (supplementary charge in respect of ring fence trades).]

Amendments (Textual)

F46. S. 45. F inserted (with effect as mentioned in s. 63 of the amending Act) by Finance Act 2002 (c. 23), s. 63, Sch. 21 para. 3

[F4745. G Plant or machinery used for less than five years in a ring fence trade

(1) Expenditure incurred by a company on the provision of plant or machinery is to be treated as never having been first-year qualifying expenditure under section 45. F if the plant or machinery—

(a) is at no time in the relevant period used in a ring fence trade carried on by the company or a company connected with it, or

(b) is at any time in the relevant period used for a purpose other than that of a ring fence trade carried on by the company or a company connected with it.

(2) For the purposes of this section " the relevant period " means whichever of the following periods, beginning with the incurring of the expenditure, first ends, namely—

(a) the period ending with the fifth anniversary of the incurring of the expenditure, or

(b) the period ending with the day preceding the first occasion on which the plant or machinery,

29

after becoming owned by the company which incurred the expenditure, is not owned by a company which is either that company or a company connected with it.

(3) All such assessments and adjustments of assessments are to be made as are necessary to give effect to subsection (1).

(4) If a person who has made a return becomes aware that, after making it, anything in it has become incorrect because of the operation of this section, he must give notice to [F39an officer of Revenue and Customs] specifying how the return needs to be amended.

(5) The notice must be given within 3 months beginning with the day on which the person first became aware that anything in the return had become incorrect because of the operation of this section.

(6) In this section " ring fence trade " has the same meaning as in section 45. F.]

Amendments (Textual)

F39. Words in Act substituted (18.4.2005) by Commissioners for Revenue and Customs Act 2005 (c. 11), s. 53. (1), Sch. 4 para. 83. (1); S.I. 2005/1126, art. 2. (2)(h)

F47. S. 45. G inserted (with effect as mentioned in s. 63 of the amending Act) by Finance Act 2002 (c. 23), s. 63, Sch. 21 para. 4

[F48. Expenditure on environmentally beneficial plant or machinery

Amendments (Textual)

F48. S. 45. H-45. J inserted (with effect in accordance with s. 167 of the amending Act) by Finance Act 2003 (c. 14), Sch. 30 para. 3

45. H(1)Expenditure is first-year qualifying expenditure if—

    (a) it is expenditure on environmentally beneficial plant or machinery that is unused and not second-hand,

    (b) it is incurred on or after 1st April 2003,

    (c) it is not long-life asset expenditure, and

    (d) it is not excluded by section 46 (general exclusions).

(2) Environmentally beneficial plant or machinery means plant or machinery in relation to which the following conditions are met—

    (a) when the expenditure is incurred, or

    (b) when the contract for the provision of the plant or machinery is entered into.

(3) The conditions are that the plant or machinery—

    (a) is of a description specified by Treasury order, and

    (b) meets the environmental criteria specified by Treasury order for plant or machinery of that description.

(4) The Treasury may make such orders under subsection (3) as appear to them appropriate to promote the use of technologies, or products, designed to remedy or prevent damage to the physical environment or natural resources.

(5) Any such order may make provision by reference to any technology list, or product list, issued by the Secretary of State (whether before or after the coming into force of this section).

Certification of environmentally beneficial plant and machinery

45. I(1)The Treasury may by order provide that, in such cases as may be specified in the order, no section 45. H allowance may be made unless a relevant certificate of environmental benefit is in force.

A " section 45. H allowance " means a first-year allowance in respect of expenditure that is first-year qualifying expenditure under section 45. H.

(2) A certificate of environmental benefit is one certifying that—

(a) particular plant or machinery, or

(b) plant or machinery constructed to a particular design,

meets the environmental criteria specified in relation to that description of plant or machinery by order under section 45. H.

(3) A relevant certification of environmental benefit means one issued—

(a) by the Secretary of State or a person authorised by the Secretary of State;

(b) in the case of plant or machinery used or for use in Scotland, by the Scottish Ministers or a person authorised by them;

(c) in the case of plant or machinery used or for use in Wales, by the National Assembly for Wales or a person authorised by it;

(d) in the case of plant or machinery used or for use in Northern Ireland, by the Department of Enterprise, Trade and Investment in Northern Ireland or a person authorised by it.

(4) If a certification of environmental benefit is revoked—

(a) the certificate is treated for the purposes of this section as if it had never been issued, and

(b) all such assessments and adjustments shall be made as are necessary as a result of the revocation.

(5) If a person who has made a tax return becomes aware that, as a result of the revocation of a certificate of environmental benefit after the return was made, the return has become incorrect, he must give notice to [F39an officer of Revenue and Customs] specifying how the return needs to be amended.

(6) The notice must be given within three months beginning with the day on which the person first became aware that anything in the tax return had become incorrect because of the revocation of the certificate.

Environmentally beneficial components of plant or machinery

45. J(1)This section applies for the purpose of apportioning expenditure incurred on plant or machinery where one or more of the components of the plant or machinery (but not all of it) is of a description specified by Treasury order under section 45. H(3).

(2) If—

(a) only one of the components is of such a description, and

(b) an amount is specified by the order in respect of that component,

the part of the expenditure that is section 45. H expenditure must not exceed that amount.

(3) If—

(a) more than one of the components is of such a description, and

(b) an amount is specified by the order in respect of each of those components,

the part of the expenditure that is section 45. H expenditure must not exceed the total of those amounts.

(4) If the expenditure is treated under this Act as incurred in instalments, the proportion of each instalment that is section 45. H expenditure is the same as the proportion of the whole expenditure that is section 45. H expenditure.

(5) Where this section applies, the expenditure is not apportioned under section 562. (3) (apportionment where property sold with other property).

(6) In this section " section 45. H expenditure " means expenditure that is first-year qualifying expenditure under section 45. H.]

46 General exclusions applying to sections 40, 44 and 45.

(1) Expenditure within any of the general exclusions in subsection (2) is not first-year qualifying expenditure under [F49any of the following provisions]—

section 40 (expenditure incurred for Northern Ireland purposes by small or medium-sized enterprises),

section 44 (expenditure incurred by small or medium-sized enterprises), F50...

section 45 (ICT expenditure incurred by small enterprises)[F51, F52...

section 45. A (expenditure on energy-saving plant or machinery)] [F53,

section 45. D (expenditure on cars with low CO2 emissions),]

[F54section 45. E (expenditure on plant or machinery for gas refuelling station)] , F55...

[F56section 45. F (expenditure on plant and machinery for use wholly in a ring fence trade)]

[F57section 45. H expenditure on environmentally beneficial plant or machinery.]

(2) The general exclusions are—

General exclusion 1

The expenditure is incurred in the chargeable period in which the qualifying activity is permanently discontinued.

General exclusion 2

The expenditure is incurred on the provision of a car (as defined by section 81).

General exclusion 3

The expenditure is of the kind described in section 94 (ships).

General exclusion 4

The expenditure is of the kind described in section 95 (railway assets).

General exclusion 5

The expenditure would be long-life asset expenditure but for paragraph 20 of Schedule 3 (transitional provisions).

General exclusion 6

The expenditure is on the provision of plant or machinery for leasing (whether in the course of a trade or otherwise).

For this purpose, the letting of a ship on charter, or of any other asset on hire, is to be regarded as leasing (whether or not it would otherwise be so regarded).

General exclusion 7

The circumstances of the incurring of the expenditure are that—

- the provision of the plant or machinery on which the expenditure is incurred is connected with a change in the nature or conduct of a trade or business carried on by a person other than the person incurring the expenditure, and

- the obtaining of a first-year allowance is the main benefit, or one of the main benefits, which could reasonably be expected to arise from the making of the change.

General exclusion 8

[F58. Any] of the following sections applies—

- section 13 (use for qualifying activity of plant or machinery provided for other purposes);

- [F59section 13. A (use for other purposes of plant or machinery provided for long funding leasing);]

- section 14 (use for qualifying activity of plant or machinery which is a gift).

This is subject to section 161 (pre-trading expenditure on mineral exploration and access).

[F60. (3)Subsection (1) is subject to the following provisions of this section.

(4) General exclusion 2 does not prevent expenditure being first-year qualifying expenditure under section 45. D.]

[F61. (5)General exclusion 6 does not prevent expenditure being first-year qualifying expenditure under any of the following provisions—

section 45. A, if the condition in subsection (6) is met,

section 45. D,

section 45. H, if the condition in subsection (6) is met.

(6) The condition is that the plant or machinery is provided for leasing under an excluded lease of background plant or machinery for a building, within the meaning given by section 70. R.]

Amendments (Textual)

F49 Words in s. 46. (1) inserted (with effect in accordance with s. 167 of the amending Act) by Finance Act 2003 (c. 14) , Sch. 30 para. 4. (1)(a)

F50. Word in s. 46. (1) repealed (with effect in accordance with s. 65 of the amending Act) by Finance Act 2001 (c. 9), s. 110, Sch. 33 Pt. 2. (4) Note

F51. Words in s. 46. (1) inserted (with effect as mentioned in s. 65 of the amending Act) by

Finance Act 2001 (c. 9), s. 65, Sch. 17 para. 3

F52. Word in s. 46. (1) repealed (with effect as mentioned in s. 59 of the amending Act) by Finance Act 2002 (c. 23), s. 141, (Sch. 40 Pt. 3. (7) note)

F53. Entry in s. 46. (1) relating to s. 45. D inserted (with effect as mentioned in s. 59 of the amending Act) by Finance Act 2002 (c. 23), s. 59, Sch. 19 para. 4. (2)

F54. Entry in s. 46. (1) relating to s. 45. E inserted (with effect as mentioned in s. 61of the amending Act) by Finance Act 2002 (c. 23), s. 61, Sch. 20 para. 4

F55 Word in s. 46. (1) repealed (with effect in accordance with s. 167 of the amending Act) by Finance Act 2003 (c. 14) , Sch. 30 para. 4. (1)(b) , 43 Pt. 3. (9)

F56. Entry in s. 46. (1) relating to s. 45. F inserted (with effect as mentioned in s. 63 of the amending Act) by Finance Act 2002 (c. 23), s. 63, Sch. 21 para. 5

F57 Words in s. 46. (1) added (with effect in accordance with s. 167 of the amending Act) by Finance Act 2003 (c. 14) , Sch. 30 para. 4. (1)(c)

F58. Word in s. 46. (2) substituted (with effect in accordance with Sch. 8 para. 15 of the amending Act) by Finance Act 2006 (c. 25), Sch. 8 para. 4. (2)(a)

F59. Words in s. 46. (2) inserted (with effect in accordance with Sch. 8 para. 15 of the amending Act) by Finance Act 2006 (c. 25), Sch. 8 para. 4. (2)(b)

F60. Entry relating to s. 46. (3)(4) inserted (with effect as mentioned in s. 59 of the amending Act) by Finance Act 2002 (c. 23), s. 59, Sch. 19 para. 4. (3)

F61. S. 46. (5)(6) substituted for s. 46. (5) (with effect in accordance with Sch. 9 para. 11. (3) of the amending Act) by Finance Act 2006 (c. 25), Sch. 9 para. 11. (2)

Expenditure of small or medium-sized enterprises

47 Expenditure of small or medium-sized enterprises: companies
(1) Use this section to decide whether expenditure incurred by a company is, for the purposes of this Chapter, incurred by—

(a) a small or medium-sized enterprise, or

(b) a small enterprise.

(2) The expenditure is incurred by a small or medium-sized enterprise if the company—

(a) qualifies (or is treated as qualifying) as small or medium-sized under the relevant companies legislation in relation to the financial year of the company in which the expenditure is incurred, and

(b) is not a member of a large group at the time when the expenditure is incurred.

(3) The expenditure is incurred by a small enterprise if the company—

(a) qualifies (or is treated as qualifying) as small under the relevant companies legislation in relation to the financial year of the company in which the expenditure is incurred, and

(b) is not a member of a large or medium-sized group at the time when the expenditure is incurred.

(4) [F62. In this section] —

(a) "the relevant companies legislation" means [F63sections 382 and 465 of the Companies Act 2006], and

(b) "financial year" has the same meaning as in [F64section 390 of the Companies Act 2006].

F65. (5). . . . .

(6) "Company" means—

(a) a company, or an oversea company, within the meaning of [F66the Companies Act 1985], or

(b) a company, or a Part XXIII company, within the meaning of [F67the Companies (Northern Ireland) Order 1986].

Amendments (Textual)

F62. Words in s. 47. (4) substituted (6.4.2008) by The Companies Act 2006 (Consequential Amendments) (Taxes and National Insurance) Order 2008 (S.I. 2008/954), arts. 1. (1), 28. (2)(a) (with art. 4)

F63. Words in s. 47. (4)(a) substituted (6.4.2008) by virtue ofThe Companies Act 2006 (Consequential Amendments) (Taxes and National Insurance) Order 2008 (S.I. 2008/954), arts. 1. (1), 28. (2)(b) (with art. 4)

F64. Words in s. 47. (4)(b) substituted (6.4.2008) by The Companies Act 2006 (Consequential Amendments) (Taxes and National Insurance) Order 2008 (S.I. 2008/954), arts. 1. (1), 28. (2)(c) (with art. 4)

F65. S. 47. (5) repealed (6.4.2008) by The Companies Act 2006 (Consequential Amendments) (Taxes and National Insurance) Order 2008 (S.I. 2008/954), arts. 1. (1), 28. (3), Sch. (with art. 4)

F66. Words in s. 47. (6)(a) substituted (6.4.2008) by The Companies Act 2006 (Consequential Amendments) (Taxes and National Insurance) Order 2008 (S.I. 2008/954), arts. 1. (1), 28. (4)(a) (with art. 4)

F67. Words in s. 47. (6)(b) substituted (6.4.2008) by The Companies Act 2006 (Consequential Amendments) (Taxes and National Insurance) Order 2008 (S.I. 2008/954), arts. 1. (1), 28. (4)(b) (with art. 4)

48 Expenditure of small or medium-sized enterprises: businesses

(1) Use this section to decide whether expenditure incurred by a business is, for the purposes of this Chapter, incurred by—

(a) a small or medium-sized enterprise, or

(b) a small enterprise.

(2) In this section "business" means—

(a) an individual,

(b) a partnership of which all the members are individuals,

(c) a registered friendly society within the meaning of Chapter II of Part XII of ICTA, or

(d) a body corporate which is not a company but is within the charge to corporation tax.

(3) The expenditure is incurred by a small or medium-sized enterprise if—

(a) the expenditure is incurred for the purposes of a qualifying activity carried on by the business, and

(b) the business passes the hypothetical company test, in relation to that expenditure, as a small or medium-sized company.

(4) The expenditure is incurred by a small enterprise if—

(a) the expenditure is incurred for the purposes of a qualifying activity carried on by the business, and

(b) the business passes the hypothetical company test, in relation to that expenditure, as a small company.

(5) To apply the hypothetical company test, assume that—

(a) the qualifying activity is carried on by a company ("the hypothetical company"),

(b) every trade, business, profession or vocation carried on by the business is carried on by the business as part of that activity,

(c) the financial years of the hypothetical company coincide with the chargeable periods of the business, and

(d) accounts of the hypothetical company for any relevant chargeable period have been duly drawn up as if that period were a financial year of the company.

(6) The business passes the hypothetical company test as a small or medium-sized company in relation to the expenditure in question if, on the assumptions in subsection (5), the company would qualify (or be treated as qualifying) as small or medium-sized under the relevant companies legislation in relation to the financial year in which the expenditure is assumed to be incurred.

(7) The business passes the hypothetical company test as a small company in relation to the expenditure in question if, on the assumptions in subsection (5), the company would qualify (or be treated as qualifying) as small under the relevant companies legislation in relation to the financial year in which the expenditure is assumed to be incurred.

(8) [F68. In this section] —

(a) "the relevant companies legislation" means [F69sections 382 and 465 of the Companies Act 2006], and

(b) "financial year" has the same meaning as in [F70section 390 of the Companies Act 2006]; and the reference in subsection (5)(d) to accounts being duly drawn up is to their being drawn up in accordance with that Act.

F71. (9). . . . .

Amendments (Textual)

F68. Words in s. 48. (8) substituted (6.4.2008) by The Companies Act 2006 (Consequential Amendments) (Taxes and National Insurance) Order 2008 (S.I. 2008/954), arts. 1. (1), 29. (2)(a) (with art. 4)

F69. Words in s. 48. (8)(a) substituted (6.4.2008) by virtue of The Companies Act 2006 (Consequential Amendments) (Taxes and National Insurance) Order 2008 (S.I. 2008/954), arts. 1. (1), 29. (2)(b) (with art. 4)

F70. Words in s. 48. (8)(b) substituted (6.4.2008) by The Companies Act 2006 (Consequential Amendments) (Taxes and National Insurance) Order 2008 (S.I. 2008/954), arts. 1. (1), 29. (2)(c) (with art. 4)

F71. S. 48. (9) repealed (6.4.2008) by The Companies Act 2006 (Consequential Amendments) (Taxes and National Insurance) Order 2008 (S.I. 2008/954), arts. 1. (1), 29. (3), Sch. (with art. 4)

49 Whether company is a member of a large or medium-sized group

(1) Use this section to decide whether, for the purposes of section 47, a company is—

(a) a member of a large group, or

(b) a member of a large or medium-sized group.

(2) Subject to subsection (4), a company is a member of a large group at the time when any expenditure is incurred if—

(a) it is at that time the parent undertaking of a group which does not qualify as small or medium-sized in relation to the financial year of the parent undertaking in which that time falls, or

(b) it is at that time a subsidiary undertaking in relation to the parent undertaking of such a group.

(3) Subject to subsection (4), a company is a member of a large or medium-sized group at the time when any expenditure is incurred if—

(a) it is at that time the parent undertaking of a group which does not qualify as small in relation to the financial year of the parent undertaking in which that time falls, or

(b) it is at that time a subsidiary undertaking in relation to the parent undertaking of such a group.

(4) If, at the time when any expenditure is incurred by a company, any arrangements exist which are such that, had effect been given to them immediately before that time, the company or a successor of the company—

(a) would, at that time, have been a member of a large group, or

(b) would, at that time, have been a member of a large or medium-sized group,

the company incurring the expenditure is to be treated as a member of a large group or (as the case may be) a large or medium-sized group at that time.

(5) For the purposes of subsections (2) and (3), the question whether—

(a) a group qualifies as small or medium-sized, or

(b) a group qualifies as small,

is to be decided by reference to the relevant companies legislation (but reading references in that legislation to a parent company as references to a parent undertaking).

(6) In subsection (5) "the relevant companies legislation" means [F72sections 383 and 466 of the Companies Act 2006.]

(7) For the purposes of subsection (4) a company is the successor of another if—

(a) it carries on a trade which, in whole or in part, the other company has ceased to carry on, and

(b) the circumstances are such that section 343 of ICTA (company reconstructions without a change of ownership) applies in relation to the two companies as the predecessor and the successor within the meaning of that section,

and "arrangements" means arrangements of any kind (whether or not in writing or legally enforceable).

[F73. (8)In this section—
"financial year" and "group" have the same meaning as in Part 15 of the Companies Act 2006;
"parent undertaking" and "subsidiary undertaking" have the same meaning as in section 1162 of that Act.]
Amendments (Textual)
F72. Words in s. 49. (6) substituted (6.4.2008) by The Companies Act 2006 (Consequential Amendments) (Taxes and National Insurance) Order 2008 (S.I. 2008/954), arts. 1. (1), 30. (2) (with art. 4)
F73. S. 49. (8) substituted (6.4.2008) by The Companies Act 2006 (Consequential Amendments) (Taxes and National Insurance) Order 2008 (S.I. 2008/954), arts. 1. (1), 30. (3) (with art. 4)

Supplementary

50 Time when expenditure is incurred
In determining whether expenditure is first-year qualifying expenditure under this Chapter, any effect of section 12 on the time at which it is to be treated as incurred is to be disregarded.
51 Disclosure of information between UK tax authorities
(1) No obligation as to secrecy or other restriction on the disclosure of information imposed by statute or otherwise prevents—
    (a) [F74. Her Majesty's Revenue and Customs] from disclosing information, for the purpose given in subsection (2), to the Department of Agriculture and Rural Development in Northern Ireland ("the Department") or an authorised officer of the Department, or
    (b) the Department or an authorised officer of the Department from disclosing information for that purpose to [F74. Her Majesty's Revenue and Customs].
(2) The purpose is assisting—
    (a) [F75the Commissioners for Her Majesty's Revenue and Customs], in carrying out [F76their] functions relating to allowances made because of section 40 (expenditure incurred for Northern Ireland purposes by small or medium-sized enterprises), or
    (b) the Department, in carrying out its functions under this Chapter.
(3) Information obtained as a result of a disclosure authorised by this section must not be disclosed except—
    (a) to [F77. Her Majesty's Revenue and Customs], the Department or an authorised officer of the Department, or
    (b) for the purposes of any proceedings connected with a matter in relation to which [F75the Commissioners for Her Majesty's Revenue and Customs] or the Department carry out the functions mentioned in subsection (2)(a) or (b).
Amendments (Textual)
F74. Words in s. 51. (1) substituted (18.4.2005) by Commissioners for Revenue and Customs Act 2005 (c. 11), s. 53. (1), Sch. 4 para. 84. (a); S.I. 2005/1126, art. 2. (2)(h)
F75. Words in Act substituted (18.4.2005) by Commissioners for Revenue and Customs Act 2005 (c. 11), s. 53. (1), Sch. 4 para. 83. (2); S.I. 2005/1126, art. 2. (2)(h)
F76. Word in s. 51. (2) substituted (18.4.2005) by Commissioners for Revenue and Customs Act 2005 (c. 11), s. 53. (1), Sch. 4 para. 84. (b); S.I. 2005/1126, art. 2. (2)(h)
F77. Words in s. 51. (3)(a) substituted (18.4.2005) by Commissioners for Revenue and Customs Act 2005 (c. 11), s. 53. (1), Sch. 4 para. 84. (c); S.I. 2005/1126, art. 2. (2)(h)

Chapter 5. Allowances and charges

Modifications etc. (not altering text)
C10 Pt. 2 modified (5.10.2004) by Energy Act 2004 (c. 20) , s. 198. (2) , Sch. 9 para. 21. (2) (with s. 38. (2)); S.I. 2004/2575 , art. 2. (1) , Sch. 1
C11 Pt. 2 restricted (5.10.2004) by Energy Act 2004 (c. 20) , s. 198. (2) , Sch. 9 para. 10 (with s.

38. (2)); S.I. 2004/2575 , art. 2. (1) , Sch. 1

52 First-year allowances

(1) A person is entitled to a first-year allowance in respect of first-year qualifying expenditure if—

    (a) the expenditure is incurred in a chargeable period to which this Act applies, and

    (b) the person owns the plant or machinery at some time during that chargeable period.

(2) Any first-year allowance is made for the chargeable period in which the first-year qualifying expenditure is incurred.

(3) The amount of the allowance is a percentage of the first-year qualifying expenditure in respect of which the allowance is made, as shown in the Table—

Table

Amount of first-year allowances

Type of first-year qualifying expenditure	Amount
Expenditure qualifying under section 40 (expenditure incurred for Northern Ireland purposes by small or medium-sized enterprises)	100%
Expenditure qualifying under section 44 (expenditure incurred by small or medium-sized enterprises)	40%
Expenditure qualifying under section 45 (ICT expenditure incurred by small enterprises)	100%
[F78Expenditure qualifying under section 45A (expenditure on energy-saving plant or machinery	100%]
[F79Expenditure qualifying under section 45D (expenditure on cars with low CO2 emissions)	100%]
[F80Expenditure qualifying under section 45E (expenditure on plant or machinery for gas refuelling station)	100%]
[F81Expenditure qualifying under section 45F (expenditure on plant and machinery for use wholly in a ring fence trade) which is long-life asset expenditure	24%
Expenditure qualifying under section 45F (expenditure on plant and machinery for use wholly in a ring fence trade) other than long-life asset expenditure	100%]
[F82Expenditure qualifying under section 45H (expenditure on environmentally beneficial plant or machinery)	100%]

[F83. In the case of expenditure qualifying under section 44, see also—

    (a) section 142 of the Finance Act 2004 (substitution of 50% in the case of expenditure incurred by a small enterprise in 2004-05 or financial year 2004);

    (b) section 30 of the Finance Act 2006 (substitution of 50% in the case of expenditure incurred by a small enterprise in 2006-07 or financial year 2006).]

    [F84. (c)section 37 of the Finance Act 2007 (substitution of 50% in the case of expenditure incurred by a small enterprise in 2007-08 or financial year 2007).]

(4) A person who is entitled to a first-year allowance may claim the allowance in respect of the whole or a part of the first-year qualifying expenditure.

(5) Subsection (1) needs to be read with section 236 (first-year allowances in respect of additional VAT liabilities) and is subject to—

section 205 (reduction of first-year allowance if plant or machinery provided partly for purposes other than those of qualifying activity),

section 210 (reduction of first-year allowance if it appears that a partial depreciation subsidy is or will be payable), and

sections 217, 223 and 241 (anti-avoidance: no first-year allowance in certain cases).

Amendments (Textual)

F78. S. 52. (3): words in Table added (with effect as mentioned in s. 65 of the amending Act) by Finance Act 2001 (c. 9), s. 65, Sch. 17 para. 4

F79. S. 52. (3): words in Table added (with effect as mentioned in s. 59 of the amending Act) by Finance Act 2002 (c. 23), s. 59, Sch. 19 para. 5

F80. S. 52. (3): words in Table added (with effect as mentioned in s. 61 of the amending Act) by Finance Act 2002 (c. 23), s. 61, Sch. 20 para. 5

F81. S. 52. (3): words in Table added (with effect as mentioned in s. 63 of the amending Act) by

Finance Act 2002 (c. 23), s. 63, Sch. 21 para. 6
F82 Words in s. 52. (3) added (with effect in accordance with s. 167 of the amending Act) by Finance Act 2003 (c. 14) , Sch. 30 para. 5
F83. Words in s. 52. (3) substituted (19.7.2006) by Finance Act 2006 (c. 25), s. 30. (3)
F84. S. 52. (3)(c) inserted (19.7.2007) by Finance Act 2007 (c. 11), s. 37. (3)
Modifications etc. (not altering text)
C12. S. 52. (3) modified (temp.) (with effect in accordance with s. 30. (2) of the amending Act) by Finance Act 2006 (c. 25), s. 30. (1)

Pooling

53 Pooling of qualifying expenditure
(1) Qualifying expenditure has to be pooled for the purpose of determining a person's entitlement to writing-down allowances and balancing allowances and liability to balancing charges.
(2) If a person carries on more than one qualifying activity, expenditure relating to the different activities must not be allocated to the same pool.
54 The different kinds of pools
(1) There are single asset pools, class pools and the main pool.
(2) A single asset pool may not contain expenditure relating to more than one asset.
(3) The following provide for qualifying expenditure to be allocated to a single asset pool—
section 74 (car above the cost threshold);
section 86 (short-life asset);
section 127 (ship);
section 206 (plant or machinery provided or used partly for purposes other than those of qualifying activity);
section 211 (payment of partial depreciation subsidy);
section 538 (contribution allowances: plant and machinery).
(4) A class pool is a pool which may contain expenditure relating to more than one asset.
(5) The following provide for qualifying expenditure to be allocated to a class pool—
section 101 (long-life assets);
section 107 (overseas leasing).
(6) Qualifying expenditure may be allocated to the main pool only if it does not fall to be allocated to a single asset pool or a class pool.

Writing-down and balancing allowances and balancing charges

55 Determination of entitlement or liability
(1) Whether a person is entitled to a writing-down allowance or a balancing allowance, or liable to a balancing charge, for a chargeable period is determined separately for each pool of qualifying expenditure and depends on—
    (a) the available qualifying expenditure in that pool for that period ("AQE"), and
    (b) the total of any disposal receipts to be brought into account in that pool for that period ("TDR").
(2) If AQE exceeds TDR, the person is entitled to a writing-down allowance or a balancing allowance for the period.
(3) If TDR exceeds AQE, the person is liable to a balancing charge for the period.
(4) The entitlement under subsection (2) is to a writing-down allowance except for the final chargeable period when it is to a balancing allowance.
(5) The final chargeable period is given by section 65.
(6) Subsection (2) is subject to section 110. (1) (overseas leasing: allowances prohibited in certain cases).
56 Amount of allowances and charges

(1) The amount of the writing-down allowance to which a person is entitled for a chargeable period is 25% of the amount by which AQE exceeds TDR.

(2) Subsection (1) is subject to—

(a) section 102 (long-life asset expenditure: 6%), and

(b) section 109 (overseas leasing: 10%).

(3) If the chargeable period is more or less than a year, the amount is proportionately increased or reduced.

(4) If the qualifying activity has been carried on for part only of the chargeable period, the amount is proportionately reduced.

(5) A person claiming a writing-down allowance may require the allowance to be reduced to a specified amount.

(6) The amount of the balancing charge to which a person is liable for a chargeable period is the amount by which TDR exceeds AQE.

(7) The amount of the balancing allowance to which a person is entitled for the final chargeable period is the amount by which AQE exceeds TDR.

Available qualifying expenditure

57 Available qualifying expenditure

(1) The general rule is that a person's available qualifying expenditure in a pool for a chargeable period consists of—

(a) any qualifying expenditure allocated to the pool for that period in accordance with section 58, and

(b) any unrelieved qualifying expenditure carried forward in the pool from the previous chargeable period under section 59.

(2) A person's available qualifying expenditure in a pool for a chargeable period also includes any amount allocated to the pool for that period under—

section 26. (3) (net costs of demolition);

section 86. (2) or 87. (2) (allocation of expenditure in short-life asset pool);

section 111. (3) (overseas leasing: standard recovery mechanism);

section 129. (1), 132. (2), 133. (3) or 137 (provisions relating to operation of single ship pool and deferment of balancing charges in respect of ships);

[F85section 161. C(2)(decommissioning expenditure incurred by person carrying on trade of oil extraction);]

section 165. (3) (abandonment expenditure incurred after cessation of ring fence trade);

section 206. (3) (plant or machinery used partly for purposes other than those of the qualifying activity);

section 211. (4) (partial depreciation subsidy paid).

(3) A person's available qualifying expenditure does not include any expenditure excluded by—

section 8. (4) or 9. (1) (rules against double relief);

section 166. (2) (transfers of interests in oil fields: anti-avoidance);

section 185. (2), 186. (2) or 187. (2) (restrictions where other claims made in respect of fixture);

section 218. (1), 224. (1), 228. (2), 242. (2), or 243. (2) (general anti-avoidance provisions).

(4) Subsection (1) is also subject to section 220 (allocation to chargeable periods of expenditure incurred on plant or machinery for leasing under finance lease).

Amendments (Textual)

F85. Words in s. 57. (2) inserted (with effect as mentioned in Sch. 20 para. 9. (1)-(4)(8) of the amending Act) by Finance Act 2001 (c. 9), s. 68, Sch. 20 para. 5. (2)

58 Initial allocation of qualifying expenditure to pools

(1) The following rules apply to the allocation of a person's qualifying expenditure to the appropriate pool.

(2) An amount of qualifying expenditure is not to be allocated to a pool for a chargeable period if

that amount has been taken into account in determining the person's available qualifying expenditure for an earlier chargeable period.

(3) Qualifying expenditure is not to be allocated to a pool for a chargeable period before that in which the expenditure is incurred.

(4) Qualifying expenditure is not to be allocated to a pool for a chargeable period unless the person owns the plant or machinery at some time in that period.

(5) If a first-year allowance is made in respect of an amount of first-year qualifying expenditure—

(a) subject to subsection (6), none of that amount is to be allocated to a pool for the chargeable period in which the expenditure is incurred, and

(b) the amount that may be allocated to a pool for any chargeable period is limited to the balance left after deducting the first-year allowance.

(6) If—

(a) a first-year allowance is made in respect of an amount of first-year qualifying expenditure,

(b) a disposal event occurs in respect of the plant or machinery in any chargeable period, and

(c) none of the balance left after deducting the first-year allowance has been allocated to a pool for an earlier chargeable period,

the balance (or some of it) must be allocated to a pool for the chargeable period in which the disposal event occurs.

(7) Subsection (6) applies even if the balance is nil (because of a 100% first-year allowance).

(8) "The appropriate pool" means whichever pool is applicable under the provisions of this Part apart from this section.

59 Unrelieved qualifying expenditure

(1) A person has unrelieved qualifying expenditure to carry forward from a chargeable period if for that period AQE exceeds TDR.

(2) The amount of the unrelieved qualifying expenditure is—

(a) the excess less the writing-down allowance made for the period, or

(b) if no writing-down allowance is claimed for the period, the excess.

(3) No amount may be carried forward as unrelieved qualifying expenditure from the final chargeable period.

Disposal events and disposal values: general

60 Meaning of "disposal receipt" and "disposal event"

(1) In this Part "disposal receipt" means a disposal value that a person is required to bring into account in accordance with—

(a) sections 61, 62 and 63 (disposal events, disposal values and the general limit on the amount of a disposal value),

(b) any of the provisions of this Part listed in section 66, or

(c) paragraph 11 of Schedule 12 to FA 1997 (finance lease or loan: receipt of major lump sum) or any other enactment,

when read with sections 64 and 264. (3) (cases in which no disposal value need be brought into account).

(2) In this Part "disposal event" means any event of a kind that requires a disposal value to be brought into account under this Part (whether under section 61. (1) or otherwise).

(3) If—

(a) qualifying expenditure has been allocated to a pool, and

(b) more than one disposal event occurs in respect of the plant or machinery,

a disposal value is required to be brought into account in the pool in connection with the first event only.

(4) In subsection (3) "disposal event" does not include a disposal event arising under—

section 72 (computer software),

sections 140 and 143 (attribution of deferred balancing charge), or section 238. (2) (additional VAT rebates).

61 Disposal events and disposal values

(1) A person who has incurred qualifying expenditure is required to bring the disposal value of the plant or machinery into account for the chargeable period in which—

    (a) the person ceases to own the plant or machinery;

    (b) the person loses possession of the plant or machinery in circumstances where it is reasonable to assume that the loss is permanent;

    (c) the plant or machinery has been in use for mineral exploration and access and the person abandons it at the site where it was in use for that purpose;

    (d) the plant or machinery ceases to exist as such (as a result of destruction, dismantling or otherwise);

    (e) the plant or machinery begins to be used wholly or partly for purposes other than those of the qualifying activity;

    [F86. (ee)the plant or machinery begins to be leased under a long funding lease (see Chapter 6. A);]

    (f) the qualifying activity is permanently discontinued.

(2) The disposal value to be brought into account depends on the disposal event, as shown in the Table—

Table

Disposal values: general

1. Disposal event | 2. Disposal value |

The net proceeds of the sale, together with—

(a) any insurance money received in respect of the plant or machinery as a result of an event affecting the price obtainable on the sale, and

(b) any other compensation of any description so received, so far as it consists of capital sums.

2. Sale of the plant or machinery where—

(a) the sale is at less than market value,

(b) there is no charge to tax under [F87. ITEPA 2003], and

(c) the condition in subsection (4) is met by the buyer.

The net amount received for the remains of the plant or machinery, together with—

(a) any insurance money received in respect of the demolition or destruction, and

(b) any other compensation of any description so received, so far as it consists of capital sums.

4. Permanent loss of the plant or machinery otherwise than as a result of its demolition or destruction. | Any insurance money received in respect of the loss and, so far as it consists of capital sums, any other compensation of any description so received. |

5. Abandonment of the plant or machinery which has been in use for mineral exploration and access at the site where it was in use for that purpose. | Any insurance money received in respect of the abandonment and, so far as it consists of capital sums, any other compensation of any description so received. |

[F885A. Commencement of the term of a long funding finance lease of the plant or machinery. | An amount equal to that which would fall to be recognised as the lessor's net investment in the lease if accounts were prepared in accordance with generally accepted accounting practice on the date on which the lessor's net investment in the lease is first recognised in the books or other financial records of the lessor. |

5B. Commencement of the term of a long funding operating lease of the plant or machinery. | An amount equal to the market value of the plant or machinery at the commencement of the term of the lease.] |

6. Permanent discontinuance of the qualifying activity followed by the occurrence of an event within any of items 1 to [F895B]. | The disposal value for the item in question. |

7. Any event not falling within any of items 1 to 6. | The market value of the plant or machinery at the time of the event. |

(3) The amounts referred to in column 2 of the Table are those received by the person required to bring the disposal value into account.

(4) The condition referred to in item 2 of the Table is met by the buyer if—

(a) the buyer's expenditure on the acquisition of the plant or machinery cannot be qualifying expenditure under this Part or Part 6 (research and development allowances), or

(b) the buyer is a dual resident investing company which is connected with the seller.

(5) In this section "mineral exploration and access" has the same meaning as in Chapter 13 (provisions affecting the mining and oil industries) and Part 5 (mineral extraction allowances).

Amendments (Textual)

F86. S. 61. (1)(ee) inserted (with effect in accordance with Sch. 8 para. 15 of the amending Act) by Finance Act 2006 (c. 25), Sch. 8 para. 5. (2)

F87. Words in s. 61. (2) substituted (with effect in accordance with s. 723. (1)(a)(b) of the amending Act) by Income Tax (Earnings and Pensions) Act 2003 (c. 1), s. 723, Sch. 6 para. 249 (with Sch. 7)

F88. S. 61. (2) Table Item 5. A 5. B inserted (with effect in accordance with Sch. 8 para. 15 of the amending Act) by Finance Act 2006 (c. 25), Sch. 8 para. 5. (3)

F89. Word in s. 61. (2) substituted (with effect in accordance with Sch. 8 para. 15 of the amending Act) by Finance Act 2006 (c. 25), Sch. 8 para. 5. (4)

Modifications etc. (not altering text)

C13 S. 61 modified (5.10.2004) by Energy Act 2004 (c. 20) , s. 198. (2) , Sch. 9 para. 9. (4) (with s. 38. (2)); S.I. 2004/2575 , art. 2. (1) , Sch. 1

C14. S. 61 modified (E.W.S.) (8.6.2005) by Railways Act 2005 (c. 14), s. 60. (2), Sch. 10 para. 2; S.I. 2005/1444, art. 2. (1), Sch. 1

C15. S. 61 modified (E.W.S.) (24.7.2005) by Railways Act 2005 (c. 14), s. 60. (2), Sch. 10 para. 22; S.I. 2005/1909, art. 2, Sch.

C16. S. 61. (2)-(4) excluded (E.W.S.) (8.6.2005) by Railways Act 2005 (c. 14), s. 60. (2), Sch. 10 para. 14. (2)(a); S.I. 2005/1444, art. 2. (1), Sch. 1

62 General limit on amount of disposal value

(1) The amount of any disposal value required to be brought into account by a person in respect of any plant or machinery is limited to the qualifying expenditure incurred by the person on its provision.

(2) Subsection (3) applies if a person who is required to bring a disposal value into account has acquired the plant or machinery as a result of a transaction which was, or a series of transactions each of which was, between connected persons.

(3) The amount of the disposal value is limited to the amount of the qualifying expenditure on the provision of the plant or machinery incurred by whichever party to the transaction, or to any of the transactions, incurred the greatest such expenditure.

(4) This section is subject to section 239 (limit on disposal value where additional VAT rebate or rebates has or have been made in respect of original expenditure).

63 Cases in which disposal value is nil

(1) If a person disposes of plant or machinery by way of gift in circumstances such that there is a charge to tax under [F90. ITEPA 2003], the disposal value of the plant or machinery is nil.

(2) If a person carrying on a relevant qualifying activity makes a gift of plant or machinery used in the course of the activity—

(a) to a charity within the meaning of section 506 of ICTA (charities: qualifying and non-qualifying expenditure),

(b) to a body listed in section 507. (1) of ICTA (various heritage bodies and museums), or

(c) for the purposes of a designated educational establishment within the meaning of [F91section 110 of ITTOIA 2005 or] section 84 of ICTA (gifts to educational establishments), the disposal value of the plant or machinery is nil.

(3) In subsection (2) "relevant qualifying activity" means a qualifying activity consisting of—

(a) a trade,

(b) an ordinary [F92property] business,

(c) a furnished holiday lettings business,

(d) an overseas property business, or

(e) a profession or vocation.

(4) Subsection (2) needs to be read with [F93section 109 of ITTOIA 2005 and] sections 83. A(4) and 84. (4) of ICTA (which provide for a charge to tax if subsection (2) applies in circumstances in which the donor or a connected person receives a benefit attributable to the gift).

(5) If expenditure is treated under section 27. (2) (expenditure on thermal insulation, safety measures, etc.) as having been incurred on plant or machinery, the disposal value of the plant or machinery is nil.

Amendments (Textual)

F90 Words in s. 63. (1) substituted (with effect in accordance with s. 723. (1)(a)(b) of the amending Act) by Income Tax (Earnings and Pensions) Act 2003 (c. 1), s. 723, Sch. 6 para. 250 (with Sch. 7)

F91 Words in s. 63. (2)(c) inserted (6.4.2005) by Income Tax (Trading and Other Income) Act 2005 (c. 5), s. 883. (1), Sch. 1 para. 535. (2) (with Sch. 2)

F92 Word in s. 63. (3)(b) substituted (6.4.2005) by Income Tax (Trading and Other Income) Act 2005 (c. 5), s. 883. (1), Sch. 1 para. 535. (3) (with Sch. 2)

F93 Words in s. 63. (4) inserted (6.4.2005) by Income Tax (Trading and Other Income) Act 2005 (c. 5), s. 883. (1), Sch. 1 para. 535. (4) (with Sch. 2)

Modifications etc. (not altering text)

C17. S. 63. (2) modifed (with effect as mentioned in s. 58. (4) of the amending Act) by Finance Act 2002 (c. 23), s. 58, Sch. 18 para. 9. (3)(c)

64 Case in which no disposal value need be brought into account

(1) A person is not required to bring a disposal value into account in a pool for a chargeable period in respect of plant or machinery if none of the qualifying expenditure is or has been taken into account in a claim in determining the person's available qualifying expenditure in the pool for that or any previous chargeable period.

(2) Subsection (3) applies if—

(a) a person ("C") has incurred qualifying expenditure on plant or machinery,

(b) C acquired the plant or machinery as a result of a transaction which was, or a series of transactions each of which was, between connected persons,

(c) any connected person (apart from C) who was a party to the transaction, or one of the series of transactions, is or has been required to bring a disposal value into account as a result of the transaction,

(d) a disposal event ("the relevant disposal event") occurs in respect of the plant or machinery at a time when it is owned by C, and

(e) none of C's qualifying expenditure is or has been taken into account in a claim in determining C's available qualifying expenditure for the chargeable period in which the relevant disposal event occurs or any previous chargeable period.

(3) If this subsection applies—

(a) subsection (1) does not apply in relation to the relevant disposal event, and

(b) C's qualifying expenditure is to be treated as allocated to the appropriate pool for the chargeable period in which the relevant disposal event occurs.

(4) In subsection (3)—

(a) "qualifying expenditure" means, if a first-year allowance has been made to C, the amount (including a nil amount) remaining after deducting the allowance, and

(b) "the appropriate pool" means whichever pool is applicable in relation to C under the provisions of this Part.

(5) A person takes expenditure into account in a claim if he takes it into account—

(a) in a tax return;

(b) by giving notice of an amendment of a tax return;

(c) in any other claim under this Part.

The final chargeable period

65 The final chargeable period

(1) The final chargeable period for—

    (a) the main pool, or

    (b) a long-life asset pool,

is the chargeable period in which the qualifying activity is permanently discontinued.

(2) The final chargeable period for a single asset pool is the first chargeable period in which any disposal event given in section 61. (1) occurs.

(3) Subsection (2) is subject to—

sections 77. (1) and 206. (4) (no final chargeable period merely because plant or machinery begins to be used partly for purposes other than those of qualifying activity);

sections 86. (2) and 87. (2) (ending of short-life asset pool at four-year cut-off without final chargeable period);

section 132. (2) (no final chargeable period for single ship pool).

(4) The final chargeable period for a class pool under section 107 (overseas leasing) is the chargeable period at the end of which the circumstances are such that there can be no more disposal receipts in any subsequent chargeable period.

List of provisions outside this Chapter about disposal values

66 List of provisions outside this Chapter about disposal values

The provisions of this Part referred to in section 60. (1)(b) are—

section 68 | hire-purchase etc.: disposal value on cessation of notional ownership |

sections 72 and 73 | grant of new software right: disposal value |

section 79 | cars: disposal value in avoidance cases |

sections 88 and 89 | short-life assets: disposal at under-value or to connected person |

section 104 | long-life assets: avoidance cases |

sections 108, 111 and 114 | overseas leasing: disposal values in various cases |

sections 132 and 143 | ships: ship used for overseas leasing etc.; attribution of amount where balancing charge deferred |

section 171 | oil production sharing contracts: disposal values on cessation of ownership |

sections 196 and 197 | fixtures: disposal values on cessation of notional ownership and in avoidance cases |

section 208 | effect of significant reduction in use of plant or machinery for purposes of qualifying activity |

section 211 | effect of payment of partial depreciation subsidy |

section 222 | anti-avoidance: limit on disposal value |

 [F94sections 228K to 228M | Disposal of plant or machinery subject to lease where income retained] |

section 229 | hire-purchase: disposal values in finance leasing and anti-avoidance cases |

sections 238 and 239 | additional VAT rebates |

Amendments (Textual)

F94. Words in s. 66 inserted (with effect in accordance with s. 84. (5)(6) of the amending Act) by Finance Act 2006 (c. 25), s. 84. (2)

Chapter 6. Hire-purchase etc. and plant or machinery provided by lessee

67 Plant or machinery treated as owned by person entitled to benefit of contract, etc.

(1) This section applies if—

    (a) a person carrying on a qualifying activity [F95or corresponding overseas activity] incurs capital expenditure on the provision of plant or machinery for the purposes of the qualifying activity [F95or corresponding overseas activity], and

(b) the expenditure is incurred under a contract providing that the person shall or may become the owner of the plant or machinery on the performance of the contract.

(2) The plant or machinery is to be treated for the purposes of this Part as owned by the person (and not by any other person) at any time when he is entitled to the benefit of the contract so far as it relates to the plant or machinery.

[F96. This subsection has effect subject to, and in accordance with, subsections (2. A) to (2. C).]

[F97. (2. A)If the contract is one which, in accordance with generally accepted accounting practice, falls (or would fall) to be treated as a lease, subsection (2. B) applies.

(2. B)Where that is the case, the plant or machinery is to be treated under subsection (2) as owned by the person at any time only if the contract falls (or would fall) to be treated by that person in accordance with generally accepted accounting practice as a finance lease.

(2. C)Where at any time the plant or machinery—

(a) is not treated under subsection (2) as owned by the person, but

(b) would be treated under that subsection as owned by the person, but for subsection (2. B), the plant or machinery is nevertheless to be treated under subsection (2) as not owned by any other person at that time.]

(3) At the time when the plant or machinery is brought into use for the purposes of the qualifying activity [F95or corresponding overseas activity], the person is to be treated for the purposes of this Part as having incurred all capital expenditure in respect of the plant or machinery to be incurred by him under the contract after that time.

(4) If a person—

(a) is treated under subsection (2) as owning plant or machinery,

(b) ceases to be entitled to the benefit of the contract in question so far as it relates to that plant or machinery, and

(c) does not then in fact become the owner of the plant or machinery, the person is to be treated as ceasing to own the plant or machinery at the time when he ceases to be entitled to the benefit of the contract.

[F98. (6)If—

(a) a person enters into two or more agreements, and

(b) those agreements are such that, if they together constituted a single contract, the condition in subsection (1)(b) would be met in relation to that person and that contract, the agreements are to be treated for the purposes of this section as parts of a single contract.

In this subsection, any reference to an agreement includes a reference to an undertaking, whether or not legally enforceable.]

[F99. (7)] This section is subject to section 69 (hire-purchase and fixtures) and subsection (3) is subject to section 229 (anti-avoidance).

[F100. (8)In this section "corresponding overseas activity" means an activity that would be a qualifying activity if the person carrying it on were resident in the United Kingdom.]

Amendments (Textual)

F95. Words in s. 67 inserted (with effect in accordance with Sch. 9 para. 12. (8) of the amending Act) by Finance Act 2006 (c. 25), Sch. 9 para. 12. (2)

F96. Words in s. 67. (2) inserted (with effect in accordance with Sch. 9 para. 12. (8) of the amending Act) by Finance Act 2006 (c. 25), Sch. 9 para. 12. (3)

F97. S. 67. (2. A)-(2. C) inserted (with effect in accordance with Sch. 9 para. 12. (8) of the amending Act) by Finance Act 2006 (c. 25), Sch. 9 para. 12. (4)

F98. S. 67. (6) inserted (with effect in accordance with Sch. 9 para. 12. (8) of the amending Act) by Finance Act 2006 (c. 25), Sch. 9 para. 12. (6)

F99. S. 67. (7) renumbered (with effect in accordance with Sch. 9 para. 12. (8) of the amending Act) by Finance Act 2006 (c. 25), Sch. 9 para. 12. (5)

F100. S. 67. (8) inserted (with effect in accordance with Sch. 9 para. 12. (8) of the amending Act) by Finance Act 2006 (c. 25), Sch. 9 para. 12. (7)

68 Disposal value on cessation of notional ownership

(1) This section applies if a person—

(a) is treated under section 67. (4) as ceasing to own plant or machinery, and

(b) is required to bring a disposal value into account as a result.

(2) If the plant or machinery has been brought into use for the purposes of the qualifying activity before the person ceases to own the plant or machinery, the disposal value is the total of—

(a) any relevant capital sums, and

(b) any capital expenditure treated under section 67. (3) as having been incurred when the plant or machinery was brought into use but which has not in fact been incurred.

(3) If the plant or machinery has not been brought into use for the purposes of the qualifying activity before the person ceases to own the plant or machinery, the disposal value is the total of any relevant capital sums.

(4) "Relevant capital sums" means capital sums that the person receives or is entitled to receive by way of consideration, compensation, damages or insurance money in respect of—

(a) his rights under the contract, or

(b) the plant or machinery.

(5) This section is subject to section 229 (anti-avoidance).

69 Hire-purchase etc. and fixtures

(1) Section 67 does not—

(a) apply to expenditure incurred on plant or machinery which is a fixture, or

(b) prevent Chapter 14 (fixtures) applying in relation to expenditure on plant or machinery incurred under such a contract as is mentioned in section 67. (1)(b).

(2) If—

(a) a person is treated under section 67. (2) as owning plant or machinery,

(b) the plant or machinery becomes a fixture, and

(c) the person is not treated under Chapter 14 as being the owner of the plant or machinery,

the person is to be treated for the purposes of this Part as ceasing to own the plant or machinery at the time when it becomes a fixture.

(3) In this section "fixture" has the meaning given by section 173. (1).

Plant or machinery provided by lessee

70 Plant or machinery provided by lessee

(1) This section applies if—

(a) under the terms of a lease, a lessee is required to provide plant or machinery,

(b) the lessee incurs capital expenditure on the provision of that plant or machinery for the purposes of a qualifying activity which the lessee carries on,

(c) the plant or machinery is not so installed or otherwise fixed in or to a building or any other description of land as to become, in law, part of that building or other land, and

(d) the lessee does not own the plant or machinery.

(2) The lessee—

(a) is to be treated as being the owner of the plant or machinery, as a result of incurring the capital expenditure, for so long as it continues to be used for the purposes of the qualifying activity, but

(b) is not required to bring a disposal value into account because the lease ends.

(3) Subsection (4) applies if—

(a) the plant or machinery continues to be used for the purposes of the lessee's qualifying activity until the lease ends,

(b) the lessor holds the lease in the course of a qualifying activity, and

(c) on or after the ending of the lease, a disposal event occurs in respect of the plant or machinery at a time when the lessor owns the plant or machinery as a result of the requirement under the terms of the lease.

(4) The lessor is required to bring a disposal value into account in the appropriate pool for the chargeable period in which the disposal event occurs.

(5) "The appropriate pool" means the pool which would be applicable under this Part in relation to the lessor's qualifying activity if—

(a) the expenditure incurred by the lessee had been qualifying expenditure incurred by the lessor, and

(b) that qualifying expenditure were being allocated to a pool for the chargeable period in which the disposal event occurs.

(6) In this section "lease" includes—

(a) an agreement for a lease if the term to be covered by the lease has begun, and

(b) any tenancy,

but does not include a mortgage (and "lessee" and "lessor" are to be read accordingly).

[F101. Lessees under long funding leases

Amendments (Textual)

F101. Ss. 70. A-70. E and cross-heading inserted (with effect in accordance with Sch. 8 para. 15 of the amending Act) by Finance Act 2006 (c. 25), Sch. 8 para. 6

70. AEntitlement to capital allowances

(1) This section applies if a person carrying on a qualifying activity incurs expenditure (whether or not of a capital nature) on the provision of plant or machinery for the purposes of the qualifying activity under a long funding lease.

(2) In the application of this Part in the case of that person, the plant or machinery is to be treated as owned by him at any time when he is the lessee under the long funding lease.

That is so whether or not the lease also falls to be regarded as a long funding lease in the application of this Part in the case of the lessor.

(3) The person is to be treated for the purposes of this Part as having incurred capital expenditure on the provision of the plant or machinery as follows.

(4) The capital expenditure is to be treated as incurred at the commencement of the term of the long funding lease.

(5) The amount of the capital expenditure varies, according to whether the long funding lease is—

(a) a long funding operating lease (subsection (6)), or

(b) a long funding finance lease (subsection (7)).

(6) If the long funding lease is a long funding operating lease, the amount of the capital expenditure is to be found in accordance with section 70. B.

(7) If the long funding lease is a long funding finance lease, the amount of the capital expenditure is to be found in accordance with section 70. C.

(8) See Chapter 6. A for interpretation of this section.

70. BLong funding operating lease: amount of capital expenditure

(1) This section applies by virtue of section 70. A(6).

(2) If the long funding lease is a long funding operating lease, the amount of the capital expenditure is the market value of the plant or machinery at the later of—

(a) the commencement of the term of the lease;

(b) the date on which the plant or machinery is first brought into use for the purposes of the qualifying activity.

(3) This section is to be construed as one with section 70. A.

70. CLong funding finance lease: amount of capital expenditure

(1) This section has effect by virtue of section 70. A(7) for the purpose of determining the amount of the capital expenditure in the case of a long funding finance lease.

(2) If the lease is one which, under generally accepted accounting practice, falls (or would fall) to be treated as a loan, this section applies as if the lease were one which, under generally accepted accounting practice, fell to be treated as a finance lease.

(3) The amount of the capital expenditure is the total of—
    (a) commencement PVMLP (see subsection (4)), and
    (b) if subsection (6) applies, the unrelievable pre-commencement rentals ("UPR"),
but subject, in a case falling within subsection (7), to the restriction imposed by subsection (8).
(4) Commencement PVMLP is the amount that would fall to be recognised as the present value, at the appropriate date, of the minimum lease payments (see section 70. YE) if appropriate accounts were prepared by the person.
(5) For the purposes of subsection (4)—
"appropriate accounts" are accounts prepared in accordance with generally accepted accounting practice on the date on which that amount is first recognised in the books or other financial records of the person;
"the appropriate date" is the later of—
    - the commencement of the term of the lease;
    - the date on which the plant or machinery is first brought into use for the purposes of the qualifying activity.
(6) This subsection applies if—
    (a) the person has paid rentals under the lease before the commencement of the term of the lease, and
    (b) in the case of some or all of those rentals, relief otherwise than by virtue of this subsection—
(i) is not available, and
(ii) if the case is one where the plant or machinery was not used for the purposes of a qualifying activity in the period before the commencement of the term of the lease, would not have been available had the plant or machinery been used in that period for the purposes of a qualifying activity,
and in any such case UPR is the amount of the rentals for which relief is not, and (in a case falling within paragraph (b)(ii)) would not have been, so available.
(7) Subsection (8) applies if the main purpose, or one of the main purposes, of entering into—
    (a) the lease,
    (b) a series of transactions of which the lease is one, or
    (c) any of the transactions in such a series,
is to obtain allowances under this Part in respect of an amount of capital expenditure that materially exceeds the market value of the leased asset at the commencement of the term of the lease.
(8) In any such case, the amount of the capital expenditure described in subsection (3) is to be restricted to an amount equal to the market value of the asset at the commencement of the term of the lease.
(9) In this section "relief" means relief by way of—
    (a) an allowance under this Act,
    (b) a deduction in computing profits for the purposes of income tax or corporation tax,
    (c) a deduction from total profits or total income for the purposes of either of those taxes.
(10) This section is to be construed as one with section 70. A.
70. DLong funding finance lease: additional expenditure: allowances for lessee
(1) This section applies where the following conditions are met—
    (a) a person is the lessee of plant or machinery under a long funding finance lease,
    (b) as a result of section 70. A, the person falls to be regarded as having incurred qualifying expenditure on the provision of the plant or machinery, and
    (c) the lessor incurs expenditure in relation to the plant or machinery,
    (d) as a result of the lessor incurring the expenditure, there is in the case of the lessee an increase (the "relevant increase") in the present value of the minimum lease payments.
(2) If the lease is one which, under generally accepted accounting practice, falls (or would fall) to be treated as a loan, this section applies as if the lease were one which, under generally accepted accounting practice, fell to be treated as a finance lease.
(3) The person is to be treated for the purposes of this Part as having incurred further capital

expenditure on the provision of the plant or machinery as follows.

(4) The person is to be treated as having incurred the expenditure on the date of first recognition.

(5) The amount of the expenditure is the amount that would fall to be recognised as the amount of the relevant increase if appropriate accounts were prepared by the person.

(6) For that purpose, "appropriate accounts" are accounts prepared in accordance with generally accepted accounting practice on the date of first recognition.

(7) For the purposes of this section, the "date of first recognition" is the date on which the relevant increase is first recognised in the books or other financial records of the person.

(8) This section is to be construed as one with section 70. A.

70. EDisposal events and disposal values

(1) This section applies where—

(a) a person is the lessee of plant or machinery under a long funding lease,

(b) as a result of section 70. A, the person falls to be regarded as having incurred qualifying expenditure on the provision of the plant or machinery, and

(c) the lease terminates.

(2) In the case of that person—

(a) the termination of the lease is a disposal event, and

(b) the person is required to bring into account a disposal value for the chargeable period in which that disposal event occurs.

(3) The amount of the disposal value varies according to whether the lease is—

(a) a long funding operating lease (see subsections (4) to (6)), or

(b) a long funding finance lease (see subsections (7) and (8)).

(4) If the lease is a long funding operating lease, the disposal value is the sum of—

(a) element A (see subsection (5)), and

(b) element B (see subsection (6)).

(5) Element A is the amount (if any) by which—

(a) the market value of the plant or machinery at the later of—

(i) the commencement of the term of the lease,

(ii) the date on which the plant or machinery is first brought into use for the purposes of the qualifying activity,

exceeds

(b) the aggregate amount of the reductions that fell to be made under section 502. K of ICTA or 148. I of ITTOIA 2005 for periods of account in which the person was the lessee.

(6) Element B is the sum of any amounts payable to the person which are calculated by reference to the termination value.

(7) If, in the case of the person, the lease is a long funding finance lease, the amount of the disposal value is found by first finding the sum of—

(a) any amounts payable to the person which are calculated by reference to the termination value, and

(b) if the lease terminates before the end of the term, the amount that would fall to be recognised as the present value, immediately before the termination, of the balance of the minimum lease payments (see subsection (8)) if appropriate accounts were prepared by the person, and then reducing that sum (but not below nil) by subtracting from it any amount payable by the person to the lessor for or in consequence of the termination.

(8) For the purposes of subsection (7)(b)—

(a) the balance of the minimum lease payments is the amount by which MLP exceeds TMLP, where—

- MLP is the amount of the minimum lease payments, and

- TMLP is the amount that would have been the minimum lease payments if the term of the lease had been such as to expire on the day of the termination, and

(b) "appropriate accounts" are accounts prepared in accordance with generally accepted accounting practice immediately before the termination of the lease.

(9) If the termination of the lease gives rise to a disposal event in the case of the person apart from

this section, that disposal event is to be ignored.

(10) This section is to be construed as one with section 70. A.]

[F102. Chapter 6. AInterpretation of provisions about long funding leases

Amendments (Textual)

F102. Pt. 2 Ch. 6. A inserted (with effect in accordance with Sch. 8 para. 15 of the amending Act) by Finance Act 2006 (c. 25), Sch. 8 para. 7

70. FIntroductory

This Chapter makes provision for the interpretation of this Part so far as relating to long funding leases.

Meaning of "long funding lease" etc

70. G"Long funding lease"

(1) A "long funding lease" is a funding lease (see section 70. J) which meets the following conditions—

    (a) it is not a short lease (see section 70. I),

    (b) it is not an excluded lease of background plant or machinery for a building (see section 70. R),

    (c) it not excluded by section 70. U (plant or machinery leased with land: low percentage value).

(2) Where, at the commencement of the term of a plant or machinery lease, the plant or machinery—

    (a) is not being used for the purposes of a qualifying activity carried on by the person concerned, but

    (b) subsequently begins to be used for the purposes of a qualifying activity carried on by that person,

the plant or machinery lease is a long funding lease if the condition in subsection (3) is met.

(3) The condition is that (apart from section 70. H) the plant or machinery lease would have been a long funding lease at its inception had the plant or machinery been used at that time for the purposes of a qualifying activity carried on by the person concerned.

(4) This section is subject, in the case of the lessee, to—

    (a) section 70. H (requirement for tax return treating lease as long funding lease);

    (b) section 70. Q (leases excluded by right of lessor etc to claim capital allowances).

(5) See also paragraph 91. A of Schedule 22 to the Finance Act 2000 (tonnage tax: certain leases to be treated as not being long funding leases).

70. HLessee: requirement for tax return treating lease as long funding lease

(1) A lease is not a long funding lease in the case of the lessee unless he makes a tax return for the initial period on the basis that he falls to be taxed in respect of the lease in accordance with the provisions of—

    (a) Chapter 5. A of Part 12 of ICTA (long funding leases: corporation tax), or

    (b) Chapter 10. A of Part 2 of ITTOIA 2005 (long funding leases: income tax).

(2) Where, in the case of a lease, a person has made a tax return for the initial period—

    (a) on the basis that he falls to be taxed in respect of the lease in accordance with those provisions, or

    (b) on the basis that he does not fall to be so taxed,

he may not make a claim for relief under the error or mistake provisions in respect of the tax return having been made on that basis.

(3) In this section—

"the error or mistake provisions" means—

- section 33 of the Taxes Management Act 1970; or
- paragraph 51 of Schedule 18 to the Finance Act 1998;
"the initial period" is the first accounting period or, as the case may be, tax year in which there is a difference in the amount of the profits or losses falling to be shown in the return, according to whether the lease is a long funding lease or not;
"tax return" means—
- a company tax return under paragraph 3 of Schedule 18 to the Finance Act 1998, or
- a return under section 8 of the Taxes Management Act 1970 (income tax: personal return).
70. I"Short lease"
(1) Construe "short lease" in accordance with this section.
(2) A lease whose term is 5 years or less is a short lease.
(3) Where the term of a lease is—
    (a) longer than 5 years, but
    (b) not longer than 7 years,
the lease is a short lease if Conditions A, B and C are met.
(4) Condition A is that the lease is one which, under generally accepted accounting practice, falls (or would fall) to be treated as a finance lease.
(5) Condition B is that—
    (a) the residual value of the plant or machinery which is implied in the terms of the lease, is not more than
    (b) 5% of the market value of the plant or machinery at the commencement of the term of the lease, as estimated at the inception of the lease.
(6) Condition C is that under the terms of the lease—
    (a) the total rentals falling due in the first reference year, if less than the total rentals falling due in the second reference year, are no more than 10% less than those rentals, and
    (b) the total rentals falling due in the final year or in any reference year after the second reference year, if greater than the total rentals falling due in the second reference year, are no more than 10% greater than those rentals.
(7) For the purposes of Condition C—
    (a) the first reference year is the period of 12 months beginning with the day next after the commencement of the term of the lease;
    (b) the other reference years are successive periods of 12 months each beginning on an anniversary of that day and ending before the last day of the term of the lease;
    (c) the final year is the period of 12 months ending with the last day of the term of the lease;
    (d) any part of the final year, other than the last day, may accordingly also be part of a reference year.
(8) In determining whether Condition C is met, exclude any variation in the rentals that results from changes in a standard published base rate for interest.
(9) Where—
    (a) a person leases an asset to another ("S") under a lease that would, apart from this subsection, be a short lease,
    (b) the inception of that lease is on or after 7th April 2006,
    (c) at or about the time of the inception of that lease, arrangements are entered into for the asset to be leased to one or more other persons under one or more other leases, and
    (d) in the aggregate, the term of the lease to S and the terms of the leases to such of those other persons as are connected with S exceed 5 years,
the lease to S is not a short lease.
70. J"Funding lease"
(1) A "funding lease" is a plant or machinery lease (see section 70. K) which at its inception meets one or more of the following tests—
    (a) the finance lease test (see section 70. N),
    (b) the lease payments test (see section 70. O),
    (c) the useful economic life test (see section 70. P).

51

(2) Subsection (1) is subject to the following provisions of this section.

(3) A plant or machinery lease is not a funding lease if—

(a) section 67 applies (plant or machinery treated as owned by person entitled to benefit of contract, etc), and

(b) the lease is the contract mentioned in that section.

(4) A plant or machinery lease is not a funding lease if—

(a) before the commencement of the term of the lease, the lessor has leased the plant or machinery under one or more other plant or machinery leases,

(b) in the aggregate, the terms of those other leases exceed 65% of the remaining useful economic life of the plant or machinery at the commencement of the term of the earliest of them, and

(c) none of those earlier leases was a funding lease.

(5) For the purposes of subsection (4), all persons who were lessors of the plant or machinery before 1st April 2006 are to be treated as if they were the same person as the first lessor of the plant or machinery on or after that date.

(6) A plant or machinery lease is not a funding lease in the case of the lessor if—

(a) before 1st April 2006, the plant or machinery had, for a period or periods totalling at least 10 years, been the subject of one or more leases, and

(b) the lessor under the plant or machinery lease was also lessor of the plant or machinery on the last day before 1st April 2006 on which the plant or machinery was the subject of a lease.

Meaning of "plant or machinery lease"

70. K"Plant or machinery lease"

(1) A "plant or machinery lease" is any of the following—

(a) any agreement or arrangement to which subsection (2) applies,

(b) any other agreement or arrangement, to the extent that subsection (3) applies to it,

(c) where plant or machinery is the subject of a sale and finance leaseback, as defined in section 221, the finance lease mentioned in subsection (1)(c) of that section,

and "lease", "lessor", "lessee" and other related expressions are to be construed accordingly.

(2) This subsection applies to an agreement or arrangement—

(a) under which a person grants to another person the right to use plant or machinery for a period, and

(b) which, in accordance with generally accepted accounting practice, falls (or would fall) to be treated as a lease.

(3) This subsection applies to an agreement or arrangement to the extent that—

(a) in accordance with generally accepted accounting practice, it falls (or would fall) to be treated as a lease, and

(b) it meets the conditions in subsection (4).

(4) The conditions are that, for the purposes of generally accepted accounting practice,—

(a) the agreement or arrangement conveys, or falls (or would fall) to be regarded as conveying, the right to use an asset, and

(b) the asset is plant or machinery.

(5) In the case of an agreement or arrangement that falls (or would fall) within subsection (2) or (3) immediately after the commencement of the term of the lease, the condition in subsection (2)(b) or (3)(a) (as the case may be) is to be taken to be met as respects any time in the pre-commencement period.

(6) For the purposes of subsection (5), the "pre-commencement period" is the period that—

(a) begins with the inception of the lease, and

(b) ends with the commencement of the term of the lease.

70. LPlant or machinery leased with other assets: separate derived leases

(1) This section applies in any case where an agreement or arrangement (the "mixed lease") at any

time relates, or is to relate, or has come to relate, to both—

(a) plant or machinery of any particular description (the "relevant plant or machinery"), and

(b) other assets (whether or not also plant or machinery).

(2) A mixed lease is an "eligible mixed lease" if—

(a) under generally accepted accounting practice, it falls (or would fall) to be treated as a lease, or

(b) the relevant plant or machinery is the subject of a sale and finance leaseback, as defined in section 221, and the mixed lease is or includes the finance lease mentioned in subsection (1)(c) of that section.

(3) In the case of an agreement or arrangement that falls (or would fall) within paragraph (a) of subsection (2) immediately after the commencement of the term of the lease, the condition in that paragraph is to be taken to be met as respects any time in the pre-commencement period.

(4) For the purposes of subsection (3), the "pre-commencement period" is the period that—

(a) begins with the inception of the lease, and

(b) ends with the commencement of the term of the lease.

(5) Where this section applies—

(a) the eligible mixed lease, so far as relating to the relevant plant or machinery, and

(b) the eligible mixed lease, so far as relating to other assets,

shall be treated for the purposes of this Part (other than this section) as if they were separate agreements or arrangements.

(6) Any such notional separate agreement or arrangement is referred to in this Part as a "derived lease".

(7) Section 70. M makes further provision with respect to derived leases of plant or machinery.

70. MDerived leases of plant or machinery: term and rentals

(1) This section has effect in any case where, as a result of applying section 70. L, there is a derived lease of the relevant plant or machinery.

(2) This section makes provision with respect to—

(a) determining whether the derived lease is a plant or machinery lease (see subsection (3)),

(b) the term of the derived lease (see subsection (4)),

(c) the rentals to be regarded as payable under the derived lease (see subsections (5) to (7)).

(3) Any question whether the derived lease—

(a) is a plant or machinery lease, or

(b) if it is such a lease, whether it is also a long funding lease,

is to be determined in accordance with the provisions of this Part.

(4) The term of the derived lease—

(a) is limited to the remaining useful economic life of the relevant plant or machinery at the commencement of the term of the derived lease, but

(b) subject to that, is to be determined in accordance with section 70. YF (the "term" of a lease).

(5) The rentals that are to be regarded as payable under the derived lease shall be such rentals (the "deemed rentals") as are just and reasonable in all the circumstances of the case.

(6) It shall be assumed that rentals under the derived lease are payable in equal instalments throughout the term of the lease, unless it is reasonable to draw a different conclusion from all the circumstances of the case.

(7) In determining the amount of any deemed rentals, regard shall be had to—

(a) all the provisions of the eligible mixed lease,

(b) the nature of the relevant plant or machinery,

(c) the value of the relevant plant or machinery at the commencement of the term of the derived lease,

(d) the amount which, at the commencement of the term of the derived lease, is expected to be the market value of the relevant plant or machinery at the end of the term of the derived lease,

(e) the remaining useful economic life of the relevant plant or machinery at the commencement of the term of the derived lease;

(f) the term of the derived lease.

(8) Expressions used in section 70. L have the same meaning in this section.

The tests for being a funding lease

70. NThe finance lease test

(1) A lease meets the finance lease test in the case of any person if the lease is one which, under generally accepted accounting practice, falls (or would fall) to be treated as a finance lease or a loan in the accounts—

(a) of that person, or

(b) where that person is the lessor, of any person connected with him.

(2) In this section "accounts", in relation to a company, includes any accounts which—

(a) relate to two or more companies of which that company is one, and

(b) are drawn up in accordance with generally accepted accounting practice.

(3) Where for any period—

(a) a person is not within the charge to income tax or corporation tax by reason of not being resident in the United Kingdom, and

(b) accounts are not prepared in accordance with international accounting standards or UK generally accepted accounting practice,

any question relating to generally accepted accounting practice is to be determined for the purposes of this section by reference to generally accepted accounting practice with respect to accounts prepared in accordance with international accounting standards.

70. OThe lease payments test

(1) A lease meets the lease payments test if—

(a) the present value of the minimum lease payments (see section 70. YE),

is equal to

(b) 80% or more of the fair value of the leased plant or machinery.

(2) The present value of the minimum lease payments is to be calculated by using the interest rate implicit in the lease.

(3) In this section "fair value" means—

(a) the market value of the leased plant or machinery,

less

(b) any grants receivable towards the purchase or use of that plant or machinery.

(4) For the purposes of this section—

(a) the interest rate implicit in the lease is the interest rate that would apply in accordance with normal commercial criteria, including, in particular, generally accepted accounting practice (where applicable), but

(b) if the interest rate implicit in the lease cannot be determined in accordance with paragraph (a), it is the temporal discount rate for the purposes of section 70 of the Finance Act 2005 (companies: film relief: valuation of "rights to guaranteed income" and "disposed rights").

70. PThe useful economic life test

A lease meets the useful economic life test if the term of the lease is more than 65% of the remaining useful economic life of the leased plant or machinery.

Leases excluded by right of lessor etc to claim capital allowances

70. QLeases excluded by right of lessor etc to claim capital allowances

(1) A lease is not a long funding lease in the case of the lessee if it is excluded by virtue of subsection (2) (but see also subsection (5)).

(2) A lease is excluded if the lessor, or any superior lessor (see subsections (7) to (9)),—

(a) is entitled, at the commencement of the term of the lease, to claim a relevant allowance (see subsection (6)),

(b) would have been so entitled at that time, but for section 70. V (tax avoidance involving international leasing),

(c) has at any earlier time been entitled to claim such an allowance, but has not been required to bring a disposal value into account in accordance with section 61. (1)(ee), or

(d) would fall within any one or more of paragraphs (a) to (c), if he had been within the charge to income tax or corporation tax at the inception of the lease and any earlier times.

(3) Where for any period the lessor, or any superior lessor, is a person—

(a) who is not within the charge to income tax or corporation tax by reason of not being resident in the United Kingdom, and

(b) who does not prepare accounts in accordance with international accounting standards or UK generally accepted accounting practice,

subsection (4) applies.

(4) In determining whether the condition in subsection (2)(d) is met in any such case, any question relating to generally accepted accounting practice in relation to that person and that period is to be determined by reference to generally accepted accounting practice with respect to accounts prepared in accordance with international accounting standards.

(5) A lease is not excluded by virtue of subsection (2) if—

(a) the inception of the lease is before 28th June 2006, and

(b) by virtue only of section 70. J(6), the lease is not a funding lease in the case of the lessor.

(6) A "relevant allowance" is an allowance under this Act in respect of the leased plant or machinery.

(7) There is a "superior lessor" only if the leased plant or machinery is the subject of a chain of superior leases.

(8) Leased plant or machinery is the subject of a chain of superior leases if—

(a) the lessor has his interest in relation to the plant or machinery under or by virtue of a lease from a third person (P), or

(b) the circumstances are as in paragraph (a), but P has his interest in relation to the plant or machinery under or by virtue of a lease from a fourth person (Q), or

(c) the circumstances are as in paragraph (b), but Q has his interest in relation to the plant or machinery under or by virtue of a lease from a fifth person (R),

and so on, where there is more than a fifth person involved.

(9) Where any leased plant or machinery is the subject of a chain of superior leases, the superior lessors are the persons described in subsection (8) as P, Q, R, and so on.

(10) Subsections (6) to (9) have effect for the interpretation of this section.

Excluded leases of background plant or machinery for a building

70. RExcluded leases of background plant or machinery for a building

(1) Construe references to an excluded lease of background plant or machinery for a building in accordance with this section.

(2) This section applies where—

(a) plant or machinery is affixed to, or otherwise installed in or on, any land which consists of or includes a building,

(b) the plant or machinery is background plant or machinery for the building (see subsections (4) and (5)),

(c) the plant or machinery is leased with the land under a mixed lease, and

(d) none of the disqualifications set out in section 70. S applies.

(3) In any such case, the derived lease of the plant or machinery is an excluded lease of background plant or machinery for a building.

(4) The background plant or machinery for a building is any plant or machinery—

(a) which is of such a description that plant or machinery of that description might reasonably be expected to be installed in, or in or on the sites of, a variety of buildings of different descriptions, and

(b) whose sole or main purpose is to contribute to the functionality of the building or its site as an environment within which activities can be carried on.

(5) Subsection (4) has effect subject to the provisions of any order under section 70. T.

70. SThe disqualifications

(1) This section sets out the disqualifications mentioned in subsection (2)(d) of section 70. R and is to be construed as one with that section.

(2) Disqualification A is that the amounts payable—

(a) under the mixed lease, or

(b) under any other arrangement,

vary, or may be varied, by reference to the value from time to time to the lessor of allowances under this Act in respect of expenditure incurred by him in the provision of the background plant or machinery for the building.

(3) Disqualification B is that the main purpose, or one of the main purposes, of entering into—

(a) the mixed lease,

(b) a series of transactions of which the mixed lease is one, or

(c) any of the transactions in such a series,

is to secure that allowances under this Act are available to the lessor in respect of expenditure incurred in the provision of background plant or machinery for a building.

70. TOrders relating to background plant or machinery for a building

(1) This section supplements section 70. R and is to be construed as one with it.

(2) The Treasury may by order prescribe—

(a) descriptions of plant or machinery to be used as examples of the kinds of plant or machinery that may be regarded as falling within the definition of background plant or machinery for a building in determining whether any particular plant or machinery does or does not fall within that definition;

(b) descriptions of plant or machinery to be deemed to be background plant or machinery for a building;

(c) descriptions of plant or machinery to be deemed not to be background plant or machinery for a building.

(3) An order under this section—

(a) may make different provision for different cases (including different descriptions of building),

(b) may contain incidental, consequential, supplemental, or transitional provision or savings.

(4) The first order made under this section may include provisions having effect in relation to times before the making of the order (but not times earlier than 1st April 2006).

Exclusion for certain plant or machinery leased with land

70. UPlant or machinery leased with land: low percentage value

(1) This section applies where—

(a) any plant or machinery (the "relevant plant or machinery") is affixed to, or otherwise installed, in or on any land,

(b) the plant or machinery is not background plant or machinery for any building situated in or on the land,

(c) the plant or machinery is leased with the land under a mixed lease, and

(d) none of the relevant disqualifications applies.

(2) For the purposes of this section the "relevant disqualifications" are the disqualifications set out in section 70. S, but for this purpose—

(a) take the reference in subsection (1) of that section to subsection (2)(d) of section 70. R as a reference to this subsection (and, accordingly, construe the second reference to that section as a reference to this section), and

(b) take references in section 70. S to background plant or machinery for a building as references to relevant plant or machinery.

(3) Where this section applies, the derived lease of the relevant plant or machinery is excluded by this section if the condition in subsection (4) is met at the commencement of the term of that lease.

(4) The condition is that AMV does not exceed both—

(a) 10% of BMV; and

(b) 5% of LMV.

(5) For that purpose—

AMV is the aggregate of—

- the market value of the relevant plant or machinery, and

- the market value of any other plant or machinery that falls within subsection (1) in the case of the leased land;

BMV is the aggregate market value of all the background plant or machinery leased with the land;

LMV is the market value of the land (including buildings and fixtures).

(6) For this purpose the market value of any land at any time is to be determined on the assumption of a sale by an absolute owner of the land free from all leases and other encumbrances.

Avoidance

70. VTax avoidance involving international leasing

(1) This section applies where matters are so arranged that there are plant or machinery leases such that—

(a) under a lease by a non-resident, an asset is provided directly or indirectly to a resident,

(b) the direct provision of the asset to the resident is by a lease which, in the case of the resident, is a long funding lease or a lease to which section 67 (hire purchase etc) applies,

(c) the asset is used by the resident for the purpose of leasing it under a lease (the "relevant lease") that would not (apart from this section) be a long funding lease in the case of the resident, and

(d) under the relevant lease, the asset is provided directly or indirectly (but by a lease) to a non-resident.

(2) Subsection (3) applies if the sole or main purpose of arranging matters in that way is to obtain a tax advantage by securing that allowances under this Part are available to a resident by virtue of—

(a) section 67 (hire purchase), or

(b) section 70. A (long funding leases).

(3) In any such case, the relevant lease is deemed to be a long funding lease in the case of the resident who is the lessor under it.

(4) The reference in this section to a person obtaining a tax advantage (see section 577. (4)) also includes a reference to a person obtaining a tax advantage within the meaning of [F103section 840. ZA of ICTA].

(5) In this section—

"non-resident" means a person who—

- is not resident in the United Kingdom, and

- does not use the plant or machinery exclusively for earning profits chargeable to tax;

"resident" means a person who—

- is resident in the United Kingdom, or

- uses the plant or machinery exclusively for earning profits chargeable to tax.

Amendments (Textual)

F103. Words in s. 70. V(4) substituted (6.4.2007) by Income Tax Act 2007 (c. 3), s. 1034. (1), Sch. 1 para. 398 (with Sch. 2)

Transfers, assignments, novations, leaseback, variations etc

70. WTransfers, assignments etc by lessor

(1) This section applies in any case where the following conditions are met—

(a) a person (the "old lessor") is lessor of plant or machinery under a plant or machinery lease (the "old lease"),

(b) during the term of the lease, the old lessor transfers the plant or machinery to another person (the "new lessor"),

(c) the transfer is not the grant of a plant or machinery lease by the old lessor,

(d) immediately after the transfer, the new lessor is the lessor of the plant or machinery under a lease ("the new lease") (whether or not the same lease as the old lease).

(2) If it is not otherwise the case,—

(a) the old lessor is to be treated as if the old lease terminated immediately before the transfer, and

(b) the new lessor is to be treated as if the new lease had been entered into immediately after the transfer.

(3) The new lessor is also to be treated as if the date of the transfer were the date of both—

(a) the inception of the new lease, and

(b) the commencement of the term of the new lease,

if it is not otherwise the case.

(4) If, immediately before the transfer, the old lease was (or was treated by virtue of this subsection as being) in the case of the old lessor a lease of either of the following descriptions—

(a) a long funding lease, or

(b) a lease which is not a long funding lease,

the new lease is to be treated in the case of the new lessor as being a lease of the same description, if the conditions in subsection (5) are met.

(5) The conditions are that—

(a) the term of the new lease is the unexpired portion of the term of the old lease, and

(b) the amounts receivable under the new lease are the same as would have been receivable under the old lease, assuming it to have continued in effect.

(6) If—

(a) it is not otherwise the case, and

(b) the conditions in subsection (5) are met,

the lessee is to be treated as if the old lease and the new lease were the same continuing lease.

(7) Any reference in this section to a transfer of plant or machinery by a person includes a reference to—

(a) any kind of disposal of, or of the person's interest in, the plant or machinery,

(b) any arrangements under which the person's interest in the plant or machinery is terminated and another person becomes lessor of the plant or machinery,

(c) in a case where the plant or machinery is a fixture and the person is treated under section 176 as the owner, any cessation of ownership under section 188, 190, 191, 192 or 192. A.

70. XTransfers, assignments etc by lessee

(1) This section applies in any case where the following conditions are met—

(a) a person (the "old lessee") is lessee of plant or machinery under a plant or machinery lease (the "old lease"),

(b) during the term of the lease, the old lessee transfers the plant or machinery to another person (the "new lessee"),

(c) the transfer is not the grant of a plant or machinery lease by the old lessee,

(d) immediately after the transfer, the new lessee is the lessee of the plant or machinery under a lease ("the new lease") (whether or not the same lease as the old lease).

(2) If it is not otherwise the case,—

(a) the old lessee is to be treated as if the old lease terminated immediately before the transfer, and

(b) the new lessee is to be treated as if the new lease had been entered into immediately after the transfer.

(3) The new lessee is also to be treated as if the date of the transfer were the date of both—

    (a) the inception of the new lease, and

    (b) the commencement of the term of the new lease,

if it is not otherwise the case.

(4) If, immediately before the transfer, the old lease was (or was treated by virtue of this subsection as being) in the case of the old lessee a lease of one of the following descriptions—

    (a) a long funding lease, or

    (b) a lease which is not a long funding lease,

the new lease is to be treated in the case of the new lessee as being a lease of the same description, if the conditions in subsection (5) are met.

(5) The conditions are that—

    (a) the term of the new lease is the unexpired portion of the term of the old lease, and

    (b) the amounts payable under the new lease are the same as would have been payable under the old lease, assuming it to have continued in effect.

(6) If—

    (a) it is not otherwise the case, and

    (b) the conditions in subsection (5) are met,

the lessor is to be treated as if the old lease and the new lease were the same continuing lease.

(7) Any reference in this section to a transfer of plant or machinery by a person includes a reference to—

    (a) any kind of disposal of, or of the person's interest in, the plant or machinery,

    (b) any arrangements under which the person's interest in the plant or machinery is terminated and another person becomes lessee of the plant or machinery,

    (c) in a case where the plant or machinery is a fixture and the person is treated under section 176 as the owner, any cessation of ownership under section 188, 190, 191, 192 or 192. A.

70. YSale and leaseback, lease and leaseback etc: lessors

(1) Where—

    (a) a person (B) transfers plant or machinery to another person (A),

    (b) the plant or machinery is directly or indirectly leased back to B, and

    (c) immediately before the commencement of the term of the lease back to B, B is the lessor of the plant or machinery to another person under a lease which is, in B's case, a long funding lease,

the lease back to B is, in the case of both A and B, a long funding lease.

(2) If, in any such case, the plant or machinery is leased back from A to B indirectly, any leases by means of which the indirect lease back from A to B is effected are also long funding leases in the case of each of the parties to them.

(3) Any reference in this section to a transfer of plant or machinery by a person includes a reference to—

    (a) any kind of disposal of, or of the person's interest in, the plant or machinery (including the grant of a lease),

    (b) any arrangements under which the person's interest in the plant or machinery is terminated and another person becomes entitled to, or to an interest in, the plant or machinery,

    (c) in a case where the plant or machinery is a fixture and the person is treated under section 176 as the owner, any cessation of ownership under section 188, 190, 191, 192 or 192. A.

70. YAChange in accountancy classification of long funding lease

(1) This section applies in any case where—

    (a) a person is lessor or lessee under a long funding lease, and

    (b) at any time after the inception of the lease, the accountancy classification of the lease as a finance lease or an operating lease changes in the relevant accounts.

(2) The person is to be treated as if—

    (a) the lease had terminated immediately before the time of the change,

    (b) another lease (the "new lease") had been entered into immediately after the time of the change, and

    (c) the new lease were a long funding lease in the case of the lessor.

(3) The person is also to be treated as if the date on which the change occurs were the date of both—

(a) the inception of the new lease, and

(b) the commencement of the term of the new lease.

(4) The cases where the accountancy classification of a long funding lease as a finance lease or an operating lease changes at any time (the "relevant time") in the relevant accounts are those set out in subsections (5) and (6).

(5) Case 1 is where—

(a) immediately before the relevant time, the lease is one that falls (or would fall) to be treated in the relevant accounts in accordance with generally accepted accounting practice as a finance lease for accounting purposes, and

(b) at the relevant time the lease becomes one that falls (or would fall) to be treated in the relevant accounts in accordance with generally accepted accounting practice as not being a finance lease for accounting purposes.

(6) Case 2 is where—

(a) immediately before the relevant time, the lease is one that falls (or would fall) to be treated in the relevant accounts in accordance with generally accepted accounting practice as not being a finance lease for accounting purposes, and

(b) at the relevant time the lease becomes one that falls (or would fall) to be treated in the relevant accounts in accordance with generally accepted accounting practice as a finance lease for accounting purposes.

(7) The Treasury may by regulations make provision for or in connection with restricting the application or operation of this section.

(8) In this section, any reference to a finance lease includes a reference to a loan.

(9) In the application of this section in relation to any person, the "relevant accounts" are the accounts—

(a) of that person, or

(b) where that person is the lessor, of any person connected with that person,

but only to the extent that the treatment of the lease in those accounts as a finance lease or otherwise falls (or would fall) to be determined by reference to that person as the lessor or lessee under the lease.

(10) Subsections (2) and (3) of section 70. N (finance lease test: group accounts, and generally accepted accounting practice for persons outside the charge to tax) also apply for the purposes of this section.

70. YBLong funding operating lease: extension of term of lease

(1) This section applies in any case where—

(a) a person is lessor or lessee under a long funding operating lease (the "existing lease"),

(b) an event occurs which has the effect of extending the term of the lease (whether by variation of the provisions of the lease, the grant or exercise of an option or in any other way), and

(c) the event is not one by reason of which, within the meaning of section 70. YA, the accountancy classification of the lease as an operating lease changes in the relevant accounts.

(2) For this purpose an event has the effect of extending the term of the lease if it meets any of the following conditions—

(a) it has the effect of making a further period a non-cancellable period;

(b) it is the grant of an option to the lessee to continue to lease the plant or machinery for a further period, where it is reasonably certain at the time the option is granted that the lessee will exercise it;

(c) it is the exercise by the lessee of an option to continue to lease the plant or machinery for a further period;

(d) it does not fall within the preceding paragraphs, but it has the effect that the lessee will continue, or is reasonably certain to continue, to lease the plant or machinery for a further period. For this purpose "further period" means a period falling wholly or partly after the end of the pre-existing term.

(3) The person is to be treated as if—

(a) the existing lease terminated at the end of the day before the effective date,

(b) another lease (the "new lease") were entered into on the effective date, and

(c) the term of the new lease were the unexpired portion of the term of the existing lease, as extended.

(4) The person is also to be treated as if the effective date were the date of both—

(a) the inception of the new lease, and

(b) the commencement of the term of the new lease.

(5) The new lease is to be taken to be a long funding operating lease.

(6) For the purposes of this section the "effective date" is the earlier of—

(a) the day after the end of the pre-existing term of the existing lease;

(b) if the rentals payable are varied as a result of or otherwise in connection with the event, the date on which the variation takes effect.

(7) In this section—

"non-cancellable period" has the same meaning as in section 70. YF (the "term" of a lease);

"pre-existing term", in relation to a lease, means the term of the lease apart from the extension in question.

70. YCExtension of term of lease that is not a long funding lease

(1) This section applies where—

(a) a person is lessor under a plant or machinery lease (the "existing lease") that is not a long funding lease, and

(b) an event occurs which has the effect of extending the term of the lease (whether by variation of the provisions of the lease, the grant or exercise of an option or in any other way).

(2) Subsection (2) of section 70. YB (events having the effect of extending the term of a lease) also has effect for the purposes of this section.

(3) Make the following assumptions—

(a) the existing lease terminates immediately before the effective date,

(b) another lease (the "new lease") is entered into on the effective date,

(c) the term of the new lease is the portion of the term of the existing lease, as extended, that remains unexpired as at the effective date;

(d) the effective date is the date of both—

(i) the inception of the new lease, and

(ii) the commencement of the term of the new lease.

(4) If, on those assumptions, the new lease would be a long funding lease, the person is to be treated on those assumptions.

(5) If subsection (4) does not apply, then, for the purposes of any subsequent application of this section or section 70. YD in the case of the existing lease, the term of the existing lease is to be taken to be the term as extended (or further extended).

(6) For the purposes of this section the "effective date" is the earlier of—

(a) the day after the end of the pre-existing term of the existing lease;

(b) if the rentals payable are varied as a result of or otherwise in connection with the event, the date on which the variation takes effect.

(7) In this section "pre-existing term", in relation to a lease, means the term of the lease apart from the extension in question.

70. YDIncrease in proportion of residual amount guaranteed: review of status

(1) This section applies where—

(a) a person is lessor under a lease (the "existing lease") that is not a long funding lease,

(b) the person enters into an arrangement which meets, or arrangements which (taken together) meet, the conditions in subsection (2).

(2) The conditions are that—

(a) as a result of the arrangement or arrangements, there is an increase, after the inception of the lease, in the proportion of the residual amount that is guaranteed as mentioned in section 70. YE(1)(b), and

(b) had the arrangement or arrangements been entered into before the inception of the lease, the lease would have been a long funding lease.

(3) The person is to be treated as if—

(a) the existing lease had terminated immediately before the time of the relevant transaction,

(b) another lease (the "new lease") had been entered into immediately after the time of the relevant transaction,

(c) the term of the new lease were the portion of the term of the existing lease that remains unexpired as at the date of the relevant transaction;

(d) the date of the relevant transaction were the date of both—

(i) the inception of the new lease, and

(ii) the commencement of the term of the new lease.

(4) For the purposes of this section, the "relevant transaction" is the arrangement or, where two or more arrangements have been entered into, the latest of them.

(5) The Treasury may by regulations make provision for or in connection with restricting the application or operation of this section.

Interpretation

70. YE"Minimum lease payments"

(1) In the case of any lease, the minimum lease payments are the minimum payments under the lease over the term of the lease (including any initial payment) together with—

(a) in the case of the lessee, so much of any residual amount as is guaranteed by him or a person connected with him, or

(b) in the case of the lessor, so much of any residual amount as is guaranteed by the lessee or a person who is not connected with the lessor.

(2) In determining the minimum payments, exclude so much of any payment as represents—

(a) charges for services, or

(b) qualifying UK or foreign tax to be paid by the lessor.

(3) In this section—

"qualifying UK or foreign tax" means any tax or duty chargeable under the law of any part of the United Kingdom, or under the law of any foreign country, other than—

- income tax,

- corporation tax,

- any tax chargeable under the law of a foreign country which is similar to income tax or corporation tax,

and here "foreign country" means any territory outside the United Kingdom;

"residual amount" means so much of the fair value of the plant or machinery subject to the lease as cannot reasonably be expected to be recovered by the lessor from the payments under the lease.

(4) In the definition of "residual amount" in subsection (3), "fair value" means—

(a) the market value of the leased plant or machinery,

less

(b) any grants receivable towards the purchase or use of that plant or machinery.

70. YFThe "term" of a lease

(1) The term of a lease is the period comprising—

(a) so much of the post-commencement period as is a non-cancellable period, and

(b) any subsequent periods which meet the conditions in subsection (2).

(2) The conditions are that—

(a) the lessee has an option to continue to lease the asset for the period (whether with or without further payment), and

(b) it is reasonably certain, at the inception of the lease, that the lessee will exercise that option.

(3) The "post-commencement period" is so much of the period of the lease as begins with the commencement of the term of the lease.

(4) A "non-cancellable period" is any period during which the lessee may terminate the lease only—

(a) upon the occurrence of some remote contingency, or

(b) upon payment by the lessee of such an additional amount that, at the inception of the lease, continuation of the lease is reasonably certain.

(5) If, at the commencement of the term of the lease,—

(a) the market value of the asset exceeds £1 million, and

(b) the estimated market value of the asset 5 years after the commencement of the term of the lease is more than half of the market value of the asset at the commencement of the term of the lease,

subsection (6) applies.

(6) If, in any such case, the term of the lease (apart from this subsection) would be 5 years or less, but—

(a) the lessee has one or more options to continue to lease the asset,

(b) on the assumption that it is reasonably certain, at the inception of the lease, that the lessee will exercise those options, the term of the lease would exceed 7 years, and

(c) on failing to exercise any one of those options, the lessee may be required to make a payment to the lessor,

it is to be assumed for the purposes of this section that any option to continue to lease the asset will be exercised, unless it is reasonably certain, at the inception of the lease, that the option will not be exercised.

(7) Subsection (6) does not apply if, leaving out of account any options that would, by virtue of that subsection, result in the term of the lease exceeding 7 years, Conditions A, B and C in section 70. I (meaning of "short lease") are met.

(8) See also section 70. YC(5) (extension, for certain purposes, of term of lease that is not a long funding lease).

70. YG"Termination amount"

(1) This section applies where plant or machinery is or has been, or is to be, leased under a long funding lease.

(2) Construe "termination amount", in the case of a long funding lease, in accordance with the following provisions of this section.

(3) If—

(a) the lease terminates as a result of a plant or machinery disposal event, or

(b) a plant or machinery disposal event occurs as a result of, or otherwise in connection with, the termination of the lease,

the termination amount is the disposal value that would have fallen to be brought into account by the lessor by reason of the plant or machinery disposal event on the assumptions in subsection (4).

(4) Those assumptions are—

(a) that section 34. A (which prevents the lessor's expenditure for long funding leasing from being qualifying expenditure) did not apply in the case of the lessor, and

(b) that the lessor had claimed all the capital allowances that would in consequence have been available to him.

(5) If—

(a) subsection (3) does not apply, and

(b) the lease is a long funding finance lease,

the termination amount is the value at which, immediately after the termination of the lease, the plant or machinery is recognised in the books or other financial records of the lessor.

(6) If—

(a) subsection (3) does not apply, and

(b) the lease is a long funding operating lease,

the termination amount is the market value of the plant or machinery immediately after the termination of the lease.

(7) For the purposes of this section a "plant or machinery disposal event" is an event that would

have been a disposal event in relation to the plant or machinery in the case of the lessor on the assumptions in subsection (4).

70. YH"Termination value"

(1) This section applies where plant or machinery is or has been, or is to be, leased under a long funding lease.

(2) Construe "termination value" in accordance with the following provisions of this section.

(3) The general rule is that the termination value of any plant or machinery is the value of the plant or machinery at or about the time when the lease terminates.

(4) Any reference to calculation by reference to the termination value includes a reference to calculation by reference to any one or more of—

(a) the proceeds of sale, if the plant or machinery is sold after the lease comes to an end,

(b) any insurance proceeds, compensation or similar sums in respect of the plant or machinery,

(c) an estimate of the market value of the plant or machinery.

(5) Any reference to calculation by reference to the termination value also includes a reference to—

(a) determination in a way which, or by reference to factors or criteria which, might reasonably be expected to produce a broadly similar result to calculation by reference to the termination value, or

(b) any other form of calculation indirectly by reference to the termination value.

70. YIGeneral definitions

(1) Construe these expressions as follows—

"absolute owner", in the application of this Chapter in relation to Scotland, means the owner;

"arrangement" includes any transaction or series of transactions;

"background plant or machinery for a building" is to be construed in accordance with sections 70. R to 70. T;

"building" includes a reference to—

- a structure,

- part of a building or structure;

"commencement", in relation to the term of a lease, means the date on and after which the lessee is entitled to exercise his right to use the complete leased asset under the lease;

for this purpose an asset is to be regarded as complete if its construction is substantially complete;

"derived lease" is to be construed in accordance with section 70. L;

"the finance lease test" means the finance lease test in section 70. N;

"fixture"—

- means any plant or machinery that is so installed or otherwise fixed in or to a building or other description of land as to become, in law, part of that building or other land, and

- includes any boiler or water-filled radiator installed in a building as part of a space or water heating system;

"funding lease" has the meaning given by section 70. J;

"inception", in relation to a plant or machinery lease, means the earliest date on which the following conditions are met—

- there is a contract in writing for the lease between the lessor and the lessee,

- either—

the contract is unconditional, or

if it is conditional, the conditions have been met,

- no terms remain to be agreed;

"initial payment", in the case of a plant or machinery lease, means a payment by the lessee—

- at or before the time when the lease is entered into, and

- in respect of the plant or machinery which is the subject of the lease;

"lease" includes any agreement or arrangement which is or includes a plant or machinery lease (and "lessor", "lessee" and other related expressions are to be construed accordingly);

"lease", in relation to land, includes—

- an underlease, sublease or any tenancy,

- in England and Wales or Northern Ireland, an agreement for a lease, underlease, sublease, or tenancy,

- in Scotland, an agreement (including missives of let not constituting a lease) under which a lease, sublease or tenancy is to be executed,

- in the case of land situated outside the United Kingdom, any interest corresponding to a lease as so defined,

and "lessor", "lessee" and other related expressions are to be construed accordingly;

"lease", in relation to plant or machinery, includes a sublease (and "lessor", "lessee" and other related expressions are to be construed accordingly);

"lessee", in relation to a lease, includes any person entitled to the lessee's interest under the lease;

"lessor", in relation to a lease, includes any person entitled to the lessor's interest under the lease;

"long funding lease" has the meaning given by section 70. G;

"long funding finance lease" means a long funding lease that meets the finance lease test by virtue of section 70. N(1)(a);

"long funding operating lease" means a long funding lease which is not a long funding finance lease;

"market value", in relation to plant or machinery, is to be construed in accordance with subsection (2);

"minimum lease payments" has the meaning given by section 70. YE;

"mixed lease" is to be construed in accordance with section 70. L;

"plant or machinery lease" has the meaning given by section 70. K (and see also sections 70. L and 70. M);

"remaining useful economic life", in the case of any leased plant or machinery, is the period—

- beginning with the commencement of the term of the lease, and

- ending when the asset is no longer used, and no longer likely to be used, by any person for any purpose as a fixed asset of a business;

"short lease" is to be construed in accordance with section 70. I;

"the term", in relation to a lease, is to be construed in accordance with section 70. YF (but see also section 70. YC(5) (extension, for certain purposes, of term of lease that is not a long funding lease));

"termination", in relation to a lease,—

- means the coming to an end of the lease, whether by effluxion of time or in any other way, and

- includes in particular the bringing to an end of the lease by any person or by operation of law,

and related expressions are to be construed accordingly;

"termination amount" is to be construed in accordance with section 70. YG;

"termination value" is to be construed in accordance with section 70. YH.

(2) The market value of any plant or machinery at any time is to be determined on the assumption of a disposal by an absolute owner free from all leases and other encumbrances.

(3) In relation to a lease, any reference to plant or machinery includes a reference to fixtures.

F104. (4). . . . .

(5) Any necessary apportionments under or by virtue of this Chapter are to be made on a just and reasonable basis.

Amendments (Textual)

F104. S. 70. YI(4) repealed (6.4.2007) by Income Tax Act 2007 (c. 3), s. 1034. (1), Sch. 1 para. 399, Sch. 3 Pt. 1 (with Sch. 2)

70. YJPower to vary the meaning of certain expressions

(1) The Treasury may by regulations make provision amending this Chapter so as to vary—

(a) the meaning of "plant or machinery lease", or

(b) the finance lease test.

(2) A statutory instrument containing regulations under this section is not to be made unless a draft of the instrument has been laid before, and approved by a resolution of, the House of Commons.]

Chapter 7. Computer software

71 Software and rights to software

(1) For the purposes of this Part computer software is treated as plant (whether or not it would constitute plant apart from this section).

(2) If a person carrying on a qualifying activity incurs capital expenditure in acquiring, for the purposes of the qualifying activity, a right to use or otherwise deal with computer software, this Part applies as if—

    (a) the right and the software to which it relates were plant,

    (b) the plant were provided for the purposes of the qualifying activity, and

    (c) so long as the person is entitled to the right, the person owned the plant as a result of incurring the capital expenditure.

72 Disposal values

(1) This section applies if a person—

    (a) has incurred qualifying expenditure on the provision of plant consisting of computer software or the right to use or otherwise deal with computer software, and

    (b) grants to another a right to use or otherwise deal with the whole or part of the computer software in circumstances in which the consideration for the grant—

(i) consists of a capital sum, or

(ii) would consist of a capital sum if the consideration were in money.

(2) The person is required to bring a disposal value into account unless—

    (a) while the person owned the computer software or the right to use or otherwise deal with the computer software, and

    (b) before the grant of the right referred to in subsection (1)(b),

there has been a disposal event falling within section 61. (1)(e) (use for purposes other than those of the qualifying activity) or 61. (1)(f) (permanent discontinuance of the qualifying activity).

(3) The disposal value to be brought into account under this section depends on the circumstances of the grant of the right, as shown in the Table—

Table

Disposal values: grant of software right

1. Circumstances of grant	2. Disposal value
1. The grant is for a consideration not consisting entirely of money.	The market value of the right granted at the time of the grant.

2. The grant is made where—

(a) it is for no consideration or at less than market value,

(b) there is no charge to tax under [F105. ITEPA 2003], and

(c) the condition in subsection (5) is met by the grantee.

The net consideration in money received in respect of the grant, together with—

(a) any insurance money received in respect of the computer software as a result of an event affecting the consideration obtainable on the grant, and

(b) any other compensation of any description so received, so far as it consists of capital sums.

(4) The amounts referred to in column 2 of the Table are those received by the person required to bring the disposal value into account.

(5) The condition referred to in item 2 of the Table is met by the grantee if—

    (a) the grantee's expenditure on the acquisition of the plant cannot be qualifying expenditure under this Part or Part 6 (research and development allowances), or

    (b) the grantee is a dual resident investing company which is connected with the grantor.

Amendments (Textual)
F105 Words in s. 72. (3) substituted (with effect in accordance with s. 723. (1)(a)(b) of the amending Act) by Income Tax (Earnings and Pensions) Act 2003 (c. 1) , s. 723 , Sch. 6 para. 251 (with Sch. 7)
Modifications etc. (not altering text)
C18. S. 72. (3)-(5) excluded (E.W.S.) (8.6.2005) by Railways Act 2005 (c. 14), s. 60. (2), Sch. 10 para. 14. (2)(a); S.I. 2005/1444, art. 2. (1), Sch. 1

73 Limit on disposal values

(1) This section applies if a person is required to bring into account a disposal value in respect of—

(a) computer software, or

(b) the right to use or otherwise deal with computer software.

(2) For the purpose only of—

(a) determining whether the limit on the disposal value under section 62 is exceeded, and

(b) reducing the amount of that disposal value so that the limit is not exceeded,

the disposal value is to be taken to be increased by the amount given in subsection (3).

(3) The amount is the total of any disposal values which, in respect of that person and that plant, fall or have fallen to be brought into account under section 72.

Chapter 8. Cars, etc.

74 Single asset pool

(1) Qualifying expenditure incurred on the provision of a car to which this section applies, if allocated to a pool, must be allocated to a single asset pool.

(2) This section applies to a car if—

(a) the car is not a qualifying hire car (as defined by section 82), F106...

(b) the capital expenditure incurred on its provision for the purposes of the qualifying activity exceeds £12,000.[F107, and

(c) the qualifying expenditure incurred on the provision of the car is not first-year qualifying expenditure under section 45. D (expenditure on cars with low CO_2 emissions)]

(3) In this Chapter "car" has the meaning given by section 81 (extended meaning of "car").

(4) The Treasury may by order increase or further increase the sums of money specified in subsection (2) and in sections 75 and 76.

Amendments (Textual)
F106. Word in s. 74. (2) repealed (with effect as mentioned in s. 59 of the amending Act) by Finance Act 2002 (c. 23), s. 141, (Sch. 40 Pt. 3. (7) note)
F107. S. 74. (2)(c) and word inserted (with effect as mentioned in s. 59 of the amending Act) by Finance Act 2002 (c. 23), s. 59, Sch. 19 para. 6
Modifications etc. (not altering text)
C19. S. 74. (2) modified by 1993 c. 34, s. 93. A(6) (as inserted (with effect as mentioned in s. 80. (2) of the inserting Act) by Finance Act 2002 (c. 23), s. 80, Sch. 24 para. 4. (with Sch. 23 para. 25))

75 General limit on amount of writing-down allowance

(1) The amount of the writing-down allowance to be made to a person for a chargeable period in respect of qualifying expenditure incurred on the provision of a car to which section 74 applies must not exceed £3,000.

(2) The limit under subsection (1) is proportionately increased or reduced if the chargeable period is more or less than a year.

(3) The amount of the writing-down allowance may be further limited under—

section 76 (expenditure met by another person),

section 77 (effect of use partly for other purposes), or

section 78 (effect of partial depreciation subsidy).

Modifications etc. (not altering text)

C20. S. 75. (1) modified by 1993 c. 34, s. 93. A(6) (as inserted (with effect as mentioned in s. 80. (2) of the inserting Act) by Finance Act 2002 (c. 23), s. 80, Sch. 24 para. 4 (with Sch. 23 para. 25))

76 Limit where part of expenditure met by another person

(1) Subsection (2) applies if, as a result of section 532 (general rule excluding contributions), only part of the capital expenditure incurred on the provision of a car to which section 74 applies is treated as incurred by a person.

(2) The amount of the writing-down allowance to be made to that person for a chargeable period in respect of the qualifying expenditure on the car must not exceed—

where—

E is the amount of capital expenditure incurred on the provision of the car, and

X is the amount of the expenditure excluded by section 532.

(3) Subsection (4) applies if—

(a) capital expenditure exceeding £12,000 is incurred on the provision of a car to which section 74 applies, and

(b) a person ("the contributor") is entitled to writing-down allowances as a result of section 538 (contribution allowances for plant and machinery).

(4) The amount of the writing-down allowance to be made to the contributor for a chargeable period in respect of his contribution to the expenditure on the car must not exceed—

where—

E is the amount of capital expenditure incurred on the provision of the car, and

C is the amount of the contribution.

(5) The limit under subsection (2) or (4) is proportionately increased or reduced if the chargeable period is more or less than a year.

Modifications etc. (not altering text)

C21. S. 76. (2) modified by 1993 c. 34, s. 93. A(6) (as inserted (with effect as mentioned in s. 80. (2) of the inserting Act) by Finance Act 2002 (c. 23), s. 80, Sch. 24 para. 4 (with Sch. 23 para. 25))

C22. S. 76. (3) modified by 1993 c. 34, s. 93. A(6) (as inserted (with effect as mentioned in s. 80. (2) of the inserting Act) by Finance Act 2002 (c. 23), s. 80, Sch. 24 para. 4 (with Sch. 23 para. 25))

C23. S. 76. (4) modified by 1993 c. 34, s. 93. A(6) (as inserted (with effect as mentioned in s. 80. (2) of the inserting Act) by Finance Act 2002 (c. 23), s. 80, Sch. 24 para. 4 (with Sch. 23 para. 25))

77 Car used partly for purposes other than those of qualifying activity

(1) In the case of a single asset pool under section 74 there is no final chargeable period or disposal event merely because the car begins to be used partly for purposes other than those of the qualifying activity.

(2) For any chargeable period in which the car is used partly for purposes other than those of the qualifying activity—

(a) any writing-down allowance or balancing allowance to which the person is entitled, or

(b) any balancing charge to which the person is liable,

must be reduced to an amount which is just and reasonable having regard to the relevant circumstances.

(3) The relevant circumstances include, in particular, the extent to which the car is used in that chargeable period for purposes other than those of the qualifying activity.

(4) In calculating under section 59 the amount of unrelieved qualifying expenditure carried forward, a reduction of a writing-down allowance under this section is to be disregarded.

(5) If this section applies, Chapter 15 (plant or machinery provided or used partly for purposes other than those of the qualifying activity) does not apply.

78 Effect of partial depreciation subsidy

(1) This section applies if—

(a) a car to which section 74 applies is in use for the purposes of the qualifying activity,

(b) there is paid to the person carrying on that activity a sum in respect of, or which takes account of, part of the depreciation of the car resulting from that use, and

(c) the sum does not fall to be taken into account as income of that person or in calculating the profits of any qualifying activity carried on by him.

(2) The amount of—

(a) any writing-down allowance or balancing allowance to which the person is entitled, or

(b) any balancing charge to which the person is liable,

must be reduced to an amount which is just and reasonable having regard to the relevant circumstances.

(3) In calculating under section 59 the amount of unrelieved qualifying expenditure carried forward, a reduction of a writing-down allowance under subsection (2) is to be disregarded.

(4) This section has effect for the chargeable period in which any such sum as is mentioned in subsection (1)(b) is first paid and for any subsequent chargeable period.

(5) If this section applies, Chapter 16 (partial depreciation subsidies) does not apply.

79 Cases where Chapter 17 (anti-avoidance) applies

(1) This section applies if—

(a) a disposal value is required to be brought into account under section 61, and

(b) the disposal event is that the person concerned ceases to own a car to which section 74 applies because of—

(i) a sale, or

(ii) the performance of a contract,

which is a relevant transaction for the purposes of Chapter 17 (anti-avoidance).

(2) The disposal value to be brought into account is—

(a) the market value of the car at the time of the event referred to in subsection (1), or

(b) if less, the capital expenditure incurred, or treated as incurred, on the provision of the car by the person disposing of it.

(3) The person acquiring the car is to be treated as having incurred capital expenditure on its provision of an amount equal to the disposal value required to be brought into account under subsection (2).

Vehicles provided for purposes of employment or office

80. Vehicles provided for purposes of employment or office

F108. . . . .

Amendments (Textual)

F108. S. 80 repealed (with effect as mentioned in s. 59. (3)(4) of the amending Act) by Finance Act 2001 (c. 9), s. 59. (2), 110, Sch. 33 Pt. 2. (1) Note

Interpretation

81 Extended meaning of "car"

In this Part "car" means a mechanically propelled road vehicle other than one—

(a) of a construction primarily suited for the conveyance of goods or burden of any description, or

(b) of a type not commonly used as a private vehicle and unsuitable for such use.

References to a car accordingly include a motor cycle.

82 Qualifying hire cars

(1) For the purposes of this Part a car is a qualifying hire car if—

(a) it is provided wholly or mainly for hire to, or the carriage of, members of the public in the ordinary course of a trade, and

(b) the case is within subsection (2), (3) or (4).

(2) The first case is where the following conditions are met—

(a) the number of consecutive days for which the car is on hire to, or used for the carriage of, the same person will normally be less than 30, and

(b) the total number of days for which it is on hire to, or used for the carriage of, the same person in any period of 12 months will normally be less than 90.

(3) The second case is where the car is provided for hire to a person who will himself use it—

(a) wholly or mainly for hire to, or for the carriage of, members of the public in the ordinary course of a trade, and

(b) in a way that meets the conditions in subsection (2).

(4) The third case is where the car is provided wholly or mainly for the use of a person in receipt of—

(a) a disability living allowance under—

(i) the Social Security Contributions and Benefits Act 1992 (c. 4), or

(ii) the Social Security Contributions and Benefits (Northern Ireland) Act 1992 (c. 7),

because of entitlement to the mobility component,

(b) a mobility supplement under a scheme made under the Personal Injuries (Emergency Provisions) Act 1939 (c. 82),

(c) a mobility supplement under an Order in Council made under section 12 of the Social Security (Miscellaneous Provisions) Act 1977 (c. 5), or

(d) any payment appearing to the Treasury to be of a similar kind and specified by them by order.

(5) For the purposes of subsection (2) persons who are connected with each other are to be treated as the same person.

Chapter 9. Short-life assets

83 Meaning of "short-life asset"

Plant or machinery in respect of which qualifying expenditure has been incurred is a short-life asset if—

(a) its treatment as a short-life asset is not ruled out by section 84, and

(b) the person incurring the expenditure elects for the plant or machinery to be treated as a short-life asset.

84 Cases in which short-life asset treatment is ruled out

Treatment of plant or machinery as a short-life asset is ruled out in any of the cases listed in column 1 of the Table, unless an exception listed in column 2 applies.

Table

 Short-life asset treatment

1. Short-life asset treatment ruled out | 2. Exception (if any) |

1. The expenditure is treated as incurred for the purposes of a qualifying activity under—

(a) section 13 (use for qualifying activity of plant or machinery provided for other purposes), or

[F109. (aa) section 13. A (use for other purposes of plant or machinery provided for long funding leasing), or]

(b) section 14 (use for qualifying activity of plant or machinery which is a gift).

2. The plant or machinery is the subject of special leasing (as defined by section 19). | |

3. The plant or machinery is a car (as defined by section 81). | The car is within section 82(4) (cars hired out to persons receiving disability allowances etc.). |

4. The expenditure is long-life asset expenditure (see Chapter 10). | |

The plant or machinery is a car which is within section 82. (4) (cars hired out to persons receiving disability allowances etc.).

The plant or machinery will be used within the designated period (as defined by section 106) for a qualifying purpose (as defined by sections 122 to 125).

6. Section 109 provides only a 10% writing-down allowance in respect of expenditure on the plant or machinery. | |

7. The plant or machinery is leased to two or more persons jointly in circumstances such that section 116 applies. | |

8. The plant or machinery is a ship. | |

9. The expenditure was incurred partly for the purposes of a qualifying activity and partly for other purposes (see Chapter 15). | |

10. The expenditure is required to be allocated to a single asset pool under section 211 (partial depreciation subsidy). | |

Amendments (Textual)

F109. Words in s. 84 inserted (with effect in accordance with Sch. 8 para. 15 of the amending Act) by Finance Act 2006 (c. 25), Sch. 8 para. 8. (2)

85 Election for short-life asset treatment: procedure

(1) An election under section 83 must specify—

    (a) the plant or machinery which is the subject of the election,

    (b) the qualifying expenditure incurred in respect of it, and

    (c) the date on which the expenditure was incurred.

(2) An election under section 83 must be made by notice given to [F39an officer of Revenue and Customs]—

    (a) for income tax purposes, on or before the normal time limit for amending a tax return for the tax year in which the relevant chargeable period ends;

    (b) for corporation tax purposes, no later than 2 years after the end of the relevant chargeable period.

(3) "The relevant chargeable period" means—

    (a) the chargeable period in which the qualifying expenditure was incurred, or

    (b) if the qualifying expenditure was incurred in different chargeable periods, the first chargeable period in which any of the qualifying expenditure was incurred.

(4) An election under section 83 is irrevocable.

(5) All such assessments and adjustments of assessments are to be made as are necessary to give effect to the election.

Amendments (Textual)

F39. Words in Act substituted (18.4.2005) by Commissioners for Revenue and Customs Act 2005 (c. 11), s. 53. (1), Sch. 4 para. 83. (1); S.I. 2005/1126, art. 2. (2)(h)

86 Short-life asset pool

(1) Qualifying expenditure in respect of a short-life asset, if allocated to a pool, must be allocated to a single asset pool (a "short-life asset pool").

(2) If the final chargeable period for the short-life asset pool has not occurred before the four-year cut-off—

    (a) the pool ends at the four-year cut-off without a final chargeable period,

    (b) the available qualifying expenditure in the pool is allocated to the main pool for the first chargeable period ending after the four-year cut-off, and

    (c) the asset ceases to be a short-life asset.

(3) In this Chapter "the four-year cut-off" means the fourth anniversary of the end of—

    (a) the chargeable period in which the qualifying expenditure was incurred on the provision of the short-life asset, or

    (b) if the qualifying expenditure was incurred in different chargeable periods, the first chargeable period in which any of the qualifying expenditure was incurred.

(4) For the purposes of subsection (2), the final chargeable period occurs before the four-year cut-off only if it ends on or before it.

87 Short-life assets provided for leasing

(1) This section applies if—

(a) plant or machinery is a short-life asset on the basis that it has been provided for leasing but will be used within the designated period for a qualifying purpose (see item 5 of the Table in section 84),

(b) in a chargeable period ending on or before the four-year cut-off, the short-life asset begins to be used otherwise than for a qualifying purpose, and

(c) the time when it begins to be so used falls within the first 4 years of the designated period.

(2) If this section applies—

(a) the short-life asset pool ends without a final chargeable period,

(b) the available qualifying expenditure in the pool is allocated to the main pool for the chargeable period in which the asset begins to be used otherwise than for a qualifying purpose, and

(c) the asset ceases to be a short-life asset.

88 Sales at under-value

If—

(a) a short-life asset is disposed of at less than market value,

(b) the disposal is not one in respect of which an election is made under section 89. (6), and

(c) there is no charge to tax under [F110. ITEPA 2003],

the disposal value to be brought into account for the purposes of Chapter 5 is the market value of the asset.

Amendments (Textual)

F110 Words in s. 88. (c) substituted (with effect in accordance with s. 723. (1)(a)(b) of the amending Act) by Income Tax (Earnings and Pensions) Act 2003 (c. 1) , s. 723 , Sch. 6 para. 252 (with Sch. 7)

Modifications etc. (not altering text)

C24. S. 88 excluded (8.6.2005) by Railways Act 2005 (c. 14), s. 60. (2), Sch. 10 para. 14. (2)(a); S.I. 2005/1444, art. 2. (1), Sch. 1

C25. S. 88 excluded (E.W.S.) (8.6.2005) by Railways Act 2005 (c. 14), s. 60. (2), Sch. 10 para. 2. (4); S.I. 2005/1444, art. 2. (1), Sch. 1

C26. S. 88 excluded (24.7.2005) by Railways Act 2005 (c. 14), s. 60. (2), Sch. 10 para. 22. (4); S.I. 2005/1909, art. 2, Sch.

89 Disposal to connected person

(1) This section applies if, at any time before the four-year cut-off, a person ("the transferor") disposes of a short-life asset to a connected person.

(2) Subject to subsection (6)—

(a) the transferor is to be treated as having sold the short-life asset to the connected person for an amount equal to the available qualifying expenditure in the short-life asset pool for the chargeable period in which the disposal occurs, and

(b) the connected person is to be treated as having incurred qualifying expenditure of the same amount in buying the short-life asset.

(3) Subject to subsection (6)—

(a) sections 217 and 218 (restrictions on first-year and other allowances in the case of certain transactions between connected persons, to obtain a tax advantage etc.), and

(b) sections 222 to 225 (further restrictions in the case of sale and finance leaseback),

do not apply to the disposal.

(4) Immediately after the disposal of the short-life asset, the connected person is to be taken to have made an election under section 83 (so that the plant or machinery is a short-life asset in his hands).

(5) In relation to the connected person, "the four-year cut-off" means the date that would have been the four-year cut-off in relation to the transferor.

(6) Subsections (2) and (3) apply in relation to a disposal only if—

(a) the transferor, and

(b) the connected person,

elect that they should apply.

(7) An election under subsection (6) must be made by notice given to [F39an officer of Revenue and Customs] no later than 2 years after the end of the chargeable period in which the disposal occurred.

Amendments (Textual)

F39. Words in Act substituted (18.4.2005) by Commissioners for Revenue and Customs Act 2005 (c. 11), s. 53. (1), Sch. 4 para. 83. (1); S.I. 2005/1126, art. 2. (2)(h)

Chapter 10. Long-life assets

90 Long-life asset expenditure

"Long-life asset expenditure" means qualifying expenditure—

(a) incurred on the provision of a long-life asset for the purposes of a qualifying activity, and

(b) not excluded from being long-life asset expenditure by any of sections 93 to 100.

91 Meaning of "long-life asset"

(1) For the purposes of this Chapter "long-life asset" means plant or machinery which—

(a) if new, can reasonably be expected to have a useful economic life of at least 25 years, and

(b) if not new, could reasonably have been expected when new to have a useful economic life of at least 25 years.

(2) "New" means unused and not second-hand.

(3) The useful economic life of plant or machinery is the period—

(a) beginning when it is first brought into use by any person for any purpose, and

(b) ending when it is no longer used or likely to be used by anyone for any purpose as a fixed asset of a business.

92 Application of Chapter to part of expenditure

(1) If, under any of the following provisions of this Chapter, this Chapter applies to part only of the capital expenditure on plant and machinery—

(a) the part to which this Chapter applies, and

(b) the part to which it does not,

are to be treated for the purposes of this Act as expenditure on separate items of plant or machinery.

(2) For the purposes of subsection (1), all such apportionments are to be made as are just and reasonable.

Expenditure excluded from being long-life asset expenditure

93 Fixtures etc.

(1) Expenditure is not long-life asset expenditure if it is incurred on the provision of plant or machinery which is a fixture in, or is provided for use in, any building used wholly or mainly—

(a) as a dwelling-house, hotel, office, retail shop or showroom, or

(b) for purposes ancillary to the use referred to in paragraph (a).

(2) In this section—

"fixture" has the meaning given by section 173. (1);

"retail shop" includes any premises of a similar character where a retail trade or business, including repair work, is carried on.

94 Ships

(1) Expenditure is not long-life asset expenditure if—

(a) it is incurred before 1st January 2011 on the provision of a ship of a sea-going kind, and

(b) each of the conditions in subsection (2) is met.

(2) The conditions are that—

(a) the ship is not an offshore installation,

F111. (b)...............................

(c) the primary use to which ships of the same kind are put by their owners (or, if their use is made available to others, those others) is a use otherwise than for sport or recreation.

F112. (3)...............................

Amendments (Textual)

F111 S. 94. (2)(b) repealed (with effect in accordance with Sch. 27 para. 11 of the amending Act) by Finance Act 2004 (c. 12) , Sch. 27 para. 8 , 42 Pt. 2. (19)

F112 S. 94. (3) repealed (with effect in accordance with Sch. 27 para. 11 of the amending Act) by Finance Act 2004 (c. 12) , Sch. 27 para. 8 , 42 Pt. 2. (19)

95 Railway assets

(1) Expenditure is not long-life asset expenditure if it is incurred before 1st January 2011 on the provision of a railway asset used by any person wholly and exclusively for the purposes of a railway business.

(2) "Railway asset" means—

(a) a locomotive, tram or other vehicle, or a carriage, wagon or other rolling stock designed or adapted for use on a railway;

(b) anything which is, or is to be, comprised in any railway station, railway track or light maintenance depot or any apparatus which is, or is to be, installed in association with such a station, track or depot.

(3) "Railway business" means a business so far as carried on to provide a service to the public for carrying goods or passengers by means of a railway in the United Kingdom or the Channel Tunnel.

(4) For the purposes of subsection (1), a railway asset of a kind described in subsection (2)(a) is not to be treated as used otherwise than wholly and exclusively for the purposes of a railway business merely because it is used to carry goods or passengers—

(a) from places inside the United Kingdom to places outside the United Kingdom, or

(b) from places outside the United Kingdom to places inside the United Kingdom.

(5) In subsections (2) and (3), "railway" has the same meaning as in section 81. (2) of the 1993 Act ("railway" includes tramways and other modes of guided transport).

(6) In this section—

"the 1993 Act" means the Railways Act 1993 (c. 43);

"goods" has the same meaning as in Part I of the 1993 Act;

"railway station" and "railway track" include—

- anything included in the definitions of "station" and "track" in section 83 of the 1993 Act, and

- anything else that would be included if in section 83 "railway" had the meaning given in section 81. (2) of the 1993 Act;

"light maintenance depot" means—

- any light maintenance depot within the meaning of Part I of the 1993 Act, and

- any land or other property which is the equivalent of such a depot in relation to anything which is a railway only when "railway" has the meaning given by section 81. (2) of the 1993 Act.

96 Cars

Expenditure is not long-life asset expenditure if it is incurred on the provision of a car (as defined by section 81).

97 Expenditure within the relevant monetary limit: general

Expenditure is not long-life asset expenditure if it is—

    (a) expenditure to which the monetary limits apply, and

    (b) incurred in a chargeable period for which the relevant monetary limit is not exceeded.

98 Expenditure to which the monetary limits apply

(1) The monetary limits apply to expenditure incurred by an individual for a chargeable period if—

    (a) the expenditure was incurred by him for the purposes of a qualifying activity carried on by him,

    (b) the whole of his time is substantially devoted in that period to the carrying on of that qualifying activity, and

    (c) the expenditure is not within subsection (4).

(2) The monetary limits apply to expenditure incurred by a partnership for a chargeable period if—

    (a) all of the members of the partnership are individuals,

    (b) the expenditure was incurred by the partnership for the purposes of a qualifying activity carried on by it,

    (c) at all times throughout that period at least half the partners for the time being devote the whole or a substantial part of their time to the carrying on of that qualifying activity, and

    (d) the expenditure is not within subsection (4).

(3) The monetary limits apply for the purposes of corporation tax to any expenditure incurred by a company for a chargeable period other than expenditure within subsection (4).

(4) Expenditure is within this subsection if it is—

    (a) incurred on the provision of a share in plant or machinery,

    (b) treated as a result of section 538 (contribution allowances: plant and machinery) as incurred on the provision of plant or machinery, or

    (c) incurred on the provision of plant or machinery for leasing (whether or not the leasing is in the course of a trade).

99 The monetary limit

(1) The monetary limit in the case of a chargeable period of 12 months is £100,000.

(2) If, in the case of an individual or partnership, the chargeable period is longer or shorter than 12 months, the monetary limit is the amount given by a proportional increase or reduction of £100,000.

(3) If, in the case of a company, the chargeable period is shorter than 12 months, the monetary limit is the amount given by a proportional reduction of £100,000.

(4) If, in a chargeable period, a company has one or more associated companies, the monetary limit for that period is—

where—

L is the monetary limit applicable under subsection (1) or (3), and

N is the number of the associated companies.

(5) Section 13. (4) and (5) of ICTA (companies which count as associated companies for the purposes of section 13. (3)) applies for the purposes of subsection (4).

Modifications etc. (not altering text)

C27. S. 99. (1) modified by 1993 c. 34, s. 93. A(6) (as inserted (with effect as mentioned in s. 80. (2) of the inserting Act) by Finance Act 2002 (c. 23), s. 80, Sch. 24 para. 4 (with Sch. 23 para. 25))

C28. S. 99. (2) modified by 1993 c. 34, s. 93. A(6) (as inserted (with effect as mentioned in s. 80. (2) of the inserting Act) by Finance Act 2002 (c. 23), s. 80, Sch. 24 para. 4 (with Sch. 23 para. 25))

C29. S. 99. (3) modified by 1993 c. 34, s. 93. A(6) (as inserted (with effect as mentioned in s. 80. (2) of the inserting Act) by Finance Act 2002 (c. 23), s. 80, Sch. 24 para. 4 (with Sch. 23 para. 25))

100 Exceeding the monetary limit

(1) The monetary limit for a chargeable period is exceeded if the total expenditure in that period that meets the conditions in subsection (2) exceeds that limit.

(2) The conditions are that the expenditure—

(a) is long-life asset expenditure, or would be long-life asset expenditure in the absence of section 97 (expenditure within monetary limit), and

(b) is expenditure to which the monetary limits apply.

(3) Subsection (4) applies if, in the case of any contract for the provision of plant or machinery, the capital expenditure which is (or is to be) incurred under the contract is (or may fall to be) treated for the purposes of this Act as incurred in different chargeable periods.

(4) All of the expenditure falling to be incurred under the contract on the provision of the plant or machinery is to be treated for the purposes of this section as incurred in the first chargeable period in which any of the expenditure is incurred.

Rules applying to long-life asset expenditure

101 Long-life asset pool

(1) Long-life asset expenditure to which this section applies, if allocated to a pool, must be allocated to a class pool ("the long-life asset pool").

(2) This section applies to long-life asset expenditure if—

(a) it is incurred on the provision of long-life assets wholly and exclusively for the purposes of a qualifying activity, and

(b) it is not expenditure which is required to be allocated to a single asset pool.

102 Writing-down allowances at 6%

(1) The amount of the writing-down allowance to which a person is entitled for a chargeable period in respect of expenditure which is long-life asset expenditure is 6% of the amount by which AQE exceeds TDR (see Chapter 5).

(2) Subsection (1) applies even if the long-life asset expenditure is in a single asset pool.

(3) In the case of expenditure which is within section 107. (2)(a) and (b) (overseas leasing which is not protected leasing), this section is subject to sections 110, 114 and 115 (allowances prohibited in certain cases etc.).

(4) Subsections (3) and (4) of section 56 (proportionate increases or reductions in amount in certain cases) apply for the purposes of subsection (1) of this section as they apply for the purposes of subsection (1) of that section.

Anti-avoidance provisions

103 Later claims

(1) Subsection (2) applies if—

(a) a person entitled to do so has made a Part 2 claim in respect of expenditure incurred on the provision of plant or machinery, and

(b) the expenditure fell to be treated as long-life asset expenditure for the purposes of the claim.

(2) If—

(a) at any time after making the Part 2 claim, that claimant or another person makes a Part 2 claim in respect of any qualifying expenditure incurred at any time (including a time before the incurring of the expenditure to which the earlier claim relates) on the provision of the same plant or machinery, and

(b) the expenditure to which the later claim relates—

(i) would not (but for this subsection) be treated for the purposes of the later claim as long-life asset expenditure, and

(ii) is not prevented from being long-life asset expenditure by any of sections 93 to 96,

this Part has effect in relation to the later claim as if the expenditure to which it relates were long-life asset expenditure.

(3) A person makes a Part 2 claim in respect of any expenditure if he—

(a) makes a tax return in which the expenditure is taken into account in determining his available qualifying expenditure for the purposes of this Part;

(b) gives notice of an amendment of a tax return which provides for the expenditure to be so taken into account;

(c) makes a claim in any other way for the expenditure to be so taken into account.

104 Disposal value of long-life assets

(1) This section applies if—

(a) section 102 (writing-down allowances at 6%) has had effect in relation to any long-life asset expenditure incurred by a person ("the taxpayer"),

(b) any disposal event occurs in relation to the long-life asset,

(c) the disposal value to be brought into account by the taxpayer would (but for this section) be less than the notional written-down value of the long-life asset, and

(d) the disposal event is part of, or occurs as a result of, a scheme or arrangement the main purpose or one of the main purposes of which is the obtaining by the taxpayer of a tax advantage under this Part.

(2) The disposal value that the taxpayer must bring into account is the notional written-down value of the long-life asset.

(3) The notional written-down value is—

where—

QE is the taxpayer's expenditure on the plant or machinery that is qualifying expenditure, and A is the total of all allowances which could have been made to the taxpayer in respect of that expenditure if—

(a) that expenditure had been the only expenditure that had ever been taken into account in determining his available qualifying expenditure,

(b) that expenditure had not been prevented by the application of a monetary limit from being long-life asset expenditure, and

(c) all allowances had been made in full.

Chapter 11. Overseas leasing

105"Leasing", "overseas leasing" etc.

(1) In this Chapter—

(a) "leasing" includes letting a ship or aircraft on charter or letting any other asset on hire, and

(b) references to a lease include a sub-lease (and references to a lessor or lessee are to be read accordingly).

(2) Plant or machinery is used for overseas leasing if it is used for the purpose of being leased to a person who—

(a) is not resident in the United Kingdom, and

(b) does not use the plant or machinery exclusively for earning profits chargeable to tax.

[F113. (2. A)In determining whether plant or machinery is used for overseas leasing, no account shall be taken of any lease finalised, within the meaning of Part 4 of Schedule 8 to the Finance Act 2006, on or after 1st April 2006.]

(3) In this Chapter "profits chargeable to tax"—

(a) includes profits chargeable under section 830. (4) of ICTA (profits from exploration and exploitation of the seabed etc.), but

(b) excludes profits arising to a person who, under double taxation arrangements, is afforded or is entitled to claim any relief from the tax chargeable on those profits.

(4) "Double taxation arrangements" means arrangements specified in an Order in Council making any such provisions as are referred to in section 788 of ICTA.

(5) "Protected leasing" of plant or machinery means—

(a) short-term leasing of the plant or machinery (as defined in section 121), or

(b) if the plant or machinery is a ship, aircraft or transport container, the use of the ship, aircraft or transport container for a qualifying purpose under section 123 or 124 (letting on charter to UK resident etc.).

(6) In this Chapter "qualifying activity" includes (subject to any provision to the contrary) any activity listed in section 15. (1) even if any profits or gains from it are not chargeable to tax.

Amendments (Textual)

F113. S. 105. (2. A) inserted (19.7.2006) by Finance Act 2006 (c. 25), Sch. 9 para. 13. (2)

106 The designated period

(1) Subject to subsection (2), the designated period, in relation to expenditure incurred by a person on the provision of plant or machinery, is the period of 10 years beginning with the date on which he first brought the plant or machinery into use.

(2) If the person who incurred the expenditure ceases to own the plant or machinery before the end of the 10 year period, the designated period ends on the date when he ceases to own it.

(3) For the purposes of subsection (2), a person is to be treated as continuing to own plant or machinery so long as it is owned by a person who—

(a) is connected with him, or

(b) acquired it from him as a result of one or more disposals on the occasion of which, or each of which [F114—

(i) there was a change in the persons carrying on the qualifying activity which did not involve all of the persons carrying on that activity before the change permanently ceasing to carry it on, or

(ii) the qualifying activity carried on by the person making the disposal was treated as continuing under section 114. (1) of ICTA (effect of partnership changes involving companies).]

F115. (4). . . . .

Amendments (Textual)

F114. Words in s. 106. (3)(b) substituted (with effect in accordance with s. 883. (1) of the amending Act) by Income Tax (Trading and Other Income) Act 2005 (c. 5), Sch. 1 para. 536. (2) (with Sch. 2)

F115. S. 106. (4) repealed (with effect in accordance with s. 883. (1) of the amending Act) by Income Tax (Trading and Other Income) Act 2005 (c. 5),, Sch. 1 para. 536. (3), 3 (with Sch. 2)

Certain expenditure to be pooled

107 The overseas leasing pool

(1) Qualifying expenditure to which this section applies, if allocated to a pool, must be allocated to a class pool ("the overseas leasing pool").

(2) This section applies to qualifying expenditure if—

(a) it is incurred on the provision of plant or machinery for leasing,

(b) the plant or machinery is at any time in the designated period used for overseas leasing which is not protected leasing, and

(c) the expenditure is not—

(i) long-life asset expenditure, or

(ii) expenditure that is required to be allocated to a single asset pool.

108 Effect of disposal to connected person on overseas leasing pool

(1) This section applies if—

(a) a person who has incurred qualifying expenditure which has been allocated to an overseas leasing pool disposes of the plant or machinery to a connected person,

[F116. (b)the disposal is one on the occasion of which—

(i) there was a change in the persons carrying on the qualifying activity which involved all of the persons carrying on that activity before the change permanently ceasing to carry it on, or

(ii) the qualifying activity carried on by the person making the disposal was not treated as continuing under section 114. (1) or 343. (2) of ICTA (effect of partnership changes involving companies or of company reconstructions), and]

(c) a disposal value is required to be brought into account on that occasion under this Part.

(2) The disposal value to be brought into account is—

(a) the market value of the plant or machinery at the time of the disposal, or

(b) if less, the qualifying expenditure incurred by the person disposing of the plant or machinery.

(3) The person acquiring the plant or machinery is to be treated for the purposes of this Part as having incurred expenditure on its provision of an amount equal to the disposal value given by subsection (2).

F117. (4). . . . .

Amendments (Textual)

F116. S. 108. (1)(b) substituted for s. 108. (1)(b) (with effect in accordance with s. 883. (1) of the amending Act)) by Income Tax (Trading and Other Income) Act 2005 (c. 5), Sch. 1 para. 537. (2) (with Sch. 2)

F117. S. 108. (4) repealed (with effect in accordance with s. 883. (1) of the amending Act) by Income Tax (Trading and Other Income) Act 2005 (c. 5), Sch. 1 para. 537. (3), 3 (with Sch. 2)

Allowances reduced or, in certain cases, prohibited

109 Writing-down allowances at 10%

(1) The amount of the writing-down allowance to which a person is entitled for a chargeable period in respect of expenditure to which this section applies is 10% of the amount by which AQE exceeds TDR (see Chapter 5).

(2) This section applies to expenditure incurred on the provision of plant or machinery for leasing if—

(a) the plant or machinery is at any time in the designated period used for overseas leasing which is not protected leasing, and

(b) the expenditure is not long-life asset expenditure.

(3) Subsection (2) applies to expenditure even if the expenditure is in a single asset pool.

(4) Subsections (3) and (4) of section 56 (proportionate increases or reductions in amount in certain cases) apply for the purposes of subsection (1) of this section as they apply for the purposes of subsection (1) of that section.

110 Cases where allowances are prohibited

(1) A person is not entitled to any writing-down or balancing allowances in respect of qualifying expenditure which is within subsection (2).

(2) Expenditure is within this subsection if—

(a) it is incurred on the provision of plant or machinery for leasing,

(b) the plant or machinery is at any time in the designated period used for overseas leasing which is not protected leasing,

(c) the plant or machinery is used otherwise than for a qualifying purpose (see sections 122 to 125), and

(d) the lease is within any of the items in the list below.

List

 Leases in relation to which allowances are prohibited

1. | The lease is expressed to be for a period of more than 13 years. |

The lease, or a separate agreement, provides for—

(a) extending or renewing the lease, or

(b) the grant of a new lease,making it possible for the plant or machinery to be leased for a period of more than 13 years.

3. | There is a period of more than one year between the dates on which any two consecutive payments become due under the lease. |

4. | Any payments are due under the lease or a collateral agreement other than periodical payments. |

If payments due under the lease or a collateral agreement are expressed as monthly amounts due over a period, any payment due for that period is not the same as any of the others.

But, for this purpose, ignore variations made under the terms of the lease which are attributable to changes in—

(a) the rate of corporation tax or income tax,

(b) the rate of capital allowances,

(c) any rate of interest where the changes are linked to changes in the rate of interest applicable to inter-bank loans, or

(d) the premiums charged for insurance of any description by a person who is not connected with the lessor or the lessee.

The lessor or a person connected with the lessor will, or may in certain circumstances, become entitled at any time to receive from the lessee or any other person a payment, other than a payment of insurance money, which is—

(a) of an amount determined before the expiry of the lease, and

(b) referable to a value of the plant or machinery at or after the expiry of the lease.

For this purpose, it does not matter whether the payment relates to a disposal of the plant or machinery.

(3) In items 4 and 5 of the list "collateral agreement" means an agreement which might reasonably be construed as being collateral to the lease.

Recovery of excess allowances

111 Excess allowances: standard recovery mechanism

(1) If—

(a) expenditure incurred by a person in providing plant or machinery has qualified for a first-year allowance or a normal writing-down allowance, and

(b) at any time in the designated period, the plant or machinery is used for overseas leasing which is not protected leasing,

the following provisions of this section have effect in relation to the person who is the owner of the plant or machinery when it is first so used.

(2) For the chargeable period in which the plant or machinery is first used as described in subsection (1)(b), the owner is—

(a) liable to a balancing charge of an amount given by subsection (4), and

(b) required to bring into account a disposal value of an amount given by that subsection.

(3) For the chargeable period following that in which the plant or machinery is first used as described in subsection (1)(b), an amount given by subsection (4) is to be allocated to whatever pool is appropriate for plant or machinery which is of that description and is provided for leasing and used for overseas leasing.

(4) The amounts are—

The balancing charge

The amount, if any, by which $F + N$ exceeds T, where—

F is the amount of any first-year allowance made in respect of the qualifying expenditure referred to in subsection (1)(a) ("E"),

N is the total of any normal writing-down allowances made in respect of E for the relevant chargeable periods, and

T is the total of the allowances that could have been made for the relevant chargeable periods if no first-year allowance or normal writing-down allowances had been or could have been made.

The disposal value

The amount, if any, by which E exceeds $(F + N)$, where E, F and N have the meaning given in relation to the amount of the balancing charge.

The amount to be allocated to the pool

The aggregate of the balancing charge and the disposal value.

(5) For the purpose of calculating N, the normal writing-down allowances that were made in respect of expenditure on an item of plant or machinery are to be determined as if that item were

the only item of plant or machinery in relation to which Chapter 5 had effect.

(6) "The relevant chargeable periods" means the chargeable period in which the qualifying expenditure was incurred and any subsequent chargeable period up to and including the one in which the plant or machinery was first used as described in subsection (1)(b).

112 Excess allowances: connected persons

(1) Section 111 applies with the modifications in subsections (2) to (4) in a case in which—

(a) the owner acquired the plant or machinery as a result of a transaction between connected persons (or a series of transactions each of which was between connected persons),

[F118. (b)the transaction (or each of the transactions) is one—

(i) which involved all of the persons carrying on the qualifying activity before the transaction permanently ceasing to carry it on, or

(ii) in respect of which the qualifying activity carried on by the person making the disposal was not treated as continuing under section 114. (1) or 343. (2) of ICTA (effect of partnership changes involving companies or of company reconstructions), and]

(c) any of the connected persons is a person to whom—

(i) a first-year allowance or a normal writing-down allowance has been made in respect of expenditure on the provision of the plant or machinery, or

(ii) a balancing allowance has been made in respect of such expenditure without a first-year allowance or normal writing-down allowance having been claimed.

(2) For the purposes of section 111. (2) and (3)—

E is the amount of the expenditure in respect of which an allowance within subsection (1)(c) has been made,

F is the amount of any first-year allowance within subsection (1)(c), and

N is the amount of any normal writing-down allowance or balancing allowance within subsection (1)(c).

(3) For the purposes of section 111. (2) and (3), any consideration paid or received on a disposal of the plant or machinery between the connected persons is to be disregarded.

(4) If a balancing allowance or a balancing charge has been made in respect of any of the transactions, the amount representing $F + N$ is to be adjusted in a just and reasonable manner.

F119. (5). . . . .

Amendments (Textual)

F118. S. 112. (1)(b) substituted for s. 112. (1)(b) (with effect in accordance with s. 883. (1) of the amending Act) by Income Tax (Trading and Other Income) Act 2005 (c. 5), Sch. 1 para. 538. (2) (with Sch. 2)

F119. S. 112. (5) repealed (with effect in accordance with s. 883. (1) of the amending Act)by Income Tax (Trading and Other Income) Act 2005 (c. 5), Sch. 1 para. 538. (3), 3 (with Sch. 2)

113 Excess allowances: special provision for ships

(1) If the plant or machinery referred to in section 111 is a ship—

(a) no allowance is to be made in respect of the ship under section 131. (3) (postponed allowances) for the first chargeable period of overseas use or any subsequent chargeable period,

(b) nothing in section 132. (2) (disposal events and single ship pool) restricts the operation of section 111, and

(c) the amount of any first-year or writing-down allowance in respect of the ship which has been postponed under section 130 and not made is to be allocated to a long-life asset pool or an overseas leasing pool for the chargeable period following the first chargeable period of overseas use.

(2) "The first chargeable period of overseas use" means the chargeable period in which the plant or machinery is first used for overseas leasing which is not protected leasing.

Recovery of allowances given in cases where prohibition applies

114 Prohibited allowances: standard recovery mechanism

(1) If—

(a) a first-year allowance, a writing-down allowance or a balancing allowance has been made in respect of expenditure incurred in providing plant or machinery, and

(b) at any time in the designated period, an event occurs such that the expenditure is brought within section 110. (2) (cases where allowances are prohibited),

the following provisions have effect in relation to the person owning the plant or machinery immediately before that event.

(2) For the chargeable period in which the event occurs, the owner is—

(a) liable to a balancing charge of an amount equal to A — R, and

(b) required to bring into account a disposal value of an amount equal to E - (A - R).

(3) For the purposes of subsection (2)—

A is the amount of any allowances within subsection (1)(a),

R is any amount previously recovered under section 111 or 112 (recovery of excess allowances), and

E is the amount of the expenditure referred to in subsection (1)(a).

(4) For the purpose of calculating A, the amount of the allowances made in respect of expenditure on an item of plant or machinery is to be determined as if that item were the only item of plant or machinery in relation to which Chapter 5 had effect.

115 Prohibited allowances: connected persons

(1) Section 114 applies with the modifications in subsection (2) in a case in which—

(a) an amount falls to be treated as a balancing charge under that section,

(b) the person on whom the balancing charge is to be imposed acquired the plant or machinery in question as a result of a transaction between connected persons (or a series of transactions each of which was between connected persons),

[F120. (c)the transaction (or each of the transactions) is one—

(i) which involved all of the persons carrying on the qualifying activity before the transaction permanently ceasing to carry it on, or

(ii) in respect of which the qualifying activity carried on by the person making the disposal was not treated as continuing under section 114. (1) or 343. (2) of ICTA (effect of partnership changes involving companies or of company reconstructions), and]

(d) a first-year allowance, a writing-down allowance or a balancing allowance in respect of expenditure on the provision of that plant or machinery has been made to any of those persons.

(2) For the purpose of calculating the balancing charge—

(a) A is the amount of any allowances within subsection (1)(d),

(b) any consideration paid or received on a disposal of the plant or machinery between the connected persons is to be disregarded, and

(c) if a balancing allowance or a balancing charge has been made in respect of any of the transactions, A is to be adjusted in a just and reasonable manner.

F121. (3). . . . .

Amendments (Textual)

F120. S. 115. (1)(c) substituted for s. 115. (1)(c) (with effect in accordance with s. 883. (1) of the amending Act) by Income Tax (Trading and Other Income) Act 2005 (c. 5), Sch. 1 para. 539. (2) (with Sch. 2)

F121. S. 115. (3) repealed (with effect in accordance with s. 883. (1) of the amending Act)by Income Tax (Trading and Other Income) Act 2005 (c. 5), Sch. 1 para. 539. (3), Sch. 3 (with Sch. 2)

Application of Chapter in relation to joint lessees

116 Mitigation of regime

(1) This section applies if—

(a) plant or machinery is leased to two or more persons jointly,

(b) at least one of them is a person who—

(i) is not resident in the United Kingdom, and

(ii) does not use the plant or machinery exclusively for earning profits chargeable to tax, and

(c) the leasing is not protected leasing.

(2) Subsection (3) applies if, at any time when the plant or machinery is leased as described in subsection (1), the lessees use the plant or machinery for the purposes of a qualifying activity or activities but not for leasing.

(3) The expenditure on the provision of the plant or machinery is to be treated as not subject to sections 107, 109 and 110 if, and to the extent to which, it appears that the profits of the qualifying activity or activities will be chargeable to tax throughout—

(a) the designated period, or

(b) if shorter, the period of the lease.

(4) Subsection (5) applies if, under subsection (3), part of the expenditure is treated as not subject to section 107, 109 or 110.

(5) Whether or not the plant or machinery continues to be leased as described in subsection (1), Chapters 5 (allowances and charges) and 10 (long-life assets) and this Chapter have effect as if—

(a) the part of the expenditure that is not subject to section 107, 109 or 110 were expenditure on the provision of a separate item of plant or machinery, and

(b) the rest were expenditure which has been incurred on the provision of another item of plant or machinery (and which is subject to those sections).

(6) All such apportionments are to be made as are necessary as a result of subsection (5).

117 Recovery of allowances in case of joint lessees

(1) If—

(a) expenditure is incurred on the provision of plant or machinery which is leased as described in section 116. (1),

(b) the whole or a part of the expenditure has qualified for a normal writing-down allowance under section 116. (3),

(c) at any time in the designated period while the plant or machinery is so leased, no lessee uses the plant or machinery for the purposes of a qualifying activity or activities the profits of which are chargeable to tax, and

(d) section 114 (recovery of prohibited allowances) does not apply at that time and has not applied at any earlier time,

sections 111 and 112 (recovery of excess allowances) apply as if the plant or machinery or (as the case may be) the separate item of plant or machinery referred to in section 116. (5)(a) had at that time begun to be used for overseas leasing which is not protected leasing.

(2) If—

(a) the whole or a part of any expenditure has qualified for—

(i) a normal writing-down allowance otherwise than as a result of section 116. (3), or

(ii) a first-year allowance,

(b) subsequently, but during the designated period, the plant or machinery is leased as described in section 116. (1),

(c) at any time in the designated period while the plant or machinery is so leased, no lessee uses the plant or machinery for the purposes of a qualifying activity or activities the profits of which are chargeable to tax, and

(d) section 114 (recovery of prohibited allowances) does not apply at that time and has not applied at any earlier time,

sections 111 and 112 (recovery of excess allowances) apply as if the plant or machinery (and not any separate item of plant or machinery referred to in section 116. (5)(a)) had at that time begun to be used for overseas leasing which is not protected leasing.

(3) Subsections (4) and (5) apply if—

(a) expenditure is incurred on the provision of plant or machinery which is leased as described in section 116. (1),

(b) the whole or a part of the expenditure has qualified for a normal writing-down allowance under section 116. (3),

(c) at the end of the designated period, the plant or machinery is leased as described in section 116. (1) but subsection (1) has not had effect, and

(d) it appears that the extent to which the plant or machinery has been used for the purposes of a qualifying activity or activities the profits of which are chargeable to tax is less than the extent of such use taken into account in determining the amount of the expenditure which qualified for a normal writing-down allowance.

(4) Sections 111 and 112 (recovery of excess allowances) apply as if—

(a) a part of the expenditure corresponding to the reduction in the extent of use referred to in subsection (3)(d) were expenditure on the provision of a separate item of plant or machinery, and

(b) the separate item of plant or machinery had been used, on the last day of the designated period, for overseas leasing which is not protected leasing.

(5) Any disposal value subsequently brought into account under this Part in respect of the plant or machinery must be apportioned by reference to the extent of its use (determined at the end of the designated period) for the purposes of a qualifying activity or activities the profits of which are chargeable to tax.

(6) If an apportionment is made under subsection (5), section 116. (6) does not apply.

Duties to supply information

118 Certificate relating to protected leasing

(1) If—

(a) expenditure is incurred on the provision of plant or machinery, and

(b) before the expenditure has qualified for a normal writing-down allowance, the plant or machinery is used for overseas leasing which is protected leasing,

a claim for a writing-down allowance which takes account of that expenditure must be accompanied by a certificate.

(2) The certificate must specify—

(a) the description of protected leasing,

(b) the person to whom the plant or machinery has been leased, and

(c) if the certificate is given by reference to a chargeable period, all the items of plant or machinery (if more than one) relevant to that period.

(3) Subsection (1) applies, for the purposes of claims to first-year allowances, as if the references to a normal writing-down allowance and to a writing-down allowance included a first-year allowance.

(4) But nothing in subsection (3) prevents subsection (1) from continuing to apply if the use for protected leasing occurs after the expenditure has qualified for one allowance and before it qualifies for another.

119 Notice of change of use of plant or machinery

(1) If—

(a) any expenditure on plant or machinery has qualified for a first-year allowance or a normal writing-down allowance, and

(b) the plant or machinery is subsequently used at any time in the designated period for overseas leasing which is not protected leasing,

the person who then owns the plant or machinery must give notice of the fact to [F39an officer of Revenue and Customs].

(2) The notice must specify—

(a) the person who is not resident in the United Kingdom to whom the plant or machinery has been leased, and

(b) if the notice is given by reference to a chargeable period, all the items of plant or machinery (if more than one) relevant to that period.

(3) The notice must be given—

(a) no later than 3 months after the end of the chargeable period in which the plant or machinery is first used for overseas leasing which is not protected leasing, or

(b) if at the end of the 3 months the person required to give the notice does not know and cannot reasonably be expected to know that the plant or machinery is being so used, within 30 days of coming to know of it.

Amendments (Textual)

F39. Words in Act substituted (18.4.2005) by Commissioners for Revenue and Customs Act 2005 (c. 11), s. 53. (1), Sch. 4 para. 83. (1); S.I. 2005/1126, art. 2. (2)(h)

120 Notice and joint lessees

(1) If expenditure is incurred on the provision of plant or machinery which is leased as described in section 116. (1) (joint lessees: mitigation of regime), the lessor must give notice to [F39an officer of Revenue and Customs].

(2) A notice under subsection (1) must specify—

(a) the names and addresses of the persons to whom the asset is jointly leased,

(b) the part of the expenditure properly attributable to each of them, and

(c) which of them (so far as the lessor knows) is resident in the United Kingdom.

(3) If circumstances occur such that section 117. (1) or (2) (recovery of allowances) applies, the person who is then the lessor must give notice of the fact to [F39an officer of Revenue and Customs].

(4) A notice under subsection (3) must specify—

(a) any of the joint lessees who is not resident in the United Kingdom to whom the plant or machinery has been leased, and

(b) if it is given by reference to a chargeable period, all the items of plant or machinery (if more than one) relevant to that period.

(5) A notice under this section must be given—

(a) no later than 3 months after the end of the chargeable period in which the plant or machinery is first leased as described in section 116. (1) or (as the case may be) in which the circumstances referred to in subsection (3) occur, or

(b) if at the end of the 3 months the person required to give the notice does not know and cannot reasonably be expected to know that the plant or machinery is being so used, within 30 days of coming to know of it.

Amendments (Textual)

F39. Words in Act substituted (18.4.2005) by Commissioners for Revenue and Customs Act 2005 (c. 11), s. 53. (1), Sch. 4 para. 83. (1); S.I. 2005/1126, art. 2. (2)(h)

Qualifying purposes

121 Meaning of "short-term leasing"

(1) Leasing of plant or machinery is short-term leasing if—

(a) the number of consecutive days for which it is leased to the same person will normally be less than 30, and

(b) the total number of days for which it is leased to that person in any period of 12 months will normally be less than 90.

(2) Leasing of plant or machinery is also short-term leasing if—

(a) the number of consecutive days for which the plant or machinery is leased to the same person will not normally exceed 365, and

(b) the total length of the periods for which it is leased in any consecutive period of 4 years within the designated period to lessees in circumstances not falling within section 125. (4) (other qualifying purposes: non-leasing use) will not exceed 2 years.

(3) If any plant or machinery is leased as a number of items which—

(a) form part of a group of items of the same or a similar description, and

(b) are not separately identifiable,

all items in the group may be treated as used for short-term leasing if substantially the whole of the items in the group are so used.

(4) For the purposes of subsections (1) and (2) persons who are connected with each other are to be treated as the same person.

122 Short-term leasing by buyer, lessee, etc.

(1) Plant or machinery is used for a qualifying purpose at any time when any of the persons listed in subsection (2) uses it for short-term leasing (as defined by section 121).

(2) The persons are—

(a) the person ("X") who incurred expenditure on the provision of the plant or machinery;

(b) a person who is connected with X;

[F122. (c)a person who acquired the plant or machinery from X as a result of a disposal on the occasion of which, or two or more disposals on the occasion of each of which—

(i) there was a change in the persons carrying on the qualifying activity which did not involve all of the persons carrying on that activity before the change permanently ceasing to carry it on, or

(ii) the qualifying activity carried on by the person making the disposal was treated as continuing under section 114. (1) of ICTA (effect of partnership changes involving companies);]

(d) a person to whom the plant or machinery is leased and who is resident in the United Kingdom;

(e) a person to whom the plant or machinery is leased, who is carrying on a qualifying activity in the United Kingdom and who uses the plant or machinery for the short-term leasing in the course of that activity.

F123. (3). . . . .

Amendments (Textual)

F122. S. 122. (2)(c) substituted (with effect in accordance with s. 883. (1) of the amending Act) by Income Tax (Trading and Other Income) Act 2005 (c. 5), , Sch. 1 para. 540. (2) (with Sch. 2)

F123. S. 122. (3) repealed (with effect in accordance with s. 883. (1) of the amending Act) by Income Tax (Trading and Other Income) Act 2005 (c. 5), Sch. 1 para. 540. (3), Sch. 3 (with Sch. 2)

123 Ships and aircraft

(1) A ship is used for a qualifying purpose at any time when it is let on charter in the course of a trade which consists of or includes operating ships by a person who is—

(a) resident in the United Kingdom or carries on the trade there, and

(b) responsible for navigating and managing the ship throughout the period of the charter and for defraying—

(i) all expenses in connection with the ship throughout that period, or

(ii) substantially all such expenses other than those directly incidental to a particular voyage or to the employment of the ship during that period.

(2) Subsection (1) applies, with the necessary modifications, in relation to aircraft as it applies in relation to ships.

(3) For the purposes of subsection (1)(b) a person is responsible for something if he—

(a) is responsible as principal, or

(b) appoints another person to be responsible in his place.

(4) Subsections (1) and (2) do not apply if the main object, or one of the main objects—

(a) of the letting of the ship or aircraft on charter,

(b) of a series of transactions of which the letting of the ship or aircraft on charter was one, or

(c) of any of the transactions in such a series,

was to obtain a writing-down allowance determined without regard to section 109 (writing-down allowances at 10%) in respect of expenditure incurred by any person on the provision of the ship or aircraft.

124 Transport containers

(1) A transport container is used for a qualifying purpose at any time when it is leased in the course of a trade which is carried on by a person who—

(a) is resident in the United Kingdom, or

(b) carries on the trade there,

and either of the conditions given below is met.

(2) The first condition is that—

(a) the person's trade consists of or includes the operation of ships or aircraft, and

(b) the container is at other times used by that person in connection with the operation of the ships or aircraft.

(3) The second condition is that the container is leased under a succession of leases to different persons who are not, or most of whom are not, connected with each other.

125 Other qualifying purposes

(1) Plant or machinery is used for a qualifying purpose at any time when subsection (2) or (4) applies.

(2) This subsection applies if any of the persons listed in subsection (3) uses the plant or machinery for the purpose of a qualifying activity without leasing it.

(3) The persons are—

(a) the person ("X") who incurred expenditure on the provision of the plant or machinery;

(b) a person who is connected with X;

[F124. (c)a person who acquired the plant or machinery from X as a result of a disposal on the occasion of which, or two or more disposals on the occasion of each of which—

(i) there was a change in the persons carrying on the qualifying activity which did not involve all of the persons carrying on that activity before the change permanently ceasing to carry it on, or

(ii) the qualifying activity carried on by the person making the disposal was treated as continuing under section 114. (1) of ICTA (effect of partnership changes involving companies).]

(4) This subsection applies if—

(a) a lessee uses the plant or machinery for the purposes of a qualifying activity without leasing it, and

(b) if he had incurred expenditure on the provision of the plant or machinery at that time, the expenditure would have fallen to be included, in whole or in part, in his available qualifying expenditure for a chargeable period.

F125. (5). . . . .

Amendments (Textual)

F124. S. 125. (3)(c) substituted (with effect in accordance with s. 883. (1) of the amending Act) by Income Tax (Trading and Other Income) Act 2005 (c. 5), Sch. 1 para. 541. (2) (with Sch. 2)

F125. S. 125. (5) repealed (with effect in accordance with s. 883. (1) of the amending Act) by Income Tax (Trading and Other Income) Act 2005 (c. 5), Sch. 1 para. 541. (3), Sch. 3 (with Sch. 2)

Minor definitions

126 Minor definitions

(1) In this Chapter "normal writing-down allowance" means a writing-down allowance of an amount determined without regard to sections 102 and 109 (reduced rates).

(2) In this Chapter any reference, in relation to any person, to expenditure having qualified for a normal writing-down allowance is to—

(a) the expenditure, or part of it, having fallen to be included in that person's available qualifying expenditure for any chargeable period, and

(b) that available qualifying expenditure being expenditure which is not subject to section 102 or 109.

(3) Any reference in this Chapter to a person's expenditure having qualified for a first-year allowance is to such an allowance having fallen to be made in respect of the whole or any part of the expenditure.

Chapter 12. Ships

127 Single ship pool

(1) Qualifying expenditure incurred on the provision of a ship for the purposes of a qualifying activity, if allocated to a pool, must be allocated to a single asset pool (a "single ship pool").

(2) Subsection (1) is subject to the exceptions given in section 128 and any election under section 129 to use the appropriate non-ship pool.

(3) In this Chapter "the appropriate non-ship pool", in relation to a ship, means the pool to which the expenditure incurred on the provision of the ship would be allocated, or would have been allocated, apart from this Chapter.

128 Expenditure which is not to be allocated to single ship pool

(1) The expenditure is not to be allocated to a single ship pool if the ship is provided for leasing unless—

　(a) the ship is not used for overseas leasing at any time in the designated period, or if it is, is used only for protected leasing, and

　(b) it appears that the ship will be used for a qualifying purpose in the designated period and will not be used for any other purpose at any time in that period.

(2) The expenditure is not to be allocated to a single ship pool if the qualifying activity for the purposes of which the ship is provided is special leasing of plant or machinery.

(3) In subsection (1) "leasing", "overseas leasing", "protected leasing", "qualifying purpose" and "designated period" have the same meaning as in Chapter 11 (overseas leasing).

129 Election to use the appropriate non-ship pool

(1) A person who has incurred qualifying expenditure on the provision of a ship may, by an election made for a chargeable period, allocate to the appropriate non-ship pool—

　(a) all or a part of any qualifying expenditure that would otherwise be allocated to a single ship pool, or

　(b) all or a part of the available qualifying expenditure in a single ship pool.

(2) An election under this section must be made by notice given to [F39an officer of Revenue and Customs]—

　(a) for income tax purposes, on or before the normal time limit for amending a tax return for the tax year in which the relevant chargeable period ends;

　(b) for corporation tax purposes, no later than 2 years after the end of the relevant chargeable period.

(3) "The relevant chargeable period" means the chargeable period for which the election is made.

Amendments (Textual)

F39. Words in Act substituted (18.4.2005) by Commissioners for Revenue and Customs Act 2005 (c. 11), s. 53. (1), Sch. 4 para. 83. (1); S.I. 2005/1126, art. 2. (2)(h)

130 Notice postponing first-year or writing-down allowance

(1) A person who is entitled to a first-year allowance for a chargeable period in respect of qualifying expenditure on the provision of a ship may, by notice, postpone all or part of the allowance.

(2) A person who is entitled to a writing-down allowance for a chargeable period in respect of qualifying expenditure allocated to a single ship pool may, by notice, postpone all or part of the allowance.

(3) A notice under this section must specify the amount postponed.

(4) A notice under this section must be given to [F39an officer of Revenue and Customs]—

　(a) for income tax purposes, on or before the normal time limit for amending a tax return for the tax year in which the relevant chargeable period ends;

　(b) for corporation tax purposes, no later than 2 years after the end of the relevant chargeable period.

(5) "The relevant chargeable period" means the chargeable period for which the person is entitled to the allowance.

(6) If a person entitled to a first-year allowance in respect of qualifying expenditure on the provision of a ship claims the allowance in respect of part of the expenditure, subsection (1)

applies to the allowance claimed.

(7) If a person entitled to a writing-down allowance in respect of qualifying expenditure allocated to a single ship pool requires the allowance to be reduced to a specified amount, subsection (2) applies to the allowance as so reduced.

Amendments (Textual)

F39. Words in Act substituted (18.4.2005) by Commissioners for Revenue and Customs Act 2005 (c. 11), s. 53. (1), Sch. 4 para. 83. (1); S.I. 2005/1126, art. 2. (2)(h)

131 Effect of postponement

(1) If a person gives notice in respect of a chargeable period under section 130—

    (a) the allowance is withheld or withdrawn to the extent that it is postponed, but

    (b) sections 57 to 59 (calculation of available qualifying expenditure) apply as if the allowance had been made to the person without any postponement.

(2) On making a claim, the person is entitled to have all or part of a postponed first-year allowance made to him as a first-year allowance for one or more subsequent chargeable periods in which he is carrying on the qualifying activity.

(3) On making a claim, the person is entitled to have all or part of a postponed writing-down allowance made to him as a writing-down allowance for one or more subsequent chargeable periods in which he is carrying on the qualifying activity.

(4) The total amount of any first-year allowances made under subsection (2) or writing-down allowances made under subsection (3) must not exceed the amount of the postponed allowance in question.

(5) A writing-down allowance made under subsection (3) is ignored for the purposes of section 59 (unrelieved qualifying expenditure).

(6) The fact that a postponed writing-down allowance is claimed for a chargeable period does not affect entitlement to, or the amount of, any other writing-down allowance to which the person is otherwise entitled for that chargeable period.

(7) A postponed allowance is not, merely because of the postponement, included in the reference in section 403. ZB(2) of ICTA (group relief) to an allowance or amount carried forward from an earlier period.

132 Disposal events and single ship pool

(1) A person is required to bring a disposal value into account in a single ship pool if the ship—

    (a) is provided for leasing, and

    (b) begins to be used otherwise than for a qualifying purpose within the first 4 years of the designated period.

(2) If any disposal event (including one under subsection (1)) occurs in relation to a single ship pool—

    (a) the available qualifying expenditure in the single ship pool is allocated, for the chargeable period in which the event occurs, to the appropriate non-ship pool,

    (b) the disposal value must be brought into account as a disposal value for that chargeable period in the appropriate non-ship pool, and

    (c) the single ship pool ends without a final chargeable period and without any liability to a balancing charge arising.

(3) Subsections (1) and (2) apply even if, as a result of an election under section 129, some of the qualifying expenditure on the provision of the ship has been allocated to the appropriate non-ship pool.

(4) In subsection (1) "leasing", "qualifying purpose" and "designated period" have the same meaning as in Chapter 11 (overseas leasing).

133 Ship not used

(1) This section applies if—

    (a) a person has incurred qualifying expenditure on the provision of a ship for the purposes of a qualifying activity, and

    (b) the ship ceases to be owned by the person without having been brought into use for the purposes of the qualifying activity.

(2) Any writing-down allowances that have previously been made in respect of qualifying expenditure in the single ship pool (or which have been postponed) must be withdrawn.
(3) The amount of any writing-down allowances withdrawn under subsection (2) is allocated, for the chargeable period in which the person ceases to own the ship, to the appropriate non-ship pool.
(4) Any adjustments required by this section are in addition to any adjustments required under section 132 (disposal events and single ship pool).

Deferment of balancing charges

134 Deferment of balancing charges: introduction
(1) Sections 135 to 156 enable a balancing charge that arises when there is a disposal event in respect of a ship to be deferred and attributed to qualifying expenditure on another ship.
(2) In this Chapter "the deferment rules" means sections 135 to 156.
135 Claim for deferment
(1) A person ("the shipowner") who is liable to a balancing charge for a chargeable period may claim deferment of all or part of the charge if—
    (a) in the chargeable period there is a disposal event ("the relevant disposal event") in respect of a ship ("the old ship"),
    (b) the old ship—
(i) was provided for the purposes of a qualifying activity carried on by the shipowner, and
(ii) was owned by the shipowner at some time in the chargeable period, and
    (c) the conditions in section 136 are met.
(2) The amount which may be deferred is subject to the limit in section 138.
(3) For income tax purposes, a claim for deferment must be made on or before the normal time limit for amending a tax return for the tax year in which the relevant chargeable period ends.
(4) "The relevant chargeable period" means the chargeable period for which the shipowner is liable to the balancing charge.
(5) For corporation tax purposes, Part IX of Schedule 18 to FA 1998 applies in relation to the making of a claim for deferment as it applies in relation to the making of a claim for an allowance.
136 Further conditions for deferment
The conditions referred to in section 135. (1)(c) are that—
    (a) the relevant disposal event is of a kind mentioned in section 61. (1)(a) to (d) (cessation of ownership, loss, abandonment, destruction etc. of ship),
    (b) the old ship was a qualifying ship immediately before the relevant disposal event,
    (c) the shipowner has not incurred a loss in respect of the qualifying activity for the chargeable period for which he is liable to the balancing charge, and
    (d) no amount in respect of the old ship has been allocated to—
(i) the overseas leasing pool,
(ii) a single asset pool under section 206 (plant or machinery provided or used partly for purposes other than those of the qualifying activity),
(iii) a single asset pool under section 211 (payment of partial depreciation subsidy), or
(iv) a pool for a qualifying activity consisting of special leasing.
137 Effect of deferment
A claim for deferment is given effect by allocating the amount deferred, for the chargeable period in respect of which the claim is made, to the appropriate non-ship pool.
138 Limit on amount deferred
(1) The amount deferred must not exceed the smallest of the following amounts—
    (a) the amount of any balancing charge which, if the claim for deferment had not been made, would have been made for the chargeable period for which deferment is claimed in the appropriate non-ship pool;
    (b) the amount given by section 139 (amount taken into account in respect of the old ship);
    (c) the amount which is, or is expected to be, the amount of expenditure on new shipping

incurred—

(i) by the shipowner or, if the shipowner is a company, by another company which is a member of the same group at the time when the expenditure is incurred, and

(ii) within the period of 6 years beginning with the relevant disposal event;

(d) the amount of the shipowner's profits or income from the qualifying activity for the chargeable period for which deferment is claimed.

(2) In determining profits or income for the purposes of subsection (1)(d)—

(a) any other amounts deferred under section 135 are to be taken into account, and

(b) any amounts brought forward under [F126section 83 of ITA 2007 or section] 393 of ICTA (losses) are to be disregarded.

Amendments (Textual)

F126. Words in s. 138. (2)(b) substituted (6.4.2007) by Income Tax Act 2007 (c. 3), s. 1034. (1), Sch. 1 para. 400 (with Sch. 2)

139 Amount taken into account in respect of old ship

(1) The amount taken into account in respect of the old ship for the purposes of section 138. (1)(b) is—

(a) amount A, if no election has been made under section 129 (election to use appropriate non-ship pool) in respect of any of the qualifying expenditure incurred on the provision of the ship, or

(b) amount B, in any other case.

(2) Amount A is the amount which falls to be brought into account as a disposal value in the appropriate non-ship pool under section 132. (2)(b) as a result of the relevant disposal event, less the available qualifying expenditure allocated to the appropriate non-ship pool under section 132. (2)(a).

(3) Amount B is—

where—

DV is the amount of the disposal value required to be brought into account in respect of the old ship,

QE is all the qualifying expenditure incurred in respect of the old ship,

WDA is the maximum amount of any writing-down allowances which (on the assumptions in subsection (4)) could have been made in respect of that qualifying expenditure for chargeable periods up to (but not including) the one in respect of which the claim for deferment is made, and

FYA is the total of any first-year allowances actually made or postponed in respect of the old ship.

(4) The assumptions are that—

(a) all the qualifying expenditure in respect of the old ship is (and has always been) allocated to the appropriate non-ship pool, and

(b) no other qualifying expenditure has been allocated to that pool.

(5) If an election is made under section 129 (election to use appropriate non-ship pool) after the determination under this section of the amount taken into account in respect of the old ship, the amount is, and is treated as always having been, amount B and not amount A.

Attribution of deferred amounts

140 Notice attributing deferred amounts to new expenditure

(1) The shipowner may, by notice to [F39an officer of Revenue and Customs], attribute all or part of an amount deferred under section 135 to expenditure on new shipping.

(2) An amount attributed under this section is attributed to an equal amount of the expenditure on new shipping.

(3) Subsection (1) is subject to subsections (4) and (5) and section 141 (deferred amounts attributed to earlier expenditure first).

(4) Subsection (1) applies only if the expenditure on new shipping is incurred—

(a) by the shipowner or, if the shipowner is a company, by another company which is a member of the same group at the time when the expenditure is incurred, and

(b) within the period of 6 years beginning with the relevant disposal event.

(5) An amount may be attributed to expenditure on new shipping only to the extent that amounts have not already been attributed to it under this section.

(6) A notice given in respect of expenditure incurred by another company does not have effect unless the other company joins the shipowner in giving it.

Amendments (Textual)

F39. Words in Act substituted (18.4.2005) by Commissioners for Revenue and Customs Act 2005 (c. 11), s. 53. (1), Sch. 4 para. 83. (1); S.I. 2005/1126, art. 2. (2)(h)

141 Deferred amounts attributed to earlier expenditure first

(1) No part of an amount deferred under section 135 is to be attributed to the whole or a part of any expenditure on new shipping ("the current expenditure") if there is other expenditure ("the earlier expenditure") which—

(a) was incurred before the current expenditure but at the same time as or after the relevant disposal event,

(b) was incurred by the shipowner or, if the shipowner is a company, by another company which was a member of the same group at the time the earlier expenditure was incurred, and

(c) is expenditure on new shipping, or would be treated as such but for an election under section 129 (election to use appropriate non-ship pool),

unless the condition in subsection (2) is met in relation to the earlier expenditure.

(2) The condition is that—

(a) amounts have been attributed to all the earlier expenditure under section 140, and

(b) the attributions have been made in the case of the amount deferred and any other amounts deferred under section 135 as a result of disposal events occurring at the same time as or before the relevant disposal event.

142 Variation of attribution

(1) The shipowner may, by notice, vary an attribution under section 140 (notice attributing deferred amounts to new expenditure).

(2) The notice must be given to [F39an officer of Revenue and Customs] on or before the time limit for the shipowner to make a claim for deferment in respect of the relevant chargeable period.

(3) For the time limit for making a claim for deferment, see section 135. (3) to (5).

(4) For the purposes of subsection (2), it is to be assumed that—

(a) the shipowner is liable to a balancing charge for the relevant chargeable period, and

(b) a claim for deferment of that balancing charge can be made for the relevant chargeable period.

(5) "The relevant chargeable period" means the earliest chargeable period in which expenditure to which the variation relates is incurred.

(6) If the person to whose expenditure the notice relates is not the shipowner, a notice under subsection (1) does not have effect unless the person joins the shipowner in giving it.

Amendments (Textual)

F39. Words in Act substituted (18.4.2005) by Commissioners for Revenue and Customs Act 2005 (c. 11), s. 53. (1), Sch. 4 para. 83. (1); S.I. 2005/1126, art. 2. (2)(h)

143 Effect of attribution

(1) This section applies if a notice is given under section 140 attributing an amount to expenditure on new shipping.

(2) The amount must be brought into account as a disposal value—

(a) for the chargeable period in which the expenditure is incurred, and

(b) in the single ship pool to which the expenditure is allocated.

144 Amounts which cease to be attributable

(1) This section applies if—

(a) an amount has been deferred under section 135, and

(b) circumstances arise in which any part of the amount ceases (otherwise than by being attributed) to be attributable.

(2) The shipowner is assumed not to have been entitled to defer so much of the amount as ceases

to be attributable.

(3) For the purposes of this section an amount is attributable if it may be attributed to expenditure on new shipping in accordance with section 140.

145 Requirement to notify where no entitlement to defer amounts

(1) This section applies if—

(a) an amount has been deferred under section 135, and

(b) circumstances arise that require the shipowner to be treated as if he was not entitled to defer all or part of the amount.

(2) The shipowner must give notice of the fact to [F39an officer of Revenue and Customs], specifying the circumstances.

(3) The notice must be given no later than 3 months after the end of the chargeable period in which the circumstances first arise.

(4) An assessment to tax chargeable as a result of the circumstances may be made at any time in the period which—

(a) begins when those circumstances arise, and

(b) ends 12 months after the shipowner gives notice of them to [F39an officer of Revenue and Customs].

(5) Subsection (4) applies in spite of any limitation on the time for making assessments.

Amendments (Textual)

F39. Words in Act substituted (18.4.2005) by Commissioners for Revenue and Customs Act 2005 (c. 11), s. 53. (1), Sch. 4 para. 83. (1); S.I. 2005/1126, art. 2. (2)(h)

Expenditure on new shipping

146 Basic meaning of expenditure on new shipping

(1) For the purposes of the deferment rules, expenditure on the provision of a ship is expenditure on new shipping if the conditions in subsection (3) are met.

(2) Subsection (1) is subject to sections 147 to 150.

(3) The conditions are that—

(a) the expenditure is qualifying expenditure incurred by a person wholly and exclusively for the purposes of a qualifying activity carried on by him,

(b) when the expenditure is incurred, it appears that the ship will—

(i) be brought into use for the purposes of the qualifying activity as a qualifying ship, and

(ii) continue to be a qualifying ship for at least 3 years after that, and

(c) the expenditure is allocated to a single ship pool.

147 Exclusions: ship previously owned

(1) Expenditure on the provision of a ship is not expenditure on new shipping if the person who incurred the expenditure—

(a) has already owned the ship in the period of 6 years ending with the time when he first owns it as a result of incurring the expenditure, or

(b) was connected at a material time with a person who owned the ship at any time during that period.

(2) For this purpose a material time is—

(a) the time when the expenditure was incurred, or

(b) any earlier time in the 6 year period beginning with the relevant disposal event.

148 Exclusions: object to secure deferment

Expenditure on the provision of a ship is not expenditure on new shipping if the object, or one of the main objects, of—

(a) the transaction by which the ship was provided for the purposes of a qualifying activity carried on by the person who incurred the expenditure,

(b) any series of transactions of which that transaction was one, or

(c) any transaction in such a series,

was to secure the deferment of a balancing charge under section 135.

149 Exclusions: later events

(1) Expenditure on the provision of a ship is not, and is treated as never having been, expenditure on new shipping if—

(a) at a time during the period mentioned in subsection (2), the ship is not a qualifying ship,

(b) the expenditure is allocated to a pool as a result of an election under section 129 (election to use appropriate non-ship pool), or

(c) section 107 applies in relation to the expenditure (overseas leasing).

(2) The period referred to in subsection (1)(a) is—

(a) the period of 3 years beginning with the time when the ship is first brought into use for the purposes of a qualifying activity carried on—

(i) by the person ("A") who incurred the expenditure, or

(ii) if earlier, by a person connected with A, or

(b) if shorter, the period beginning with that time and ending when neither A nor a person connected with A owns the ship.

150 Exclusions where expenditure not incurred by shipowner

(1) Expenditure on the provision of a ship is not, and is treated as never having been, expenditure on new shipping if—

(a) it is incurred by a company which is a member of the same group as the shipowner at the time when the expenditure is incurred, and

(b) subsection (2) or (4) applies.

(2) This subsection applies (subject to subsection (3)) if—

(a) the ship ceases to be owned by the company before it has been brought into use for the purposes of a qualifying activity carried on by the company, or

(b) a disposal event occurs in respect of the ship within 3 years of its first being brought into use for the purposes of a qualifying activity carried on by the company.

(3) But subsection (2) does not apply if the event which would otherwise result in that subsection applying is, or is the result of, the total loss of the ship or irreparable damage to it.

(4) This subsection applies if—

(a) after the expenditure is incurred, there is a time when the company and the shipowner are not members of the same group, and

(b) if the ship is brought into use for the purposes of a qualifying activity carried on by the company, that time is within 3 years of the ship first being so brought into use.

(5) A time falling after the total loss of the ship or irreparable damage to it is to be disregarded for the purposes of subsection (4).

(6) In this section "irreparable damage", in relation to a ship, means damage that puts it in a condition in which it is impossible, or not commercially worthwhile, to undertake the repairs required for restoring it to its previous use.

Qualifying ships

151 Basic meaning of qualifying ship

(1) For the purposes of the deferment rules, a ship is a qualifying ship if it is—

(a) of a sea-going kind, and

(b) registered as a ship with a gross tonnage of 100 tons or more in a register of shipping established and maintained under the law of any country or territory.

(2) This is subject to sections 152 to 154.

152 Ships under 100 tons

(1) This section applies if the relevant disposal event is, or results from—

(a) the total loss of the old ship, or

(b) damage to the old ship that puts it in a condition in which it is impossible, or not commercially worthwhile, to undertake the repairs required for restoring it to its previous use.

(2) A registered ship may be a qualifying ship for the purposes of—

    (a) section 136. (b) (further conditions for deferment), or

    (b) sections 146. (3)(b) and 149. (1)(a) (expenditure on new shipping),

even if it is not registered as a ship with a gross tonnage of 100 tons or more.

(3) In subsection (2) "registered ship" means a ship registered in a register of shipping established and maintained under the law of any country or territory.

153 Ships which are not qualifying ships

(1) A ship is not a qualifying ship if the primary use to which ships of the same kind as that ship are put—

    (a) by the persons who own them, or

    (b) by others to whom they are made available,

is use for sport or recreation.

[F127. (2)A ship is not a qualifying ship at any time when it is an offshore installation.]

F128. (3). . . . .

Amendments (Textual)

F127 S. 153. (2) substituted (with effect in accordance with Sch. 27 para. 11 of the amending Act) by Finance Act 2004 (c. 12) , Sch. 27 para. 9. (2)

F128 S. 153. (3) repealed (with effect in accordance with Sch. 27 para. 11 of the amending Act) by Finance Act 2004 (c. 12) , Sch. 27 para. 9. (3) , 42 Pt. 2. (19)

154 Further registration requirement

(1) If—

    (a) a person ("A") has incurred expenditure on the provision of a ship, and

    (b) there is a time in the qualifying period, but more than 3 months after the beginning of that period, when the ship is not registered in a relevant register,

the ship is not a qualifying ship after that time.

(2) The qualifying period is—

    (a) the period of 3 years beginning with the time when the ship is first brought into use for the purposes of a qualifying activity carried on—

(i) by A, or

(ii) if earlier, by a person connected with A, or

    (b) if shorter, the period beginning with that time and ending when neither A nor a person connected with A owns the ship.

(3) In determining the qualifying period for the old ship, a qualifying activity carried on at any time by a person ("B") is taken to be carried on at that time by a person connected with A if—

    (a) it is subsequently carried on by A or a person connected with A, and

    [F129. (b)the only changes in the persons carrying it on between the time that B does so and the time that A or a person connected with A does so are changes—

(i) which do not involve all of the persons carrying it on before the changes permanently ceasing to carry it on, or

(ii) in respect of which the qualifying activity is treated as continuing under section 343. (2) of ICTA.]

(4) In this section "relevant register" means a register of shipping established and maintained—

    (a) under the laws of any part of the British Islands, or

    (b) under the laws of any country or territory which, at a time in the qualifying period for the ship, is an EEA State or a colony.

(5) "EEA State" means a State which is a contracting party to the Agreement on the European Economic Area signed at Oporto on 2nd May 1992 as adjusted by the Protocol signed at Brussels on 17th March 1993 (except that for the period before the Agreement came into force in relation to Liechtenstein it does not include the State of Liechtenstein).

Amendments (Textual)

F129 S. 154. (3)(b) substituted (6.4.2005) by Income Tax (Trading and Other Income) Act 2005 (c. 5) , s. 883. (1) , Sch. 1 para. 542 (with Sch. 2)

Deferment of balancing charges: supplementary provisions

155 Change in the persons carrying on the qualifying activity

(1) This section applies if—

(a) a person is carrying on the qualifying activity previously carried on by the shipowner, and

[F130. (b)the only changes in the persons carrying on the qualifying activity since the shipowner carried it on are changes—

(i) which do not involve all of the persons carrying it on before the changes permanently ceasing to carry it on, or

(ii) in respect of which the qualifying activity is treated as continuing under section 343. (2) of ICTA.]

(2) For the purposes of the deferment rules—

(a) expenditure incurred by a person mentioned in subsection (1)(a) for the purposes of the qualifying activity is to be treated as incurred by the shipowner, and

(b) in relation to the giving of any notice, a reference to the shipowner is to be read as a reference to the person carrying on the qualifying activity when the notice is given or is required to be given.

Amendments (Textual)

F130 S. 155. (1)(b) substituted (6.4.2005) by Income Tax (Trading and Other Income) Act 2005 (c. 5) , s. 883. (1) , Sch. 1 para. 543 (with Sch. 2)

156 Connected persons

(1) For the purposes of the deferment rules a person ("B") is connected with another person ("A") at any time if, at that time—

(a) B is connected (in the sense given in [F131 section 575]) with A,

(b) B is carrying on a qualifying activity previously carried on by A and the condition in subsection (2) is met, or

(c) B is connected (in the sense given in [F132 section 575]) with a person who is carrying on a qualifying activity previously carried on by A and the condition in subsection (2) is met.

[F133. (2)The condition is that the only changes in the persons carrying on the qualifying activity since A carried it on are changes—

(a) which do not involve all of the persons carrying it on before the changes permanently ceasing to carry it on, or

(b) in respect of which the qualifying activity is treated as continuing under section 343. (2) of ICTA.]

(3) If expenditure is incurred by a person who is not the shipowner, the persons connected with him at any time include any person connected with the shipowner at that time as a result of subsection (1).

Amendments (Textual)

F131. Words in s. 156. (1)(a) substituted (6.4.2007) by Income Tax Act 2007 (c. 3), s. 1034. (1), Sch. 1 para. 401 (with Sch. 2)

F132. Words in s. 156. (1)(c) substituted (6.4.2007) by Income Tax Act 2007 (c. 3), s. 1034. (1), Sch. 1 para. 401 (with Sch. 2)

F133 S. 156. (2) substituted (6.4.2005) by Income Tax (Trading and Other Income) Act 2005 (c. 5) , s. 883. (1) , Sch. 1 para. 544 (with Sch. 2)

Further provisions

157 Adjustment of assessments etc.

(1) All such assessments and adjustments of assessments are to be made as are necessary to give effect to this Chapter.

(2) Subsection (1) does not apply for the purposes of section 145 (see instead section 145. (4) and (5)).

158 Members of same group

For the purposes of this Chapter two companies are members of the same group at any time if they would be treated as members of the same group of companies at that time for the purposes of Chapter IV of Part X of ICTA (group relief).

Chapter 13. Provisions affecting mining and oil industries

159 Meaning of "mineral extraction trade" etc.

In this Chapter—

"mineral extraction trade", and

"mineral exploration and access"

have the same meaning as in Part 5 (mineral extraction allowances).

160 Expenditure treated as incurred for purposes of mineral extraction trade

For the purposes of this Part, expenditure incurred by a person—

(a) on the provision of plant or machinery for mineral exploration and access, and

(b) in connection with a mineral extraction trade carried on by him,

is to be treated as incurred for the purposes of that trade.

161 Pre-trading expenditure on mineral exploration and access

(1) This section applies if a person—

(a) incurs pre-trading expenditure on the provision of plant or machinery for the purposes of mineral exploration and access, and

(b) owns the plant or machinery on the first day of trading.

But this is subject to subsection (5).

(2) The person is to be treated for the purposes of this Part as if he had—

(a) sold the plant or machinery immediately before the first day of trading, and

(b) on that first day incurred capital expenditure on the provision of the plant or machinery for the purposes of the trade.

(3) The amount of the capital expenditure that the person is to be treated as having incurred is an amount equal to—

(a) the pre-trading expenditure, or

(b) if there has been an actual sale and re-acquisition before the first day of trading, the amount last incurred on the provision of the plant or machinery.

(4) In this section—

(a) "pre-trading expenditure" means capital expenditure incurred before the day on which a person begins to carry on a mineral extraction trade, and

(b) "the first day of trading", in relation to a person's pre-trading expenditure, means the day on which that person begins to carry on the mineral extraction trade.

(5) This section does not apply if the plant or machinery on which the pre-trading expenditure was incurred is sold, demolished, destroyed or abandoned before the first day of trading (but see section 402 (mineral extraction allowances: pre-trading expenditure on plant or machinery)).

[F134 Expenditure connected with reuse etc. of offshore oil infrastructure

Amendments (Textual)

F134. Ss. 161. A-161. D and crossheading inserted (with effect as mentioned in Sch. 20 para. 9. (1)-(4)(8) of the amending Act) by Finance Act 2001 (c. 9), s. 68, Sch. 20 para. 5. (1)

161. A Meaning of "offshore infrastructure"

(1) In sections 161. C and 161. D " offshore infrastructure " means—

(a) an offshore installation within the meaning given by section 44 of the Petroleum Act 1998 (c. 17) or a part of such an installation, or

(b) something that would be, or would be a part of, an offshore installation within that meaning if in subsection (3) of that section " relevant waters " meant waters in a foreign sector of the continental shelf and other foreign tidal waters, or

(c) a pipeline within the meaning of section 26 of that Act, or a part of such a pipeline, that is in, under or over waters in—

(i) the territorial sea adjacent to the United Kingdom, or

(ii) an area designated under section 1. (7) of the Continental Shelf Act 1964 (c. 29), or

(d) a pipeline within the meaning of section 26 of the Petroleum Act 1998 (c. 17), or a part of such a pipeline, that is in, under or over waters in a foreign sector of the continental shelf.

(2) In subsection (1)(b) and (d)—

" foreign sector of the continental shelf " means an area within which rights are exercisable with respect to the sea bed and subsoil and their natural resources by a country or territory outside the United Kingdom;

" foreign tidal waters " means tidal waters in an area within which rights are exercisable with respect to the bed and subsoil of the body of water in question and their natural resources by a country or territory outside the United Kingdom.

161. B Meaning of "decommissioning expenditure"

(1) In sections 161. C and 161. D " decommissioning expenditure " means expenditure in connection with—

(a) preserving plant or machinery pending its reuse or demolition,

(b) preparing plant or machinery for reuse, or

(c) arranging for the reuse of plant or machinery.

(2) It is immaterial for the purposes of subsection (1)(a) whether the plant or machinery is reused, is demolished or is partly reused and partly demolished.

(3) It is immaterial for the purposes of subsection (1)(b) and (c) whether the plant or machinery is in fact reused.

161. C Expenditure related to reuse etc. qualifies for writing-down allowances

(1) This section applies where—

(a) a person carrying on a trade of oil extraction incurs decommissioning expenditure, and

(b) the plant or machinery concerned—

(i) has been brought into use for the purposes of the trade, and

(ii) is, or was when last in use for those purposes, offshore infrastructure.

(2) The decommissioning expenditure is allocated to the appropriate pool for the chargeable period in which it is incurred.

(3) Subsection (2) is subject to sections 161. D and 164. (4).

(4) In subsection (2) " the appropriate pool " means the pool to which the expenditure on the plant or machinery concerned has been or would be allocated in accordance with this Part.

161. D Exceptions to section 161. C(2)

(1) Subsection (2) of section 161. C does not apply to decommissioning expenditure on UK infrastructure unless it is incurred in connection with measures taken, wholly or substantially, in order to comply with—

(a) an abandonment programme within the meaning given by section 29 of the Petroleum Act 1998 (c. 17), or

(b) any condition to which the approval of such a programme is subject.

(2) Subsection (2) of section 161. C does not apply to expenditure in respect of which an allowance or deduction could be made apart from that subsection in taxing, or computing, the person's income for any tax purpose.

(3) For the purposes of subsection (1), decommissioning expenditure is " on UK infrastructure " if the plant or machinery concerned—

(a) is offshore infrastructure within section 161. A(1)(a) or (c), or

(b) is not offshore infrastructure but was offshore infrastructure within section 161. A(1)(a) or (c) when last in use for the purposes of the trade.]

Provisions relating to ring fence trades

162 Ring fence trade a separate qualifying activity

(1) If a person carries on a ring fence trade, it is a separate qualifying activity for the purposes of this Part.

(2) In this Chapter "ring fence trade" means activities which—

(a) fall within [F135the definition of "oil-related activities" in section 16. (2) of ITTOIA 2005 or within] [F135the definition of "oil-related activities" in section 16. (2) of ITTOIA 2005 or within] any of paragraphs (a) to (c) of section 492. (1) of ICTA (oil extraction activities, the acquisition, enjoyment or exploitation of oil rights, etc.), and

(b) constitute a separate trade (whether as a result of [F136section 16. (1) of ITTOIA 2005 or] [F136section 16. (1) of ITTOIA 2005 or] section 492. (1) of ICTA or otherwise).

Amendments (Textual)

F135 Words in s. 162. (2)(a) inserted (6.4.2005) by Income Tax (Trading and Other Income) Act 2005 (c. 5) , s. 883. (1) , Sch. 1 para. 545. (a) (with Sch. 2)

F136 Words in s. 162. (2)(b) inserted (6.4.2005) by Income Tax (Trading and Other Income) Act 2005 (c. 5) , s. 883. (1) , Sch. 1 para. 545. (b) (with Sch. 2)

163 Meaning of "abandonment expenditure"

(1) In sections 164 and 165 "abandonment expenditure" means expenditure which meets the requirements in subsections (2) to (4).

(2) The expenditure must have been incurred—

(a) for the purposes of, or in connection with, the closing down of an oil field or of any part of an oil field, and

(b) on the [F137decommissioning] plant or machinery—

(i) which has been brought into use for the purposes of a ring fence trade, and

(ii) which is, or forms part of, an offshore installation or a submarine pipeline [F138or which, when last in use for the purposes of a ring-fence trade, was, or formed part of, such an installation or pipeline.]

(3) The [F139decommissioning] of the plant or machinery must be carried out, wholly or substantially, to comply with—

(a) an abandonment programme, or

(b) any condition to which the approval of an abandonment programme is subject.

(4) The plant or machinery must not be replaced.

[F140. (4. A) In this section " decommissioning ", in relation to any plant or machinery, means—

(a) demolishing the plant or machinery,

(b) preserving the plant or machinery pending its reuse or demolition,

(c) preparing the plant or machinery for reuse, or

(d) arranging for the reuse of the plant or machinery.

(4. B)In determining whether expenditure is incurred on preserving plant or machinery pending its reuse or demolition, it is immaterial whether the plant or machinery is reused, is demolished or is partly reused and partly demolished.

(4. C)In determining whether expenditure is incurred on preparing plant or machinery for reuse, or on arranging for the reuse of plant or machinery, it is immaterial whether the plant or machinery is in fact reused.]

(5) In this section—

(a) "oil field" has the same meaning as in Part I of OTA 1975, and

(b) "abandonment programme", "offshore installation" and "submarine pipeline" have the same meaning as in Part IV of the Petroleum Act 1998 (c. 17).

Amendments (Textual)

F137. Words in s. 163. (2)(b) substituted (with effect as mentioned in Sch. 20 para. 9. (1)(5)(8) of the amending Act) by Finance Act 2001 (c. 9), s. 68, Sch. 20 Pt. 2 para. 6. (2)

F138. Words in s. 163. (2)(b)(ii) inserted (with effect as mentioned in Sch. 20 para. 9. (1)(5)(8) of the amending Act) by Finance Act 2001 (c. 9), s. 68, Sch. 20 Pt. 2 para. 6. (3)

F139. Word in s. 163. (3) substituted (with effect as mentioned in Sch. 20 para. 9. (1)(5)(8) of the amending Act) by Finance Act 2001 (c. 9), s. 68, Sch. 20 Pt. 2 para. 6. (4)

F140. S. 163. (4. A)-(4. C) inserted (with effect as mentioned in Sch. 20 para. 9. (1)(5)(8) of the amending Act) by Finance Act 2001 (c. 9), s. 68, Sch. 20 Pt. 2 para. 6. (5)

164 Abandonment expenditure incurred before cessation of ring fence trade

(1) If a person carrying on a ring fence trade incurs abandonment expenditure, [F141and the plant or machinery concerned has been brought into use for the purposes of that trade,] he may elect to have a special allowance made to him.

(2) The election—

(a) must be made by notice to [F39an officer of Revenue and Customs] no later than 2 years after the end of the chargeable period in which the abandonment expenditure is incurred, and

(b) is irrevocable.

(3) The election must specify—

(a) the abandonment expenditure to which it relates, and

[F142. (b)where the plant or machinery concerned has been or is to be demolished, any amounts received for its remains.]

(4) If a person makes an election under this section—

(a) he is entitled to a special allowance F143... for the chargeable period in which the abandonment expenditure is incurred, and

[F144. (b)neither of sections 26. (3) and 161. C(2)(net cost of demolition where plant or machinery not replaced, or cost of preparing for reuse, added to existing pool) applies.]

[F145. (5)The amount of the special allowance for a chargeable period is equal to so much of the abandonment expenditure to which the election relates as is incurred in that period.

(6) If plant or machinery is demolished, the total of any special allowances in respect of expenditure on decommissioning the plant or machinery is reduced by any amount received for the remains of the plant or machinery.

Here " decommissioning " has the meaning given by section 163. (4. A).

(7) Effect is given to subsection (6) by setting the amount (until wholly utilised)—

first, against any special allowance for the chargeable period in which the amount is received (as previously reduced in giving effect to subsection (6));

second, against special allowances for earlier chargeable periods (as so reduced and taking later such periods before earlier ones); and

third, against special allowances for later chargeable periods (as so reduced and taking earlier such periods before later ones).]

Amendments (Textual)

F39. Words in Act substituted (18.4.2005) by Commissioners for Revenue and Customs Act 2005 (c. 11), s. 53. (1), Sch. 4 para. 83. (1); S.I. 2005/1126, art. 2. (2)(h)

F141 Words in s. 164. (1) inserted (retrospectively) by Finance Act 2001 (c. 9) , s. 68 , Sch. 20 Pt. 2 paras. 7. (2) , 9. (9)

F142. S. 164. (3)(b) substituted (with effect as mentioned in Sch. 20 para. 9. (1)(5)(8) of the amending Act) by Finance Act 2001 (c. 9), s. 68, Sch. 20 Pt. 2 para. 7. (3)

F143. Words in s. 164. (4)(a) repealed (with effect as mentioned in Sch. 20 para.9. (1)(5)(8) of the amending Act) by Finance Act 2001 (c. 9), s. 68, 110, Sch. 20 Pt. 2 para. 7. (4), Sch. 33 Pt. 2. (5) Note 1

F144. S. 164. (4)(b) substituted (with effect as mentioned in Sch. 20 para. 9. (1)(5)(8) of the amending Act) by Finance Act 2001 (c. 9), s. 68, Sch. 20 Pt. 2 para. 7. (5)

F145. S. 164. (5)-(7) substituted (with effect as mentioned in Sch. 20 para. 9. (1)(5)(8) of the amending Act) for s. 164. (5) by Finance Act 2001 (c. 9), s. 68, Sch. 20 Pt. 2 para. 7. (6)

165 Abandonment expenditure within 3 years of ceasing ring fence trade

(1) This section applies if—

(a) a person ("the former trader") has ceased to carry on a ring fence trade,

(b) the former trader incurs abandonment expenditure F146... within the post-cessation period, and

(c) the abandonment expenditure is not otherwise deductible in calculating the income of the former trader for any tax purpose.

(2) "The post-cessation period" means the period of 3 years immediately following the last day on which the former trader carried on the ring fence trade.

(3) If this section applies—

(a) an amount equal to the relevant abandonment cost is allocated to the appropriate pool for the chargeable period in which the former trader ceased to carry on the ring fence trade, and

(b) [F147where any of the abandonment expenditure was incurred on the demolition of plant or machinery,]any amount received within the post-cessation period for the remains of the plant or machinery does not constitute income of the former trader for any tax purpose.

(4) In subsection (3)—

"the appropriate pool" means the pool to which the expenditure on the demolished plant or machinery has been allocated, and

"the relevant abandonment cost" means the amount by which the abandonment expenditure exceeds any amounts received within the post-cessation period for the remains of [F148any plant or machinery on whose demolition any of the abandonment expenditure was incurred].

(5) All such adjustments, by discharge or repayment of tax or otherwise, are to be made as are necessary to give effect to this section.

Amendments (Textual)

F146 Words in s. 165. (1)(b) repealed (retrospectively) by Finance Act 2001 (c. 9) , s. 68 , 110 , Sch. 20 Pt. 2 para. 8. (2) , Sch. 33 Pt. 2. (5) , Note 2

F147. Words in s. 165. (3)(b) inserted (with effect as mentioned in Sch. 20 para. 9. (1)(5)(8) of the amending Act) by Finance Act 2001 (c. 9), s. 68, Sch. 20 para. 8. (3)

F148. Words in s. 165. (4) substituted (with effect as mentioned in Sch. 20 para. 9. (1)(5)(8) of the amending Act) by Finance Act 2001 (c. 9), s. 68, Sch. 20 para. 8. (4)

Transfers of interests in oil fields: anti-avoidance

166 Transfers of interests in oil fields: anti-avoidance

(1) This section applies if—

(a) there is, for the purposes of Schedule 17 to FA 1980, a transfer by a participator in an oil field of the whole or part of his interest in the field, and

(b) as part of the transfer, the old participator disposes of, and the new participator acquires—

(i) plant or machinery used, or expected to be used, in connection with the field, or

(ii) a share in such plant or machinery.

(2) The amount, if any, by which the new participator's expenditure exceeds the old participator's disposal value is to be left out of account in determining the new participator's available qualifying expenditure.

(3) In subsection (2)—

(a) "the new participator's expenditure" means the expenditure incurred by the new participator on the acquisition of the plant or machinery, and

(b) "the old participator's disposal value" means the disposal value to be brought into account by the old participator as a result of the disposal of the plant or machinery to the new participator.

(4) In this section—

(a) "oil field" and "participator" have the same meaning as in Part I of OTA 1975,

(b) "the old participator" means the participator whose interest in the oil field is wholly or partly transferred, and

(c) "the new participator" means the person to whom the interest in the oil field is transferred.

(5) Nothing in this section affects the operation of Chapter 17 (anti-avoidance).

Oil production sharing contracts

167 Oil production sharing contracts

(1) Sections 168 to 170 apply if—

(a) a person ("the contractor") is entitled to an interest in a contract made with, or with the authorised representative of, the government of a country or territory in which oil is or may be produced, and

(b) the contract provides (among other things) for any plant or machinery of a description specified in the contract which—

(i) is provided by the contractor, and

(ii) has an oil-related use under the contract,

to be transferred (immediately or later) to the government or representative.

(2) For the purposes of this section and sections 168 to 170, plant or machinery has an oil-related use if it is used—

(a) to explore for, win access to or extract oil,

(b) for the initial storage or treatment of oil, or

(c) for other purposes ancillary to the extraction of oil.

(3) In this section and sections 168 to 170 "oil" has the meaning given by section 556. (3).

168 Expenditure on plant or machinery incurred by contractor

(1) This section applies if—

(a) the contractor incurs capital expenditure on the provision of plant or machinery of a description specified in the contract,

(b) the plant or machinery is to have an oil-related use under the contract, for the purposes of a trade of oil extraction carried on by the contractor,

(c) the amount of the expenditure is commensurate with the value of the contractor's interest under the contract, and

(d) the plant or machinery is transferred to the government or representative in accordance with the contract.

(2) Despite the transfer, the plant or machinery is to be treated for the purposes of this Part as owned by the contractor (and not by any other person) until—

(a) it ceases to be owned by the government or representative, or

(b) it ceases to be used, or held for use, by any person under the contract.

This is subject to section 170. (2).

169 Expenditure on plant or machinery incurred by participator

(1) This section applies if—

(a) a person ("the participator") acquires an interest in the contract from—

(i) the contractor, or

(ii) another person who has acquired it (directly or indirectly) from the contractor,

(b) the participator incurs capital expenditure on the provision of plant or machinery,

(c) the plant or machinery is to have an oil-related use under the contract, for the purposes of a trade of oil extraction carried on by the participator,

(d) the amount of the expenditure is commensurate with the value of the participator's interest under the contract, and

(e) the plant or machinery is transferred to the government or representative in accordance with the contract.

(2) Despite the transfer, the plant or machinery is to be treated for the purposes of this Part as owned by the participator (and not by any other person) until—

(a) it ceases to be owned by the government or representative, or

(b) it ceases to be used, or held for use, by any person under the contract.

This is subject to section 170. (2).

170 Participator's expenditure attributable to plant or machinery

(1) This section applies if—

(a) a person ("the relevant participator") acquires an interest in the contract from—

(i) the contractor, or

(ii) another person who has acquired it (directly or indirectly) from the contractor, and

(b) some of the expenditure incurred by the relevant participator to acquire the interest in the contract is attributable to plant or machinery which—

(i) is treated by section 168 as owned by the contractor, or

(ii) is treated by section 169 or subsection (2) as owned by another person ("the other participator").

(2) The plant or machinery is to be treated for the purposes of this Part as owned by the relevant participator (and not by any other person) until—

(a) it ceases to be owned by the government or representative, or

(b) it ceases to be used, or held for use, by any person under the contract.

This is subject to a later application of this subsection.

(3) The person who, until subsection (2) applies, is treated as owning the plant or machinery is to be treated for the purposes of this Part as if he had disposed of it for a consideration equal to the relevant participator's expenditure attributable to it.

(4) The relevant participator is to be treated for the purposes of this Part as if—

(a) he had incurred capital expenditure of an amount given by subsection (5), and

(b) he owned the plant or machinery (in accordance with subsection (2)) as a result of having incurred that expenditure.

(5) The amount of that expenditure is—

(a) the amount of the relevant participator's expenditure attributable to the plant or machinery, or

(b) if less, the disposal value to be brought into account by the contractor or the other participator as a result of subsection (3).

(6) The expenditure attributable to plant or machinery for the purposes of this section is to be determined having regard to what is just and reasonable in the circumstances.

171 Disposal values on cessation of ownership

(1) This section applies if a person treated as owning plant or machinery under section 168. (2), 169. (2) or 170. (2) ceases to be treated as owning it solely as a result of one of those provisions.

(2) If the person receives capital compensation, the disposal value to be brought into account is the amount of the compensation.

(3) If the person does not receive capital compensation, the disposal value to be brought into account is nil.

Modifications etc. (not altering text)

C30. S. 171 excluded (E.W.S.) (8.6.2005) by Railways Act 2005 (c. 14), s. 60. (2), Sch. 10 para. 14. (2)(a); S.I. 2005/1444, art. 2. (1), Sch. 1

Chapter 14. Fixtures

172 Scope of Chapter etc.

(1) This Chapter applies to determine entitlement to allowances under this Part in respect of expenditure on plant or machinery that is, or becomes, a fixture.

(2) For the purposes of this Part, ownership of plant or machinery that is, or becomes, a fixture is determined under this Chapter.

[F149. (2. A)Subsections (1) and (2) are subject to section 172. A.]

(3) The provisions of this Chapter that treat a person as being the owner of a fixture (see sections 176 to 184 and 193 to [F150195. B]) are subject to the provisions of this Chapter which treat a person as ceasing to be the owner of a fixture (see sections 188 to [F151192. A]).

(4) References in this Chapter to a person being treated—

(a) as the owner of plant or machinery, or

(b) as ceasing to be the owner of plant or machinery,

are to be read as references to the person being so treated for the purposes of this Part.

(5) This Chapter does not affect any entitlement a person has to an allowance as a result of section

538 (contribution allowances for plant and machinery).

Amendments (Textual)

F149. S. 172. (2. A) inserted (with effect in accordance with Sch. 8 para. 15 of the amending Act) by Finance Act 2006 (c. 25), Sch. 8 para. 9. (1)

F150. Word in s. 172. (3) substituted (with effect as mentioned in s. 66 of the amending Act) by Finance Act 2001 (c. 9), s. 66, Sch. 18 para. 1. (a)

F151. Word in s. 172. (3) substituted (with effect as mentioned in s. 66 of the amending Act) by Finance Act 2001 (c. 9), s. 66, Sch. 18 para. 1. (b)

[F152172. ALong funding leases etc: cases where this Chapter does not apply.

(1) This section applies where plant or machinery that is or becomes a fixture is the subject of a long funding lease (see Chapter 6. A).

(2) This section also applies if, in any such case,—

(a) the lessee under the long funding lease is or becomes the lessor of some or all of the plant or machinery under a further lease, and

(b) the further lease is not itself a long funding lease within subsection (1).

(3) This Chapter does not apply to determine the entitlement of the lessor or the lessee (under either lease) to allowances under this Part in respect of expenditure on the plant or machinery.

(4) This Chapter does not apply to determine whether the lessor or the lessee (under either lease) is to be treated as the owner of the plant or machinery.]

Amendments (Textual)

F152. S. 172. A inserted (with effect in accordance with Sch. 8 para. 15 of the amending Act) by Finance Act 2006 (c. 25), Sch. 8 para. 9. (2)

173 Meaning of "fixture" and "relevant land"

(1) In this Chapter "fixture"—

(a) means plant or machinery that is so installed or otherwise fixed in or to a building or other description of land as to become, in law, part of that building or other land, and

(b) includes any boiler or water-filled radiator installed in a building as part of a space or water heating system.

(2) In this Chapter "relevant land", in relation to a fixture means—

(a) the building or other description of land of which the fixture becomes part, or

(b) in the case of a boiler or water-filled radiator which is a fixture as a result of subsection (1)(b), the building in which it is installed as part of a space or water heating system.

174 Meaning of "equipment lease" and "lease"

(1) In this Chapter "equipment lease" means—

(a) an agreement entered into in the circumstances given in subsection (2), or

(b) a lease entered into under or as a result of such an agreement.

(2) The circumstances are that—

(a) a person incurs capital expenditure on the provision of plant or machinery for leasing,

(b) an agreement is entered into for the lease, directly or indirectly from that person, of the plant or machinery to another person,

(c) the plant or machinery becomes a fixture, and

(d) the agreement is not an agreement for the plant or machinery to be leased as part of the relevant land.

(3) In this Chapter—

"equipment lessor" means the person from whom (directly or indirectly) the equipment lease provides for the plant or machinery to be leased, and

"equipment lessee" means the person to whom the equipment lease provides for the plant or machinery to be leased.

(4) Except in the context of leasing plant or machinery, any reference in this Chapter to a lease is to—

(a) any leasehold estate in or, in Scotland, lease of, the land (whether in the nature of a head-lease, sub-lease or under-lease), or

(b) any agreement to acquire such an estate or, in Scotland, lease;

and, in relation to such an agreement, "grant" is to be read accordingly.

175 Meaning of "interest in land", etc.

(1) In this Chapter "interest in land" means—

(a) the fee simple estate in the land or an agreement to acquire such an estate,

(b) in relation to Scotland, the interest of the owner or an agreement to acquire such an interest,

(c) a lease,

(d) an easement or servitude or an agreement to acquire an easement or servitude, and

(e) a licence to occupy land.

(2) If an interest in land is—

(a) conveyed or assigned by way of security, and

(b) subject to a right of redemption,

the person with the right of redemption is treated for the purposes of this Chapter as having that interest, and not the creditor.

[F153 175. A Meaning of "energy services agreement"

(1) In this Chapter " energy services agreement " means an agreement entered into by an energy services provider (" the energy services provider ") and another person (" the client ") that makes provision, with a view to saving energy or using energy more efficiently, for—

(a) the design of plant or machinery, or one or more systems incorporating plant or machinery,

(b) obtaining and installing the plant or machinery,

(c) the operation of the plant or machinery,

(d) the maintenance of the plant or machinery, and

(e) the amount of any payments in respect of the operation of the plant or machinery to be linked (wholly or in part) to energy savings or increases in energy efficiency resulting from the provision or operation of the plant or machinery.

(2) In this Chapter " energy services provider " means a person carrying on a qualifying activity consisting wholly or mainly in the provision of energy management services.]

Amendments (Textual)

F153. S. 175. A inserted by (with effect as mentioned in s. 66 of the amending Act) by Finance Act 2001 (c. 9), s. 66, Sch. 18 para. 2

Persons who are treated as owners of fixtures

176 Person with interest in relevant land having fixture for purposes of qualifying activity

(1) If—

(a) a person incurs capital expenditure on the provision of plant or machinery for the purposes of a qualifying activity carried on by him,

(b) the plant or machinery becomes a fixture, and

(c) that person has an interest in the relevant land at the time the plant or machinery becomes a fixture,

that person is to be treated, on and after that time, as the owner of the fixture as a result of incurring the expenditure.

(2) If there are two or more persons with different interests in the relevant land who would be treated as the owner of the same fixture as a result of subsection (1), one interest only is taken into account under that subsection.

(3) The interest to be taken into account is given by the following rules—

Rule 1

If one of the interests is an easement or servitude or any agreement to acquire an easement or servitude, that interest is the interest to be taken into account.

Rule 2

If Rule 1 does not apply, but one of the interests is a licence to occupy land, that interest is the interest to be taken into account.

Rule 3

In any other case—

(a) except in Scotland, the interest to be taken into account is the interest which is not in reversion (at law or in equity and whether directly or indirectly) on any other interest in the relevant land which is held by any of the persons referred to in subsection (2), and

(b) in Scotland, the interest to be taken into account is the interest of whichever of the persons referred to in subsection (2) has, or last had, the right of use of the relevant land.

(4) Subsection (1) is subject to [F154sections 177. (4) and 180. A(4)] .

Amendments (Textual)

F154. Words in s. 176. (4) substituted (with effect as mentioned in s. 66 of the amending Act) by Finance Act 2001 (c. 9), s. 66, Sch. 18 para. 3

177 Equipment lessors

(1) If—

(a) the conditions in—

(i) section 178 (equipment lessee has qualifying activity etc.),

(ii) section 179 (equipment lessor has right to sever fixture that is not part of building), or

(iii) section 180 (equipment lease is part of affordable warmth programme),

are met in relation to an equipment lease,

(b) the equipment lessor and the equipment lessee are not connected persons, and

(c) they elect that this section should apply,

the equipment lessor is to be treated, on and after the relevant time, as the owner of the fixture as a result of incurring the capital expenditure on the provision of the plant or machinery that is the subject of the equipment lease.

(2) The relevant time for the purposes of subsection (1) is (unless subsection (3) applies) the time when the equipment lessor incurs the expenditure.

(3) If—

(a) the conditions in section 178 are met in relation to an equipment lease (but the conditions in sections 179 and 180 are not), and

(b) the equipment lessor incurs the capital expenditure before the equipment lessee begins to carry on the qualifying activity,

the relevant time is the time when the equipment lessee begins to carry on the qualifying activity.

(4) If an election is made under this section, the equipment lessee is not to be treated under section 176 as the owner of the fixture.

(5) An election under this section must be made by notice to the [F39an officer of Revenue and Customs]—

(a) for income tax purposes, on or before the normal time limit for amending a tax return for the tax year in which the relevant chargeable period ends;

(b) for corporation tax purposes, no later than 2 years after the end of the relevant chargeable period.

(6) "The relevant chargeable period" means the chargeable period in which the capital expenditure was incurred.

Amendments (Textual)

F39. Words in Act substituted (18.4.2005) by Commissioners for Revenue and Customs Act 2005 (c. 11), s. 53. (1), Sch. 4 para. 83. (1); S.I. 2005/1126, art. 2. (2)(h)

178 Equipment lessee has qualifying activity etc.

The conditions referred to in section 177. (1)(a)(i) are that—

(a) the equipment lease is for the lease of the plant or machinery for the purposes of a qualifying activity which is, or is to be, carried on by the equipment lessee,

(b) if the equipment lessee had incurred the capital expenditure incurred by the equipment lessor on the provision of the plant or machinery that is the subject of the equipment lease, he would, as a result of section 176, have been entitled to an allowance in respect of it, and

(c) the equipment lease is not for the lease of the plant or machinery for use in a dwelling-house.

179 Equipment lessor has right to sever fixture that is not part of building

(1) The conditions referred to in section 177. (1)(a)(ii) are that—

(a) the plant or machinery becomes a fixture by being fixed to land that is neither a building nor part of a building,

(b) the equipment lessee has an interest in the land when taking possession of the plant or machinery under the equipment lease,

(c) under the terms of the equipment lease, the equipment lessor is entitled to sever the plant or machinery, at the end of the period for which it is leased, from the land to which it is fixed at that time,

(d) under the terms of the equipment lease, the equipment lessor will own the plant or machinery on its severance in accordance with the equipment lease,

(e) the nature of the plant or machinery and the way in which it is fixed to land are such that its use on one set of premises does not, to any material extent, prevent it from being used, once severed, for the same purposes on a different set of premises,

(f) the equipment lease is one which under [F155generally accepted accounting practice] falls (or would fall) to be treated in the accounts of the equipment lessor as an operating lease, and

(g) the equipment lease is not for the lease of the plant or machinery for use in a dwelling-house.

(2) F156. . . . .

Amendments (Textual)

F155 Words in s. 179. (1)(f) substituted (24.7.2002) by Finance Act 2002 (c. 23) , s. 103. (4)(g)

F156. S. 179. (2) repealed (with effect as mentioned in s. 107 of the amending Act) by Finance Act 2002 (c. 23), s. 141, Sch. 40 Pt. 3. (16)

180 Equipment lease is part of affordable warmth programme

(1) The conditions referred to in section 177. (1)(a)(iii) are that—

(a) the plant or machinery which is the subject of the equipment lease consists of a boiler, heat exchanger, radiator or heating control that is installed in a building as part of a space or water heating system,

(b) the expenditure of the equipment lessor is incurred before 1st January 2008, and

(c) the equipment lease is approved for the purposes of this section as entered into as part of the affordable warmth programme.

(2) The approval mentioned in subsection (1)(c) may be given, with the consent of the Treasury—

(a) by the Secretary of State;

(b) in the case of buildings in Scotland, by the Scottish Ministers;

(c) in the case of buildings in Wales, by the National Assembly for Wales;

(d) in the case of buildings in Northern Ireland, by the Department for Social Development in Northern Ireland.

(3) If an approval is withdrawn, it is to be treated for the purposes of subsection (1)(c) as never having had effect.

[F157180. A Energy services providers

(1) If—

(a) an energy services agreement is entered into,

(b) the energy services provider incurs capital expenditure under the agreement on the provision of plant or machinery,

(c) the plant or machinery becomes a fixture,

(d) at the time the plant or machinery becomes a fixture—

(i) the client has an interest in the relevant land, and

(ii) the energy services provider does not,

(e) the plant or machinery—

(i) is not provided for leasing, and

(ii) is not provided for use in a dwelling-house,

(f) the operation of the plant or machinery is carried out wholly or substantially by the energy services provider or a person connected with him,

(g) the energy services provider and the client are not connected persons, and

(h) they elect that this section should apply,

the energy services provider is to be treated, on and after the time at which he incurs the expenditure, as the owner of the fixture as a result of incurring the expenditure.

(2) But if the client would not have been entitled to a section 176 allowance in respect of the expenditure if he had incurred it, subsection (1) does not apply unless the plant or machinery belongs to a class of plant or machinery specified by Treasury order.

(3) In subsection (2) a " section 176 allowance " means an allowance to which a person is entitled as a result of section 176.

(4) If an election is made under this section, the client is not to be treated under section 176 as the owner of the fixture.

(5) An election under this section must be made by notice to [F39an officer of Revenue and Customs]—

(a) for income tax purposes, on or before the normal time limit for amending a tax return for the tax year in which the relevant chargeable period ends;

(b) for corporation tax purposes, no later than 2 years after the end of the relevant chargeable period.

(6) The " relevant chargeable period " means the chargeable period in which the capital expenditure was incurred.]

Amendments (Textual)

F39. Words in Act substituted (18.4.2005) by Commissioners for Revenue and Customs Act 2005 (c. 11), s. 53. (1), Sch. 4 para. 83. (1); S.I. 2005/1126, art. 2. (2)(h)

F157. S. 180. A inserted (with effect as mentioned in s. 66 of the amending Act) by Finance Act 2001 (c. 9), s. 66, Sch. 18 para. 4

181 Purchaser of land giving consideration for fixture

(1) If—

(a) after any plant or machinery has become a fixture, a person ("the purchaser") acquires an interest in the relevant land,

(b) that interest was in existence before the purchaser's acquisition of it, and

(c) the consideration which the purchaser gives for the interest is or includes a capital sum that, in whole or in part, falls to be treated for the purposes of this Part as expenditure on the provision of the fixture,

the purchaser is to be treated, on and after the time of the acquisition, as the owner of the fixture as a result of incurring that expenditure.

[F158. (2)Subsection (1) does not apply, and is to be treated as never having applied, if, immediately after the time of the acquisition, a person has a prior right in relation to the fixture.]

(3) For the purposes of [F159subsection (2), a person] has a prior right in relation to the fixture if he—

(a) is treated as the owner of the fixture immediately before the time referred to in [F160subsection (2)] as a result of incurring expenditure on the provision of the fixture,

(b) is not so treated as a result of section 538 (contribution allowances for plant and machinery),

(c) is entitled to an allowance in respect of that expenditure, and

(d) makes or has made a claim in respect of that expenditure.

(4) Subsection (1) is subject to [F161sections 182 and 182. A] .

Amendments (Textual)

F158. S. 181. (2) substituted (with effect as mentioned in s. 69. (2) of the amending Act) by Finance Act 2001 (c. 9), s. 69. (1), Sch. 21 para. 2. (1)

F159. Words in s. 181. (3) substituted (with effect as mentioned in s. 69. (2) of the amending Act) by Finance Act 2001 (c. 9), s. 69. (1), Sch. 21 para. 2. (2)(a)

F160. Words in s. 181. (3) substituted (with effect as mentioned in s. 69. (2) of the amending Act) by Finance Act 2001 (c. 9), s. 69. (1), Sch. 21 para. 2. (2)(b)

F161. Words in s. 181. (4) substituted (with effect as mentioned in s. 66 of the amending Act) by Finance Act 2001 (c. 9), s. 66, Sch. 18 para. 5

Modifications etc. (not altering text)

182 Purchaser of land discharging obligations of equipment lessee

(1) If—

(a) after any plant or machinery has become a fixture, a person ("the purchaser") acquires an interest in the relevant land,

(b) that interest was in existence before the purchaser's acquisition of it,

(c) before that acquisition, the plant or machinery was let under an equipment lease, and

(d) in connection with that acquisition, the purchaser pays a capital sum to discharge the obligations of the equipment lessee under the equipment lease,

the purchaser is to be treated, on and after the time of the acquisition, as the owner of the fixture as a result of incurring expenditure, consisting of that capital sum, on the provision of the fixture.

[F162. (2)Subsection (1) does not apply, and is to be treated as never having applied, if, immediately after the time of the acquisition, a person has a prior right in relation to the fixture.

(3) Section 181. (3)(test for whether person has a prior right) applies for the purposes of subsection (2).]

Amendments (Textual)

F162. S. 182. (2)(3) substituted (with effect as mentioned in s. 69. (2) of the amending Act) by Finance Act 2001 (c. 9), s. 69. (1), Sch. 21 para. 2. (3)

Modifications etc. (not altering text)

[F163182. A Purchaser of land discharging obligations of client under energy services agreement

(1) If—

(a) after any plant or machinery has become a fixture, a person (" the purchaser ") acquires an interest in the relevant land,

(b) that interest was in existence before the purchaser's acquisition of it,

(c) before that acquisition, the plant or machinery was provided under an energy services agreement, and

(d) in connection with that acquisition, the purchaser pays a capital sum to discharge the obligations of the client under the energy services agreement,

the purchaser is to be treated, on and after the time of the acquisition, as the owner of the fixture as a result of incurring expenditure, consisting of that capital sum, on the provision of the fixture.

(2) Subsection (1) does not apply, and is to be treated as never having applied, if, immediately after the time of the acquisition, a person has a prior right in relation to the fixture.

(3) Section 181. (3) (test for whether person has a prior right) applies for the purposes of subsection (2).]

Amendments (Textual)

F163. S. 182. A inserted (with effect as mentioned in s. 66 of the amending Act) by Finance Act 2001 (c. 9), s. 66, Sch. 18 para. 6

183 Incoming lessee where lessor entitled to allowances

(1) If—

(a) after any plant or machinery has become a fixture, a person ("the lessor") who has an interest in the relevant land grants a lease,

(b) the lessor is entitled to an allowance in respect of the fixture for the chargeable period in which the lease is granted or would be if he were within the charge to tax,

(c) the consideration which the lessee gives for the lease is or includes a capital sum that, in whole or in part, falls to be treated for the purposes of this Part as expenditure on the provision of the fixture,

(d) the lessor and the lessee are not connected persons, and

(e) the lessor and the lessee make an election under this section,

the lessee is to be treated, on and after the time when the lease is granted, as the owner of the fixture as a result of incurring that expenditure.

(2) An election under this section must be made by notice to [F39an officer of Revenue and Customs] within 2 years after the date on which the lease takes effect.

Amendments (Textual)

F39. Words in Act substituted (18.4.2005) by Commissioners for Revenue and Customs Act 2005 (c. 11), s. 53. (1), Sch. 4 para. 83. (1); S.I. 2005/1126, art. 2. (2)(h)

184 Incoming lessee where lessor not entitled to allowances

(1) If—

(a) after any plant or machinery has become a fixture, a person ("the lessor") who has an interest in the relevant land grants a lease,

(b) the lessor is not within section 183. (1)(b),

(c) before the lease is granted, the fixture has not been used for the purposes of a qualifying activity carried on by the lessor or any person connected with the lessor, and

(d) the consideration which the lessee gives for the lease is or includes a capital sum that, in whole or in part, falls to be treated for the purposes of this Part as expenditure on the provision of the fixture,

the lessee is to be treated, on and after the time when the lease is granted, as the owner of the fixture as a result of incurring that expenditure.

[F164. (2)Subsection (1) does not apply, and is to be treated as never having applied, if, immediately after the time when the lease is granted, a person has a prior right in relation to the fixture.

(3) Section 181. (3)(test for whether person has a prior right) applies for the purposes of subsection (2).]

Amendments (Textual)

F164. S. 184. (2)(3) substituted (with effect as mentioned in s. 69. (2) of the amending Act) by Finance Act 2001 (c. 9), s. 69. (1), Sch. 21 para. 2. (4)

Restrictions on amount of qualifying expenditure

185 Fixture on which a plant and machinery allowance has been claimed

(1) This section applies if—

(a) a person ("the current owner") is treated as the owner of a fixture as a result of incurring capital expenditure ("new expenditure") on its provision,

(b) the plant or machinery is treated as having been owned at a relevant earlier time by any person ("the past owner") as a result of incurring other expenditure,

(c) the plant or machinery is within paragraph (b) otherwise than as a result of section 538 (contribution allowances for plant and machinery), and

(d) the past owner is or has been required to bring the disposal value of the plant or machinery into account (as a result of having made a claim in respect of that other expenditure).

(2) If the new expenditure exceeds the maximum allowable amount, the excess—

(a) is to be left out of account in determining the current owner's qualifying expenditure, or

(b) if the new expenditure has already been taken into account for this purpose, is to be treated as expenditure that should never have been taken into account.

(3) The maximum allowable amount is—

where—

D is the disposal value of the plant or machinery which the past owner has been or is required to bring into account, and

I is any of the new expenditure that is treated under section 25 (building alterations in connection with installation) as expenditure on the provision of the plant or machinery.

(4) If more than one disposal event has occurred requiring the past owner to bring the disposal value of the plant or machinery into account, the maximum allowable amount is calculated by reference only to the most recent of those events.

(5) For the purposes of this section, the current owner and the past owner may be the same person.

(6) In subsection (1)(b) "relevant earlier time" means (subject to subsection (7)) any time before the earliest time when the current owner is treated as owning the plant or machinery as a result of incurring the new expenditure.

(7) If, before the earliest time when the current owner is treated as owning the plant or machinery as a result of incurring the new expenditure—

(a) any person has ceased to own the plant or machinery as a result of a sale,

(b) the sale was not a sale of the plant or machinery as a fixture, and

(c) the buyer and seller were not connected persons at the time of the sale,

the relevant earlier time does not include any time before the seller ceased to own the plant or machinery.

186 Fixture on which an industrial buildings allowance has been made

(1) This section applies if—

(a) a person ("the past owner") has at any time claimed an allowance to which he is entitled under Part 3 (industrial buildings allowances) in respect of expenditure which was or included expenditure on the provision of plant or machinery,

(b) the past owner has transferred the interest which is the relevant interest for the purposes of Part 3, and

(c) the current owner of the plant or machinery makes a claim in respect of expenditure ("new expenditure") incurred—

(i) on the provision of the plant or machinery, and

(ii) at a time when it is a fixture in the building.

(2) If the new expenditure exceeds the maximum allowable amount, the excess is to be left out of account in determining the current owner's qualifying expenditure.

(3) The maximum allowable amount is—

where—

F is the part of the consideration for the transfer by the past owner that is attributable to the fixture,

T is the total consideration for that transfer, and

R is the residue of qualifying expenditure attributable to the relevant interest immediately after that transfer, calculated on the assumption that the transfer was a sale of the relevant interest.

(4) For the purposes of this section the current owner of the plant or machinery is—

(a) the person to whom the past owner transferred the relevant interest, or

(b) any person who is subsequently treated as the owner of the plant or machinery.

(5) In this section "building" and "residue of qualifying expenditure" have the same meaning as in Part 3.

187 Fixture on which a research and development allowance has been made

(1) This section applies if—

(a) a person has at any time claimed an allowance to which he is entitled under Part 6 (research and development allowances) in respect of qualifying expenditure under that Part ("Part 6 expenditure"),

(b) an asset representing the whole or part of the Part 6 expenditure ("the Part 6 asset") has ceased to be owned by that person ("the past owner"),

(c) the Part 6 asset was or included plant or machinery, and

(d) the current owner makes a claim under this Part in respect of expenditure ("new expenditure") incurred—

(i) on the provision of the plant or machinery, and

(ii) at a time when it is a fixture.

(2) If the new expenditure exceeds the maximum allowable amount, the excess is to be left out of account in determining the current owner's qualifying expenditure.

(3) The maximum allowable amount is—

where—

F is the part of the consideration for the disposal of the Part 6 asset by the past owner that is attributable to the fixture,

T is the total consideration for that disposal, and

A is an amount equal to whichever is the smaller of—

(a) the disposal value of the Part 6 asset when the past owner ceased to own it, and

(b) so much of the Part 6 expenditure as related to the provision of the Part 6 asset.

(4) For the purposes of this section the current owner of the plant or machinery is—

(a) the person who acquired the Part 6 asset from the past owner, or

(b) any person who is subsequently treated as the owner of the plant or machinery.

Cessation of ownership of fixtures

188 Cessation of ownership when person ceases to have qualifying interest

(1) This section applies if a person is treated as the owner of a fixture under—

(a) section 176 (person with interest in land having fixture for purposes of qualifying activity),

(b) section 181 (purchaser of land giving consideration for fixture),

(c) section 182 (purchaser of land discharging obligations of equipment lessee),

[F165. (ca)section 182. A (purchaser of land discharging obligations of client under energy services agreement),]

(d) section 183 (incoming lessee where lessor entitled to allowances), or

(e) section 184 (incoming lessee where lessor not entitled to allowances).

(2) If the person ceases at any time to have the qualifying interest, he is to be treated as ceasing to be the owner of the fixture at that time.

(3) In this Chapter "the qualifying interest" means—

(a) if section 176, 181 [F166, 182 or 182. A] applies, the interest in the relevant land referred to in that section, and

(b) if section 183 or 184 applies, the lease referred to in that section.

(4) This section is subject to section 189.

Amendments (Textual)

F165. S. 188. (1)(ca) inserted (with effect as mentioned in s. 66 of the amending Act) by Finance Act 2001 (c. 9), s. 66, Sch. 18 para. 7. (2)

F166. Words in s. 188. (3)(a) substituted (with effect as mentioned in s. 66 of the amending Act) by Finance Act 2001 (c. 9), s. 66, Sch. 18 para. 7. (3)

189 Identifying the qualifying interest in special cases

(1) If—

(a) a person's qualifying interest is an agreement to acquire an interest in land, and

(b) that interest is subsequently transferred or granted to that person,

the interest transferred or granted is to be treated as the qualifying interest.

(2) If a person's qualifying interest ceases to exist as a result of its being merged in another interest acquired by that person, that other interest is to be treated as the qualifying interest.

(3) If—

(a) the qualifying interest is a lease, and

(b) on its termination, a new lease of the relevant land (with or without other land) is granted to the lessee,

the new lease is to be treated as the qualifying interest.

(4) If—

(a) the qualifying interest is a licence, and

(b) on its termination, a new licence to occupy the relevant land (with or without other land) is granted to the licensee,

the new licence is to be treated as the qualifying interest.

(5) If—

(a) the qualifying interest is a lease, and

(b) with the consent of the lessor, the lessee remains in possession of the relevant land after the termination of the lease without a new lease being granted to him,

the qualifying interest is to be treated as continuing so long as the lessee remains in possession of the relevant land.

190 Cessation of ownership of lessor where section 183 applies

(1) This section applies if a lessee is treated under section 183 (incoming lessee where lessor entitled to allowances) as the owner of a fixture.

(2) The lessor is to be treated as ceasing to be the owner of the fixture when the lessee begins to be treated as the owner.

191 Cessation of ownership on severance of fixture

If—

(a) a person is treated as the owner of the fixture as a result of any provision of this Chapter,

(b) the fixture is permanently severed from the relevant land (so that it ceases to be a fixture), and

(c) once it is severed, it is not in fact owned by that person,

that person is to be treated as ceasing to be the owner of the fixture when it is severed.

192 Cessation of ownership of equipment lessor

(1) This section applies if an equipment lessor is treated under section 177 as the owner of a fixture.

(2) If—

(a) the equipment lessor at any time assigns his rights under the equipment lease, or

(b) the financial obligations of the equipment lessee under an equipment lease are at any time discharged (on the payment of a capital sum or otherwise),

the equipment lessor is to be treated as ceasing to be the owner of the fixture at that time (or, as the case may be, at the earliest of those times).

(3) The reference in subsection (2)(b) to the equipment lessee is, in a case where the financial obligations of the equipment lessee have become vested in another person (by assignment, operation of law or otherwise), a reference to the person in whom the obligations are vested when the capital sum is paid.

[F167192. A Cessation of ownership of energy services provider

(1) This section applies if an energy services provider is treated under section 180. A as the owner of a fixture.

(2) If—

(a) the energy services provider at any time assigns his rights under the energy services agreement, or

(b) the financial obligations of the client in respect of the fixture under an energy services agreement are at any time discharged (on the payment of a capital sum or otherwise),

the energy services provider is to be treated as ceasing to be the owner of the fixture at that time (or, as the case may be, the earliest of those times).

(3) The reference in subsection (2)(b) to the client is, in a case where the financial obligations of the client have become vested in another person (by assignment, operation of law or otherwise), a reference to the person in whom the obligations are vested when the capital sum is paid.]

Amendments (Textual)

F167. S. 192. A inserted (with effect as mentioned in s. 66 of the amending Act) by Finance Act 2001 (c. 9), s. 66, Sch. 18 para. 8

Acquisition of ownership of fixture when another ceases to own it

193 Acquisition of ownership by lessor or licensor on termination of lease or licence

If, on the termination of a lease or licence, the outgoing lessee or licensee is treated under section 188 as ceasing to be the owner of a fixture, the lessor or licensor is to be treated, on and after the termination of the lease or licence, as the owner of the fixture.

194 Acquisition of ownership by assignee of equipment lessor

(1) If section 192. (2)(a) applies (cessation of ownership of equipment lessor as a result of assignment), the assignee is to be treated, on and after the assignment—

(a) as having incurred expenditure, consisting of the consideration given by him for the assignment, on the provision of the fixture, and

(b) as being the owner of the fixture.

(2) For the purposes of section 192 (and subsection (1) and section 195) the assignee is to be treated as being an equipment lessor who owns the fixture under section 177.

195 Acquisition of ownership by equipment lessee

(1) If section 192. (2)(b) applies (discharge of obligations of equipment lessee) because the equipment lessee has paid a capital sum, the equipment lessee is to be treated—

(a) as having incurred expenditure, consisting of the capital sum, on the provision of the fixture, and

(b) as being, on and after the time of payment, the owner of the fixture.

(2) Section 192. (3) (assignee of equipment lessee) applies in relation to subsection (1).

[F168195. A Acquisition of ownership by assignee of energy services provider

(1) If section 192. A(2)(a) applies (cessation of ownership of energy services provider as a result of assignment), the assignee is to be treated, on and after the assignment—

(a) as having incurred expenditure, consisting of the consideration given by him for the assignment, on the provision of the fixture, and

(b) as being the owner of the fixture.

(2) For the purposes of section 192. A (and subsection (1) and section 195. B) the assignee is to be treated as being an energy services provider who owns the fixture under section 180. A.

Amendments (Textual)

F168. Ss, 195. A, 195. B inserted (with effect as mentioned in s. 66 of the amending Act) by Finance Act 2001 (c. 9), s. 66, Sch. 18 para. 9

195. B Acquisition of ownership by client

(1) If section 192. A(2)(b) applies (discharge of obligations of client) because the client has paid a capital sum, the client is to be treated—

(a) as having incurred expenditure, consisting of the capital sum, on the provision of the fixture, and

(b) as being, on and after the time of payment, the owner of the fixture.

(2) Section 192. A(3)(assignee of client) applies in relation to subsection (1).]

Amendments (Textual)

F168. Ss, 195. A, 195. B inserted (with effect as mentioned in s. 66 of the amending Act) by Finance Act 2001 (c. 9), s. 66, Sch. 18 para. 9

Disposal values

196 Disposal values in relation to fixtures: general

(1) The disposal value to be brought into account in relation to a fixture depends on the nature of the disposal event, as shown in the Table—

Table

Disposal values: fixtures

1. Disposal event | 2. Disposal value |

The part of the sale price that—

(a) falls to be treated for the purposes of this Part as expenditure incurred by the purchaser on the provision of the fixture, or

(b) would fall to be so treated if the purchaser were entitled to an allowance.

2. Cessation of ownership of the fixture under section 188 because of a sale of the qualifying interest where—

(a) the sale is at less than market value, and

(b) the condition in subsection (2) is met by the purchaser.

The part of the price that would be treated for the purposes of this Part as expenditure by the purchaser on the provision of the fixture if—

(a) the qualifying interest were sold at market value,

(b) that sale took place immediately before the event which causes the former owner to be treated as ceasing to be the owner of the fixture, and

(c) that event were disregarded in determining that market value.

3. Cessation of ownership of the fixture under section 188 where—

(a) neither item 1 nor 2 applies, but

(b) the qualifying interest continues in existence after that time or would so continue but for its becoming merged in another interest.

If the person receives a capital sum, by way of compensation or otherwise, by reference to the fixture, the amount of the capital sum.

In any other case, nil.

5. Cessation of ownership of the fixture under section 190 because the lessee has become the owner under section 183. | The part of the capital sum given by the lessee for the lease referred to in section 183 that falls to be treated for the purposes of this Part as the lessee's expenditure on the provision of the fixture. |

6. Cessation of ownership of the fixture under section 191 (severance). | The market value of the fixture at the time of the severance. |

7. Cessation of ownership of the fixture because section 192(2)(a) (assignment of rights) applies. | The consideration given by the assignee for the assignment. |

8. Cessation of ownership of the fixture because section 192(2)(b) (discharge of equipment lessee's obligations) applies on the payment of a capital sum. | The capital sum paid to discharge the financial obligations of the equipment lessee. |

[F1698A. Cessation of ownership of the fixture because section 192A(2)(a)(assignment of rights) applies. | The consideration given by the assignee for the assignment. |

8B. Cessation of ownership of the fixture because section 192A(2)(b) (discharge of client's obligations) applies on the payment of a capital sum. | The capital sum paid to discharge the financial obligations of the client.] |

The part of the sale price that—

(a) falls to be treated as expenditure incurred by the purchaser on the provision of the fixture, or

(b) would fall to be so treated if the purchaser were entitled to an allowance.

The net amount received for the remains of the fixture, together with—

(a) any insurance money received in respect of the demolition or destruction, and

(b) any other compensation of any description so received, so far as it consists of capital sums.

11. Permanent discontinuance of the qualifying activity followed by the permanent loss of the fixture otherwise than as a result of its demolition or destruction. | Any insurance money received in respect of the loss and, so far as it consists of capital sums, any other compensation of any description so received. |

12. The fixture begins to be used wholly or partly for purposes other than those of the qualifying activity. | The part of the price that would fall to be treated for the purposes of this Part as expenditure incurred by the purchaser on the provision of the fixture if the qualifying interest were sold at market value. |

(2) The condition referred to in item 2 of the Table is met by the purchaser if—

   (a) the purchaser's expenditure on the provision of the fixture cannot be qualifying expenditure under this Part or Part 6 (research and development allowances), or

   (b) the purchaser is a dual resident investing company which is connected with the former owner.

(3) Items 1 and 5 of the Table are subject to sections 198 and 199 (election to fix apportionment on sale of qualifying interest or grant of lease).

(4) Section 192. (3) (assignee of equipment lessee) applies in relation to item 8 of the Table.

[F170. (4. A)Section 192. A(3)(assignee of client) applies in relation to item 8. B of the Table.]

(5) Nothing in sections 188 to [F171192. A] or this section prevents a disposal value having to be brought into account under Chapter 5 because of a disposal event not dealt with in these sections.

(6) This section is subject to section 197.

Amendments (Textual)

F169. S. 196. (1) Table, items 8. A, 8. B inserted (with effect as mentioned in s. 66 of the amending Act) by Finance Act 2001 (c. 9), s. 66, Sch. 18 para. 10. (2)

F170. S. 196. (4. A) inserted (with effect as mentioned in s. 66 of the amending Act) by Finance Act 2001 (c. 9), s. 66, Sch. 18 para. 10. (3)

F171. Words in s. 196. (5) substituted (with effect as mentioned in s. 66 of the amending Act) by Finance Act 2001 (c. 9), s. 66, Sch. 18 para. 10. (4)

Modifications etc. (not altering text)

C33 S. 196 excluded (E.W.S.) (8.6.2005) by Railways Act 2005 (c. 14) , s. 60. (2) , Sch. 10 para. 14. (2)(a) ; S.I. 2005/1444 , art. 2. (1) , Sch. 1

C34 S. 196 modified (E.W.S.) (8.6.2005) by Railways Act 2005 (c. 14) , s. 60. (2) , Sch. 10 para. 3 ; S.I. 2005/1444 , art. 2. (1) , Sch. 1

C35. S. 196 modified (E.W.S.) (24.7.2005) by Railways Act 2005 (c. 14), s. 60. (2), Sch. 10 para. 23; S.I. 2005/1909, art. 2, Sch.

197 Disposal values in avoidance cases

(1) This section applies if—

(a) a person ("the taxpayer") is treated under this Chapter as the owner of any plant or machinery as a result of incurring any expenditure,

(b) any disposal event occurs in relation to the plant or machinery,

(c) the disposal value to be brought into account by the taxpayer would (but for this section) be less than the notional written-down value of the plant or machinery, and

(d) the disposal event is part of, or occurs as a result of, a scheme or arrangement the main purpose or one of the main purposes of which is the obtaining by the taxpayer of a tax advantage under this Part.

(2) The disposal value that the taxpayer must bring into account is the notional written-down value of the plant or machinery.

(3) The notional written-down value is—

where—

QE is the taxpayer's expenditure on the plant or machinery that is qualifying expenditure,

A is the total of all allowances which could have been made to the taxpayer in respect of that expenditure if—

(a) that expenditure had been the only expenditure that had ever been taken into account in determining his available qualifying expenditure, and

(b) all allowances had been made in full.

Election to fix apportionment

198 Election to apportion sale price on sale of qualifying interest

(1) This section applies if the disposal value of a fixture is required to be brought into account in accordance with item 1 of the Table in section 196 (sale of qualifying interest at not less than market value, etc.).

(2) The seller and the purchaser may jointly, by an election, fix the amount that is to be treated—

(a) for the purposes of item 1 of the Table, and

(b) for the other purposes of this Part,

as the part of the sale price that is expenditure incurred by the purchaser on the provision of the fixture.

(3) The amount fixed by the election must not exceed—

(a) the amount of the capital expenditure which was treated as incurred by the seller on the provision of the fixture or of the plant or machinery which became the fixture, or

(b) the actual sale price.

(4) If an election fixes the amount to be treated as the part of the sale price—

(a) the remaining amount (if any) of the sale price is to be treated for the purposes of this Act as expenditure attributable to the acquisition of the property which is not the fixture but is acquired for that amount, and

(b) if there is no remaining amount, the expenditure so attributable is to be treated for the purposes of this Act as nil.

(5) This section is subject to—

(a) sections 186 and 187 (fixtures on which industrial buildings allowance or research and development allowance has been made),

(b) section 197 (disposal values in avoidance cases), and

(c) sections 200 and 201 (further provisions about elections).

199 Election to apportion capital sum given by lessee on grant of lease

(1) This section applies if the disposal value of a fixture is required to be brought into account in accordance with item 5 of the Table in section 196 (on acquisition of ownership by incoming lessee under section 183).

(2) The persons who are the lessor and the lessee for the purposes of section 183 may jointly, by an election, fix the amount that is to be treated—

(a) for the purposes of item 5 of the Table, and

(b) for the other purposes of this Part,

as the part of the capital sum that is expenditure incurred by the lessee on the provision of the fixture.

(3) The amount fixed by the election must not exceed—

(a) the amount of the capital expenditure which was treated as incurred by the lessor on the provision of the fixture or of the plant or machinery which became the fixture, or

(b) the actual capital sum.

(4) If an election fixes the amount to be treated as the part of the capital sum—

(a) the remaining amount (if any) of the capital sum is to be treated for the purposes of this Act as expenditure attributable to the acquisition of the property which is not the fixture but is acquired for that amount, and

(b) if there is no remaining amount, the expenditure so attributable is to be treated for the purposes of this Act as nil.

(5) This section is subject to—

(a) sections 186 and 187 (fixtures on which industrial buildings allowance or research and development allowance has been made),

(b) section 197 (disposal values in avoidance cases), and

(c) sections 200 and 201 (further provisions about elections).

200 Elections under sections 198 and 199: supplementary

(1) In this section and section 201, references to an election are to an election under section 198 or 199.

(2) An apportionment made by an election has effect in place of any apportionment that would otherwise be made under sections 562, 563 and 564. (1) (apportionment and procedure for determining apportionment).

(3) An election is irrevocable.

(4) If, as a result of circumstances arising after the making of an election, the maximum amount which could be fixed by the election is reduced to an amount which is less than the amount specified in the election, the election is to be treated, for the purposes of this Act, as having specified the amount to which the maximum is reduced.

201 Elections under sections 198 and 199: procedure

(1) An election must be made by notice to [F39an officer of Revenue and Customs] no later than 2 years after the date when—

(a) the purchaser acquires the qualifying interest, in the case of an election under section 198, or

(b) the lessee is granted the lease, in the case of an election under section 199.

(2) The amount fixed by an election must be quantified at the time when the election is made.

(3) The notice must state—

(a) the amount fixed by the election,

(b) the name of each of the persons making the election,

(c) information sufficient to identify the plant or machinery,

(d) information sufficient to identify the relevant land,

(e) particulars of—

(i) the interest acquired by the purchaser, in the case of an election under section 198, or

(ii) the lease granted to the lessee, in the case of an election under section 199, and

(f) the tax district references of each of the persons making the election.

(4) If a person—

(a) has joined in making an election, and

(b) subsequently makes a tax return for a period which is the first period for which he is making a tax return in which the election has an effect for tax purposes in his case,

a copy of the notice containing the election must accompany the return.

(5) The following provisions do not apply to the election—

(a) section 42 of, and Schedule 1. A to, TMA 1970 (claims and elections for income tax purposes);

(b) paragraphs 54 to 60 of Schedule 18 to FA 1998 (claims and elections for corporation tax purposes).

(6) References in this section to a tax return, in the case of an election for the purposes of a trade, profession or business carried on by persons in partnership, are to be read, in relation to those persons, as references to a return under section 12. AA of TMA 1970 (partnership returns).

Amendments (Textual)

F39. Words in Act substituted (18.4.2005) by Commissioners for Revenue and Customs Act 2005 (c. 11), s. 53. (1), Sch. 4 para. 83. (1); S.I. 2005/1126, art. 2. (2)(h)

Further provisions

202 Interpretation

(1) Any reference in this Chapter to a person being entitled to an allowance in respect of expenditure on the provision of a fixture includes the person having a pool to which expenditure on the provision of the fixture has been allocated.

But this is subject to subsection (2).

(2) If—

(a) expenditure on the provision of the fixture has been allocated to a pool, and

(b) the person is required under section 61. (1) to bring the disposal value of the fixture into account in the pool,

the person is not entitled to an allowance in respect of the expenditure allocated to that pool for any chargeable period after that in which the disposal event occurs.

(3) For the purposes of this Chapter, a person makes a claim in respect of expenditure if he—

(a) makes a claim for an allowance in respect of that expenditure,

(b) makes a tax return in which that expenditure is taken into account in determining his available qualifying expenditure for the purposes of this Part, or

(c) gives notice of an amendment of a tax return which provides for that expenditure to be so taken into account.

203 Amendment of returns etc.

(1) If a person who has made a tax return ("the taxpayer") becomes aware that, after making it, anything in it has become incorrect for any of the reasons given in subsection (2), the taxpayer must give notice to [F39an officer of Revenue and Customs] specifying how the return needs to be amended.

(2) The reasons are that—

(a) an approval given for the purposes of section 180 (affordable warmth programme) has been withdrawn;

(b) section 181. (2), 182. (2) [F172, 182. A(2)] or 184. (2) (another person has a prior right) applies in the taxpayer's case;

(c) section 185 (restriction on qualifying expenditure where another person has claimed an allowance) applies in the taxpayer's case;

(d) an election is made under section 198 or 199 (election to fix apportionment);

(e) section 200. (4) (reduction in amount which can be fixed by an election) applies in the taxpayer's case.

(3) The notice must be given within 3 months beginning with the day on which the taxpayer first became aware that anything contained in the tax return had become incorrect for any of the reasons given in subsection (2).

(4) All such assessments and adjustments of assessments are to be made as are necessary to give effect to this Chapter.

Amendments (Textual)

F39. Words in Act substituted (18.4.2005) by Commissioners for Revenue and Customs Act 2005 (c. 11), s. 53. (1), Sch. 4 para. 83. (1); S.I. 2005/1126, art. 2. (2)(h)

F172. Words in s. 203. (2)(b) inserted (with effect as mentioned in s. 66 of the amending Act) by Finance Act 2001 (c. 9), s. 66, Sch. 18 para. 11

204 Appeals etc.

(1) Subsections (2) and (3) apply if—

(a) any question arises as to whether any plant or machinery has become, in law, part of a building or other land, and

(b) that question is material to the tax liability (for whatever period) of two or more persons.

(2) The question is to be determined, for the purposes of the tax of all the persons concerned, by the Special Commissioners.

(3) The Special Commissioners must determine the question in the same way as an appeal, but all the persons concerned are entitled—

(a) to appear before and be heard by the Special Commissioners, or

(b) to make representations to them in writing.

(4) Subsections (5) and (6) apply if any question relating to an election under section 198 or 199 (apportionments) arises for determination by any body of Commissioners for the purposes of any proceedings before them.

(5) The Commissioners must determine the question separately from any other questions in those proceedings.

(6) Each of the persons who has joined in making the election is entitled—

(a) to appear before and be heard by the Commissioners, or

(b) to make representations to them in writing;

and the Commissioners' determination has effect as if made in an appeal to which each of those persons was a party.

Chapter 15. Asset provided or used only partly for qualifying activity

205 Reduction of first-year allowances

(1) If it appears that a person carrying on a qualifying activity has incurred expenditure on the provision of plant or machinery—

(a) partly for the purposes of the qualifying activity, and

(b) partly for other purposes,

any first-year allowance to which he is entitled in respect of the expenditure must be reduced to an amount which is just and reasonable having regard to the relevant circumstances.

(2) The relevant circumstances include, in particular, the extent to which it appears that the plant

or machinery is likely to be used for purposes other than those of the qualifying activity in question.

(3) In calculating for the purposes of section 58 the balance left after deducting a first-year allowance, a reduction under subsection (1) is to be disregarded.

206 Single asset pool etc.

(1) Qualifying expenditure to which this subsection applies, if allocated to a pool, must be allocated to a single asset pool.

(2) Subsection (1) applies to qualifying expenditure incurred by a person carrying on a qualifying activity—
    (a) partly for the purposes of the qualifying activity, and
    (b) partly for other purposes.

(3) If a person is required to bring a disposal value into account in a pool for a chargeable period because the plant or machinery begins to be used partly for purposes other than those of the qualifying activity, an amount equal to that disposal value is allocated (as expenditure on the plant or machinery) to a single asset pool for that chargeable period.

(4) In the case of a single asset pool under subsection (1), there is no final chargeable period or disposal event merely because the plant or machinery begins to be used partly for purposes other than those of the qualifying activity.

207 Reduction of allowances and charges on expenditure in single asset pool

(1) This section applies if a person's expenditure is in a single asset pool under section 206. (1) or (3).

(2) The amount of—
    (a) any writing-down allowance or balancing allowance to which the person is entitled, or
    (b) any balancing charge to which the person is liable,
must be reduced to an amount which is just and reasonable having regard to the relevant circumstances.

(3) The relevant circumstances include, in particular, the extent to which it appears that the plant or machinery was used in the chargeable period in question for purposes other than those of the person's qualifying activity.

(4) In calculating under section 59 the amount of unrelieved qualifying expenditure carried forward, a reduction of a writing-down allowance under subsection (2) is to be disregarded.

(5) If a person entitled to a writing-down allowance for a chargeable period—
    (a) does not claim the allowance, or
    (b) claims less than the full amount of the allowance,
the unrelieved qualifying expenditure carried forward from the period is to be treated as not reduced or (as the case may be) only proportionately reduced.

208 Effect of significant reduction in use for purposes of qualifying activity

(1) This section applies if—
    (a) expenditure is allocated to a single asset pool under this Chapter,
    (b) there is such a change of circumstances as would make it appropriate for any reduction falling to be made under section 207—
(i) for the chargeable period in which the change takes place ("the relevant chargeable period"), or
(ii) for any subsequent chargeable period,

to represent a larger proportion of the amount reduced than would have been appropriate apart from the change,

(c) no disposal value in respect of the plant or machinery would, apart from this section, fall to be brought into account for the relevant chargeable period, and

(d) the market value of the plant or machinery at the end of the relevant chargeable period exceeds the available qualifying expenditure in that pool for that period by more than £1 million.

(2) If this section applies—

(a) a disposal value is required to be brought into account in the single asset pool for the relevant chargeable period, and

(b) section 206 applies as if, at the beginning of the following chargeable period, expenditure had been incurred on the provision of the plant or machinery of an amount equal to the disposal value brought into account as a result of paragraph (a).

Modifications etc. (not altering text)

C36. S. 208. (1) modified by 1993 c. 34, s. 93. A(6) (as inserted (with effect as mentioned in s. 80. (2) of the inserting Act) by Finance Act 2002 (c. 23), s. 80, Sch. 24 para. 4) (with Sch. 23 para. 25))

Chapter 16. Partial depreciation subsidies

209 Meaning of "partial depreciation subsidy"

In this Chapter "partial depreciation subsidy" means a sum which—

(a) is payable directly or indirectly to a person who has incurred qualifying expenditure for the purposes of a qualifying activity,

(b) is in respect of, or takes account of, part of the depreciation of the plant or machinery resulting from its use for the purposes of that activity, and

(c) does not fall to be taken into account as income of that person or in calculating the profits of any qualifying activity carried on by him.

210 Reduction of first-year allowances

(1) If—

(a) a person has incurred qualifying expenditure for the purposes of a qualifying activity carried on by him, and

(b) it appears that a partial depreciation subsidy is, or will be, payable to him in the period during which the plant or machinery will be used for the purposes of that qualifying activity, the amount of any first-year allowance in respect of that expenditure must be reduced to an amount which is just and reasonable having regard to the relevant circumstances.

(2) In calculating for the purposes of section 58 the balance left after deducting a first-year allowance, a reduction under subsection (1) is to be disregarded.

211 Single asset pool etc.

(1) Qualifying expenditure to which this subsection applies, if allocated to a pool, must be allocated to a single asset pool.

(2) Subsection (1) applies to qualifying expenditure if a partial depreciation subsidy relating to the plant or machinery has been paid to the person who incurred the expenditure.

(3) Subsection (4) applies if—

(a) qualifying expenditure has been allocated to a pool, and

(b) a partial depreciation subsidy relating to the plant or machinery is paid to that person.

(4) For the chargeable period in which the partial depreciation subsidy is paid—

(a) the person is required to bring a disposal value into account in the pool referred to in subsection (3), and

(b) an amount equal to the disposal value is allocated (as expenditure on the plant or machinery) to a single asset pool.

(5) If qualifying expenditure in respect of any plant or machinery is in a single asset pool under this section, there is no further allocation of that qualifying expenditure because a further partial depreciation subsidy is paid in respect of that plant or machinery.

212 Reduction of allowances and charges on expenditure in single asset pool

(1) This section applies if expenditure is in a single asset pool under section 211. (1) or (4).

(2) The amount of—

(a) any writing-down allowance or balancing allowance to which the person is entitled, or

(b) any balancing charge to which the person is liable,

must be reduced to an amount which is just and reasonable having regard to the relevant circumstances.

(3) In calculating under section 59 the amount of unrelieved qualifying expenditure carried forward, a reduction of a writing-down allowance under subsection (2) is to be disregarded.

(4) If a person entitled to a writing-down allowance for a chargeable period—

(a) does not claim the allowance, or

(b) claims less than the full amount of the allowance,

the unrelieved qualifying expenditure carried forward from the period is to be treated as not reduced or (as the case may be) only proportionately reduced.

Chapter 17. Anti-avoidance

213 Relevant transactions: sale, hire-purchase (etc.) and assignment

(1) For the purposes of this Chapter, a person ("B") enters into a relevant transaction with another ("S") if—

(a) S sells plant or machinery to B,

(b) B enters into a contract with S providing that B shall or may become the owner of plant or machinery on the performance of the contract, or

(c) S assigns to B the benefit of a contract providing that S shall or may become the owner of plant or machinery on the performance of the contract.

(2) For the purposes of this Chapter, references to B's expenditure under a relevant transaction are references—

(a) in the case of a sale within subsection (1)(a), to B's capital expenditure on the provision of the plant or machinery by purchase,

(b) in the case of a contract within subsection (1)(b), to B's capital expenditure under the contract so far as it relates to the plant or machinery, or

(c) in the case of an assignment within subsection (1)(c), to B's capital expenditure under the contract so far as it relates to the plant or machinery or is by way of consideration for the assignment.

(3) If—

(a) B is treated under section 14 (use for qualifying activity of plant or machinery which is a gift) as having incurred capital expenditure on the provision of plant or machinery, and

(b) the donor of the plant or machinery was S,

B is to be treated for the purposes of this Chapter as having incurred capital expenditure on the provision of the plant or machinery by purchasing it from S.

Restrictions on allowances

214 Connected persons

Allowances under this Part are restricted under sections 217 and 218 if—

(a) B enters into a relevant transaction with S, and

(b) B and S are connected with each other.

215 Transactions to obtain allowances

Allowances under this Part are restricted under sections 217 and 218 if—

(a) B enters into a relevant transaction with S, and

(b) it appears that the sole or main benefit which (but for this section) might have been expected to accrue to B or S, or to any other party, from—

(i) the relevant transaction, or

(ii) transactions of which the relevant transaction is one,

was obtaining an allowance under this Part.

216 Sale and leaseback, etc.

(1) Allowances under this Part are restricted under sections 217 and 218 if—

(a) B enters into a relevant transaction with S, and

(b) the plant or machinery—

(i) continues to be used for the purposes of a qualifying activity carried on by S, or

(ii) is used after the date of the transaction for the purposes of a qualifying activity carried on by S or by a person (other than B) who is connected with S, without having been used since that date for the purposes of any other qualifying activity except that of leasing the plant or machinery.

(2) In this section—

"the date of the transaction" means the date of the sale, the making of the contract or the assignment referred to in section 213. (1)(a) to (c), and

"qualifying activity" includes any activity listed in section 15. (1) even if any profits or gains from it are not chargeable to tax.

217 No first-year allowance for B's expenditure

(1) If this section applies as a result of section 214, 215 or 216, a first-year allowance is not to be made in respect of B's expenditure under the relevant transaction.

(2) Any first-year allowance which is prohibited by subsection (1), but which has already been made, is to be withdrawn.

(3) If plant or machinery is the subject of a sale and finance leaseback (as defined in section 221) section 223 applies instead of this section.

218 Restriction on B's qualifying expenditure

(1) If this section applies as a result of section 214, 215 or 216, the amount, if any, by which B's expenditure under the relevant transaction exceeds D is to be left out of account in determining B's available qualifying expenditure.

D is defined in subsections (2) and (3).

(2) If S is required to bring a disposal value into account under this Part because of the relevant transaction, D is that disposal value.

(3) If S is not required to bring a disposal value into account under this Part because of the relevant transaction, D is whichever of the following is the smallest—

(a) the market value of the plant or machinery;

(b) if S incurred capital expenditure on the provision of the plant or machinery, the amount of that expenditure;

(c) if a person connected with S incurred capital expenditure on the provision of the plant or machinery, the amount of that expenditure.

(4) If plant or machinery is the subject of a sale and finance leaseback (as defined in section 221), section 224 or 225 applies instead of this section.

[F173. Finance leases and certain operating leases]

Amendments (Textual)

F173. S. 219 cross-heading substituted (with effect in accordance with Sch. 9 para. 15. (6) of the amending Act) by Finance Act 2006 (c. 25), Sch. 9 para. 15. (5)

219 Meaning of "finance lease"

(1) In this Chapter "finance lease" means any arrangements—

(a) which provide for plant or machinery to be leased or otherwise made available by a person ("the lessor") to another person ("the lessee"), and

(b) which, under [F174generally accepted accounting practice]—

(i) fall (or would fall) to be treated, in the accounts of the lessor or a person connected with the lessor, as a finance lease or a loan, or

(ii) are comprised in arrangements which fall (or would fall) to be so treated.

(2) F175. . . . .

(3) In this section "accounts", in relation to a company, includes any accounts which—

(a) relate to two or more companies of which that company is one, and

[F176. (b)are drawn up in accordance with generally accepted accounting practice.]

Amendments (Textual)

F174. Words in s. 219. (1) substituted (24.7.2002) by Finance Act 2002 (c. 23), s. 103. (4)(g)

F175. S. 219. (2) repealed (with effect as mentioned in s. 107 of the amending Act) by Finance Act 2002 (c. 23), s. 141, Sch. 40 Pt. 3. (16)

F176. S. 219. (3)(b) substituted (7.4.2005) by Finance Act 2005 (c. 7), Sch. 4 para. 33

220 Allocation of expenditure to a chargeable period

[F177. (A1)Subsection (1) applies to a company for a chargeable period if—

(a) at the end of the ICTA period of account which is the basis period for the chargeable period, the company is a member of a group, and

(b) the last day of that ICTA period of account is not also the last day of an ICTA period of account of the principal company of the group.]

(1) Subject to subsection (2), if [F178the company] incurs at any time in [F179the chargeable period] capital expenditure on the provision of plant or machinery for leasing under a finance lease [F180or under a qualifying operating lease (see subsection (4))] —

(a) the part of the expenditure which is proportional to the part of that chargeable period falling before that time is not to be taken into account in determining that [F181company's] available qualifying expenditure for that period, but

(b) this does not prevent that part of the expenditure being taken into account in determining that [F181company's] available qualifying expenditure for any subsequent chargeable period.

(2) Subsection (1)(a) does not apply to a chargeable period if a disposal event occurs in that period in respect of the plant or machinery.

[F182. (3)The following provisions have effect for the interpretation of this section.

(4) A "qualifying operating lease" is a plant or machinery lease that meets the following conditions—

(a) it is not a finance lease,

(b) it is a funding lease,

(c) its term is longer than 4 years but not longer than 5 years.

(5) An ICTA period of account is the basis period for a chargeable period if the chargeable period coincides with, or falls within, the ICTA period of account.

(6) An "ICTA period of account" is a period of account as defined in section 832. (1) of ICTA.

(7) The provisions of section 170. (3) to (6) of TCGA 1992 apply to determine for the purposes of this section—

(a) whether a company is member of a group, and

(b) which company is the principal company of the group.

(8) But, in applying those provisions for the purposes of this section, a company ("the subsidiary

company") that does not have ordinary share capital is to be treated as being a qualifying 75% subsidiary of another company ("the parent company") if the parent company—

(a) has control of the subsidiary companyF183..., and

(b) is beneficially entitled to the appropriate proportion of profits and assets.

(9) The parent company is beneficially entitled to the appropriate proportion of profits and assets if (and only if) it—

(a) is beneficially entitled to at least 75% of any profits available for distribution to equity holders of the subsidiary company, and

(b) would be beneficially entitled to at least 75% of any assets of the subsidiary company available for distribution to its equity holders on a winding-up.

(10) The provisions of Schedule 18 to ICTA (equity holders and profits or assets etc) also apply for the purposes of this section.

(11) In this section, the following expressions have the same meaning as in Chapter 6. A of Part 2 (interpretation of provisions about long funding leases)—

"funding lease",

"plant or machinery lease",

"term", in relation to a lease.]

Amendments (Textual)

F177. S. 220. (A1) inserted (with effect in accordance with Sch. 9 para. 15. (6) of the amending Act) by Finance Act 2006 (c. 25), Sch. 9 para. 15. (2)

F178. Words in s. 220. (1) substituted (with effect in accordance with Sch. 9 para. 15. (6) of the amending Act) by Finance Act 2006 (c. 25), Sch. 9 para. 15. (3)(a)

F179. Words in s. 220. (1) substituted (with effect in accordance with Sch. 9 para. 15. (6) of the amending Act) by Finance Act 2006 (c. 25), Sch. 9 para. 15. (3)(b)

F180. Words in s. 220. (1) inserted (with effect in accordance with Sch. 9 para. 15. (6) of the amending Act) by Finance Act 2006 (c. 25), Sch. 9 para. 15. (3)(c)

F181. Word in s. 220. (1) substituted (with effect in accordance with Sch. 9 para. 15. (6) of the amending Act) by Finance Act 2006 (c. 25), Sch. 9 para. 15. (3)(d)

F182. S. 220. (3)-(11) inserted (with effect in accordance with Sch. 9 para. 15. (6) of the amending Act) by Finance Act 2006 (c. 25), Sch. 9 para. 15. (4)

F183. Words in s. 220. (8)(a) omitted (6.4.2007) by virtue of Income Tax Act 2007 (c. 3), s. 1034. (1), Sch. 1 para. 402, Sch. 3 Pt. 1 (with Sch. 2)

Sale and finance leasebacks

221 Meaning of "sale and finance leaseback"

(1) For the purposes of this section and sections 222 to 228, plant or machinery is the subject of a sale and finance leaseback if—

(a) B enters into a relevant transaction with S,

(b) after the date of the transaction, the plant or machinery—

(i) continues to be used for the purposes of a qualifying activity carried on by S,

(ii) is used for the purposes of a qualifying activity carried on by S or by a person (other than B) who is connected with S, without having been used since that date for the purposes of any other qualifying activity except that of leasing the plant or machinery, or

(iii) is used for the purposes of a non-qualifying activity carried on by [F184. S or by a person (other than B) who is connected with S] , without having been used since that date for the purposes of a qualifying activity except that of leasing the plant or machinery, and

(c) it is directly or indirectly as a consequence of having been leased under a finance lease that the plant or machinery is available to be so used after that date.

(2) In this section—

"the date of the transaction" means the date of the sale, the making of the contract or the assignment referred to in section 213. (1)(a) to (c), "non-qualifying activity" means any activity which is not a qualifying activity, and "qualifying activity" includes any activity listed in section 15. (1) even if any profits or gains from it are not chargeable to tax.

Amendments (Textual)

F184. Words in s. 221. (1)(b)(iii) substituted (with effect as mentioned in s. 69. (2) of the amending Act) by Finance Act 2001 (c. 9), s. 69. (1), Sch. 21 para. 3

222 Disposal value restricted

(1) If—

    (a) plant or machinery is the subject of a sale and finance leaseback, and

    (b) S is required to bring a disposal value into account under this Part because of the relevant transaction,

the disposal value is whichever of the amounts in subsection (2) is the smallest.

(2) The amounts are—

    (a) the disposal value that S would be required to bring into account apart from subsection (1);

    (b) the market value of the plant or machinery;

    (c) if S incurred capital expenditure on the provision of the plant or machinery, the notional written-down value of that capital expenditure;

    (d) if a person connected with S incurred capital expenditure on the provision of the plant or machinery, the notional written-down value of that capital expenditure.

(3) The notional written-down value is—

where—

QE is the expenditure incurred by S, or the person connected with S, on the plant or machinery,

A is the total of all allowances which could have been made to S, or the person connected with S, in respect of that expenditure if—

(a) that expenditure had been qualifying expenditure,

(b) that expenditure had been the only expenditure that had ever been taken into account in determining his available qualifying expenditure,

(c) that expenditure had been treated as long-life asset expenditure only if it is in fact such expenditure, and

(d) all allowances had been made in full.

(4) This section does not apply if the finance lease or any transaction or series of transactions of which it forms a part makes provision such as is described in section 225. (1) (sale and finance leasebacks: B's qualifying expenditure if lessor not bearing non-compliance risk).

223 No first-year allowance for B's expenditure

(1) If plant or machinery is the subject of a sale and finance leaseback, a first-year allowance is not to be made in respect of B's expenditure under the relevant transaction.

(2) Any first-year allowance which is prohibited by subsection (1), but which has already been made, is to be withdrawn.

224 Restriction on B's qualifying expenditure

(1) If plant or machinery is the subject of a sale and finance leaseback the amount, if any, by which B's expenditure under the relevant transaction exceeds D is to be left out of account in determining B's available qualifying expenditure.

D is defined in subsections (2) and (3).

(2) If S is required to bring a disposal value into account under this Part because of the relevant transaction, D is that disposal value (determined in accordance with section 222).

(3) If S is not required to bring a disposal value into account under this Part because of the relevant transaction, D is whichever of the following is the smallest—

    (a) the market value of the plant or machinery;

    (b) if S incurred capital expenditure on the provision of the plant or machinery, the notional written-down value of that capital expenditure;

    (c) if a person connected with S incurred capital expenditure on the provision of the plant or machinery, the notional written-down value of that capital expenditure.

(4) In this section "the notional written-down value", in relation to expenditure incurred by a

person on the provision of plant or machinery, has the meaning given by section 222. (3).

(5) This section does not apply if the finance lease or any transaction or series of transactions of which it forms a part makes provision such as is described in section 225. (1).

225 B's qualifying expenditure if lessor not bearing non-compliance risk

(1) This section applies if plant or machinery is the subject of a sale and finance leaseback, and the finance lease, or any transaction or series of transactions of which it forms a part, makes provision which—

(a) removes from the lessor the whole, or the greater part, of any risk, which would otherwise fall directly or indirectly on the lessor, of any person sustaining a loss if payments under the lease are not made in accordance with its terms, and

(b) does so otherwise than by means of guarantees from persons connected with the lessee.

(2) In such a case the following are not qualifying expenditure for the purposes of this Part —

(a) B's expenditure under the relevant transaction;

(b) if the lessor is a different person from B, the expenditure incurred by the lessor on the provision of the plant or machinery.

(3) For the purposes of determining whether this section applies, the lessor and the persons connected with the lessor are treated as the same person.

226 Qualifying expenditure limited in subsequent transactions

(1) Subsection (2) applies if—

(a) plant or machinery has been the subject of a sale and finance leaseback,

(b) S was required to bring a disposal value into account under this Part because of the relevant transaction,

(c) at any time after that event, a person ("P") becomes the owner of the plant or machinery as a result of incurring capital expenditure, and

(d) P's allowances are not restricted by any other provision of this Chapter.

(2) The amount of P's qualifying expenditure is limited to the sum of—

(a) the amount given by section 222 as the amount of S's disposal value, and

(b) so much of the actual amount of the expenditure as is treated as expenditure on the provision of plant or machinery under section 25 (building alterations connected with installation of plant or machinery).

Sale and leaseback or sale and finance leaseback: election for special treatment

227 Circumstances in which election may be made

(1) Section 228 applies if—

(a) B enters into a relevant transaction with S,

(b) the plant or machinery—

(i) is within section 216. (1)(b) (sale and leaseback), or

(ii) is the subject of a sale and finance leaseback (see section 221),

(c) the conditions set out in subsection (2) are met, and

(d) B and S elect that section 228 should apply.

(2) The conditions are—

(a) that S incurred capital expenditure on the provision of the plant or machinery,

(b) that the plant or machinery was unused and not second-hand at or after the time when it was acquired by S,

(c) that the plant or machinery was acquired by S otherwise than as a result of a transaction to which section 217, 218, 223 or 224 applies,

(d) that the relevant transaction is effected not more than 4 months after the first occasion on which the plant or machinery is brought into use by any person for any purpose, and

(e) that S has not—

(i) made a claim for an allowance under this Act in respect of expenditure incurred on the provision of the plant or machinery,

(ii) made a tax return in which such expenditure is taken into account in determining his available qualifying expenditure for the purposes of this Part, or

(iii) given notice of any such amendment of a tax return as provides for such expenditure to be so taken into account.

(3) In subsection (2)(b) and (c), the references to the plant or machinery being acquired by S are, in a case where the relevant transaction between S and B falls within section 213. (1)(c) (assignment), references to the making of the contract the benefit of which S assigns to B.

(4) An election under this section—

(a) must be made by notice to [F39an officer of Revenue and Customs] no later than 2 years after the date of the transaction, and

(b) is irrevocable.

(5) Nothing in—

(a) section 42 of, or Schedule 1. A to, TMA 1970 (claims and elections for income tax purposes), or

(b) paragraphs 54 to 60 of Schedule 18 to FA 1998 (claims and elections for corporation tax purposes),

applies to such an election.

(6) In subsection (4) "the date of the transaction" means the date of the sale, the making of the contract or the assignment referred to in section 213. (1)(a) to (c).

Amendments (Textual)

F39. Words in Act substituted (18.4.2005) by Commissioners for Revenue and Customs Act 2005 (c. 11), s. 53. (1), Sch. 4 para. 83. (1); S.I. 2005/1126, art. 2. (2)(h)

228 Effect of election: relaxation of restriction on B's qualifying expenditure, etc.

(1) The effect of an election under section 227 in relation to B is that subsections (2) and (3) apply instead of section 218 or 224 (restriction on B's qualifying expenditure).

(2) The amount, if any, by which B's expenditure under the relevant transaction exceeds D is to be left out of account in determining B's available qualifying expenditure.

(3) D is whichever of the following is the smaller—

(a) if S incurred capital expenditure on the provision of the plant or machinery, the amount of that expenditure;

(b) if a person connected with S incurred capital expenditure on the provision of the plant or machinery, the amount of that expenditure.

(4) Nothing in subsections (1) to (3) prevents section 225 from applying.

(5) The effect of an election under section 227 in relation to S is—

(a) that no allowance is to be made to S under this Act in respect of the capital expenditure on the provision of the plant or machinery, and

(b) that the whole of that expenditure must be left out of account in determining the amount for any period of Ss' available qualifying expenditure for the purposes of this Part.

[F185. Finance leaseback: parties' income and profits

Amendments (Textual)

F185. Ss. 228. A-228. J and cross-heading inserted (with effect in accordance with s. 134. (3) of the amending Act) by Finance Act 2004 (c. 12), s. 134

228. AApplication of sections 228. B to 228. E

(1) Sections 228. B to 228. E apply where—

(a) plant or machinery is the subject of a sale and finance leaseback for the purposes of section 221, and

(b) section 222 (restriction of disposal value) applies.

(2) [F186. Sections 228. B and 228. C] also apply, with the modifications set out in section 228. F, where plant or machinery is the subject of a lease and finance leaseback (as defined in section 228.

F).

Amendments (Textual)

F186. Words in s. 228. A(2) substituted (with effect in accordance with Sch. 5 para. 17. (5)-(7) of the amending Act) by Finance Act 2007 (c. 11), Sch. 5 para. 17. (2)

228. BLessee's income or profits: deductions

(1) For the purpose of income tax or corporation tax, in calculating the lessee's income or profits for a period of account the amount deducted in respect of amounts payable under the leaseback may not exceed the permitted maximum.

(2) The permitted maximum is the total of—

(a) finance charges shown in the accounts, and

(b) depreciation, taking the value of the plant or machinery at the beginning of the leaseback to be the restricted disposal value.

(3) In relation to a period of account during which the leaseback terminates, the permitted maximum shall also include an amount calculated in accordance with subsection (4).

(4) The calculation is—

where—

" Current Book Value " means the net book value of the leased plant or machinery immediately before the termination,

" Original Consideration " means the consideration payable to S for entering into the relevant transaction, and

" Original Book Value " means the net book value of the leased plant or machinery at the beginning of the leaseback.

228. CLessee's income or profits: termination of leaseback

(1) Subsection (2) applies where the leaseback terminates.

(2) For the purpose of the calculation of income tax or corporation tax, the income or profits of the lessee from the relevant qualifying activity for the period in which the termination occurs shall be increased by an amount calculated in accordance with subsection (3).

(3) The calculation is—

where—

" Net Consideration " means—

- (a)   the consideration payable to S for entering into the relevant transaction, minus

- (b)   the restricted disposal value,

" Current Book Value " means the net book value of the leased plant or machinery immediately before the termination, and

" Original Book Value " means the net book value of the leased plant or machinery at the beginning of the leaseback.

(4) In this section " relevant qualifying activity " means the qualifying activity for the purposes of which the leased plant or machinery was used immediately before the termination.

(5) Section 228. B has no effect on the treatment for the purposes of income tax or corporation tax of amounts received by way of refund on the termination of a leaseback of amounts payable under it.

(6) In subsection (5), " amounts received by way of refund " includes any amount that would be so received in respect of the lessee's interest under the leaseback if any amounts due to the lessor under the leaseback were disregarded.

228. DLessor's income or profits

(1) This section applies in relation to the calculation of the lessor's income or profits for a period of account for the purpose of income tax or corporation tax.

(2) Where—

(a) an amount receivable in respect of the lessor's interest under the leaseback falls to be taken into account in that calculation, and

(b) that amount is reduced by an amount due to the lessee under the leaseback,

that reduction shall be disregarded when taking the amount receivable into account.

(3) The amounts receivable in respect of the lessor's interest under the leaseback that fall to be

taken into account in that calculation may be disregarded to the extent that they exceed the permitted threshold (whether or not subsection (2) applies).

(4) The permitted threshold is the total of—

    (a) gross earnings, and

    (b) the allowable proportion of the capital repayment.

(5) In subsection (4)(a) " gross earnings " means the amount shown in the lessor's accounts in respect of the lessor's gross earnings under the leaseback.

(6) In subsection (4)(b) " allowable proportion of the capital repayment " means the amount obtained by this calculation—

where—

" Investment Reduction For Period " means the amount shown in the lessor's accounts in respect of the reduction in net investment in the leaseback, and

" Net Investment " means the amount shown in the lessor's accounts as the lessor's net investment in the leaseback at the beginning of its term.

(7) This section does not apply to a leaseback if the lessee is a lessee by way of an assignment made before 17 March 2004.

Modifications etc. (not altering text)

C37. S. 228. D modified (19.7.2007) by Finance Act 2007 (c. 11), Sch. 5 para. 17. (9)

228. ELessor's income or profits: termination of leaseback

(1) Subsection (2) applies where—

    (a) the leaseback terminates,

    (b) the lessor disposes of the plant or machinery, and

    (c) the amount of the disposal value required to be brought into account because of that disposal is limited by section 62.

(2) For the purpose of income tax or corporation tax, in calculating the lessor's income or profits for the period in which the termination occurs the amount deducted in respect of any amount refunded to the lessee may not exceed the amount to which the disposal value is limited by section 62.

228. FLease and finance leaseback

(1) [F187. Sections 228. B and 228. C] apply, with the following modifications, where plant or machinery is the subject of a lease and finance leaseback.

(2) In determining the permitted maximum for the purposes of section 228. B, depreciation shall be disregarded.

(3) In the calculation under section 228. C(3), the amount of the consideration referred to in subsection (6)(b) of this section shall be substituted for the Net Consideration.

F188. (4). . . . .

(5) Plant or machinery is the subject of a lease and finance leaseback if—

    (a) a person ("S") leases the plant or machinery to another ("B"),

    (b) after the date of that transaction, the use of the plant or machinery falls within sub-paragraph (i), (ii) or (iii) of section 221. (1)(b), and

    (c) it is directly as a consequence of having been leased under a finance lease that the plant or machinery is available to be so used after that date.

(6) For the purposes of subsection (5), S leases the plant or machinery to B only if—

    (a) S grants B rights over the plant or machinery,

    (b) consideration is given for that grant, and

    (c) S is not required to bring all of that consideration into account under this Part.

(7) Plant or machinery is not the subject of a lease and finance leaseback for the purposes of this section in any case where the condition in subsection (6)(c) is met only because of an election under section 199 made before 18 May 2004.

(8) In the application of [F189sections 228. B and 228. C] in relation to a lease and finance leaseback—

    (a) references to the lessee are references to the person referred to as S in this section, F190...

    F191. (b). . . . .

Amendments (Textual)

F187. Words in s. 228. F(1) substituted (with effect in accordance with Sch. 5 para. 17. (5)-(7) of the amending Act) by Finance Act 2007 (c. 11), Sch. 5 para. 17. (3)(a)

F188. S. 228. F(4) repealed (with effect in accordance with Sch. 5 para. 17. (5)-(7) of the amending Act) by Finance Act 2007 (c. 11), Sch. 5 para. 17. (3)(b), Sch. 27 Pt. 2. (3)

F189. Words in s. 228. F(8) substituted (with effect in accordance with Sch. 5 para. 17. (5)-(7) of the amending Act) by Finance Act 2007 (c. 11), Sch. 5 para. 17. (3)(c)

F190. Word in s. 228. F(8)(a) repealed (with effect in accordance with Sch. 5 para. 17. (5)-(7) of the amending Act) by Finance Act 2007 (c. 11), Sch. 5 para. 17. (3)(c), Sch. 27 Pt. 2. (3)

F191. S. 228. F(8)(b) repealed (with effect in accordance with Sch. 5 para. 17. (5)-(7) of the amending Act) by Finance Act 2007 (c. 11), Sch. 5 para. 17. (3)(c), Sch. 27 Pt. 2. (3)

228. GLeaseback not accounted for as finance lease in accounts of lessee

(1) Sections 228. B and 228. C are subject to this section in their application in relation to a leaseback that is not accounted for as a finance lease in the accounts of the lessee.

(2) Subsection (3) applies where the leaseback is accounted for as a finance lease in the accounts of a person connected with the lessee; and in that subsection " relevant calculation " means the calculation of—

(a) the permitted maximum for the purposes of section 228. B, or

(b) the amount by which the income or profits of the lessee are to be increased in accordance with section 228. C.

(3) Where an amount that falls to be used for the purposes of a relevant calculation—

(a) cannot be ascertained by reference to the lessee's accounts because the leaseback is not accounted for as a finance lease in those accounts, but

(b) can be ascertained by reference to the connected person's accounts for one or more periods, that amount as ascertained by reference to the connected person's accounts shall be used for the purposes of the relevant calculation.

(4) Subsections (5) and (6) apply in a case where the leaseback is not accounted for as a finance lease in the accounts of a person connected with the lessee.

(5) Sections 228. B and 228. C do not apply in relation to the leaseback.

(6) If the term of the leaseback begins on or after 18 May 2004 then, for the purposes of income tax or corporation tax, the income or profits of the lessee from the relevant qualifying activity for the period of account during which the term of the leaseback begins shall be increased by—

(a) the net consideration for the purposes of section 228. C(3) (in the case of a sale and finance leaseback), or

(b) the consideration referred to in section 228. F(6)(b) (in the case of a lease and finance leaseback).

(7) For the purposes of this section the leaseback is accounted for as a finance lease in a person's accounts if—

(a) the leaseback falls, under generally accepted accounting practice, to be treated in that person's accounts as a finance lease or loan, or

(b) in a case where the leaseback is comprised in other arrangements, those arrangements fall, under generally accepted accounting practice, to be so treated.

228. HSections 228. A to 228. G: supplementary

(1) In sections 228. A to 228. G—

" lessee " does not include a person who is lessee by way of an assignment;

the " net book value "of leased plant or machinery means the book value of the plant or machinery having regard to any relevant entry in the lessee's accounts, but—

- also having regard to depreciation up to the time in question, and

- disregarding any revaluation gains or losses and any impairments;

" restricted disposal value " means the disposal value under section 222;

" termination " in relation to a leaseback includes (except in section 228. E)—

- the assignment of the lessee's interest,

- the making of any arrangements (apart from an assignment of the lessee's interest) under which a person other than the lessee becomes liable to make some or all payments under the leaseback, and

- a variation as a result of which the leaseback ceases to be a finance lease.

(2) In a case where accounts drawn up are not correct accounts, or no accounts are drawn up—

(a) the provisions of sections 228. A to 228. G apply as if correct accounts had been drawn up, and

(b) amounts referred to in any of those sections as shown in accounts are those that would have been shown in correct accounts.

(3) In a case where accounts are drawn up in reliance upon amounts derived from an earlier period of account for which correct accounts were not drawn up, or no accounts were drawn up, amounts referred to in sections 228. A to 228. G as shown in the accounts for the later period are those that would have been shown if correct accounts had been drawn up for the earlier period.

(4) In subsections (2) and (3) " correct accounts " means accounts drawn up in accordance with generally accepted accounting practice.

228. JPlant or machinery subject to further operating lease

(1) This section applies where—

(a) plant or machinery is the subject of—

(i) a sale and finance leaseback, or

(ii) a lease and finance leaseback, and

(b) some or all of the plant or machinery becomes, while the subject of the leaseback, also the subject of a lease in relation to which the following conditions are met—

(i) the term of the lease begins on or after 18 May 2004;

(ii) S, or a person connected with S, is the lessee under the lease;

(iii) the lease is not accounted for as a finance lease in the accounts of the lessee.

(2) For the purpose of income tax or corporation tax, in calculating the lessee's income or profits for a period of account the amount deducted in respect of amounts payable under the operating lease shall not exceed the relevant amount.

(3) Subsections (4) and (5) apply in relation to the calculation of the lessor's income or profits for a period of account for the purpose of income tax or corporation tax.

(4) Where—

(a) an amount receivable in respect of the lessor's interest under the operating lease falls to be taken into account in that calculation, and

(b) that amount is reduced by an amount due to the lessee under the operating lease, that reduction shall be disregarded when taking the amount receivable into account.

(5) The amounts receivable in respect of the lessor's interest under the operating lease that fall to be taken into account in that calculation may be disregarded to the extent that they exceed the relevant amount (whether or not subsection (4) applies).

(6) Where only some of the plant or machinery is the subject of the operating lease, subsections (2) to (5) shall apply subject to such apportionments as may be just and reasonable.

(7) For the purposes of this section a lease is accounted for as a finance lease in a person's accounts if—

(a) the lease falls, under generally accepted accounting practice, to be treated in that person's accounts as a finance lease or loan, or

(b) in a case where the lease is comprised in other arrangements, those arrangements fall, under generally accepted accounting practice, to be so treated.

(8) In this section—

" lease and finance leaseback " has the meaning given in section 228. F;

" lessee " means the lessee under the operating lease;

" lessor " means the lessor under the operating lease;

" operating lease " means the lease referred to in subsection (1)(b);

" relevant amount " means an amount equal to the permitted maximum under section 228. B as it applies in relation to the leaseback.]

[F192. Disposal of plant or machinery subject to lease where income retained

Amendments (Textual)
F192. Ss. 228. K-228. M and cross-heading inserted (with effect in accordance with s. 84. (5)(6) of the amending Act) by Finance Act 2006 (c. 25), s. 84. (3)

228. KDisposal of plant or machinery subject to lease where income retained

(1) This section applies for corporation tax purposes if—

(a) on any day ("the relevant day") a person ("the lessor") carries on a business of leasing plant or machinery (the "leasing business"),

(b) on the relevant day the lessor sells or otherwise disposes of any relevant plant or machinery subject to a lease to another person,

(c) the lessor remains entitled immediately after the disposal to some or all of the rentals under the lease in respect of the plant or machinery which are payable on or after the relevant day, and

(d) the lessor is required to bring a disposal value of the plant or machinery into account under this Part.

(2) The disposal value to be brought into account is determined as follows.

(3) If the amount or value of the consideration for the disposal exceeds the limit that would otherwise be imposed on the amount of the disposal value by section 62 (general limit) or 239 (limit on disposal value where additional VAT rebate)—

(a) that limit is not to apply, and

(b) the whole of the amount or value of the consideration for the disposal is to be the disposal value to be brought into account.

(4) In any other case, the disposal value to be brought into account is the sum of—

(a) the amount or value of the consideration for the disposal, and

(b) the value of the rentals under the lease in respect of the plant or machinery (see subsections (7) and (8)) which are payable on or after the relevant day and to which the lessor remains entitled immediately after the disposal,

but subject to the limit imposed on the amount of the disposal value by section 62 or 239.

(5) If—

(a) any of the rentals under the lease are receivable by the lessor on or after the relevant day, and

(b) the value of any of those rentals is represented in the amount of the disposal value under subsection (4)(b),

the amount of those rentals that is equal to their value as so represented is left out of account in calculating the income of the lessor's leasing business for corporation tax purposes.

(6) If, in determining under subsection (5) the amount of any rental to be so left out of account, it is necessary to apportion the amount of the rental, the apportionment is to be made on a just and reasonable basis.

(7) For the purposes of this section, the value of any rentals under the lease in respect of the plant or machinery is taken to be the amount of the net present value of the rentals (see section 228. L).

(8) If any land or other asset which is not plant or machinery is subject to the lease, the value of any rentals under the lease in respect of the plant or machinery is taken to be so much of the amount of the net present value of the rentals as, on a just and reasonable basis, relates to the plant or machinery.

(9) This section is supplemented by—

(a) section 228. L (which provides rules for determining the net present value of the rentals), and

(b) section 228. M (which defines other expressions used in this section).

228. LDetermining the net present value of the rentals for purposes of s.228. K

(1) For the purposes of section 228. K, the amount of the net present value of the rentals is calculated as follows—

Step 1

Find the amount ("RI") of each rental payment—

    (a) which is payable at any time during the term of the lease, and

    (b) which is payable on or after the relevant day.

Step 2

For each rental payment find the day ("the payment day") on which it becomes payable.

Step 3

For each rental payment find the number of days in the period ("P") which—

    (a) begins with the relevant day, and

    (b) ends with the payment day.

Step 4

Calculate the net present value of each payment ("NPVRI") by applying the following formula—where—

T is the temporal discount rate, and

i is the number of days in P divided by 365.

Step 5

Add together each amount of NPVRI determined under step 4.

(2) For the purposes of this section the "term" of a lease has the meaning given in Chapter 6. A of this Part.

(3) For the purposes of this section the "temporal discount rate" is 3.5% or such other rate as may be specified by regulations made by the Treasury.

(4) The regulations may make such provision as is mentioned in subsection (3)(b) to (f) of section 178 of FA 1989 (power of Treasury to set rates of interest).

(5) Subsection (5) of that section (power of Commissioners to specify rate by order in certain circumstances) applies in relation to regulations under this section as it applies in relation to regulations under that section.

228. MOther definitions for the purposes of s.228. K

(1) This section applies for the purposes of section 228. K.

(2) "Business of leasing plant or machinery"—

    (a) has the same meaning as in Part 2 of Schedule 10 to FA 2006 (sale etc of lessor companies etc) (if the business is carried on otherwise than in partnership), or

    (b) has the same meaning as in Part 3 of that Schedule (if the business is carried on in partnership).

(3) "Lease" includes—

    (a) an underlease, sublease, tenancy or licence, and

    (b) an agreement for any of those things.

(4) "Relevant plant or machinery", in relation to a business of leasing plant or machinery, means plant or machinery on whose provision expenditure is incurred wholly or partly for the purposes of the business.]

Miscellaneous and supplementary

229 Hire-purchase etc.

(1) This section applies if—

    (a) a person carrying on a qualifying activity incurs capital expenditure on the provision of plant or machinery for the purposes of the qualifying activity, and

    (b) the expenditure is incurred under a contract providing that the person shall or may become the owner of the plant or machinery on the performance of the contract.

(2) If—

    (a) the person assigns the benefit of the contract to another before the plant or machinery is brought into use, and

    (b) the circumstances are such that allowances to the assignee fall to be restricted under this

Chapter,

section 68. (3) (disposal value where person ceases to be entitled to benefit of contract before plant or machinery brought into use) does not apply.

(3) If the expenditure is incurred on the provision of plant or machinery for leasing under a finance lease—

(a) section 67. (3) (expenditure due to be incurred under contract treated as incurred when plant or machinery brought into use), and

(b) section 68 (disposal values where person ceases to be entitled to benefit of contract),

do not apply.

(4) Subsection (5) applies if—

(a) a person is treated under section 67. (4) as ceasing to own plant or machinery, and

(b) as a result of subsection (2) or (3), section 68. (3) or (as the case may be) section 68 does not apply.

(5) If this subsection applies—

(a) the disposal value is the total of—

(i) any relevant capital sums, and

(ii) any capital expenditure that the person would have incurred if he had wholly performed the contract, but

(b) the person is to be treated, for the purpose only of bringing the disposal value into account, as having incurred the capital expenditure mentioned in paragraph (a)(ii) in the relevant chargeable period.

(6) "Relevant capital sums" means capital sums that the person receives or is entitled to receive by way of consideration, compensation, damages or insurance money in respect of—

(a) his rights under the contract, or

(b) the plant or machinery.

(7) The relevant chargeable period, for the purposes of subsection (5)(b), is the chargeable period in which the person is treated under section 67. (4) as ceasing to own the plant or machinery.

230 Exception for manufacturers and suppliers

(1) The restrictions in sections 217 and 218 do not apply in relation to any plant or machinery if—

(a) the relevant transaction is within section 213. (1)(a) or (b), and

(b) the conditions in subsection (3) are met.

(2) The restrictions in sections 222 to 225 do not apply in relation to any plant or machinery if—

(a) the plant or machinery is the subject of a sale and finance leaseback which is within section 213. (1)(a) or (b), and

(b) the conditions in subsection (3) are met.

(3) The conditions are that—

(a) the plant or machinery has never been used before the sale or the making of the contract,

(b) S's business, or part of S's business, is the manufacture or supply of plant or machinery of that class, and

(c) the sale is effected or the contract made in the ordinary course of that business.

231 Adjustments of assessments etc.

All such assessments and adjustments of assessments are to be made as are necessary to give effect to this Chapter.

232 Meaning of connected person

(1) For the purposes of this Chapter one person is to be treated as connected with another if—

(a) they would be treated as connected under [F193section 575], or

(b) they are to be treated as connected under subsection (2).

(2) If—

(a) a public authority has at any time acquired plant or machinery from another public authority otherwise than by purchase, and

(b) it is directly or indirectly as a consequence of having been leased under a finance lease that the plant or machinery is available for any use to which it is put,

the authority from whom the plant or machinery was acquired is to be treated, in relation to that plant or machinery, as connected with the acquiring authority and with every person connected with the acquiring authority.

(3) In subsection (2), "public authority" includes the Crown or any government or local authority.

(4) Subsection (2) does not apply in relation to section 219 (meaning of "finance lease").

Amendments (Textual)

F193. Words in s. 232. (1)(a) substituted (6.4.2007) by Income Tax Act 2007 (c. 3), s. 1034. (1), Sch. 1 para. 403 (with Sch. 2)

233 Additional VAT liabilities and rebates

This Chapter needs to be read with sections 241 to 245 (provision for cases where a person involved in a relevant transaction or a sale and finance leaseback incurs an additional VAT liability or receives an additional VAT rebate).

Chapter 18. Additional VAT liabilities and rebates

234 Introduction

For the purposes of this Chapter—

(a) "additional VAT liability" and "additional VAT rebate" have the meaning given by section 547,

(b) the time when—

(i) a person incurs an additional VAT liability, or

(ii) an additional VAT rebate is made to a person,

is given by section 548, and

(c) the chargeable period in which an additional VAT liability or an additional VAT rebate accrues is given by section 549.

Additional VAT liability

235 Additional VAT liability treated as qualifying expenditure

(1) This section applies if a person—

(a) has incurred qualifying expenditure ("the original expenditure"), and

(b) incurs an additional VAT liability in respect of the original expenditure at a time when the plant or machinery is provided for the purposes of the qualifying activity.

(2) The additional VAT liability is to be treated as qualifying expenditure—

(a) which is incurred on the same plant or machinery as the original expenditure, and

(b) which may be taken into account in determining the person's available qualifying expenditure for the chargeable period in which the additional VAT liability accrues.

236 Additional VAT liability generates first-year allowance

(1) Subsection (2) applies if—

(a) the original expenditure was first-year qualifying expenditure, and

(b) the additional VAT liability is incurred at a time when the plant or machinery is provided for the purposes of the qualifying activity.

(2) The additional VAT liability is to be regarded for the purposes of this Part as first-year qualifying expenditure which—

(a) is incurred on the same plant or machinery and is the same type of first-year qualifying expenditure as the original expenditure, and

(b) entitles the person incurring the liability to a first-year allowance for the chargeable period in which the liability accrues.

(3) Subsections (3) and (4) of section 52 apply to first-year qualifying expenditure constituted by the additional VAT liability as they apply to other first-year qualifying expenditure.

(4) This section is subject to sections 237 and 241.

237 Exceptions to section 236.

(1) An additional VAT liability is not first-year qualifying expenditure if at the time when the

liability is incurred the plant or machinery is used for overseas leasing which is not protected leasing.

(2) An additional VAT liability is not first-year qualifying expenditure if, at the time when the liability is incurred, the original expenditure is treated under section 43 (plant or machinery subsequently primarily for use outside Northern Ireland) as expenditure which was never first-year qualifying expenditure.

Additional VAT rebate

238 Additional VAT rebate generates disposal value

(1) This section applies if—

    (a) a person has incurred qualifying expenditure ("the original expenditure"),

    (b) an additional VAT rebate is made to the person in respect of the original expenditure, and

    (c) the person owns the plant or machinery on which the original expenditure was incurred at any time in the chargeable period in which the rebate is made.

(2) If (apart from this section) there would not be a disposal value to be brought into account in respect of the plant or machinery for the chargeable period in which the rebate accrues, the amount of the rebate must be brought into account as a disposal value for that chargeable period.

(3) If (apart from this section) there would be a disposal value to be brought into account in respect of the plant or machinery for the chargeable period in which the rebate accrues, the amount of the rebate must be brought into account as an addition to that disposal value.

239 Limit on disposal value where additional VAT rebate

(1) Subsection (2) applies if—

    (a) a person is required to bring a disposal value into account in respect of any plant or machinery, and

    (b) any additional VAT rebate or rebates has or have been made to him in respect of the original expenditure.

(2) The amount of the disposal value is limited to the amount of the original expenditure reduced by the total of any additional VAT rebates accruing in previous chargeable periods in respect of that expenditure.

But this is subject to subsections (3) to (6).

(3) Subsection (4) applies if the disposal value is required to be brought into account by section 238. (2) (disposal value for additional VAT rebate on its own).

(4) The amount of the disposal value to be brought into account is limited to the amount of the original expenditure reduced by the amount of any disposal values brought into account in respect of the plant or machinery as a result of any earlier event.

(5) If—

    (a) the person required to bring the disposal value into account has acquired the plant or machinery as a result of a transaction which was, or a series of transactions each of which was, between connected persons, and

    (b) an additional VAT rebate has been made to any party to the transaction, or to any of the transactions,

the amount of the disposal value is limited to the greatest relevant expenditure of any of the parties.

(6) The relevant expenditure of a party is that party's qualifying expenditure on the provision of the plant or machinery, less any additional VAT rebate made to that party.

Short-life assets: balancing allowance

240 Additional VAT liability

(1) This section applies if a person—

    (a) was entitled to a balancing allowance for the final chargeable period for a short-life asset pool for a qualifying activity,

(b) has incurred, after the end of that period, an additional VAT liability in respect of the original expenditure on the provision of the short-life asset, and

(c) has not brought the liability into account in determining the amount of the balancing allowance.

(2) The person is entitled to a further balancing allowance, of an amount equal to the additional VAT liability, for the chargeable period of the qualifying activity in which the additional VAT liability accrues.

Anti-avoidance

241 No first-year allowance in respect of additional VAT liability

(1) This section applies if—

(a) one person ("B") enters into a transaction with another person ("S") which is a relevant transaction for the purposes of Chapter 17 (anti-avoidance), and

(b) a first-year allowance in respect of B's expenditure under the relevant transaction is prohibited by section 217. (1) or 223. (1).

(2) A first-year allowance is not to be made in respect of any additional VAT liability incurred by B in respect of his expenditure under the relevant transaction.

(3) Any first-year allowance which is prohibited by subsection (2), but which has already been made, is to be withdrawn.

242 Restriction on B's qualifying expenditure: general

(1) This section applies instead of section 218 (restriction on B's qualifying expenditure in case other than sale and finance leaseback) if—

(a) apart from this subsection, section 218 would apply, and

(b) an additional VAT liability has been incurred by, or an additional rebate has been made to, any of the persons mentioned in that section.

(2) The amount, if any, by which E exceeds D is to be left out of account in determining B's available qualifying expenditure.

E and D are defined in subsections (3) to (6).

(3) Except where subsection (6) applies, E is the sum of—

(a) B's expenditure under the relevant transaction, and

(b) any additional VAT liability incurred by B in respect of that expenditure.

(4) If S is required to bring a disposal value into account under this Part because of the relevant transaction, D is that disposal value.

(5) If S is not required to bring a disposal value into account under this Part because of the relevant transaction, D is whichever of the following is the smallest—

(a) the market value of the plant or machinery;

(b) if S incurred capital expenditure on the provision of the plant or machinery, the amount of that expenditure—

(i) increased by the amount of any additional VAT liability incurred by S in respect of that expenditure, and

(ii) reduced by the amount of any additional VAT rebate made to S in respect of that expenditure;

(c) if a person connected with S incurred capital expenditure on the provision of the plant or machinery, the amount of that expenditure—

(i) increased by the amount of any additional VAT liability incurred by that person in respect of that expenditure, and

(ii) reduced by the amount of any additional VAT rebate made to that person in respect of that expenditure.

(6) If—

(a) S is not required to bring a disposal value into account under this Part because of the relevant transaction,

(b) the smallest amount under subsection (5) is the market value of the plant or machinery, and

(c) that value is determined inclusive of value added tax,

E is the amount of B's expenditure under the relevant transaction.

243 Restriction on B's qualifying expenditure: sale and finance leaseback

(1) This section applies instead of section 224 (restriction on B's qualifying expenditure in case of sale and finance leaseback) if—

(a) apart from this subsection, section 224 would apply, and

(b) an additional VAT liability has been incurred by B.

(2) The amount, if any, by which E exceeds D is to be left out of account in determining B's available qualifying expenditure.

E and D are defined in subsections (3) to (7).

(3) Except where subsection (7) applies, E is the sum of—

(a) B's expenditure under the relevant transaction, and

(b) any additional VAT liability incurred by B in respect of that expenditure.

(4) If S is required to bring a disposal value into account under this Part because of the relevant transaction, D is that disposal value (determined in accordance with section 222).

(5) If S is not required to bring a disposal value into account under this Part because of the relevant transaction, D is whichever of the following is the smallest—

(a) the market value of the plant or machinery;

(b) if S incurred capital expenditure on the provision of the plant or machinery, the notional written-down value of that capital expenditure;

(c) if a person connected with S incurred capital expenditure on the provision of the plant or machinery, the notional written-down value of that capital expenditure.

(6) In this section "the notional written-down value", in relation to expenditure incurred by a person on the provision of plant or machinery, has the meaning given by section 222. (3).

(7) If—

(a) S is not required to bring a disposal value into account under this Part because of the relevant transaction,

(b) the smallest amount under subsection (5) is the market value of the plant or machinery, and

(c) that value is determined inclusive of value added tax,

E is the amount of B's expenditure under the relevant transaction.

244 B's qualifying expenditure if lessor not bearing non-compliance risk

An additional VAT liability is not qualifying expenditure for the purposes of this Part if—

(a) section 225 (restriction on B's qualifying expenditure if lessor not bearing compliance risk) applies, and

(b) the additional VAT liability is incurred—

(i) by B, in respect of the expenditure referred to in section 225. (2)(a), or

(ii) by the lessor, in respect of the expenditure referred to in section 225. (2)(b).

245 Effect of election under section 227 on additional VAT liability

(1) This section applies if—

(a) an election is made under section 227 (sale and leaseback or sale and finance leaseback: election for special treatment), and

(b) an additional VAT liability is incurred by S in respect of the capital expenditure incurred on the provision of the plant or machinery to which the election relates.

(2) The effect of the election is—

(a) that no allowance is to be made to S under this Act in respect of the additional VAT liability, and

(b) that the additional VAT liability must be left out of account in determining Ss' available qualifying expenditure for any period.

246 Miscellaneous

(1) All such assessments and adjustments of assessments are to be made as are necessary to give effect to sections 241 to 245.

(2) Section 232 (meaning of connected person) applies for the purposes of sections 242 and 243.

Chapter 19. Giving effect to allowances and charges

247 Trades
If the qualifying activity of a person who is entitled or liable to an allowance or charge for a chargeable period is a trade, the allowance or charge is to be given effect in calculating the profits of that person's trade, by treating—
  (a) the allowance as an expense of the trade, and
  (b) the charge as a receipt of the trade.

Property businesses

248 Ordinary [F194property] businesses
If the qualifying activity of a person who is entitled or liable to an allowance or charge for a chargeable period is an ordinary [F195property] business, the allowance or charge is to be given effect in calculating the profits of that business, by treating—
  (a) the allowance as an expense of that business, and
  (b) the charge as a receipt of that business.
Amendments (Textual)
F194 Word in s. 248 substituted (6.4.2005) by Income Tax (Trading and Other Income) Act 2005 (c. 5) , s. 883. (1) , Sch. 1 para. 546. (b) (with Sch. 2)
F195 Word in s. 248 substituted (6.4.2005) by Income Tax (Trading and Other Income) Act 2005 (c. 5) , s. 883. (1) , Sch. 1 para. 546. (a) (with Sch. 2)
249 Furnished holiday lettings businesses
(1) If the qualifying activity of a person who is entitled or liable to an allowance or charge for a chargeable period is a furnished holiday lettings business, the allowance or charge is to be given effect in calculating the profits of that business, by treating—
  (a) the allowance as an expense of that business, and
  (b) the charge as a receipt of that business.
(2) Section 503 of ICTA (letting of furnished holiday accommodation treated as trade for purposes of loss relief rules, etc.) applies to profits calculated in accordance with subsection (1).
250 Overseas property businesses
If the qualifying activity of a person who is entitled or liable to an allowance or charge for a chargeable period is an overseas property business, the allowance or charge is to be given effect in calculating the profits of that business, by treating—
  (a) the allowance as an expense of that business, and
  (b) the charge as a receipt of that business.

Activities analogous to trades

251 Professions and vocations
If the qualifying activity of a person who is entitled or liable to an allowance or charge for a chargeable period is carrying on a profession or vocation, the allowance or charge is to be given effect in calculating the profits or gains of that person's profession or vocation, by treating—
  (a) the allowance as an expense of the profession or vocation, and
  (b) the charge as a receipt of the profession or vocation.
252 Mines, transport undertakings etc.
If the qualifying activity of a person who is entitled or liable to an allowance or charge for a chargeable period is a concern listed in [F196section 12. (4) of ITTOIA 2005 or] section 55. (2) of ICTA (mines, transport undertakings etc.) the allowance or charge is to be given effect in calculating the profits of the concern under [F197. Chapter 2 of Part 2 of ITTOIA 2005 or, as the

case may be, under] Case I of Schedule D, by treating—
(a) the allowance as an expense of the concern, and
(b) the charge as a receipt of the concern.

Amendments (Textual)
F196 Words in s. 252 inserted (6.4.2005) by Income Tax (Trading and Other Income) Act 2005 (c. 5) , s. 883. (1) , Sch. 1 para. 547. (a) (with Sch. 2)
F197 Words in s. 252 inserted (6.4.2005) by Income Tax (Trading and Other Income) Act 2005 (c. 5) , s. 883. (1) , Sch. 1 para. 547. (b) (with Sch. 2)

[F198. Companies with investment business]

Amendments (Textual)
F198 Pt. 2 Ch. 19. (crossheading)(investment companies) substituted (with effect in accordance with art. 1. (2) of the commencing S.I.) by Finance Act 2004, Sections 38 to 40 and 45 and Schedule 6 (Consequential Amendments of Enactments) Order 2004 (S.I. 2004/2310) , art. 1. (2) , Sch. para. 54. (3)
253[F198. Companies with investment business]
(1) This section applies if the qualifying activity of a person entitled to an allowance or liable to a charge for a chargeable period is [F199managing the investment business].
(2) The allowance is, as far as possible, to be given effect by deducting the amount of the allowance from any income for the period of the business; and section 75. (4) of ICTA (addition of allowances to company's expenses of management) applies only in so far as it cannot be given effect in this way.
(3) The charge is to be given effect by treating the amount of the charge as income of the business.
(4) Except as provided by subsections (2) and (3), the Corporation Tax Acts apply in relation to the allowance or charge as if they were required to be given effect in calculating the profits of that person's trade for the purposes of Case I of Schedule D.
(5) Corresponding allowances or charges in the case of the same plant or machinery are not to be made under this Part both under this section and in another way.
(6) Expenditure to which this section applies is not to be taken into account otherwise than under this Part or as provided by section 75. (4) of ICTA.
(7) This section is subject to sections 768. B(8) and 768. C(11) of ICTA.
Amendments (Textual)
F199 Words in s. 253. (1) substituted (with effect in accordance with art. 1. (2) of the commencing S.I.) by Finance Act 2004, Sections 38 to 40 and 45 and Schedule 6 (Consequential Amendments of Enactments) Order 2004 (S.I. 2004/2310) , art. 1. (2) , Sch. para. 54. (2)

Life assurance business

254 Introductory
(1) Sections 255 and 256 apply if a company which is carrying on any life assurance business is entitled or liable to any allowances or charges for a chargeable period in respect of plant or machinery consisting of a management asset.
(2) In this Chapter "management asset" has the same meaning as in Chapter 1 of Part 12 (life assurance business).
255 Apportionment of allowances and charges
[F200. (1)Except where subsection (3) applies, any allowance to which the company is entitled, and any charge to which it is liable, for a chargeable period in respect of a management asset must be apportioned between basic life assurance and general annuity business, gross roll-up business and PHI business in accordance with subsections (1. A) and (1. B).]
[F200. (1. A)The allowance or charge is to be apportioned to a category of business using the formula—

where—

A is the amount of the allowance or charge,

B is the mean of the opening and closing liabilities of that category of business, and

C is the mean of the opening and closing liabilities of all the categories of business mentioned in subsection (1) which are carried on by the company.

(1. B)If C is nil or below nil, the allowance or charge to be apportioned to a category of business is such as is just and reasonable.]

F201. (2). . . . .

(3) If—

(a) the company is charged to tax under [F202section 436. A of ICTA (gross roll-up business)], and

(b) the management asset in respect of which it is entitled to an allowance or liable to a charge for a chargeable period is [F203held for the purposes of a permanent establishment outside the United Kingdom at or through which the company carries on gross roll-up business], the allowance or charge must be allocated (without any apportionment) to that business.

Amendments (Textual)

F200. S. 255. (1)-(1. B) substituted for s. 255. (1)(1. A) (with effect in accordance with s. 38. (2) of the amending Act) by Finance Act 2007 (c. 11), Sch. 7 para. 69. (2) (with Sch. 7 Pt. 2)

F201. S. 255. (2) repealed (with effect in accordance with s. 38. (2) of the amending Act) by Finance Act 2007 (c. 11), Sch. 7 para. 69. (3), Sch. 27 Pt. 2. (7) (with Sch. 7 Pt. 2)

F202. Words in s. 255. (3)(a) substituted (with effect in accordance with s. 38. (2) of the amending Act) by Finance Act 2007 (c. 11), Sch. 7 para. 69. (4)(a) (with Sch. 7 Pt. 2)

F203. Words in s. 255. (3)(b) substituted (with effect in accordance with s. 38. (2) of the amending Act) by Finance Act 2007 (c. 11), Sch. 7 para. 69. (4)(b) (with Sch. 7 Pt. 2)

Modifications etc. (not altering text)

C38. S. 255 modified by The Friendly Societies (Modification of the Corporation Tax Acts) Regulations 2005 (S.I. 2005/2014), reg. 43. A (as inserted (with effect in accordance with reg. 1. (2) of the amending S.I.) by S.I. 2007/2134, regs. 1. (1), 33)

C39. S. 255 modified (with effect in accordance with reg. 1. (2)(3) of the amending S.I.) by The Insurance Companies (Tax Exempt Business) Regulations 2007 (S.I. 2007/2145), regs. 1. (1), 15

C40. S. 255 modified (with effect in accordance with reg. 1 of the amending S.I.) by The Overseas Life Insurance Companies Regulations 2006 (S.I. 2006/3271), regs. 1, 36 (as amended (with effect in accordance with reg. 1. (2) of the amending S.I.) by S.I. 2007/2146, regs. 1. (1), 21)

256 Different giving effect rules for different categories of business

(1) Subsection (2) applies if a company—

(a) carries on basic life assurance and general annuity business, and

[F204. (b)is charged to tax under the I minus E basis in respect of its life assurance business.]

(2) If this subsection applies—

(a) any allowances (or parts of allowances) to which the company is entitled in respect of the basic life assurance and general annuity business are to be given effect by treating them as [F205expenses payable which fall to brought into account at Step 3 in section 76. (7)] of ICTA, and

(b) any charges (or parts of charges) to which the company is liable in respect of that business are to be given effect by treating the amount of the charges (or parts of charges) as income under Case VI of Schedule D for the chargeable period in question.

(3) Subsection (4) applies if, for a chargeable period, a company is charged to tax under [F206section 436. A of ICTA (gross roll-up business)].

(4) If this subsection applies, then, for the purpose of calculating the [F207profits] under Case VI of Schedule D for the chargeable period in question—

(a) any allowances (or parts of allowances) to which the company is entitled in respect of [F208gross roll-up business] are to be given effect by treating them as an expense of [F208its gross roll-up business], and

(b) any charges (or parts of charges) to which the company is liable in respect of [F209gross roll-up business] are to be given effect by treating them as receipts of [F209its gross roll-up business].

Amendments (Textual)

F204. S. 256. (1)(b) substituted (with effect in accordance with s. 39. (2) of the amending Act) by Finance Act 2007 (c. 11), Sch. 8 para. 23 (with Sch. 8 Pt. 2)

F205. Words in s. 256. (2)(a) substituted (with effect in accordance with art. 1. (2) of the amending S.I.) by Finance Act 2004, Sections 38 to 40 and 45 and Schedule 6 (Consequential Amendments of Enactments) Order 2004 (S.I. 2004/2310), art. 1. (2), Sch. para. 55. (2)

F206. Words in s. 256. (3) substituted (with effect in accordance with s. 38. (2) of the amending Act) by Finance Act 2007 (c. 11), Sch. 7 para. 70. (2) (with Sch. 7 Pt. 2)

F207. Word in s. 256. (4) substituted (with effect in accordance with s. 38. (2) of the amending Act) by Finance Act 2007 (c. 11), Sch. 7 para. 70. (3)(a) (with Sch. 7 Pt. 2)

F208. Words in s. 256. (4)(a) substituted (with effect in accordance with s. 38. (2) of the amending Act) by Finance Act 2007 (c. 11), Sch. 7 para. 70. (3)(b) (with Sch. 7 Pt. 2)

F209. Words in s. 256. (4)(b) substituted (with effect in accordance with s. 38. (2) of the amending Act) by Finance Act 2007 (c. 11), Sch. 7 para. 70. (3)(c) (with Sch. 7 Pt. 2)

Modifications etc. (not altering text)

C41. S. 256 modified (1.1.2002) by S.I. 1997/473, reg. 53. C (as inserted by S.I. 2001/3975, reg. 8)

C42. S. 256 modified (with effect in accordance with reg. 1. (2) of the commencing S.I.) by The Friendly Societies (Modification of the Corporation Tax Acts) Regulations 2005 (S.I. 2005/2014), regs. 1. (1), 44

257 Supplementary

(1) Allowances and charges to which sections 255 and 256 apply are not to be given effect otherwise than in accordance with those sections.

(2) Subsection (1) does not prevent any allowance which is to be given effect under those sections from being taken into account in any calculation for the purposes of—

    [F210. (a)section 85. A(3) of the Finance Act 1989 (excess adjusted Case I profits), or

    (b) section 89 of that Act (policy holders' share of profits).]

F211. (3). . . . .

Amendments (Textual)

F210. S. 257. (2)(a)(b) substituted (with effect in accordance with s. 39. (2) of the amending Act) by Finance Act 2007 (c. 11), Sch. 8 para. 24 (with Sch. 8 Pt. 2)

F211. S. 257. (3) repealed (with effect in accordance with Sch. 10 para. 17. (2) of the amending Act) by Finance Act 2007 (c. 11), Sch. 10 para. 14. (8)(a), Sch. 27 Pt. 2. (10)

Special leasing of plant or machinery

258 Special leasing: income tax

(1) This section applies for income tax purposes if the qualifying activity of a person entitled or liable to an allowance or charge for a chargeable period ("the current tax year") is special leasing of plant or machinery.

(2) Subject to subsection (3), the allowance is to be given effect by deducting it from the person's income for the current tax year from any qualifying activity the person has of special leasing of plant or machinery.

(3) If the plant or machinery leased under the special leasing was not used for the whole or any part of the current tax year for the purposes of a qualifying activity carried on by the lessee—

    (a) the allowance, or

    (b) a proportionate part of it,

is to be given effect by deducting the allowance, or the part of the allowance, from the person's income for the current tax year from that special leasing only.

[F212. (3. A)The allowance or (as the case may be) the proportionate part of the allowance is given effect at Step 2 of the calculation in section 23 of ITA 2007.]

(4) Any charge is to be given effect by treating the charge as income to be [F213assessed to income tax].

(5) If the amount to be deducted from a description of income specified in subsection (2) or (3) exceeds the person's income of that description for the current tax year, the excess must be deducted from the person's income of the same description for the next tax year, and so on for subsequent tax years.

(6) For the purposes of this section, income from special leasing of plant or machinery includes any charge treated as income under subsection (4).

(7) In this section, references to deducting an allowance (or a part of an allowance) from income include setting it off against income.

Amendments (Textual)

F212. S. 258. (3. A) inserted (6.4.2007) by Income Tax Act 2007 (c. 3), s. 1034. (1), Sch. 1 para. 404 (with Sch. 2)

F213 Words in s. 258. (4) substituted (6.4.2005) by Income Tax (Trading and Other Income) Act 2005 (c. 5) , s. 883. (1) , Sch. 1 para. 548 (with Sch. 2)

259 Special leasing: corporation tax (general)

(1) This section applies for corporation tax purposes if the qualifying activity of a company entitled or liable to an allowance or charge for a chargeable period ("the current accounting period") is special leasing of plant or machinery.

(2) Subject to subsection (3), the allowance is to be given effect by deducting it from the company's income for the current accounting period from any qualifying activity it has of special leasing of plant or machinery.

(3) If the plant or machinery leased under the special leasing was not used for the whole or any part of the current accounting period for the purposes of a qualifying activity carried on by the lessee—

    (a) the allowance, or

    (b) a proportionate part of it,

is to be given effect by deducting the allowance, or the part of the allowance, from the company's income for the current accounting period from that special leasing only.

(4) Any charge is to be given effect by treating the charge as income from special leasing of plant or machinery.

260 Special leasing: corporation tax (excess allowance)

(1) This section applies if the amount to be deducted from a description of income specified in section 259. (2) or (3) exceeds the company's income of that description for the current accounting period.

(2) Subject to subsections (3) to (6), the excess must (if the company remains within the charge to tax) be deducted from the company's income of the same description for the next accounting period (and so on for subsequent accounting periods).

(3) The company may, on making a claim, require the excess to be deducted from any profits—

    (a) of the current accounting period, and

    (b) if the company was then within the charge to tax, of any previous accounting period ending within the carry-back period.

(4) The carry-back period is a period which—

    (a) is of the same length as the current accounting period, and

    (b) ends at the start of the current accounting period.

(5) If the preceding accounting period began before the start of the carry-back period, the total amount of deductions that may be made from the profits of the preceding accounting period under—

    (a) subsection (3), and

    (b) any corresponding provision of the Corporation Tax Acts relating to losses,

must not exceed a part of those profits proportionate to the part of the period falling within the carry-back period.

(6) A claim under subsection (3) must be made no later than 2 years after the end of the current accounting period.

(7) If the deduction of the allowance (or of part of it) was subject to the restriction in section 259. (3)—

(a) subsections (3) to (6), and

(b) section 403 of ICTA (group relief),

do not apply in relation to the allowance (or part of it).

(8) In this section "profits" has the same meaning as in section 6 of ICTA (charge to corporation tax etc.).

261 Special leasing: life assurance business

In the case of a company which is carrying on any life assurance business—

(a) subsections (3) to (6) of section 260, and

(b) section 403 of ICTA (group relief),

do not apply in relation to an allowance to which the company is entitled under section 19 (special leasing of plant or machinery).

[F214261. ASpecial leasing: leasing partnerships

(1) This section applies for corporation tax purposes if—

(a) a company carries on a business in partnership with other persons in a chargeable period of the partnership,

(b) the business ("the leasing business") is, on any day in that period, a business of leasing plant or machinery,

(c) the company is entitled to an allowance under section 19 (special leasing of plant or machinery) for any chargeable period comprised (wholly or partly) in the chargeable period of the partnership, and

(d) the interest of the company in the leasing business during the chargeable period of the partnership is not determined on an allowable basis.

(2) Subsections (3) to (6) of section 260 do not apply in relation to the allowance.

(3) For the purposes of this section—

(a) "business of leasing plant or machinery" has the same meaning as in Part 3 of Schedule 10 to FA 2006 (sale etc of lessor companies etc), and

(b) section 785. ZA of ICTA applies for determining whether the interest of the company in the leasing business during the chargeable period of the partnership is determined on an allowable basis.]

Amendments (Textual)

F214. S. 261. A inserted (with effect in accordance with s. 83. (4)-(6) of the amending Act) by Finance Act 2006 (c. 25), s. 83. (3)

Employments and offices

262 Employments and offices

If the qualifying activity of a person who is entitled or liable to an allowance or charge for a chargeable period is an employment or office, the allowance or charge is to be given effect, by treating—

(a) the allowance as [F215a deduction from the taxable earnings from] the employment or office, and

(b) the charge as [F216earnings] of the employment or office.

Amendments (Textual)

F215 Words in s. 262. (a) substituted (with effect in accordance with s. 723. (1)(a)(b) of the amending Act) by Income Tax (Earnings and Pensions) Act 2003 (c. 1) , s. 723 , Sch. 6 para. 253. (a) (with Sch. 7)

F216 Word in s. 262. (b) substituted (with effect in accordance with s. 723. (1)(a)(b) of the amending Act) by Income Tax (Earnings and Pensions) Act 2003 (c. 1) , s. 723 , Sch. 6 para. 253.

(b) (with Sch. 7)

Chapter 20. Supplementary provisions

263 Qualifying activities carried on in partnership

(1) This section applies if—

    (a) a qualifying activity has been set up and is at any time carried on in partnership,

    (b) there has been a change in the persons engaged in carrying on the qualifying activity, and

    [F217. (c)the following condition is met.]

[F218. (1. A)The condition is that—

    (a) the change does not involve all of the partners permanently ceasing to carry on the qualifying activity, or

    (b) the change does not result in the qualifying activity being treated under section 18 or 362 of ITTOIA 2005 as permanently ceasing to be carried on by a company or treated as discontinued under section 337. (1) of ICTA (companies beginning or ceasing to carry on trade etc.).]

(2) In this section—

"the present partners" means the person or persons for the time being carrying on the qualifying activity,

"the partners at the time of the event" means the person or persons carrying on the qualifying activity at the time of the event in question,

"predecessors"—

    - in relation to the present partners, means their predecessors in carrying on the qualifying activity, and

    - in relation to the partners at the time of the event, means their predecessors in carrying on the qualifying activity, and

"qualifying activity"—

    - does not include an employment or office, but

    - includes any other activity listed in section 15. (1) even if any profits or gains from it are not chargeable to tax.

(3) Any first-year allowance or writing-down allowance under this Part is to be made to the present partners.

(4) The amount of any allowance arising under subsection (3) is to be calculated as if—

    (a) the present partners had at all times been carrying on the qualifying activity, and

    (b) everything done to or by their predecessors in carrying on the qualifying activity had been done to or by the present partners.

(5) If any event occurs which gives rise or may give rise to a balancing allowance or a balancing charge under this Part, the allowance or charge is to be made to or on the partners at the time of the event.

(6) The amount of any allowance or charge arising under subsection (5) is to be calculated as if—

    (a) the partners at the time of the event had at all times been carrying on the qualifying activity, and

    (b) everything done to or by their predecessors in carrying on the qualifying activity had been done to or by the partners at the time of the event.

Amendments (Textual)

F217. S. 263. (1)(c) substituted(with effect in accordance with s. 883. (1) of the amending Act) by Income Tax (Trading and Other Income) Act 2005 (c. 5), Sch. 1 para. 549. (2) (with Sch. 2)

F218. S. 263. (1. A) inserted (with effect in accordance with s. 883. (1) of the amending Act) by Income Tax (Trading and Other Income) Act 2005 (c. 5), Sch. 1 para. 549. (3) (with Sch. 2)

264 Partnership using property of a partner

(1) Subsection (2) applies if—

    (a) a qualifying activity is carried on in partnership,

    (b) plant or machinery is used for the purposes of the qualifying activity, and

(c) the plant or machinery is owned by one or more of the partners but is not partnership property.

(2) The same allowances, deductions and charges are to be made under this Part in respect of the plant or machinery as would fall to be made if—

(a) the plant or machinery had at all material times been owned by all the partners and been partnership property, and

(b) everything done by or to any of the partners in relation to that plant or machinery had been done by or to all the partners.

(3) The disposal value of plant or machinery is not required to be brought into account if—

(a) the plant or machinery is used for the purposes of a qualifying activity carried on in partnership,

(b) a sale or gift of the plant or machinery is made by one or more of the partners to one or more of the partners, and

(c) the plant or machinery continues to be used after the sale or gift for the purposes of the qualifying activity.

(4) The references in this section to use for the purposes of a qualifying activity do not include use—

(a) as a result of a letting by the partner or partners in question to the partnership, or

(b) in consideration of the making to the partner or partners in question of any payment which may be deducted in calculating the profits of the qualifying activity.

265 Successions: general

(1) This section applies if—

(a) a person ("the successor") succeeds to a qualifying activity which until that time was carried on by another person ("the predecessor"), and

[F219. (b)the following condition is met.]

[F220. (1. A)The condition is that—

(a) all of the persons carrying on the qualifying activity before the succession permanently cease to carry it on, or

(b) the qualifying activity is treated under section 18 or 362 of ITTOIA 2005 as permanently ceasing to be carried on by a company or treated as discontinued under section 337. (1) of ICTA (companies beginning or ceasing to carry on trade etc.).]

(2) Relevant property is to be treated for the purposes of this Part as if—

(a) it had been sold to the successor when the succession takes place, and

(b) the net proceeds of the sale were the market value of the property.

(3) "Relevant property" means any property which—

(a) immediately before the succession, was owned by the predecessor and was either in use or provided and available for use for the purposes of the discontinued qualifying activity, and

(b) immediately after the succession, and without being sold, is either in use or provided and available for use for the purposes of the new qualifying activity.

(4) No entitlement to a first-year allowance arises under this section.

(5) In this section "qualifying activity"—

(a) does not include an employment or office, but

(b) includes any other activity listed in section 15. (1) even if any profits or gains from it are not chargeable to tax.

Amendments (Textual)

F219. S. 265. (1)(b) substituted (with effect in accordance with s. 883. (1) of the amending Act) by Income Tax (Trading and Other Income) Act 2005 (c. 5), Sch. 1 para. 550. (2) (with Sch. 2)

F220. S. 265. (1. A) inserted (with effect in accordance with s. 883. (1) of the amending Act) by Income Tax (Trading and Other Income) Act 2005 (c. 5), Sch. 1 para. 550. (3) (with Sch. 2)

266 Election where predecessor and successor are connected persons

(1) This section applies if a person ("the successor") succeeds to a qualifying activity which was until that time carried on by another person ("the predecessor") and—

(a) the two persons are connected with each other,

(b) each of them is within the charge to tax on the profits of the qualifying activity, and

(c) the successor is not a dual resident investing company.

(2) If this section applies, the predecessor and the successor may jointly elect for the provisions of section 267 to have effect.

(3) The election may be made whether or not any plant or machinery has actually been sold or transferred.

(4) The election must be made by notice to the [F39an officer of Revenue and Customs] within 2 years after the date on which the succession takes effect.

(5) For the purposes of this section, the predecessor and the successor are connected with each other if any of the following conditions is met—

(a) they would be treated as connected persons under [F221 section 575];

(b) one of them is a partnership and the other has the right to a share in that partnership;

(c) one of them is a body corporate and the other has control over that body;

(d) both of them are partnerships and another person has the right to a share in both of them;

(e) both of them are bodies corporate, or one of them is a partnership and the other is a body corporate, and (in either case) another person has control over both of them.

(6) In subsection (5) any reference to a right to a share in a partnership is to be read as a reference to a right to a share of the assets or income of the partnership.

(7) Sections 104, 108 and 265 (disposal value of long-life assets, effect of disposal to connected person on overseas leasing pool and general provisions about successions) do not apply if an election is made under this section [F222. (but see section 267. A)].

(8) This section does not apply if section 561 applies (transfer of UK trade to a company in another member State).

Amendments (Textual)

F39. Words in Act substituted (18.4.2005) by Commissioners for Revenue and Customs Act 2005 (c. 11), s. 53. (1), Sch. 4 para. 83. (1); S.I. 2005/1126, art. 2. (2)(h)

F221. Words in s. 266. (5)(a) substituted (6.4.2007) by Income Tax Act 2007 (c. 3), s. 1034. (1), Sch. 1 para. 405 (with Sch. 2)

F222. Words in s. 266. (7) inserted (with effect in accordance with s. 85. (5) of the amending Act) by Finance Act 2006 (c. 25), s. 85. (2)

267 Effect of election

(1) If an election is made under section 266, the following provisions have effect.

(2) For the purposes of making allowances and charges under this Part, relevant plant or machinery is treated as sold by the predecessor to the successor—

(a) when the succession takes place, and

(b) at a price which gives rise to neither a balancing allowance nor a balancing charge.

(3) "Relevant plant or machinery" means any plant or machinery which—

(a) immediately before the succession, was owned by the predecessor, and was either in use or provided and available for use for the purposes of the qualifying activity, and

(b) immediately after the succession, is owned by the successor, and is either in use or provided and available for use for the purposes of the qualifying activity.

(4) Allowances and charges are to be made under this Part to or on the successor as if everything done to or by the predecessor had been done to or by the successor.

(5) All such assessments and adjustments of assessments are to be made as are necessary to give effect to the election.

[F223. (6)This section is subject to section 267. A.]

Amendments (Textual)

F223. S. 267. (6) inserted (with effect in accordance with s. 85. (5) of the amending Act) by Finance Act 2006 (c. 25), s. 85. (3)

[F224267. ARestriction on effect of election

(1) This section applies for corporation tax purposes if—

(a) on any day ("the relevant day") a person ("the predecessor") carries on a business of leasing plant or machinery,

148

(b) on the relevant day another person ("the successor") succeeds to the business, and

(c) the predecessor and the successor make an election under section 266.

(2) Neither—

(a) section 266. (7), nor

(b) the provisions of section 267,

have effect in relation to any plant or machinery which, in determining whether the business is a business of leasing plant or machinery on the relevant day, is qualifying leased plant or machinery.

(3) In this section "business of leasing plant or machinery"—

(a) has the same meaning as in Part 2 of Schedule 10 to FA 2006 (sale etc of lessor companies etc) (if the business is carried on otherwise than in partnership), or

(b) has the same meaning as in Part 3 of that Schedule (if the business is carried on in partnership).]

Amendments (Textual)

F224. S. 267. A inserted (with effect in accordance with s. 85. (5) of the amending Act) by Finance Act 2006 (c. 25), s. 85. (4)

268 Successions by beneficiaries

(1) This section applies if—

(a) a person succeeds to a qualifying activity as a beneficiary under the will or on the intestacy of a deceased person who carried on the qualifying activity,

[F225. (b)all of the persons carrying on the qualifying activity before the succession permanently cease to carry it on, and]

(c) the beneficiary elects by notice to [F39an officer of Revenue and Customs] for this section to apply.

(2) In relation to the succession and any previous succession occurring on or after the death of the deceased, relevant plant or machinery is treated as if it had been sold to the beneficiary when the succession takes place.

(3) The net proceeds of the sale are treated as being the lesser of—

(a) the market value of the plant or machinery, and

(b) the unrelieved qualifying expenditure which would have been taken into account in calculating the amount of a balancing allowance for the appropriate chargeable period if the disposal value of the plant or machinery had been nil.

"Appropriate chargeable period" means the chargeable period in which the deceased person's qualifying activity was permanently discontinued.

(4) "Relevant plant or machinery" means plant or machinery which—

(a) was previously owned by the deceased,

(b) passes to the beneficiary with the qualifying activity, and

(c) is either used or provided and available for use by the beneficiary for the purposes of the qualifying activity.

(5) Subsections (6) and (7) apply if the beneficiary is required to bring a disposal value into account in respect of relevant plant or machinery.

(6) The provisions limiting the amount of the disposal value of property, that is—

(a) section 62 (limit on disposal value: general), and

(b) section 239 (limit on disposal value where additional VAT rebate),

apply in relation to the beneficiary to limit the disposal value by reference to expenditure incurred by the deceased or additional VAT rebates made to the deceased.

(7) Section 73 (limit on disposal value: software and rights to software) applies as if the previous disposal values to be taken into account in determining whether the limit under those provisions is exceeded were those of the deceased.

(8) In this section "qualifying activity"—

(a) does not include an employment or office, but

(b) includes any other activity listed in section 15. (1) even if any profits or gains from it are not chargeable to tax.

Amendments (Textual)

F39. Words in Act substituted (18.4.2005) by Commissioners for Revenue and Customs Act 2005 (c. 11), s. 53. (1), Sch. 4 para. 83. (1); S.I. 2005/1126, art. 2. (2)(h)

F225 S. 268. (1)(b) substituted for s. 268. (1)(b) (6.4.2005) by Income Tax (Trading and Other Income) Act 2005 (c. 5) , s. 883. (1) , Sch. 1 para. 551 (with Sch. 2)

Miscellaneous

269 Use of plant or machinery for business entertainment

(1) If—

    (a) a person carrying on a qualifying activity, or

    (b) an employee of that person,

provides business entertainment in connection with that activity, the use of plant or machinery for providing the entertainment is to be treated as use for purposes other than those of that activity.

(2) For the purposes of this section—

    (a) "entertainment" includes hospitality of any kind, and

    (b) the use of an asset for providing entertainment includes the use of an asset for providing anything incidental to the entertainment.

(3) "Business entertainment" does not include anything provided by a person for employees unless its provision for them is incidental to its provision for others.

(4) "Business entertainment" does not include the use of plant or machinery for the provision of anything by a person if—

    (a) it is a function of that person's qualifying activity to provide it, and

    (b) it is provided by that person in the ordinary course of that qualifying activity—

(i) for payment, or

(ii) free of charge with the object of advertising to the public generally.

(5) For the purposes of this section—

    (a) directors of a company, or

    (b) persons engaged in the management of a company,

are to be regarded as employed by the company.

270 Shares in plant or machinery

(1) This Part applies in relation to a share in plant or machinery as it applies (under section 571) in relation to a part of plant or machinery.

(2) For the purposes of this Part, a share in plant or machinery is treated as used for the purposes of a qualifying activity so long as, and only so long as, the plant or machinery is used for the purposes of the qualifying activity.

Application of Part to thermal insulation, safety measures, etc.

27 Application of Part to thermal insulation, safety measures, etc.

(1) Subsection (2) has effect in relation to expenditure if—

    (a) it is expenditure to which any of sections 28 to 33 applies, and

    (b) an allowance under Part 2 or a deduction in respect of the expenditure could not, in the absence of this section, be made in calculating the income from the qualifying activity in question.

(2) This Part (including in particular section 11. (4)) applies as if—

    (a) the expenditure were capital expenditure on the provision of plant or machinery for the purposes of the qualifying activity in question, and

    (b) the person who incurred the expenditure owned plant or machinery as a result of incurring it.

Part 3. Industrial buildings allowances

Part 3. Industrial buildings allowances

Modifications etc. (not altering text)
C2. Pt. 3 modified (24.2.2003) by Proceeds of Crime Act 2002 (c. 29), s. 458. (1), Sch. 10 para. 18 (with Sch. 10 para. 21); S.I. 2003/120, art. 2, Sch. (with arts. 3 4) (as amended (20.2.2003) by S.I. 2003/333, art. 14)
C3 Pt. 3 modified (5.10.2004) by Energy Act 2004 (c. 20) , s. 198. (2) , Sch. 4 para. 5 ; S.I. 2004/2575 , art. 2. (1) , Sch. 1
C4. Pt. 3 modified (E.W.S.) (8.6.2005) by Railways Act 2005 (c. 14), s. 60. (2), Sch. 10 para. 4; S.I. 2005/1444, art. 2. (1), Sch. 1
C5. Pt. 3 modified (8.6.2005) by Railways Act 2005 (c. 14), s. 60. (2), Sch. 10 para. 15; S.I. 2005/1444, art. 2. (1), Sch. 1
C6. Pt. 3 modified (24.7.2005) by Railways Act 2005 (c. 14), s. 60. (2), Sch. 10 para. 24; S.I. 2005/1909, art. 2, Sch.
C7. Pt. 3 restricted (19.7.2007) by Finance Act 2007 (c. 11), s. 36. (1)-(3), (7)

Chapter 1. Introduction

271 Industrial buildings allowances

(1) Allowances are available under this Part if—
   (a) expenditure has been incurred on the construction of a building or structure,
   (b) the building or structure is (or, in the case of an initial allowance, is to be)—
(i) in use for the purposes of a qualifying trade,
(ii) a qualifying hotel,
(iii) a qualifying sports pavilion, or
(iv) in relation to qualifying enterprise zone expenditure, a commercial building or structure, and
   (c) the expenditure incurred on the construction of the building or structure, or other expenditure, is qualifying expenditure.
(2) In the rest of this Part—
   (a) "building" is short for "building or structure", and
   (b) "industrial building" means, subject to Chapter 2 (which defines terms used in subsection (1)(b) etc.), a building or structure which is within subsection (1)(b).
(3) Allowances under this Part are made to the person who for the time being has the relevant interest in the building (see Chapter 3) in relation to the qualifying expenditure (see Chapter 4).

272 Expenditure on the construction of a building

(1) For the purposes of this Part, expenditure on the construction of a building does not include expenditure on the acquisition of land or rights in or over land.
(2) This Part has effect in relation to capital expenditure incurred by a person on repairs to a part of a building as if it were capital expenditure on the construction of that part of the building for the first time.
(3) For the purposes of subsection (2), expenditure incurred for the purposes of a trade on repairs to a building is to be treated as capital expenditure if it is not expenditure that would be allowed to be deducted in calculating the profits of the trade for tax purposes.

273 Preparation of sites for plant or machinery

(1) Subsection (2) applies if—

(a) capital expenditure is or has been incurred in preparing, cutting, tunnelling or levelling land for the purposes of preparing the land as a site for the installation of plant or machinery, and

(b) no allowance could (apart from this section) be made in respect of that expenditure under this Part or Part 2 (plant and machinery allowances).

(2) This Part has effect in relation to the expenditure as if—

(a) the purpose of incurring the expenditure were to prepare the land as a site for the construction of a building, and

(b) the installed plant or machinery were a building.

Chapter 2. Industrial buildings

274 Trades and undertakings which are "qualifying trades"

(1) "Qualifying trade" means—

(a) a trade of a kind described in Table A, or

(b) an undertaking of a kind described in Table B, if the undertaking is carried on by way of trade.

Table A

Trades which are "qualifying trades"

1. | Manufacturing | A trade consisting of manufacturing goods or materials. |

A trade consisting of subjecting goods or materials to a process.

This includes (subject to section 276. (3)) maintaining or repairing goods or materials.

A trade consisting of storing goods or materials—

(a) which are to be used in the manufacture of other goods or materials,

(b) which are to be subjected, in the course of a trade, to a process,

(c) which, having been manufactured or produced or subjected, in the course of a trade, to a process, have not yet been delivered to any purchaser, or

(d) on their arrival in the United Kingdom from a place outside the United Kingdom.

A trade consisting of—

(a) ploughing or cultivating land occupied by another,

(b) carrying out any other agricultural operation on land occupied by another, or

(c) threshing another's crops.

For this purpose "crops" includes vegetable produce.

A trade consisting of working land outside the United Kingdom used for—

(a) growing and harvesting crops,

(b) husbandry, or

(c) forestry.

For this purpose "crops" includes vegetable produce and "harvesting crops" includes the collection of vegetable produce (however effected).

6. | Fishing | A trade consisting of catching or taking fish or shellfish. |

7. | Mineral extraction | A trade consisting of working a source of mineral deposits. "Mineral deposits" includes any natural deposits capable of being lifted or extracted from the earth, and for this purpose geothermal energy is to be treated as a natural deposit. "Source of mineral deposits" includes a mine, an oil well and a source of geothermal energy. |

Table B

Undertakings which are "qualifying trades" if carried on by way of trade

1. | Electricity | An undertaking for the generation, transformation, conversion, transmission or distribution of electrical energy. |

2. | Water | An undertaking for the supply of water for public consumption. |

3. | Hydraulic power | An undertaking for the supply of hydraulic power. |

4. | Sewerage | An undertaking for the provision of sewerage services within the meaning of the Water Industry Act 1991 (c. 56) [F1or the Water and Sewerage Services (Northern Ireland) Order 2006]. |

5. | Transport | A transport undertaking. |

A highway undertaking, that is, so much of any undertaking relating to the design, building, financing and operation of roads as is carried on—

(a) for the purposes of, or

(b) in connection with,

the exploitation of highway concessions.

7. | Tunnels | A tunnel undertaking. |

8. | Bridges | A bridge undertaking. |

9. | Inland navigation | An inland navigation undertaking. |

A dock undertaking.

A dock includes—

(a) any harbour, and

(b) any wharf, pier, jetty or other works in or at which vessels can ship or unship merchandise or passengers,

other than a pier or jetty primarily used for recreation.

(2) Item 6 of Table B needs to be read with Chapter 9 (application of this Part to highway undertakings).

Amendments (Textual)

F1. Words in s. 274. (1) added (N.I.) (1.4.2007) by The Water and Sewerage Services (Northern Ireland) Order 2006 (S.I. 2006/3336), art. 1. (2), Sch. 12 para. 44 (with arts. 8. (8), 121. (3), 307); S.R. 2007/194, art. 2. (2), Sch. Pt. 2 (with Sch. 2)

275 Building used for welfare of workers

A building is in use for the purposes of a qualifying trade if it is—

   (a) provided by the person carrying on the qualifying trade for the welfare of workers employed in that qualifying trade, and

   (b) in use for the welfare of such workers.

276 Parts of trades and undertakings

(1) Sections 274 and 275 apply in relation to part of a trade or undertaking as they apply in relation to a trade or undertaking.

But this is subject to subsections (2) and (3).

(2) If—

   (a) a building is in use for the purpose of a trade or undertaking, and

   (b) part only of the trade or undertaking is a qualifying trade,

the building is in use for the purposes of the qualifying trade only if it is in use for the purposes of that part of the trade or undertaking.

(3) Maintaining or repairing goods or materials is not a qualifying trade if—

   (a) the goods or materials are employed in a trade or undertaking,

   (b) the maintenance or repair is carried out by the person employing the goods or materials, and

   (c) the trade or undertaking is not itself a qualifying trade.

277 Exclusion of dwelling-houses, retail shops, showrooms, hotels and offices etc.

(1) A building is not in use for the purposes of a qualifying trade if it is in use as, or as part of, or for any purpose ancillary to the purposes of—

   (a) a dwelling-house;

   (b) a retail shop, or premises of a similar character where a retail trade or business (including repair work) is carried on;

   (c) a showroom;

   (d) a hotel;

   (e) an office.

(2) Subsection (3) is about buildings constructed for occupation by, or for the welfare of persons

employed—

(a) on, or in connection with, working land outside the United Kingdom which is used as described in item 5 of Table A in section 274 (foreign plantations), or

(b) at, or in connection with, working a source of mineral deposits as defined in item 7 of Table A (mineral extraction).

(3) Subsection (1) does not apply to a building which this subsection is about if the building—

(a) is likely to be of little or no value to the person carrying on the trade when the land or source is no longer worked, or

(b) will cease to be owned by that person on the ending of a foreign concession under which the land or source is worked.

(4) "Foreign concession" means a right or privilege granted by the government of, or any municipality or other authority in, a territory outside the United Kingdom.

(5) Subsection (1) is subject to section 283 (non-industrial part of building disregarded).

278 Building used by more than one licensee

A building used by more than one licensee of the same person is not in use for the purposes of a qualifying trade unless each licensee uses it, or the part to which the licence relates, for the purposes of a qualifying trade.

Qualifying hotels and sports pavilions

279 Qualifying hotels

(1) A hotel is a qualifying hotel if the following conditions are met—

(a) the accommodation in the hotel is in a building of a permanent nature,

(b) the hotel is open for at least 4 months during April to October, and

(c) when the hotel is open during April to October—

(i) it has 10 or more letting bedrooms,

(ii) the sleeping accommodation it offers consists wholly or mainly of letting bedrooms, and

(iii) the services provided for guests normally include the provision of breakfast and an evening meal, the making of beds and the cleaning of rooms.

(2) Whether a hotel meets the conditions in subsection (1)(b) and (c) at any time in a chargeable period is to be determined by reference to the period given under subsections (3) to (5) ("the reference period").

(3) If the hotel was in use for the purposes of a trade carried on by—

(a) the person claiming the allowance, or

(b) a lessee occupying the hotel under a lease to which the relevant interest is reversionary, throughout the 12 month period ending with the last day of the chargeable period, the reference period is that 12 month period.

(4) If the hotel was first used for the purposes of a trade carried on as described in subsection (3) after the beginning of the 12 month period referred to there, the reference period is the 12 month period beginning with the date on which it was first so used.

(5) If a hotel does not qualify under subsection (3) because it had fewer than 10 letting bedrooms until too late a date, the reference period is the 12 month period beginning with the date when it had 10 or more letting bedrooms.

(6) A hotel is not to be treated as meeting the conditions in subsection (1)(b) and (c) at any time in a chargeable period after it has ceased altogether to be used.

(7) A building (whether or not on the same site as any other part of the hotel) which is—

(a) provided by the person carrying on the trade for the welfare of workers employed in the hotel, and

(b) in use for the welfare of such workers,

is to be treated for the purposes of this section as part of the hotel.

(8) If a qualifying hotel is carried on by an individual (alone or in partnership), accommodation which, when the hotel is open during April to October, is normally used as a dwelling by—

(a) that individual, or

(b) a member of his family or household,

is to be treated for the purposes of this section as not being part of the hotel.

(9) In this section—

"building" does not include a structure, and

"letting bedroom" means a private bedroom available for letting to the public generally and not normally in the same occupation for more than one month.

280 Qualifying sports pavilions

A building is a qualifying sports pavilion if it is—

(a) occupied by a person carrying on a trade, and

(b) used as a sports pavilion for the welfare of all or any of the workers employed in that trade.

Commercial buildings (enterprise zones)

281 Commercial buildings (enterprise zones)

For the purposes of this Part as it applies in relation to qualifying enterprise zone expenditure, "commercial building" means a building which is used—

(a) for the purposes of a trade, profession or vocation, or

(b) as an office or offices (whether or not for the purposes of a trade, profession or vocation), and which is not in use as, or as part of, a dwelling-house.

Supplementary provisions

282 Buildings outside the United Kingdom

A building outside the United Kingdom which is in use for the purposes of a trade is not an industrial building at any time when the profits of the trade are not assessable in accordance with the rules [F2that apply in calculating trade profits for income tax purposes or that apply to Case I of Schedule D for corporation tax purposes].

Amendments (Textual)

F2 Words in s. 282 substituted (6.4.2005) by Income Tax (Trading and Other Income) Act 2005 (c. 5) , s. 883. (1) , Sch. 1 para. 552 (with Sch. 2)

283 Non-industrial part of building disregarded

(1) This section applies if, apart from this section, but taking into account section 571 (parts of buildings etc.)—

(a) part of a building would be an industrial building, and

(b) part ("the non-industrial part") would not.

(2) If the qualifying expenditure relating to the non-industrial part is no more than 25% of the qualifying expenditure relating to the whole of the building, the whole of the building is an industrial building.

284 Roads on industrial estates etc.

(1) A road on an industrial estate is an industrial building if the estate consists wholly or mainly of buildings that are treated under this Part as industrial buildings.

(2) For the purposes of this Part as it applies in relation to qualifying enterprise zone expenditure, "industrial estate" includes an area (such as a business park) which consists wholly or mainly of commercial buildings.

285 Cessation of use and temporary disuse of building

For the purposes of this Part—

(a) a building is not to be regarded as ceasing altogether to be used merely because it falls temporarily out of use, and

(b) if a building is an industrial building immediately before a period of temporary disuse, it is to be treated as being an industrial building during the period of temporary disuse.

Chapter 3. The relevant interest in the building

286 General rule as to what is the relevant interest

(1) The relevant interest in relation to any qualifying expenditure is the interest in the building to which the person who incurred the expenditure on the construction of the building was entitled when the expenditure was incurred.

(2) Subsection (1) is subject to the following provisions of this Chapter and to sections 342 (highway undertakings) and 359 (provisions applying on termination of lease).

(3) If—

(a) the person who incurred the expenditure on the construction of the building was entitled to more than one interest in the building when the expenditure was incurred, and

(b) one of those interests was reversionary on all the others,

the reversionary interest is the relevant interest.

287 Interest acquired on completion of construction

For the purposes of determining the relevant interest, a person who—

(a) incurs expenditure on the construction of a building, and

(b) is entitled to an interest in the building on or as a result of the completion of the construction,

is treated as having had that interest when the expenditure was incurred.

288 Effect of creation of subordinate interest

(1) An interest does not cease to be the relevant interest merely because of the creation of a lease or other interest to which that interest is subject.

(2) This is subject to any election under section 290.

289 Merger of leasehold interest

If the relevant interest is a leasehold interest which is extinguished on—

(a) being surrendered, or

(b) the person entitled to the interest acquiring the interest which is reversionary on it,

the interest into which the leasehold interest merges becomes the relevant interest when the leasehold interest is extinguished.

290 Election to treat grant of lease exceeding 50 years as sale

(1) Subsection (2) applies if—

(a) expenditure has been incurred on the construction of a building,

(b) a lease of the building is granted out of the interest which is the relevant interest in relation to the expenditure,

(c) the duration of the lease exceeds 50 years, and

(d) the lessor and the lessee elect for subsection (2) to apply.

(2) This Part applies as if—

(a) the grant of the lease were a sale of the relevant interest by the lessor to the lessee at the time when the lease takes effect,

(b) any capital sum paid by the lessee in consideration for the grant of the lease were the purchase price on the sale, and

(c) the interest out of which the lease was granted had at that time ceased to be, and the interest granted by the lease had at that time become, the relevant interest.

(3) The election has effect in relation to all the expenditure—

(a) in relation to which the interest out of which the lease is granted is the relevant interest, and

(b) which relates to the building (or buildings) that is (or are) the subject of the lease.

291 Supplementary provisions with respect to elections

(1) No election may be made under section 290 by a lessor and lessee who are connected persons unless—

(a) the lessor is a body discharging statutory functions, and

(b) the lessee is a company of which it has control.

(2) No election may be made under section 290 if it appears that the sole or main benefit which may be expected to accrue to the lessor from the grant of the lease and the making of an election is obtaining a balancing allowance.

(3) Whether the duration of a lease exceeds 50 years is to be determined—

(a) in accordance with section 38. (1) to (4) and (6) of ICTA, and

(b) without regard to section 359. (3) (new lease granted as a result of the exercise of an option treated as continuation of old lease).

(4) An election under section 290 must be made by notice to [F3an officer of Revenue and Customs] within 2 years after the date on which the lease takes effect.

(5) All such adjustments, by discharge or repayment of tax or otherwise, are to be made as are necessary to give effect to the election.

Amendments (Textual)

F3. Words in Act substituted (18.4.2005) by Commissioners for Revenue and Customs Act 2005 (c. 11), s. 53. (1), Sch. 4 para. 83. (1); S.I. 2005/1126, art. 2. (2)(h)

Chapter 4. Qualifying expenditure

292 Meaning of "qualifying expenditure"

In this Part "qualifying expenditure" means expenditure which is qualifying expenditure under—

section 294 | capital expenditure on construction of a building |

section 295 | purchase of unused building where developer not involved |

section 296 | purchase of building which has been sold unused by developer |

section 301 | qualifying expenditure on sale within 2 years of first use where all of expenditure is qualifying enterprise zone expenditure |

section 303 | qualifying expenditure on sale within 2 years of first use where part of expenditure is qualifying enterprise zone expenditure. |

293 Meaning of references to carrying on a trade as a developer

For the purposes of this Chapter—

(a) a developer is a person who carries on a trade which consists in whole or in part in the construction of buildings with a view to their sale, and

(b) an interest in a building is sold by the developer in the course of the development trade if the developer sells it in the course of the trade or (as the case may be) that part of the trade that consists in the construction of buildings with a view to their sale.

Qualifying expenditure

294 Capital expenditure on construction of a building

If—

(a) capital expenditure is incurred on the construction of a building, and

(b) the relevant interest in the building has not been sold or, if it has been sold, it has been sold only after the first use of the building,

the capital expenditure is qualifying expenditure.

295 Purchase of unused building where developer not involved

(1) This section applies if—

(a) expenditure is incurred on the construction of a building,

(b) the relevant interest in the building is sold before the building is first used,

(c) a capital sum is paid by the purchaser for the relevant interest, and

(d) section 296 (purchase of building which has been sold unused by developer) does not apply.

(2) The lesser of—

(a) the capital sum paid by the purchaser for the relevant interest, and

(b) the expenditure incurred on the construction of the building,

is qualifying expenditure.

(3) The qualifying expenditure is to be treated as incurred by the purchaser when the capital sum became payable.

(4) If the relevant interest is sold more than once before the building is first used, subsection (2) has effect only in relation to the last of those sales.

296 Purchase of building which has been sold unused by developer

(1) This section applies if—

(a) expenditure is incurred by a developer on the construction of a building, and

(b) the relevant interest in the building is sold by the developer in the course of the development trade before the building is first used.

(2) If—

(a) the sale of the relevant interest by the developer was the only sale of that interest before the building is used, and

(b) a capital sum is paid by the purchaser for the relevant interest,

the capital sum is qualifying expenditure.

(3) If—

(a) the sale by the developer was not the only sale before the building is used, and

(b) a capital sum is paid by the purchaser for the relevant interest on the last sale,

the lesser of that capital sum and the price paid for the relevant interest on its sale by the developer is qualifying expenditure.

(4) The qualifying expenditure is to be treated as incurred by the purchaser when the capital sum referred to in subsection (2)(b) or (3)(b) became payable.

297 Purchase of used building from developer

(1) This section applies if—

(a) expenditure is incurred by a developer on the construction of a building, and

(b) the relevant interest is sold by the developer in the course of the development trade after the building has been used.

(2) This Part has effect in relation to the person to whom the relevant interest is sold as if—

(a) the expenditure on the construction of the building had been qualifying expenditure,

(b) all appropriate writing-down allowances had been made to the developer, and

(c) any appropriate balancing adjustment had been made on the occasion of the sale.

(3) This section is subject to sections 301 and 303 (purchase of building in enterprise zone within 2 years of first use).

Qualifying enterprise zone expenditure

298 The time limit for qualifying enterprise zone expenditure

(1) For the purposes of sections 299 to 304, the time limit for expenditure on the construction of a building on a site in an enterprise zone is—

(a) 10 years after the site was first included in the zone, or

(b) if the expenditure is incurred under a contract entered into within those 10 years, 20 years after the site was first included in the zone.

(2) In those sections "EZ building" is short for "building on a site in an enterprise zone".

(3) In this Part "enterprise zone" means an area designated as such by an order—

(a) made by the Secretary of State [F4, the Scottish Ministers or the National Assembly for Wales,] under powers conferred by Schedule 32 to the Local Government, Planning and Land Act 1980 (c. 65), or

(b) in Northern Ireland, made by the Department of the Environment under Article 7 of the Enterprise Zones (Northern Ireland) Order 1981 (S.I.1981/607 (N.I.15)).

Amendments (Textual)

F4. Words in s. 298. (3) inserted (with effect as mentioned in s. 69. (2) of the amending Act) by Finance Act 2001 (c. 9), s. 69. (1), Sch. 21 para. 5

299 Application of section 294.

If—

(a) capital expenditure is incurred on the construction of an EZ building, and

(b) the expenditure is incurred within the time limit,

the qualifying expenditure given by section 294 is qualifying enterprise zone expenditure.

300 Application of sections 295 and 296.

If—

(a) expenditure is incurred on the construction of an EZ building, and

(b) all the expenditure is incurred within the time limit,

any qualifying expenditure given by sections 295 and 296 in relation to that expenditure is qualifying enterprise zone expenditure.

301 Purchase of building within 2 years of first use

(1) This section applies if—

(a) expenditure is incurred on the construction of an EZ building,

(b) all the expenditure is incurred within the time limit,

(c) the relevant interest in the building is sold—

(i) after the building has been used, but

(ii) within the period of 2 years beginning with the date on which the building was first used, and

(d) that sale ("the relevant sale") is the first sale in that period after the building has been used.

(2) If this section applies—

(a) any balancing adjustment which falls to be made on the occasion of the relevant sale is to be made, and

(b) the residue of qualifying expenditure immediately after the relevant sale is to be disregarded for the purposes of this Part.

(3) If a capital sum is paid by the purchaser for the relevant interest on the relevant sale—

(a) the purchaser is to be treated as having incurred qualifying expenditure that is qualifying enterprise zone expenditure of an amount given in subsection (4), (6) or (7), and

(b) in relation to that qualifying enterprise zone expenditure, this Part applies as if the building had not been used before the date of the relevant sale.

(4) Unless subsection (6) or (7) applies, the amount of the qualifying enterprise zone expenditure is the lesser of—

(a) the capital sum paid by the purchaser for the relevant interest on the relevant sale, and

(b) the expenditure incurred on the construction of the building.

(5) Subsections (6) and (7) apply if—

(a) the expenditure incurred on the construction of the EZ building was incurred by a developer, and

(b) the relevant interest in the building has been sold by the developer in the course of the development trade.

(6) If the sale by the developer is the relevant sale, the amount of the qualifying enterprise zone expenditure is the capital sum paid by the purchaser for the relevant interest on that sale.

(7) If the sale by the developer is not the relevant sale, the amount of the qualifying enterprise zone expenditure is the lesser of—

    (a) the capital sum paid by the purchaser for the relevant interest on the relevant sale, and

    (b) the price paid for the relevant interest on its sale by the developer.

(8) The qualifying expenditure is to be treated as incurred when the capital sum on the relevant sale became payable.

Part of expenditure within time limit for qualifying enterprise zone expenditure

302 Qualifying enterprise zone expenditure where section 295 or 296 applies

(1) This section applies if—

    (a) expenditure is incurred on the construction of an EZ building,

    (b) only a part of the expenditure is incurred within the time limit, and

    (c) the circumstances are as described in—

(i) section 295. (1) (purchase of unused building where developer not involved), or

(ii) section 296. (1) (purchase of building which has been sold unused by developer).

(2) Only a part of the qualifying expenditure given by section 295. (2) or 296. (2) or (3) (as the case may be) is qualifying enterprise zone expenditure.

(3) The part of the qualifying expenditure that is qualifying enterprise zone expenditure is— where—

QE is the qualifying expenditure,

E is the part of the expenditure on the construction of the EZ building that is incurred within the time limit, and

T is the total expenditure on the construction of the building.

303 Purchase of building within 2 years of first use

(1) This section applies if—

    (a) expenditure is incurred on the construction of an EZ building,

    (b) only a part of the expenditure is incurred within the time limit,

    (c) the relevant interest in the building is sold—

(i) after the building has been used, but

(ii) within the period of 2 years beginning with the date on which the building was first used, and

    (d) that sale ("the relevant sale") is the first sale in that period after the building has been used.

(2) If this section applies—

    (a) any balancing adjustment which falls to be made on the occasion of the relevant sale is to be made, and

    (b) the residue of qualifying expenditure immediately after the relevant sale is to be disregarded for the purposes of this Part.

(3) If a capital sum is paid by the purchaser for the relevant interest on the relevant sale—

    (a) the purchaser is to be treated as having incurred qualifying expenditure—

(i) part of which is qualifying enterprise zone expenditure ("Z"), and

(ii) part of which is not ("N"), and

    (b) in relation to that qualifying expenditure, this Part applies as if the building had not been used before the date of the relevant sale.

(4) Unless section 304 (cases where developer involved) applies—

and

L is the lesser of—

(a) the capital sum paid for the relevant interest on the relevant sale, and

(b) the expenditure incurred on the construction of the building,

E is the part of the expenditure on the construction of the EZ building that is incurred within the time limit, and

T is the total expenditure on the construction of the building.

(5) Any qualifying expenditure arising under this section or section 304 is to be treated as incurred when the capital sum on the relevant sale became payable.

304 Application of section 303 where developer involved

(1) This section applies if section 303 applies but—

    (a) the expenditure on the construction of the building was incurred by a developer, and

    (b) the relevant interest in the building has been sold by the developer in the course of the development trade;

and in this section Z, N, E and T have the same meaning as in section 303.

(2) If the sale by the developer is the relevant sale—

and

where—

C is the capital sum paid for the relevant interest by the purchaser, and

L is the lesser of—

(a) the capital sum paid for the relevant interest on the relevant sale, and

(b) the expenditure incurred on the construction of the building.

(3) If the sale by the developer is not the relevant sale—

and

where D is the lesser of—

(a) the price paid for the relevant interest on its sale by the developer, and

(b) the capital sum paid for the relevant interest on the relevant sale.

Chapter 5. Initial allowances

305 Initial allowances for qualifying enterprise zone expenditure

(1) A person who has incurred qualifying enterprise zone expenditure is entitled to an initial allowance in respect of the expenditure if the building on which the expenditure is incurred is to be an industrial building—

    (a) occupied by that person or a qualifying lessee, or

    (b) used by a qualifying licensee.

(2) In this section—

"qualifying lessee" means a lessee under a lease to which the relevant interest is reversionary, and

"qualifying licensee" means a licensee of—

    - the person incurring the qualifying expenditure, or

    - a lessee of the person incurring the qualifying expenditure.

306 Amount of initial allowance and period for which allowance made

(1) The amount of the initial allowance is 100% of the qualifying enterprise zone expenditure.

(2) A person claiming an initial allowance under this section may require the allowance to be reduced to a specified amount.

(3) The initial allowance is made for the chargeable period in which the qualifying expenditure is incurred.

(4) For the purposes of subsection (3), expenditure incurred for the purposes of a trade, profession or vocation by a person about to carry it on is to be treated as if it had been incurred on the first day on which the person carries on the trade, profession or vocation.

307 Building not industrial building when first used etc.

(1) No initial allowance is to be made under section 305 if, when the building is first used, it is not an industrial building.

(2) An initial allowance which has been made in respect of a building which is to be an industrial building is to be withdrawn if, when the building is first used, it is not an industrial building.

(3) An initial allowance which has been made in respect of a building which has not been used is to be withdrawn if the person to whom the allowance was made sells the relevant interest before the building is first used.

(4) All such assessments and adjustments of assessments are to be made as are necessary to give effect to this section.

308 Grants affecting entitlement to initial allowances

(1) No initial allowance is to be made in respect of expenditure to the extent that it is taken into account for the purposes of a relevant grant or relevant payment made towards that expenditure.

(2) A grant or payment is relevant if it is—

    (a) a grant made under section 32, 34 or 56. (1) of the Transport Act 1968 (c. 73),

    (b) a payment made under section 56. (2) of the Transport Act 1968, or

    (c) a grant made under section 101 of the Greater London Authority Act 1999 (c. 29),

which is declared by the Treasury by order to be relevant for the purposes of the withholding of initial allowances.

(3) If a relevant grant or relevant payment towards the expenditure is made after the making of an initial allowance, the allowance is to be withdrawn to that extent.

(4) If the amount of the grant or payment is repaid by the grantee to the grantor, in whole or in part, the grant or payment is treated, to that extent, as never having been made.

(5) All such assessments and adjustments of assessments are to be made as are necessary to give effect to subsection (3) or (4).

(6) Any such assessment or adjustment is not out of time if it is made within 3 years of the end of the chargeable period in which the grant, payment or repayment was made.

Chapter 6. Writing-down allowances

309 Entitlement to writing-down allowance

(1) A person is entitled to a writing-down allowance for a chargeable period if—

    (a) qualifying expenditure has been incurred on a building,

    (b) at the end of that chargeable period, the person is entitled to the relevant interest in the building in relation to that expenditure, and

    (c) at the end of that chargeable period, the building is an industrial building.

(2) A person claiming a writing-down allowance may require the allowance to be reduced to a specified amount.

310 Basic rule for calculating amount of allowance

(1) The basic rule is that the writing-down allowance for a chargeable period is—

    (a) in the case of qualifying enterprise zone expenditure, 25% of the expenditure, and

    (b) in the case of other qualifying expenditure, 4% of the expenditure.

(2) The allowance is proportionately increased or reduced if the chargeable period is more or less than a year.

(3) This basic rule does not apply if section 311 applies.

311 Calculation of allowance after sale of relevant interest

(1) If a relevant event occurs, the writing-down allowance for any chargeable period ending after the event is—
where—
RQE is the amount of the residue of qualifying expenditure immediately after the event,
A is the length of the chargeable period, and
B is the length of the period from the date of the event to the end of the period of 25 years beginning with the day on which the building was first used.
(2) On any later relevant event, the writing-down allowance is further adjusted in accordance with this section.
(3) "Relevant event" means—
    (a) a sale of the relevant interest in the building which is a balancing event to which section 314 applies, or
    (b) an event which is a relevant event for the purposes of this section under section 347 or 349 (additional VAT liabilities and rebates).

312 Allowance limited to residue of qualifying expenditure

(1) The amount of the writing-down allowance for a chargeable period is limited to the residue of qualifying expenditure.
(2) For this purpose the residue is ascertained immediately before writing off the writing-down allowance at the end of the chargeable period.

313 Meaning of "the residue of qualifying expenditure"

The residue of qualifying expenditure is the qualifying expenditure that has not yet been written off in accordance with Chapter 8.
Modifications etc. (not altering text)
C8 S. 313 applied (5.10.2004) by Energy Act 2004 (c. 20) , s. 198. (2) , Sch. 4 para. 6 ; S.I. 2004/2575 , art. 2. (1) , Sch. 1

Chapter 7. Balancing adjustments

314 When balancing adjustments are made
(1) A balancing adjustment is made if—
    (a) qualifying expenditure has been incurred on a building, and
    (b) a balancing event occurs while the building is an industrial building or after it has ceased to be an industrial building.
(2) A balancing adjustment is either a balancing allowance or a balancing charge and is made for the chargeable period in which the balancing event occurs.
(3) A balancing allowance or balancing charge is made to or on the person entitled to the relevant interest in the building immediately before the balancing event.
(4) No balancing adjustment is made if the balancing event occurs more than 25 years after the building was first used.
(5) If more than one balancing event within section 315. (1) occurs during a period when the building is not an industrial building, a balancing adjustment is made only on the first of them.
315 Main balancing events
(1) The following are balancing events for the purposes of this Part—
    (a) the relevant interest in the building is sold;
    (b) if the relevant interest is a lease, the lease ends otherwise than on the person entitled to it

acquiring the interest reversionary on it;

 (c) the building is demolished or destroyed;

 (d) the building ceases altogether to be used (without being demolished or destroyed);

 (e) if the relevant interest depends on the duration of a foreign concession, the concession ends.

(2) "Foreign concession" means a right or privilege granted by the government of, or any municipality or other authority in, a territory outside the United Kingdom.

(3) Other balancing events are provided for by—

section 328 (realisation of capital value where site of building is in enterprise zone);

section 343 (ending of highway concession);

section 350 (additional VAT rebates and balancing adjustments);

and a balancing event under this section may also occur as a result of section 317 (hotel not qualifying hotel for 2 years).

316 Proceeds from main balancing events

(1) References in this Part to the proceeds from a balancing event within section 315. (1) are to the amounts received or receivable in connection with the event, as shown in the Table—

Table

Balancing events and proceeds

1. Balancing event	2. Proceeds from event
1. The sale of the relevant interest.	The net proceeds of the sale.

The net amount received for the remains of the building, together with—

(a) any insurance money received in respect of the demolition or destruction, and

(b) any other compensation of any description so received, so far as it consists of capital sums.

3. The building ceases altogether to be used. | Any compensation of any description received in respect of the event, so far as it consists of capital sums. |

4. A foreign concession ends. | Any compensation payable in respect of the relevant interest. |

(2) The amounts referred to in column 2 of the Table are those received or receivable by the person whose entitlement to a balancing allowance or liability to a balancing charge is in question.

317 Balancing event where hotel not qualifying hotel for 2 years

(1) This section applies if—

 (a) a building ceases to be a qualifying hotel otherwise than on the occurrence of a balancing event which is within section 315. (1), and

 (b) after the building ceases to be a qualifying hotel, a period of 2 years elapses—

(i) in which it is not a qualifying hotel, and

(ii) without the occurrence of a balancing event.

(2) This Part has effect as if—

 (a) the relevant interest in the building had been sold at the end of the 2 year period, and

 (b) the net proceeds of the sale were equal to the market value of that interest.

(3) Subsection (2) does not affect section 285 (building treated as industrial building during period of temporary disuse).

(4) But a building is not to be treated under section 285. (b) as continuing to be a qualifying hotel for more than 2 years after the end of the chargeable period in which it falls temporarily out of use.

(5) This section does not apply to qualifying enterprise zone expenditure.

Calculation of balancing adjustments

318 Building an industrial building etc. throughout

(1) This section provides for balancing adjustments where the building was—

 (a) an industrial building, or

 (b) used for research and development,

for the whole of the relevant period of ownership.

(2) A balancing allowance is made if—

 (a) there are no proceeds from the balancing event, or

(b) the proceeds from the balancing event are less than the residue of qualifying expenditure immediately before the event.

(3) The amount of the balancing allowance is the amount of—

(a) the residue (if there are no proceeds);

(b) the difference (if the proceeds are less than the residue).

(4) A balancing charge is made if the proceeds from the balancing event are more than the residue, if any, of qualifying expenditure immediately before the event.

(5) The amount of the balancing charge is the amount of—

(a) the difference, or

(b) the proceeds (if the residue is nil).

319 Building not an industrial building etc. throughout

(1) This section provides for balancing adjustments where the building was not—

(a) an industrial building, or

(b) used for research and development,

for a part of the relevant period of ownership.

(2) A balancing allowance is made if—

(a) there are no proceeds from the balancing event or the proceeds are less than the starting expenditure, and

(b) the net allowances made are less than the adjusted net cost of the building.

(3) The amount of the balancing allowance is the amount of the difference between the adjusted net cost of the building and the net allowances made.

(4) A balancing charge is made if the proceeds from the balancing event are equal to or more than the starting expenditure.

(5) The amount of the balancing charge is an amount equal to the net allowances made.

(6) A balancing charge is also made if—

(a) there are no proceeds from the balancing event or the proceeds are less than the starting expenditure, and

(b) the net allowances made are more than the adjusted net cost of the building.

(7) The amount of the balancing charge is the amount of the difference between the net allowances made and the adjusted net cost of the building.

320 Overall limit on balancing charge

The amount of a balancing charge made on a person must not exceed the amount of the net allowances made.

Meaning of "the relevant period of ownership" etc.

321 The relevant period of ownership

The relevant period of ownership is the period beginning—

(a) with the day on which the building was first used for any purpose, or

(b) if the relevant interest has been sold after that day, with the day following that on which the sale (or the last such sale) occurred,

and ending with the day on which the balancing event occurs.

322 Starting expenditure

(1) This section gives the starting expenditure for the purposes of this Chapter.

(2) If the person to or on whom the balancing allowance or balancing charge falls to be made is the person who incurred the qualifying expenditure, that expenditure is the starting expenditure.

(3) Otherwise, the starting expenditure is the residue of qualifying expenditure at the beginning of the relevant period of ownership.

(4) If section 340 (treatment of demolition costs) applies, the starting expenditure is increased by an amount equal to the net cost of the demolition.

323 Adjusted net cost

The amount of the adjusted net cost is—

where—

S is the starting expenditure,

P is the amount of any proceeds from the balancing event,

I is the number of days in the relevant period of ownership on which the building was an industrial building or used for research and development, and

R is the number of days in the whole of the relevant period of ownership.

324 Net allowances

For the purposes of this Chapter, the amount of the net allowances made, in relation to any qualifying expenditure, is—

where—

I is the amount of any initial allowances made to the person in relation to that qualifying expenditure,

WDA is the amount of any writing-down allowances made to the person for chargeable periods ending on or before the date of the balancing event giving rise to the balancing adjustment,

RDA is the amount of any allowances under Part 6 (research and development allowances) made to the person for such chargeable periods, and

B is the amount of any balancing charges made on the person for such chargeable periods.

Balancing allowances restricted where sale subject to subordinate interest

325 Balancing allowances restricted where sale subject to subordinate interest

(1) This section applies if—

    (a) the relevant interest in a building is sold subject to a subordinate interest,

    (b) the person entitled to the relevant interest immediately before the sale ("the former owner") would, apart from this section, be entitled to a balancing allowance under this Chapter as a result of the sale, and

    (c) condition A or B is met.

(2) Condition A is that—

    (a) the former owner,

    (b) the person who acquires the relevant interest, and

    (c) the person to whom the subordinate interest was granted,

or any two of them, are connected persons.

(3) Condition B is that it appears that the sole or main benefit which might have been expected to accrue to the parties or any of them from the sale or the grant, or transactions including the sale or grant, was the obtaining of an allowance under this Part.

(4) For the purpose of deciding what balancing adjustment is to be made in a case to which this section applies, the net proceeds to the former owner of the sale are to be increased—

    (a) by an amount equal to any premium receivable by him for the grant of the subordinate interest, and

    (b) if no rent, or no commercial rent, is payable in respect of the subordinate interest, by the amount by which the proceeds would have been greater if a commercial rent had been payable and the relevant interest had been sold in the open market.

(5) But the net proceeds of the sale are not to be treated as being greater than the amount which secures that no balancing allowance is made.

(6) If the terms on which a subordinate interest is granted are varied before the sale of the relevant interest—

    (a) any capital consideration for the variation is to be treated for the purposes of this section as a premium for the grant of the interest, and

    (b) the question whether any, and if so what, rent is payable in respect of the interest is to be determined by reference to the terms in force immediately before the sale.

(7) If this section applies in relation to a sale to deny or reduce a balancing allowance, the residue

of qualifying expenditure immediately after the sale is nevertheless calculated as if the balancing allowance had been made or not reduced.

326 Interpretation of section 325.

(1) In section 325—

"commercial rent" means such rent as may reasonably be expected to have been required in respect of the subordinate interest (having regard to any premium payable for the grant of the interest) if the transaction had been at arm's length;

"premium" includes any capital consideration, except so much of any sum as corresponds to [F5—

-] [F6, or

- an amount brought into account as a receipt in calculating the profits of a UK property business under sections 277 to 281 of ITTOIA 2005 that is calculated by reference to the sum;] an amount of rent or profits falling to be calculated by reference to that sum under section 34 of ICTA;

"subordinate interest" means an interest in or right over the building, whether granted by the former owner or anyone else.

(2) In section 325 and this section—

"capital consideration" means consideration which consists of a capital sum or would be a capital sum if it had consisted of a money payment, and

"rent" includes any consideration which is not capital consideration.

Amendments (Textual)

F5. Word in s. 326. (1) inserted (with effect in accordance with s. 883. (1) of the amending Act) by Income Tax (Trading and Other Income) Act 2005 (c. 5), Sch. 1 para. 553. (a) (with Sch. 2)

F6. S. 326. (1)(b) and word inserted (with effect in accordance with s. 883. (1) of the amending Act) by Income Tax (Trading and Other Income) Act 2005 (c. 5), Sch. 1 para. 553. (b) (with Sch. 2)

Qualifying enterprise zone expenditure: effect of realising capital value

327 Capital value provisions: application of provisions

Sections 328 to 331 apply only if expenditure on the construction of a building has been incurred—

(a) at a time—

(i) when the site of the building was wholly or mainly in an enterprise zone, and

(ii) which was not more than 10 years after the site was first included in the zone, or

(b) under a contract entered into at such a time.

328 Balancing adjustment on realisation of capital value

(1) There is a balancing event if, while the building is an industrial building or after it has ceased to be one, any capital value is realised.

(2) No balancing allowance is to be made because of a balancing event under this section.

(3) The amount of capital value realised is to be treated as the proceeds from the balancing event.

(4) If a balancing event under this section occurs—

(a) section 319 (balancing adjustment where building not an industrial building etc. throughout) has effect as if, immediately after the balancing event, the starting expenditure were reduced by the amount of capital value realised, and

(b) if the net proceeds of a sale of the relevant interest fall to be increased under section 325. (4) (balancing allowances restricted where sale subject to subordinate interest), those proceeds as so increased are reduced by the amount of any capital value realised before the sale.

(5) Capital value is realised if an amount of capital value is paid which is attributable to an interest in land ("the subordinate interest") to which the relevant interest in the building is or will be subject.

(6) The capital value is realised on the making of the payment.

(7) The amount of capital value realised is the amount of capital value that is attributable to the subordinate interest under section 329.

329 Capital value that is attributable to subordinate interest

(1) Capital value is attributable to the subordinate interest if it is paid—

(a) in consideration of the grant of the subordinate interest,

(b) instead of any rent payable by the person entitled to the subordinate interest,

(c) in consideration of the assignment of such rent, or

(d) in consideration of—

(i) the surrender of the subordinate interest, or

(ii) the variation or waiver of any of the terms on which it was granted.

(2) If—

(a) no premium is given in consideration of the grant of the subordinate interest or any premium so given is less than the commercial premium, and

(b) no commercial rent is payable in respect of the subordinate interest,

capital value is attributable under subsection (1)(a) as if the commercial premium had been paid on and in consideration of the grant of the subordinate interest.

(3) If any value given instead of any rent payable by the person entitled to the subordinate interest is less than the commercial amount, capital value is attributable under subsection (1)(b) as if the commercial amount had been paid.

(4) If—

(a) any rent payable in respect of the subordinate interest is assigned, but

(b) no value is given in consideration of the assignment or any value so given is less than the commercial amount,

capital value is attributable under subsection (1)(c) as if the commercial amount had been given on and in consideration of the assignment.

(5) If—

(a) the subordinate interest is surrendered, or any of the terms on which the subordinate interest was granted are varied or waived, but

(b) no value is given in consideration of the surrender, variation or waiver or any value so given is less than the commercial amount,

capital value is attributable under subsection (1)(d) as if the commercial amount had been given on and in consideration of the surrender, variation or waiver.

(6) Capital value is not attributable to the subordinate interest if it is paid in consideration of the grant of a lease to which an election under section 290 (treating grant of lease exceeding 50 years as sale) applies.

330 Exception for payments more than 7 years after agreement

(1) Capital value is not realised for the purposes of section 328 if the payment is made more than 7 years after—

(a) the agreement under which the qualifying expenditure was incurred was entered into, or

(b) if that agreement was conditional, the time when the agreement became unconditional.

(2) If an agreement is made to pay in respect of any event an amount of capital value which would be attributable to the subordinate interest, and—

(a) the agreement is made, or if conditional becomes unconditional, before the end of the period of 7 years referred to in subsection (1), and

(b) the event occurs, or any payment in consideration of the event is made, after the end of that period,

the event or payment is treated for the purposes of subsection (1) as occurring or made before the end of the 7 years.

(3) Subsection (1) does not apply if arrangements—

(a) under which the person entitled to the relevant interest acquired it, or

(b) which were made in connection with its acquisition,

include provision which requires, or makes substantially more likely, any of the events set out in subsection (4).

(4) The events are—

(a) the subsequent sale of the relevant interest;

(b) the subsequent grant of an interest in land out of the relevant interest;

(c) any other event on which capital value attributable to the subordinate interest would be paid or treated as paid.

331 Capital value provisions: interpretation

(1) "Capital value" means any capital sum—

(a) including what would have been a capital sum if it had been a money payment (and references to payment are to be read accordingly), but

(b) excluding so much of any sum as corresponds to [F7—

(i)   ] [F8, or

(ii) an amount brought into account as a receipt in calculating the profits of a UK property business under sections 277 to 281 of ITTOIA 2005 that is calculated by reference to the sum.] an amount of rent or profits calculated by reference to that sum under section 34 of ICTA (premiums etc. treated as rent).

(2) "Interest in land" means—

(a) a leasehold estate in the land, whether in the nature of a head lease, sub-lease or under-lease;

(b) an easement or servitude;

(c) a licence to occupy land.

(3) References to granting an interest in land include agreeing to grant any such interest.

(4) In section 329—

"commercial amount" means the amount that would have been given if the transaction had been at arm's length,

"commercial premium" means the premium that would have been given if the transaction had been at arm's length, and

"commercial rent" means such rent as may reasonably be expected to have been required in respect of the subordinate interest (having regard to any premium paid in consideration of the grant of the interest) if the transaction had been at arm's length.

(5) In the application of section 329 to Scotland, references to assignment are to be read as references to assignation.

Amendments (Textual)

F7. Word in s. 331. (1)(b) inserted (with effect in accordance with s. 883. (1) of the amending Act)by Income Tax (Trading and Other Income) Act 2005 (c. 5), Sch. 1 para. 554. (a) (with Sch. 2)

F8. S. 331. (1)(b)(ii) and word inserted (with effect in accordance with s. 883. (1) of the amending Act) by Income Tax (Trading and Other Income) Act 2005 (c. 5), Sch. 1 para. 554. (b) (with Sch. 2)

Chapter 8. Writing off qualifying expenditure

Modifications etc. (not altering text)

C9 Pt. 3 Ch. 8 applied (5.10.2004) by Energy Act 2004 (c. 20) , s. 198. (2) , Sch. 4 para. 6 ; S.I. 2004/2575 , art. 2. (1) , Sch. 1

332 Introduction

For the purposes of this Part qualifying expenditure is written off to the extent and at the times specified in this Chapter.

333 Writing off initial allowances

If an initial allowance is made in respect of the qualifying expenditure, the amount of the allowance is written off at the time when the building is first used.

334 Writing off writing-down allowances

(1) If a writing-down allowance is made in respect of the qualifying expenditure, the amount of the allowance is written off at the end of the chargeable period for which the allowance is made.
(2) If a balancing event occurs at the end of the chargeable period referred to in subsection (1), the amount written off under that subsection is to be taken into account in calculating the residue of qualifying expenditure immediately before the event to determine what balancing adjustment (if any) is to be made.

335 Writing off research and development allowances

(1) If an allowance under Part 6 (research and development allowances) is made in respect of the qualifying expenditure, the amount of the allowance is written off at the end of the chargeable period for which the allowance is made.
(2) If a balancing event occurs at the end of the chargeable period referred to in subsection (1), the amount written off under that subsection is to be taken into account in calculating the residue of qualifying expenditure immediately before that event to determine what balancing adjustment (if any) is to be made.

336 Writing off expenditure when building not an industrial building

(1) This section applies if for any period or periods between—
    (a) the time when the building was first used for any purpose, and
    (b) the time when the residue of qualifying expenditure falls to be ascertained,
the building was not an industrial building.
(2) An amount equal to the notional writing-down allowances for the period or periods is written off at the time when the residue falls to be ascertained.
(3) The notional writing-down allowances are the allowances that would have been made for the period or periods in question (if the building had remained an industrial building), at such rate or rates as would have been appropriate having regard to any relevant sale.
(4) In subsection (3) "relevant sale" means a sale of the relevant interest as a result of which a balancing adjustment falls to be made under section 314.

337 Writing off or increase of expenditure where balancing adjustment made

(1) This section applies if the relevant interest in the building is sold.
(2) If a balancing allowance is made, the amount by which the residue of qualifying expenditure before the sale exceeds the net proceeds of the sale is written off at the time of the sale.
(3) If a balancing charge is made, the amount of the residue of qualifying expenditure is increased at the time of the sale by the amount of the charge.
(4) But if the balancing charge is made under section 319. (6) (difference between net allowances made and adjusted net cost), the residue of qualifying expenditure immediately after the sale is limited to the net proceeds of the sale.

338 Writing off capital value which has been realised

If a balancing event within section 328 occurs (realisation of capital value), an amount equal to any capital value realised is written off at the time of the event.

339 Crown or other person not within the charge to tax entitled to the relevant interest

(1) This section applies if at any time—
   (a) the Crown, or
   (b) a person who is not within the charge to tax,
("A") is entitled to the relevant interest in a building.
(2) Sections 333 to 338 (writing off qualifying expenditure) have effect as if all writing-down allowances and balancing adjustments had been made as could have been made if—
   (a) a person ("B") who—
(i) is not the Crown,
(ii) is within the charge to tax, and
(iii) is not a company,
had been entitled to the relevant interest, and
   (b) the other assumptions in subsection (3) had been made.
(3) The assumptions are that—
   (a) while A was entitled to the relevant interest, all things which were done in relation to the building—
(i) by or to A, or
(ii) by or to a person using the building under the authority of A,
were done by or to B for the purposes of, and in the course of, a trade carried on by B,
   (b) any sale of the relevant interest in the building by or on behalf of A was made in connection with the termination of the trade carried on by B, and
   (c) B's periods of account for that trade had, in the case of each tax year, ended immediately before the beginning of the next tax year.

340 Treatment of demolition costs

(1) This section applies if—
   (a) a building is demolished, and
   (b) the person to or on whom any balancing allowance or balancing charge is or might be made is the person incurring the cost of the demolition.
(2) The net cost of the demolition is added to the residue of qualifying expenditure immediately before the demolition.
(3) "The net cost of the demolition" means the amount, if any, by which the cost of the demolition exceeds any money received for the remains of the property.
(4) If this section applies, neither the cost of the demolition nor the net cost of the demolition is treated for the purposes of any Part of this Act other than Part 10 (assured tenancy allowances) as expenditure on any other property replacing the property demolished.

Chapter 9. Highway undertakings

341 Carrying on of highway undertakings

(1) For the purposes of this Part the carrying on of a highway undertaking is to be treated as the carrying on of an undertaking by way of trade; and accordingly references in this Part (except

sections 274 and 276) to a trade include a highway undertaking.

(2) For the purposes of this Part a person carrying on a highway undertaking is to be treated as occupying, for the purposes of the undertaking, any road in relation to which it is carried on.

(3) In this Chapter "highway undertaking" has the meaning given in item 6 of Table B in section 274.

(4) In that item and this Chapter "highway concession", in relation to a road, means—

(a) a right to receive sums from [F9the relevant authority] because the road is or will be used by the general public, or

(b) if the road is a toll road, the right to charge tolls in respect of the road.

[F10. (5) In subsection (4) " the relevant authority " means—

(a) the Secretary of State,

(b) the Scottish Ministers,

(c) the National Assembly for Wales, or

(d) the Department for Regional Development in Northern Ireland.]

Amendments (Textual)

F9. Words in s. 341. (4) substituted (with effect as mentioned in s. 69. (2) of the amending Act) by Finance Act 2001 (c. 9), s. 69. (1), Sch. 21 para. 6. (1)

F10. S. 341. (5) inserted (with effect as mentioned in s. 69. (2) of the amending Act) by Finance Act 2001 (c. 9), s. 69. (1), Sch. 21 para. 6. (2)

342 The relevant interest

(1) For the purposes of Chapter 3 (the relevant interest in the building) as it applies to expenditure incurred on the construction of a road, a highway concession is not to be treated as an interest in the road.

(2) But if the person who incurred the expenditure on the construction of the road—

(a) was not entitled to an interest in the road when he incurred the expenditure, but

(b) was at that time entitled to a highway concession in respect of the road,

the highway concession is to be treated as the relevant interest in relation to that expenditure.

(3) Any question as to what is the relevant interest is to be determined on the assumption that, if section 344 (renewed or new concession treated as extension of earlier concession) applies, the renewed or new concession is a continuation of the earlier concession.

343 Balancing adjustment on ending of concession

(1) If—

(a) the relevant interest is a highway concession, and

(b) the concession is brought to or comes to an end without being treated as extended under section 344,

the ending of the concession is a balancing event.

(2) The proceeds from such a balancing event are—

(a) any insurance money received by the person entitled to the highway concession in respect of any qualifying expenditure, and

(b) other compensation so received so far as it consists of capital sums.

344 Cases where highway concession is to be treated as extended

(1) A highway concession in respect of a road is to be treated as extended if—

(a) the person entitled to the concession takes up a renewed concession in respect of the whole or a part of the road, or

(b) that person or a person connected with him takes up a new concession in respect of—

(i) the whole or a part of the road, or

(ii) a road that includes the whole or a part of the road.

(2) But the concession is to be treated as extended only—

(a) to the extent that the concession which has in fact ended, and the renewed or new concession, relate to the same road, and

(b) for the period of the renewed or new concession.

(3) A person takes up a renewed or new concession if he is afforded, whether or not under legally enforceable arrangements, an opportunity to be granted the renewed or new concession and takes advantage of the opportunity.

(4) For the purposes of subsection (3) it does not matter whether the renewed or new concession is on the same terms as the previous concession or on modified terms.

(5) If—

(a) a highway concession is treated as extended under this section, and

(b) the period of the extension is different in relation to different parts of the road in relation to which the concession has been granted,

such apportionments are to be made for the purposes of section 343 as are just and reasonable.

Chapter 10. Additional VAT liabilities and rebates

345 Introduction

For the purposes of this Chapter—

(a) "additional VAT liability" and "additional VAT rebate" have the meaning given by section 547,

(b) the time when—

(i) a person incurs an additional VAT liability, or

(ii) an additional VAT rebate is made to a person,

is given by section 548, and

(c) the chargeable period in which, and the time when, an additional VAT liability or an additional VAT rebate accrues are given by section 549.

Additional VAT liabilities

346 Additional VAT liabilities and initial allowances

(1) This section applies if—

(a) a person was entitled to an initial allowance in respect of qualifying enterprise zone expenditure,

(b) the person entitled to the relevant interest in relation to that expenditure incurs an additional VAT liability in respect of that expenditure,

(c) the additional VAT liability is incurred at a time when the building is, or is to be, an industrial building—

(i) occupied by the person entitled to the relevant interest or a qualifying lessee, or

(ii) used by a qualifying licensee, and

(d) the additional VAT liability is incurred not more than 10 years after the site of the building was first included in the enterprise zone.

(2) If this section applies, the person entitled to the relevant interest is entitled to an initial allowance on the amount of the additional VAT liability.

(3) The amount of the initial allowance is 100% of the amount of the additional VAT liability.

(4) A person claiming an initial allowance under this section may require the allowance to be reduced to a specified amount.

(5) The allowance is made for the chargeable period in which the additional VAT liability accrues.

(6) The persons mentioned in subsection (1)(a) and (b) need not be the same.

347 Additional VAT liabilities and writing-down allowances

(1) This section applies if the person entitled to the relevant interest in relation to qualifying expenditure incurs an additional VAT liability in respect of that expenditure.

(2) If this section applies—

(a) the additional VAT liability is treated as qualifying expenditure, and

(b) the amount of the residue of qualifying expenditure is accordingly increased at the time when the liability accrues by the amount of the liability.

(3) The incurring of the additional VAT liability is a relevant event for the purposes of section 311 (calculation of writing-down allowances) that is to be treated as occurring at the time when the liability accrues.

348 Additional VAT liabilities and writing off initial allowances

If an initial allowance is made in respect of an additional VAT liability incurred after the building is first used, the amount of the allowance is written off at the time when the liability accrues.

Additional VAT rebates

349 Additional VAT rebates and writing-down allowances

(1) This section applies if—

(a) an additional VAT rebate is made in respect of qualifying expenditure to the person entitled to the relevant interest in relation to that qualifying expenditure, and

(b) immediately before the rebate accrues, the residue of that qualifying expenditure is equal to, or greater than, the amount of the rebate.

(2) The making of the additional VAT rebate is a relevant event for the purposes of section 311 (calculation of writing-down allowances) that is to be treated as occurring at the time when the rebate accrues.

350 Additional VAT rebates and balancing adjustments

(1) If an additional VAT rebate is made in respect of qualifying expenditure to the person entitled to the relevant interest in relation to that qualifying expenditure—

(a) the making of the rebate is a balancing event for the purposes of this Part, but

(b) the making of balancing adjustments as a result of the event is subject to subsections (2) and (3).

(2) No balancing allowance is to be made as a result of the event.

(3) A balancing charge is not to be made as a result of the event unless—

(a) the amount of the additional VAT rebate is more than the amount of the residue of qualifying expenditure immediately before the time when the rebate accrues, or

(b) there is no such residue.

(4) The amount of the balancing charge is—

(a) the amount of the difference, or

(b) the amount of the rebate (if there is no residue).

(5) If a balancing charge is made under this section, the starting expenditure is reduced by the amount of that charge in a case where section 322. (2) applies (person subject to balancing adjustment is the person who incurred the qualifying expenditure).

351 Additional VAT rebates and writing off qualifying expenditure

If an additional VAT rebate is made in respect of qualifying expenditure, an amount equal to the rebate is written off at the time when the rebate accrues.

Chapter 11. Giving effect to allowances and charges

352 Trades

(1) An allowance or charge to which a person is entitled or liable under this Part is to be given

effect in calculating the profits of that person's trade, by treating—

(a) the allowance as an expense of the trade, and

(b) the charge as a receipt of the trade.

(2) In the case of a person who—

(a) is entitled to an allowance or liable to a charge in respect of a commercial building, and

(b) occupies the building in the course of a profession or vocation,

the references in subsection (1) to a trade are to be read as references to the profession or vocation.

(3) Subsection (1) is subject to the following provisions of this Chapter.

353 Lessors and licensors

(1) This section applies if—

(a) a person is entitled or liable to an allowance or charge for a chargeable period ("the relevant period"), but

(b) his interest in the building in question is or was subject to a lease or a licence at the relevant time.

(2) If the person's interest in the building is an asset of [F11a UK property business, or a Schedule A business,] carried on by him at any time in the relevant period, the allowance or charge is to be given effect in calculating the profits of that business for the relevant period, by treating—

(a) the allowance as an expense of that business, and

(b) the charge as a receipt of that business.

(3) If the person's interest in the building is an asset of an overseas property business carried on by him at any time in the relevant period, the allowance or charge is to be given effect in calculating the profits of the overseas property business for the relevant period, by treating—

(a) the allowance as an expense of that business, and

(b) the charge as a receipt of that business.

[F12. (3. A) If the person is within the charge to income tax in respect of the allowance or charge and his interest in the building is not an asset of any property business carried on by him at any time in the relevant period, the allowance or charge is to be given effect by treating him as if he had been carrying on a UK property business in that period and as if—

(a) the allowance were an expense of that business, and

(b) the charge were a receipt of that business.]

(4) If [F13the person is a company within the charge to corporation tax in respect of the allowance or charge and its] interest in the building is not an asset of any property business carried on by [F14it] at any time in the relevant period, the allowance or charge is to be given effect by treating [F15the company] as if [F16it] had been carrying on a Schedule A business in that period and as if—

(a) the allowance were an expense of that business, and

(b) the charge were a receipt of that business.

(5) In subsection (1) "the relevant time" means—

(a) in relation to an initial allowance, the time when the expenditure was incurred or any subsequent time before the building is used for any purpose;

(b) in relation to a writing-down allowance, the end of the relevant period;

(c) in relation to a balancing allowance or balancing charge, the time immediately before the event giving rise to the allowance or charge.

Amendments (Textual)

F11. Words in s. 353. (2) substituted (with effect in accordance with s. 883. (1) of the amending Act) by Income Tax (Trading and Other Income) Act 2005 (c. 5), Sch. 1 para. 555. (2) (with Sch. 2)

F12. S. 353. (3. A) inserted (with effect in accordance with s. 883. (1) of the amending Act) by Income Tax (Trading and Other Income) Act 2005 (c. 5), Sch. 1 para. 555. (3) (with Sch. 2)

F13. Words in s. 353. (4) substituted (with effect in accordance with s. 883. (1) of the amending

Act) by Income Tax (Trading and Other Income) Act 2005 (c. 5), Sch. 1 para. 555. (4)(a) (with Sch. 2)

F14. Word in s. 353. (4) substituted (with effect in accordance with s. 883. (1) of the amending Act) by Income Tax (Trading and Other Income) Act 2005 (c. 5), Sch. 1 para. 555. (4)(b) (with Sch. 2)

F15. Words in s. 353. (4) substituted (with effect in accordance with s. 883. (1) of the amending Act) by Income Tax (Trading and Other Income) Act 2005 (c. 5), Sch. 1 para. 555. (4)(c) (with Sch. 2)

F16. Word in s. 353. (4) substituted (with effect in accordance with s. 883. (1) of the amending Act) by Income Tax (Trading and Other Income) Act 2005 (c. 5), Sch. 1 para. 555. (4)(d) (with Sch. 2)

354 Buildings temporarily out of use

(1) This section applies if a person is entitled to an allowance or liable to a charge for a chargeable period during which the building is treated as an industrial building under section 285 (building still industrial building despite temporary disuse).

(2) If, when the building was last in use as an industrial building—

(a) it was in use for the purposes of a trade which has since been permanently discontinued, or

(b) the relevant interest in the building was subject to a lease or a licence which has since come to an end,

section 353. (4) applies to the person as if the relevant interest were subject to a lease or licence at the relevant time.

(3) If—

(a) the person is liable to a balancing charge, and

(b) when the building was last in use as an industrial building, it was in use as an industrial building for the purposes of a trade which was carried on by the person but which has since been permanently discontinued,

the same deductions may be made from the amount of the balancing charge as may be made under [F17section 254 of ITTOIA 2005 or] section 105 of ICTA (deductions allowed in case of post-cessation receipts) from an amount chargeable to tax under [F18. Chapter 18 of Part 2 of ITTOIA 2005 or, as the case may be, under] section 103 or 104. (1) of ICTA.

(4) Subsection (3) does not affect the making of any deduction allowed under any other provision of the Tax Acts.

(5) For the purposes of this section the permanent discontinuance of a trade does not include an event treated as a permanent discontinuance under [F19section 18 of ITTOIA 2005 or section 337. (1) of ICTA (effect of company ceasing to trade etc).]

(6) In this section "trade", in relation to a commercial building, includes a profession or vocation.

Amendments (Textual)

F17 Words in s. 354. (3) inserted (6.4.2005) by Income Tax (Trading and Other Income) Act 2005 (c. 5) , s. 883. (1) , Sch. 1 para. 556. (2)(a) (with Sch. 2)

F18 Words in s. 354. (3) inserted (6.4.2005) by Income Tax (Trading and Other Income) Act 2005 (c. 5) , s. 883. (1) , Sch. 1 para. 556. (2)(b) (with Sch. 2)

F19 Words in s. 354. (5) substituted (6.4.2005) by Income Tax (Trading and Other Income) Act 2005 (c. 5) , s. 883. (1) , Sch. 1 para. 556. (3) (with Sch. 2)

355 Buildings for miners etc.: carry-back of balancing allowances

(1) This section applies if—

(a) a trade consists of or includes the working of a source of mineral deposits (within the meaning of item 7 of Table A in section 274),

(b) a balancing allowance falls to be made under this Part for the last chargeable period in which the trade is carried on,

(c) the event giving rise to the allowance is—

(i) the source of mineral deposits ceasing to be worked, or

(ii) the coming to an end of a foreign concession,

(d) the allowance is made for expenditure on a building which was constructed for occupation by, or for the welfare of, persons employed at or in connection with the working of the source of mineral deposits, and

(e) full effect cannot be given to the allowance because there are insufficient profits for that chargeable period.

(2) If this section applies, the person entitled to the allowance may claim that the balance of the allowance is to be given for the last preceding chargeable period, and so on for other preceding chargeable periods.

[F20. (2. A)For income tax purposes the allowance is given effect at Step 2 of the calculation in section 23 of ITA 2007.]

(3) But allowances are not to be given under subsection (2) for chargeable periods amounting in total to more than 5 years; but a proportionately reduced allowance may be given for a chargeable period of which part is required to make up the 5 years.

(4) In counting the 5 years, include any period for which an allowance might be made but cannot be given effect because there are insufficient profits.

(5) If this section applies to a company, no allowance may be given under this section so as to create or increase a loss in any accounting period.

(6) If this section applies to a company and a claim is made both under this section and under section 393. A(1) of ICTA (relief for company trading losses)—

(a) effect is to be given to the claim under that section before this section is applied, and

(b) for the purposes of giving effect to the claim under that section, the allowance for which the claim under this section is made is to be disregarded.

Amendments (Textual)

F20. S. 355. (2. A) inserted (6.4.2007) by Income Tax Act 2007 (c. 3), s. 1034. (1), Sch. 1 para. 406 (with Sch. 2)

Chapter 12. Supplementary provisions

356 Apportionment of sums partly referable to non-qualifying assets

(1) If the sum paid for the sale of the relevant interest in a building is attributable—

(a) partly to assets representing expenditure for which an allowance can be made under this Part, and

(b) partly to assets representing other expenditure,

only so much of the sum as on a just and reasonable apportionment is attributable to the assets referred to in paragraph (a) is to be taken into account for the purposes of this Part.

(2) Subsection (1) applies to other proceeds from a balancing event in respect of a building as it applies to a sum given for the sale of the relevant interest in the building.

(3) Subsection (1) does not affect any other provision of this Act requiring an apportionment of the proceeds of a balancing event.

357 Arrangements having an artificial effect on pricing

(1) If—

(a) the relevant interest in a building is sold,

(b) related arrangements have been entered into, at or before the time when the sale price is fixed, which had the effect at that time of enhancing the value of the relevant interest, and

(c) the arrangements contain a provision which has an artificial effect on pricing (see subsection (4)),

the sum paid on the sale of the relevant interest is to be treated for the purposes of arriving at qualifying expenditure as reduced to what it would have been if the arrangements had not contained the provision having that artificial effect.

(2) If—

(a) qualifying expenditure is equal to a price paid on a sale of the relevant interest in a building,

(b) related arrangements have been entered into, at or before the time when the sale price is fixed, which had the effect at that time of enhancing the value of the relevant interest, and

(c) the arrangements contain a provision which has an artificial effect on pricing,

the proceeds from any balancing event subsequently occurring in relation to the building are to be treated for the purposes of this Part as reduced to what they would have been if the arrangements had not contained the provision having that artificial effect.

(3) "Related arrangements" means arrangements between two or more persons which relate—

(a) to an interest in or right over the building, or

(b) to other arrangements made with respect to such an interest or right;

and for this purpose it is immaterial whether the interest or right in question is granted by the person entitled to the relevant interest or another person.

(4) Arrangements contain a provision having an artificial effect on pricing to the extent that they go beyond what could reasonably have been regarded as required in comparable commercial transactions by the market conditions prevailing when the arrangements were entered into.

(5) "Comparable commercial transactions" means transactions—

(a) involving interests in or rights over buildings of the same kind as (or of a similar kind to) the building to which the arrangements relate, and

(b) made by persons dealing with each other at arm's length in the open market.

358 Requisitioned land

(1) This section applies in relation to any period ("period of requisition") for which compensation—

(a) is payable, or

(b) but for any agreement would be payable,

under section 2. (1)(a) of the Compensation (Defence) Act 1939 (c. 75).

(2) This Part has effect in relation to the period of requisition as if the Crown had been in possession of the land for that period under a lease.

(3) If a person carrying on a trade is authorised by the Crown to occupy the land (or part of it) during the whole or a part of the period of requisition, this Part has effect as if the Crown had granted a sub-lease of the land (or that part of it) to the occupier.

(4) If subsection (2) or (3) applies, references in this Part to—

(a) the surrender of a leasehold interest,

(b) a leasehold interest being extinguished on the person entitled to it acquiring the interest which is reversionary on it, or

(c) the merger of a leasehold interest,

apply (with the necessary modifications) in relation to the lease under subsection (2) or the sub-lease under subsection (3).

(5) If the person who (subject to the rights of the Crown) is entitled to possession of the land pays any sum to—

(a) the Crown, or

(b) if subsection (3) applies, the occupier,

in respect of a building constructed on the land during the period of requisition, the sum is to be treated for the purposes of this Part as paid in consideration of the surrender of the lease or sub-lease (as the case may be).

359 Provisions applying on termination of lease

(1) This section applies for the purposes of this Part if a lease is terminated.

(2) If, with the consent of the lessor, the lessee of a building remains in possession of the building after the termination without a new lease being granted to him the lease is treated as continuing so long as the lessee remains in possession.

(3) If on the termination a new lease is granted to the lessee as a result of the exercise of an option available to him under the terms of the first lease, the second lease is treated as a continuation of the first.

(4) If on the termination the lessor pays a sum to the lessee in respect of a building comprised in the lease, the lease is treated as if it had come to an end by surrender in consideration of the payment.

(5) If on the termination—

(a) another lease is granted to a different lessee, and

(b) in connection with the transaction that lessee pays a sum to the person who was the lessee under the first lease,

the two leases are to be treated as if they were the same lease which had been assigned by the lessee under the first lease to the lessee under the second lease in consideration of the payment.

360 Meaning of "lease" etc.

(1) In this Part "lease" includes—

(a) an agreement for a lease if the term to be covered by the lease has begun, and

(b) any tenancy,

but does not include a mortgage (and "lessee", "lessor" and "leasehold interest" are to be read accordingly).

(2) In the application of this Part to Scotland—

(a) "leasehold interest" (or "leasehold estate") means the interest of a tenant in property subject to a lease, and

(b) any reference to an interest which is reversionary on a leasehold interest or on a lease is to be read as a reference to the interest of the landlord in the property subject to the leasehold interest or lease.

Part of expenditure within time limit for qualifying enterprise zone expenditure

302 Qualifying enterprise zone expenditure where section 295 or 296 applies

(1) This section applies if—

(a) expenditure is incurred on the construction of an EZ building,

(b) only a part of the expenditure is incurred within the time limit, and

(c) the circumstances are as described in—

(i) section 295. (1) (purchase of unused building where developer not involved), or

(ii) section 296. (1) (purchase of building which has been sold unused by developer).

(2) Only a part of the qualifying expenditure given by section 295. (2) or 296. (2) or (3) (as the case may be) is qualifying enterprise zone expenditure.

(3) The part of the qualifying expenditure that is qualifying enterprise zone expenditure is— where—

QE is the qualifying expenditure,

E is the part of the expenditure on the construction of the EZ building that is incurred within the time limit, and

T is the total expenditure on the construction of the building.

303 Purchase of building within 2 years of first use

(1) This section applies if—

    (a) expenditure is incurred on the construction of an EZ building,

    (b) only a part of the expenditure is incurred within the time limit,

    (c) the relevant interest in the building is sold—

(i) after the building has been used, but

(ii) within the period of 2 years beginning with the date on which the building was first used, and

    (d) that sale ("the relevant sale") is the first sale in that period after the building has been used.

(2) If this section applies—

    (a) any balancing adjustment which falls to be made on the occasion of the relevant sale is to be made, and

    (b) the residue of qualifying expenditure immediately after the relevant sale is to be disregarded for the purposes of this Part.

(3) If a capital sum is paid by the purchaser for the relevant interest on the relevant sale—

    (a) the purchaser is to be treated as having incurred qualifying expenditure—

(i) part of which is qualifying enterprise zone expenditure ("Z"), and

(ii) part of which is not ("N"), and

    (b) in relation to that qualifying expenditure, this Part applies as if the building had not been used before the date of the relevant sale.

(4) Unless section 304 (cases where developer involved) applies—

and

L is the lesser of—

(a) the capital sum paid for the relevant interest on the relevant sale, and

(b) the expenditure incurred on the construction of the building,

E is the part of the expenditure on the construction of the EZ building that is incurred within the time limit, and

T is the total expenditure on the construction of the building.

(5) Any qualifying expenditure arising under this section or section 304 is to be treated as incurred when the capital sum on the relevant sale became payable.

304 Application of section 303 where developer involved

(1) This section applies if section 303 applies but—

    (a) the expenditure on the construction of the building was incurred by a developer, and

    (b) the relevant interest in the building has been sold by the developer in the course of the development trade;

and in this section Z, N, E and T have the same meaning as in section 303.

(2) If the sale by the developer is the relevant sale—

and

where—

C is the capital sum paid for the relevant interest by the purchaser, and

L is the lesser of—

(a) the capital sum paid for the relevant interest on the relevant sale, and

(b) the expenditure incurred on the construction of the building.

(3) If the sale by the developer is not the relevant sale—

and

where D is the lesser of—

(a) the price paid for the relevant interest on its sale by the developer, and

(b) the capital sum paid for the relevant interest on the relevant sale.

Part 3A Business Premises Renovation Allowances

[F1. Part 3. ABusiness Premises Renovation Allowances

Amendments (Textual)
F1. Pt. 3. A inserted (11.4.2007 with effect in accordance with s. 92 of the amending Act) by Finance Act 2005 (c. 7), Sch. 6 para. 1; S.I. 2007/949, art. 2

Chapter 1. INTRODUCTION

360. ABusiness premises renovation allowances

(1) Allowances are available under this Part if a person incurs qualifying expenditure in respect of a qualifying building.
(2) Allowances under this Part are made to the person who—
    (a) incurred the expenditure, and
    (b) has the relevant interest in the qualifying building.

Chapter 2. QUALIFYING EXPENDITURE

360. BMeaning of "qualifying expenditure"

(1) In this Part " qualifying expenditure " means capital expenditure incurred before the expiry date on, or in connection with—
    (a) the conversion of a qualifying building into qualifying business premises,
    (b) the renovation of a qualifying building if it is or will be qualifying business premises, or
    (c) repairs to a qualifying building or, where the qualifying building is part of a building, to the building of which the qualifying building forms part, to the extent that the repairs are incidental to expenditure within paragraph (a) or (b).
(2) In subsection (1) " the expiry date " means—
    (a) the fifth anniversary of the day appointed under section 92 of the Finance Act 2005, or
    (b) such later date as the Treasury may prescribe by regulations.
(3) Expenditure is not qualifying expenditure if it is incurred on or in connection with—
    (a) the acquisition of land or rights in or over land,
    (b) the extension of a qualifying building (except to the extent required for the purpose of providing a means of getting to or from qualifying business premises),
    (c) the development of land adjoining or adjacent to a qualifying building, or
    (d) the provision of plant and machinery, other than plant or machinery which is or becomes a fixture as defined by section 173. (1).
(4) For the purposes of this section, expenditure incurred on repairs to a building is to be treated as capital expenditure if it is not expenditure that would be allowed to be deducted in calculating the profits of a property business, or of a trade, profession or vocation, for tax purposes.
(5) The Treasury may by regulations make further provision as to expenditure which is, or is not, qualifying expenditure.

Chapter 3. QUALIFYING BUILDINGS AND QUALIFYING

BUSINESS PREMISES

360. CMeaning of "qualifying building"

(1) In this Part " qualifying building ", in relation to any conversion or renovation work, means any building or structure, or part of a building or structure, which—

(a) is situated in an area which, on the date on which the conversion or renovation work began, was a disadvantaged area,

(b) was unused throughout the period of one year ending immediately before that date,

(c) on that date, had last been used—

(i) for the purposes of a trade, profession or vocation, or

(ii) as an office or offices (whether or not for the purposes of a trade, profession or vocation),

(d) on that date, had not last been used as, or as part of, a dwelling, and

(e) in the case of part of a building or structure, on that date had not last been occupied and used in common with any other part of the building or structure other than a part—

(i) as respects which the condition in paragraph (b) is met, or

(ii) which had last been used as a dwelling.

(2) In this section " disadvantaged area " means—

(a) an area designated as a disadvantaged area for the purposes of this section by regulations made by the Treasury, or

(b) if no regulations are made under paragraph (a), an area for the time being designated as a disadvantaged area for the purposes of Schedule 6 to the Finance Act 2003 (stamp duty land tax: disadvantaged areas relief).

(3) Regulations under subsection (2)(a) may—

(a) designate specified areas as disadvantaged areas, or

(b) provide for areas of a description specified in the regulations to be designated as disadvantaged areas.

(4) If regulations under subsection (2)(a) so provide, the designation of an area as a disadvantaged area shall have effect for such period as may be specified in or determined in accordance with the regulations.

(5) Regulations under subsection (2)(a) may—

(a) make different provision for different cases, and

(b) contain such incidental, supplementary, consequential or transitional provision as appears to the Treasury to be necessary or expedient.

(6) Where a building or structure (or part of a building or structure) which would otherwise be a qualifying building is on the date mentioned in subsection (1)(a) situated partly in a disadvantaged area and partly outside it, only so much of the expenditure incurred in accordance with section 360. B as, on a just and reasonable apportionment, is attributable to the part of the building or structure located in the disadvantaged area is to be treated as qualifying expenditure.

(7) The Treasury may by regulations make further provision as to the circumstances in which a building or structure or part of a building or structure is, or is not, a qualifying building.

360. DMeaning of "qualifying business premises"

(1) In this Part " qualifying business premises " means any premises in respect of which the following requirements are met—

(a) the premises must be a qualifying building,

(b) the premises must be used, or available and suitable for letting for use,—

(i) for the purposes of a trade, profession or vocation, or

(ii) as an office or offices (whether or not for the purposes of a trade, profession or vocation),

(c) the premises must not be used, or available for use as, or as part of, a dwelling.

(2) In this section " premises " means any building or structure or part of a building or structure.

(3) For the purposes of this Part, if premises are qualifying business premises immediately before a period when they are temporarily unsuitable for use for the purposes mentioned in subsection (1)(b), they are to be treated as being qualifying business premises during that period.

(4) The Treasury may by regulations make further provision as to the circumstances in which premises are, or are not, qualifying business premises.

Chapter 4. THE RELEVANT INTEREST IN THE QUALIFYING BUILDING

360. EGeneral rule as to what is the relevant interest

(1) The relevant interest in a qualifying building in relation to any qualifying expenditure is the interest in the qualifying building to which the person who incurred the qualifying expenditure was entitled when it was incurred.

(2) Subsection (1) is subject to the following provisions of this Chapter and to section 360. Z3 (provisions applying on termination of lease).

(3) If—

(a) the person who incurred the qualifying expenditure was entitled to more than one interest in the qualifying building when the expenditure was incurred, and

(b) one of those interests was reversionary on all the others,

the reversionary interest is the relevant interest in the qualifying building.

(4) An interest does not cease to be the relevant interest merely because of the creation of a lease or other interest to which that interest is subject.

(5) If—

(a) the relevant interest is a leasehold interest, and

(b) that interest is extinguished on the person entitled to it acquiring the interest which is reversionary on it,

the interest into which the leasehold interest merges becomes the relevant interest when the leasehold interest is extinguished.

360. FInterest acquired on completion of conversion

For the purposes of determining the relevant interest in a qualifying building, a person who—

(a) incurs expenditure on the conversion of a qualifying building into qualifying business premises, and

(b) is entitled to an interest in the qualifying building on or as a result of the completion of the conversion,

is treated as having had that interest when the expenditure was incurred.

Chapter 5. INITIAL ALLOWANCES

360. GInitial allowances

(1) A person who has incurred qualifying expenditure in respect of any qualifying building is entitled to an initial allowance in respect of the expenditure.

(2) The amount of the initial allowance is 100% of the qualifying expenditure.

(3) A person claiming an initial allowance under this section may require the allowance to be reduced to a specified amount.

(4) The initial allowance is made for the chargeable period in which the qualifying expenditure is incurred.

360. HPremises not qualifying business premises or relevant interest sold before premises first used or let

(1) No initial allowance is to be made under section 360. G if, at the relevant time, the qualifying building does not constitute qualifying business premises.

(2) An initial allowance which has been made in respect of a qualifying building which is to be qualifying business premises is to be withdrawn if—

(a) the qualifying building does not constitute qualifying business premises at the relevant time, or

(b) the person to whom the allowance was made has sold the relevant interest in the qualifying building before the relevant time.

(3) All such assessments and adjustments of assessments are to be made as are necessary to give effect to this section.

(4) In this section " the relevant time " means the time when the premises are first used by the person with the relevant interest or, if they are not so used, the time when they are first suitable for letting for either of the purposes mentioned in section 360. D(1)(b).

Chapter 6. WRITING-DOWN ALLOWANCES

360. IEntitlement to writing-down allowances

(1) A person is entitled to a writing-down allowance for a chargeable period if he has incurred qualifying expenditure in respect of a qualifying building and, at the end of the chargeable period—

(a) the person is entitled to the relevant interest in the qualifying building,

(b) the person has not granted a long lease of the qualifying building out of the relevant interest in consideration of the payment of a capital sum, and

(c) the qualifying building constitutes qualifying business premises.

(2) In subsection (1)(b) " long lease " means a lease the duration of which exceeds 50 years.

(3) Whether the duration of a lease exceeds 50 years is to be determined—

(a) in accordance with section 303 of ITTOIA 2005, and

(b) without regard to section 360. Z3. (3) of this Act (new lease granted as a result of the exercise of an option treated as continuation of old lease).

(4) A person claiming a writing-down allowance may require the allowance to be reduced to a specified amount.

360. JAmount of allowance

(1) The writing-down allowance for a chargeable period is 25% of the qualifying expenditure.

(2) The allowance is proportionately increased or reduced if the chargeable period is more or less than a year.

(3) The amount of the writing-down allowance for a chargeable period is limited to the residue of qualifying expenditure.

(4) For this purpose the residue is ascertained immediately before writing off the writing-down allowance at the end of the chargeable period.

360. K Meaning of " the residue of qualifying expenditure "

The residue of qualifying expenditure is the qualifying expenditure that has not yet been written off in accordance with Chapter 9.

Chapter 7. GRANTS IN RESPECT OF QUALIFYING EXPENDITURE

360. LGrants affecting entitlement to allowances

(1) No initial allowance or writing-down allowance under this Part is to be made in respect of expenditure to the extent that it is taken into account for the purposes of a relevant grant or relevant payment made towards that expenditure.
(2) A grant or payment is relevant if it is—
    (a) a notified State aid other than an allowance under this Part, or
    (b) a grant or subsidy, other than a notified State aid, which the Treasury by order declares to be relevant for the purposes of the withholding of initial allowances or writing-down allowances.
(3) For the purposes of subsection (2), " notified State aid " means a State aid notified to and approved by the European Commission.
(4) If a relevant grant or relevant payment towards the expenditure is made after the making of an initial allowance or a writing-down allowance, the allowance is to be withdrawn to that extent.
(5) If the amount of the relevant grant or relevant payment is repaid by the grantee to the grantor, in whole or in part, the grant or payment is treated, to that extent, as never having been made.
(6) All such assessments and adjustments of assessments are to be made as are necessary to give effect to subsection (4) or (5).
(7) Any such assessment or adjustment is not out of time if it is made within 3 years of the end of the chargeable period in which the grant, payment or adjustment was made.

Chapter 8. BALANCING ADJUSTMENTS

360. MWhen balancing adjustments are made

(1) A balancing adjustment is made if—
    (a) qualifying expenditure has been incurred in respect of a qualifying building, and
    (b) a balancing event occurs.
(2) A balancing adjustment is either a balancing allowance or a balancing charge and is made for the chargeable period in which the balancing event occurs.
(3) A balancing allowance or balancing charge is made to or on the person who incurred the qualifying expenditure.
(4) No balancing adjustment is made if the balancing event occurs more than 7 years after the time when the premises were first used, or suitable for letting, for either of the purposes mentioned in section 360. D(1)(b).
(5) If more than one balancing event within section 360. N occurs, a balancing adjustment is made only on the first of them.

360. NBalancing events

(1) The following are balancing events for the purposes of this Part—

    (a) the relevant interest in the qualifying building is sold;

    (b) a long lease of the qualifying building is granted out of the relevant interest in consideration of the payment of a capital sum;

    (c) if the relevant interest is a lease, the lease ends otherwise than on the person entitled to it acquiring the interest reversionary on it;

    (d) the person who incurred the qualifying expenditure dies;

    (e) the qualifying building is demolished or destroyed;

    (f) the qualifying building ceases to be qualifying business premises (without being demolished or destroyed).

(2) Section 360. I(2) and (3) (meaning of "long lease") applies for the purposes of subsection (1)(b).

360. OProceeds from balancing events

(1) References in this Part to the proceeds from a balancing event are to the amounts received or receivable in connection with the event, as shown in the Table—

TABLE: BALANCING EVENTS AND PROCEEDS

1 Balancing Event | 2 Proceeds from event |

1 The sale of the relevant interest. | The net proceeds of the sale. |

If the capital sum paid in consideration of the grant is less than the commercial premium, the commercial premium.

In any other case, the capital sum paid in consideration of the grant.

3 The coming to an end of a lease, where a person entitled to the lease and a person entitled to any superior interest are connected persons. | The market value of the relevant interest in the qualifying building at the time of the event. |

4 The death of the person who incurred the qualifying expenditure. | The residue of qualifying expenditure immediately before the death. |

The net amount received for the remains of the qualifying building, together with

    -    any insurance money received in respect of the demolition or destruction, and

    -    any other compensation of any description so received, so far as it consists of capital sums.

6 The qualifying building ceases to be qualifying business premises. | The market value of the relevant interest in the qualifying building at the time of the event. |

(2) The amounts referred to in column 2 of the Table are those received or receivable by the person who incurred the qualifying expenditure.

(3) In Item 2 of the Table " the commercial premium " means the premium that would have been given if the transaction had been at arm's length.

360. PCalculation of balancing adjustments

(1) A balancing allowance is made if—

    (a) there are no proceeds from the balancing event, or

    (b) the proceeds from the balancing event are less than the residue of qualifying expenditure immediately before the event.

(2) The amount of the balancing allowance is the amount of—

    (a) the residue (if there are no proceeds);

    (b) the difference (if the proceeds are less than the residue).

(3) A balancing charge is made if the proceeds from the balancing event are more than the residue, if any, of qualifying expenditure immediately before the event.

(4) The amount of the balancing charge is the amount of—

    (a) the difference, or

    (b) the proceeds (if the residue is nil).

(5) The amount of a balancing charge made on a person must not exceed the total amount of—

(a) any initial allowances made to the person in respect of the expenditure, and

(b) any writing-down allowances made to the person in respect of the expenditure for chargeable periods ending on or before the date of the balancing event giving rise to the balancing adjustment.

Chapter 9. WRITING OFF QUALIFYING EXPENDITURE

360. QIntroduction

For the purposes of this Part qualifying expenditure is written off to the extent and at the times specified in this Chapter.

360. RWriting off initial allowances and writing-down allowances

(1) If an initial allowance is made in respect of the qualifying expenditure, the amount of the allowance is written off at the time when the qualifying business premises are first used, or suitable for letting for use, for either of the purposes mentioned in section 360. D(1)(b).

(2) If a writing-down allowance is made in respect of the qualifying expenditure, the amount of the allowance is written off at the end of the chargeable period for which the allowance is made.

(3) If a balancing event occurs at the end of the chargeable period referred to in subsection (2), the amount written off under that subsection is to be taken into account in calculating the residue of qualifying expenditure immediately before the event to determine what balancing adjustment (if any) is to be made.

360. STreatment of demolition costs

(1) This section applies if—

(a) a qualifying building is demolished, and

(b) the person who incurred the qualifying expenditure incurs the cost of the demolition.

(2) The net cost of the demolition is added to the residue of qualifying expenditure immediately before the demolition.

(3) " The net cost of the demolition " means the amount, if any, by which the cost of the demolition exceeds any money received for the remains of the qualifying building.

(4) If this section applies, neither the cost of the demolition nor the net cost of the demolition is treated for the purposes of any Part of this Act as expenditure on any other property replacing the qualifying building demolished.

Chapter 10. ADDITIONAL VAT LIABILITIES AND REBATES

360. TIntroduction

For the purposes of this Chapter—

(a) " additional VAT liability " and " additional VAT rebate " have the meanings given by section 547,

(b) the time when—

(i) a person incurs an additional VAT liability, or

(ii) an additional VAT rebate is made to a person,

is given by section 548, and

    (c) the chargeable period in which, and the time when, an additional VAT liability or an additional VAT rebate accrues are given by section 549.

360. U Additional VAT liabilities and initial allowances

(1) This section applies if—

    (a) a person was entitled to an initial allowance under this Part in respect of qualifying expenditure on a qualifying building,

    (b) that person incurs an additional VAT liability in respect of that expenditure, and

    (c) the additional VAT liability is incurred at a time when the qualifying building is, or is about to be, qualifying business premises.

(2) If this section applies, the person entitled to the relevant interest is entitled to an initial allowance on the amount of the additional VAT liability.

(3) The amount of the initial allowance is 100% of the amount of the additional VAT liability.

(4) A person claiming an initial allowance under this section may require the allowance to be reduced to a specified amount.

(5) The allowance is made for the chargeable period in which the additional VAT liability accrues.

360. V Additional VAT liabilities and writing-down allowances

(1) This section applies if the person entitled to the relevant interest in relation to qualifying expenditure incurs an additional VAT liability in respect of that expenditure.

(2) If this section applies—

    (a) the additional VAT liability is treated as qualifying expenditure, and

    (b) the amount of the residue of qualifying expenditure is accordingly increased at the time when the liability accrues by the amount of the liability.

360. W Additional VAT liabilities and writing off initial allowances

If an initial allowance is made in respect of an additional VAT liability incurred after the qualifying business premises are first used or suitable for letting for business use, the amount of the allowance is written off at the time when the liability accrues.

360. X Additional VAT rebates and balancing adjustments

(1) If an additional VAT rebate is made in respect of qualifying expenditure to the person entitled to the relevant interest in relation to that qualifying expenditure—

    (a) the making of the rebate is a balancing event for the purposes of this Part, but

    (b) the making of balancing adjustments as a result of the event is subject to subsections (2) and (3).

(2) No balancing allowance is to be made as a result of the event.

(3) A balancing charge is not to be made as a result of the event unless—

    (a) the amount of the additional VAT rebate is more than the amount of the residue of qualifying expenditure immediately before the time when the rebate accrues, or

    (b) there is no such residue.

(4) The amount of the balancing charge is—

    (a) the amount of the difference, or

    (b) the amount of the rebate (if there is no residue).

360. Y Additional VAT rebates and writing off qualifying expenditure

If an additional VAT rebate is made in respect of qualifying expenditure, an amount equal to the rebate is written off at the time when the rebate accrues.

Chapter 11. SUPPLEMENTARY PROVISIONS

360. ZGiving effect to allowances and charges: trades

(1) An allowance or charge to which a person is entitled or liable under this Part is to be given effect in calculating the profits of that person's trade, by treating—
    (a) the allowance as an expense of the trade, and
    (b) the charge as a receipt of the trade.
(2) In the case of a person who—
    (a) is entitled to an allowance or liable to a charge in respect of a qualifying building, and
    (b) occupies that building in the course of a profession or vocation,
the references in subsection (1) to a trade are to be read as references to the profession or vocation.
(3) Subsection (1) is subject to the following provisions of this Chapter.

360. Z1. Giving effect to allowances and charges: lessors and licensees

(1) This section applies if—
    (a) a person is entitled or liable to an allowance or charge under this Part for a chargeable period (" the relevant period "), but
    (b) his interest in the building in question is or was subject to a lease or a licence at any time in that period.
(2) If the person's interest in the building is an asset of a property business carried on by him at any time in the relevant period, the allowance or charge is to be given effect in calculating the profits of that business for the relevant period by treating—
    (a) the allowance as an expense of that business, and
    (b) the charge as a receipt of that business.
(3) If the person's interest in the building is not an asset of a property business carried on by him at any time in the relevant period, the allowance or charge is to be given effect by treating him as if he had been carrying on a property business in that period and as if—
    (a) the allowance were an expense of that business, and
    (b) the charge were a receipt of that business.

360. Z2. Apportionment of sums partly referable to non-qualifying assets

(1) If the sum paid for the sale of the relevant interest in a qualifying building is attributable—
    (a) partly to assets representing expenditure for which an allowance can be made under this Part, and
    (b) partly to assets representing other expenditure,
only so much of the sum as on a just and reasonable apportionment is attributable to the assets

referred to in paragraph (a) is to be taken into account for the purposes of this Part.

(2) Subsection (1) applies to other proceeds from a balancing event in respect of a qualifying building as it applies to a sum given for the sale of the relevant interest in the qualifying building.

(3) Subsection (1) does not affect any other provision of this Act requiring an apportionment of the proceeds of a balancing event.

360. Z3. Provisions applying on termination of lease

(1) This section applies for the purposes of this Part if a lease is terminated.

(2) If, with the consent of the lessor, the lessee of the qualifying building remains in possession of the qualifying building after the termination without a new lease being granted to him, the lease is treated as continuing so long as the lessee remains in possession.

(3) If on the termination a new lease is granted to a lessee as a result of the exercise of an option available to him under the terms of the first lease, the second lease is treated as a continuation of the first.

(4) If on the termination the lessor pays a sum to the lessee in respect of business premises comprised in the lease, the lease is treated as if it had come to an end by surrender in consideration of the payment.

(5) If on the termination—

(a) another lease is granted to a different lessee, and

(b) in connection with the transaction that lessee pays a sum to the person who was the lessee under the first lease,

the two leases are to be treated as if they were the same lease which had been assigned by the lessee under the first lease to the lessee under the second lease in consideration of the payment.

360. Z4 Meaning of "lease" etc.

(1) In this Part " lease " includes—

(a) an agreement for a lease if the term to be covered by the lease has begun, and

(b) any tenancy,

 but does not include a mortgage (and " lessee ", " lessor " and " leasehold interest " are to be read accordingly).

(2) In the application of this Part to Scotland—

(a) " leasehold interest " or " leasehold estate " means the interest of a tenant in property subject to a lease, and

(b) any reference to an interest which is reversionary on a leasehold interest or on a lease is to be read as a reference to the interest of the landlord in the property subject to the leasehold interest or lease.]

Part 4. Agricultural buildings allowances

Part 4. Agricultural buildings allowances

Modifications etc. (not altering text)
C2. Pt. 4 restricted (19.7.2007) by Finance Act 2007 (c. 11), s. 36. (4)-(7)

Chapter 1. Introduction

361 Agricultural buildings allowances

(1) Allowances are available under this Part if—

(a) capital expenditure has been incurred on the construction of a building (such as a farmhouse, farm building or cottage) or on the construction of fences or other works,

(b) the expenditure was incurred—

(i) by a person having a freehold or leasehold interest in land in the United Kingdom occupied wholly or mainly for the purposes of husbandry, and

(ii) for the purposes of husbandry on that land, and

(c) the expenditure, or other expenditure, is qualifying expenditure.

(2) In this Part—

(a) "agricultural building" means a building, fence or other works referred to in subsection (1)(a), and

(b) "the related agricultural land" means the land referred to in subsection (1)(b).

(3) Allowances under this Part are made to the person who for the time being has the relevant interest (see Chapter 2) in relation to the qualifying expenditure (see Chapter 3).

362 Meaning of "husbandry"

(1) In this Part "husbandry" includes—

(a) any method of intensive rearing of livestock or fish on a commercial basis for the production of food for human consumption, and

(b) the cultivation of short rotation coppice.

(2) "Short rotation coppice" has the meaning given by section 154. (3) of FA 1995 (meaning for general tax purposes: tree species planted at high density where stems harvested at intervals of less than 10 years).

363 Expenditure on the construction of a building

For the purposes of this Part, expenditure on the construction of a building does not include expenditure incurred on the acquisition of land or rights in or over land.

Chapter 2. The relevant interest

364 General rule as to what is the relevant interest

(1) The relevant interest in relation to any qualifying expenditure is the freehold or leasehold interest in the related agricultural land to which the person who incurred the expenditure on the construction of the agricultural building was entitled when the expenditure was incurred.

(2) Subsection (1) is subject to the following provisions of this Chapter.

(3) If, when the expenditure was incurred—

(a) the person was entitled to freehold and leasehold interests or to more than one leasehold interest in the related agricultural land, and

(b) one of those interests was reversionary on all the others,

the reversionary interest is the relevant interest.

365 Effect of creation of subordinate lease

An interest does not cease to be the relevant interest merely because of the creation of a lease or other interest to which that interest is subject.

366 Interest conveyed or assigned by way of security

If an interest in land is—
    (a) conveyed or assigned by way of security, and
    (b) subject to a right of redemption,
the person with the right of redemption is treated for the purposes of this Part as having that interest, and not the creditor.

367 Merger of leasehold interest

(1) If the relevant interest is a leasehold interest which is extinguished on—
    (a) being surrendered, or
    (b) the person entitled to it acquiring the interest which is reversionary on it,
the interest into which the leasehold interest merges becomes the relevant interest when the leasehold interest is extinguished.

(2) If the person who owns the interest into which the leasehold interest is merged is not the same as the person who owned the leasehold interest, the relevant interest is to be treated for the purposes of this Part as acquired by the owner of the interest into which the leasehold interest is merged.

(3) Subsection (1) does not apply if a new lease of the whole or a part of the related agricultural land is granted to take effect on the extinguishment of the former leasehold interest.

368 Provisions applying on ending of lease

(1) This section applies if—
    (a) a lease which is the relevant interest comes to an end, and
    (b) section 367. (1) does not apply.

(2) If a new lease of the whole or a part of the related agricultural land is granted to the same lessee, the lessee is to be treated as continuing to have the same relevant interest in the whole of the related agricultural land.

(3) If—
    (a) a new lease of the whole or a part of the related agricultural land is granted to a different lessee, and
    (b) that lessee ("the incoming lessee") makes a payment to the outgoing lessee in respect of assets representing the qualifying expenditure,
the incoming lessee is to be treated as acquiring the relevant interest in the whole of the related agricultural land.

(4) In any other case, the former lease and the interest of the lessor under it are to be treated as the same interest; and so the relevant interest in the whole of the related agricultural land is to be treated as acquired by the lessor.

Chapter 3. Qualifying expenditure

369 Capital expenditure on construction of agricultural building

(1) If—
    (a) capital expenditure has been incurred on the construction of an agricultural building,
    (b) the expenditure was incurred for the purposes of husbandry as mentioned in section 361, and

(c) the relevant interest has not been sold or, if it has been sold, has been sold only after the first use of the building,

the capital expenditure is qualifying expenditure.

(2) Subsections (3) and (4) apply if the capital expenditure has been incurred on the construction of a farmhouse.

(3) If the accommodation and amenities of the farmhouse are proportionate to the nature and extent of the farm, only one third of the capital expenditure is to be taken into account under subsection (1).

(4) If they are disproportionate, only such part of the expenditure as is just and reasonable (and not exceeding one third) is to be taken into account under subsection (1).

(5) If—

(a) the capital expenditure is incurred on the construction of any agricultural building other than a farmhouse, and

(b) the building is to be used partly for the purposes of husbandry on the related agricultural land and partly for other purposes,

only such part of the expenditure as, on a just and reasonable apportionment, is referable to use for the purposes of husbandry is to be taken into account under subsection (1).

370 Purchase of relevant interest before first use of agricultural building

(1) This section applies if—

(a) capital expenditure has been incurred on the construction of an agricultural building,

(b) the expenditure was incurred for the purposes of husbandry as mentioned in section 361,

(c) the relevant interest is sold before the building is first used, and

(d) a capital sum is paid by the purchaser for the relevant interest.

(2) The lesser of—

(a) the capital expenditure incurred on the construction of the agricultural building, and

(b) the capital sum paid by the purchaser,

is qualifying expenditure.

(3) For the purposes of subsections (1) and (2)—

(a) capital expenditure incurred on the construction of the agricultural building does not include any amount excluded from being taken into account under section 369. (3) to (5), and

(b) the capital sum paid by the purchaser for the relevant interest does not include any amount which, on a just and reasonable apportionment, is attributable to assets representing expenditure in respect of which an allowance cannot be made under this Part.

(4) Subsection (3)(b) does not affect sections 562, 563 and 564. (1) (apportionment and procedure for determining apportionment).

(5) The qualifying expenditure is to be treated as incurred when the capital sum became payable.

(6) If the relevant interest is sold more than once before the building is first used, subsection (2) has effect only in relation to the last of those sales.

371 Different relevant interests in different parts of the related agricultural land

If a person is entitled to different relevant interests in different parts of the related agricultural land—

(a) the expenditure is to be apportioned between those parts on a just and reasonable basis, and

(b) this Part applies as if the person had incurred the expenditure apportioned to each part separately.

Chapter 4. Writing-down allowances

372 Entitlement to writing-down allowance

(1) A person is entitled to a writing-down allowance for a chargeable period if—

(a) qualifying expenditure has been incurred,

(b) at any time during that chargeable period he is entitled to the relevant interest in relation to the qualifying expenditure, and

(c) that time falls within the writing-down period.

(2) The writing-down period, in relation to qualifying expenditure incurred by a person, is 25 years beginning with the first day of the chargeable period of that person in which the qualifying expenditure was incurred.

(3) A person claiming a writing-down allowance may require the allowance to be reduced to a specified amount.

373 Basic rule for calculating amount of allowance

(1) The basic rule is that the writing-down allowance for a chargeable period is 4% of the qualifying expenditure.

(2) The allowance is proportionately increased or reduced if the chargeable period is more or less than a year.

374 First use of building not for purposes of husbandry, etc.

(1) No writing-down allowance is to be made under section 372 if, when the agricultural building is first used, it is not used for the purposes of husbandry.

(2) Any writing-down allowance which has been made in respect of an agricultural building which has not been used is to be withdrawn if—

(a) when the building is first used, it is not used for the purposes of husbandry, or

(b) the person to whom the allowance was made sells the relevant interest before the building is first used.

(3) All such assessments and adjustments of assessments are to be made as are necessary to give effect to this section.

375 Effect of acquisition of relevant interest after first use of building

(1) This section applies if—

(a) a person ("the former owner") would be entitled to an allowance under this Part in respect of any expenditure if he continued to be the owner of the relevant interest, and

(b) another person ("the new owner") acquires the relevant interest in the whole or a part of the related agricultural land.

(2) For the purposes of subsection (1)(b), it is immaterial whether the relevant interest is acquired by transfer, by operation of law or otherwise.

(3) The former owner—

(a) is not entitled to an allowance for any chargeable period after that in which the acquisition occurs, and

(b) if the acquisition occurs during a chargeable period, is entitled only to an appropriate part of any writing-down allowance for that period.

(4) The new owner—

(a) is entitled to allowances for the chargeable period in which the acquisition occurs and for subsequent chargeable periods falling wholly or partly within the writing-down period, and

(b) if the acquisition occurs during a chargeable period, is entitled only to an appropriate part of any writing-down allowance for that period.

(5) If the new owner acquires the relevant interest in part only of the related agricultural land, subsections (3) and (4) apply to so much only of the allowance as is properly referable to that part of the agricultural land as if it were a separate allowance.

376 Calculation of allowance after acquisition

(1) This section applies if—

(a) section 375 applies, and

(b) the acquisition is a balancing event under section 381 (as a result of an election made in accordance with section 382).

(2) The writing-down allowance for a chargeable period ending after the event is—
where—

RQE is the residue of qualifying expenditure immediately after the event,

A is the length of the chargeable period, and

B is the length of the period from the date of the event to the end of the writing-down period.

(3) On any later acquisition that is a balancing event under section 381, the writing-down allowance is further adjusted in accordance with this section.

(4) The residue of qualifying expenditure immediately after a balancing event is calculated as mentioned in section 386, taking into account any balancing adjustment falling to be made on the event.

(5) For this purpose, any balancing allowance on that or any previous balancing event which is reduced or denied under section 389 (sale subject to subordinate interest) is to be treated as having been made in full.

(6) The allowance is proportionately reduced if the person entitled to the allowance is not entitled to the relevant interest in relation to the expenditure in question during part of the chargeable period.

377 Chargeable period when balancing adjustment made

A person is not entitled to a writing-down allowance for a chargeable period in which a balancing allowance or balancing charge is made to or on him in respect of the qualifying expenditure.

378 Allowance limited to residue of qualifying expenditure

(1) The amount of a writing-down allowance for a chargeable period is limited to the residue of qualifying expenditure immediately before it is made or would, apart from this section, be made.

(2) The residue of qualifying expenditure is calculated in accordance with section 386.

379 Final writing-down allowance

(1) In this section "the final writing-down allowance" means the writing-down allowance which is made—

(a) to the person who is entitled to the relevant interest when the writing-down period ends, and

(b) for the chargeable period in which it ends.

(2) If the final writing-down allowance would, apart from this section, be less than the amount of the residue of qualifying expenditure immediately before it is made, the allowance is increased to

that amount.

(3) When determining the residue of qualifying expenditure under section 386 for the purposes of subsection (2), assume that all such writing-down allowances have been made to the persons who have been entitled to the relevant interest during the writing-down period as could have been made if each of them—

(a) had been entitled to allowances, and

(b) had claimed allowances in full.

Chapter 5. Balancing adjustments

380 When balancing adjustments are made

(1) A balancing adjustment is made if—

(a) qualifying expenditure has been incurred, and

(b) a balancing event occurs in a chargeable period for which a person would (apart from this section) be entitled to a writing-down allowance.

(2) A balancing adjustment is either a balancing allowance or a balancing charge and is made for the chargeable period in which the balancing event occurs.

(3) A balancing allowance or balancing charge is made to or on the person entitled to the relevant interest in relation to the qualifying expenditure immediately before the balancing event.

381 Balancing events (on making an election)

(1) Any event described in subsection (2) is a balancing event, but only if an election is made in accordance with section 382 for it to be treated as such.

(2) The events are—

(a) the relevant interest is acquired as mentioned in section 375;

(b) the agricultural building is demolished or destroyed;

(c) the agricultural building ceases altogether to be used (without being demolished or destroyed).

382 Requirements as to elections

(1) An election relating to an event within section 381. (2)(a) must be made jointly by the former owner and the new owner.

(2) No election relating to such an event may be made if it appears that the sole or main benefit which might have been expected to accrue to the parties, or any of them, from—

(a) the acquisition, or

(b) transactions of which the acquisition is one,

is the obtaining of an allowance, or a greater allowance, under this Part.

(3) In determining for the purposes of subsection (2) what benefit might have been expected to accrue, sections 568 and 573 (sales treated as being for alternative amount) are to be disregarded.

(4) An election relating to an event within section 381. (2)(b) or (c) must be made by the person entitled to the relevant interest immediately before the event.

(5) No election relating to any event may be made if any person by whom the election is to be made is not within the charge to tax.

(6) The election must be made by notice given to the [F1an officer of Revenue and Customs]—

(a) for income tax purposes, on or before the normal time limit for amending a tax return for the tax year in which the relevant chargeable period ends;

(b) for corporation tax purposes, no later than 2 years after the end of the relevant chargeable period.

(7) "The relevant chargeable period" means the chargeable period in which the event in question occurs.

Amendments (Textual)

F1. Words in Act substituted (18.4.2005) by Commissioners for Revenue and Customs Act 2005 (c. 11), s. 53. (1), Sch. 4 para. 83. (1); S.I. 2005/1126, art. 2. (2)(h)

383 Proceeds from balancing events

(1) References in this Part to the proceeds from a balancing event are to the amounts received or receivable in connection with the event, as shown in the Table—
Table
Balancing events and proceeds

1. Balancing event	2. Proceeds from event
1. The sale of the relevant interest.	The net proceeds of the sale.
2. The acquisition of the relevant interest under section 368(3) (ending of lease where incoming lessee makes payment to outgoing lessee).	The net amount of the payment to the outgoing lessee.

The net amount received for the remains of the building, together with—

(a) any insurance money received in respect of the demolition or destruction, and

(b) any other compensation of any description so received, so far as it consists of capital sums.

4. The agricultural building ceases altogether to be used. | Any compensation of any description received in respect of the event, so far as it consists of capital sums. |

(2) The amounts referred to in column 2 of the Table are those received or receivable by the person whose entitlement to a balancing allowance or liability to a balancing charge is in question.

384 Exclusion of proportion of proceeds

(1) The amounts referred to in column 2 of the Table in section 383 do not include any amount which, on a just and reasonable apportionment, is attributable to assets representing expenditure in respect of which an allowance cannot be made under this Part.

(2) If the qualifying expenditure in respect of which the balancing adjustment is made was restricted as a result of—

(a) subsection (3) or (4) of section 369 (restrictions on expenditure on farmhouse), or

(b) subsection (5) of that section (restriction on expenditure on buildings to be used partly for purposes other than husbandry),

a corresponding proportion only of the amounts referred to in the Table in section 383 is to be treated as proceeds from the balancing event.

(3) Subsection (1) does not affect sections 562, 563 and 564. (1) (apportionment and procedure for determining apportionment).

Calculation of balancing adjustments

385 Calculation of balancing adjustment

(1) A balancing allowance is made if—

(a) there are no proceeds from the balancing event, or

(b) the proceeds from the balancing event are less than the residue of qualifying expenditure immediately before the event.

(2) The amount of the balancing allowance is the amount of—

(a) the residue (if there are no proceeds);

(b) the difference (if the proceeds are less than the residue).

(3) A balancing charge is made if the proceeds from the balancing event are more than the residue of qualifying expenditure immediately before the event.

(4) The amount of the balancing charge is the amount of the difference.

386 The residue of qualifying expenditure

The residue of qualifying expenditure at any time is—

where—

QE is the amount of qualifying expenditure,

B is the total amount of balancing charges previously made under this Part in respect of the expenditure, and

A is the total amount of any allowances (including balancing allowances) previously made under this Part in respect of that expenditure (whether to the same or to different persons).

387 Overall limit on balancing charge

The amount of a balancing charge made on a person in respect of any qualifying expenditure must not exceed the total allowances made under this Part to the person in respect of the expenditure for chargeable periods ending before that in which the balancing event occurs.

388 Acquisition of relevant interest in part of land, etc.

(1) This section applies if a balancing event relates to—

(a) the acquisition of the relevant interest in part only of the related agricultural land in which the interest subsisted when the qualifying expenditure was incurred, or

(b) only part of the agricultural building.

(2) Entitlement or liability to, and the amount of, the balancing adjustment, are determined by reference to the part of the qualifying expenditure that is properly attributable to the part of the related agricultural land or (as the case may be) the part of the agricultural building.

(3) Section 377 (no writing-down allowance for qualifying expenditure for the chargeable period in which a balancing adjustment is made) applies to the part of the qualifying expenditure referred to in subsection (2).

389 Balancing allowances restricted where sale subject to subordinate interest etc.

(1) This section applies if—

(a) the relevant interest is sold subject to a subordinate interest,

(b) the person entitled to the relevant interest immediately before the sale ("the former owner") would, apart from this section, be entitled to a balancing allowance under this Chapter as a result of the sale, and

(c) condition A or B is met.

(2) Condition A is that—

(a) the former owner,

(b) the person who acquires the relevant interest, and

(c) the person to whom the subordinate interest was granted,

or any two of them, are connected persons.

(3) Condition B is that it appears that the sole or main benefit which might have been expected to accrue to the parties or any of them from the sale or the grant, or transactions including the sale or grant, was the obtaining of an allowance under this Part.

(4) For the purpose of deciding what balancing adjustment is to be made in a case to which this section applies, the net proceeds to the former owner of the sale are to be increased—

(a) by an amount equal to any premium receivable by him for the grant of the subordinate interest, and

(b) if no rent, or no commercial rent, is payable in respect of the subordinate interest, by the amount by which the proceeds would have been greater if a commercial rent had been payable and the relevant interest had been sold in the open market.

(5) But the net proceeds of the sale are not to be treated as being greater than the amount which secures that no balancing allowance is made.

(6) If the terms on which a subordinate interest is granted are varied before the sale of the relevant interest—

(a) any capital consideration for the variation is to be treated for the purposes of this section as a premium for the grant of the interest, and

(b) the question whether any, and if so what, rent is payable in respect of the interest is to be determined by reference to the terms in force immediately before the sale.

(7) If this section applies in relation to a sale to deny or reduce a balancing allowance, the residue of qualifying expenditure immediately after the sale is nevertheless calculated as if the balancing allowance had been made or not reduced.

390 Interpretation of section 389.

(1) In section 389—

"commercial rent" means such rent as may reasonably be expected to have been required in respect of the subordinate interest (having regard to any premium payable for the grant of the interest) if the transaction had been at arm's length;

"premium" includes any capital consideration, except so much of any sum as corresponds to [F2—

]
- [F3, or
- an amount brought into account as a receipt in calculating the profits of a UK property business under sections 277 to 281 of ITTOIA 2005 that is calculated by reference to the sum;] an amount of rent or profits falling to be calculated by reference to that sum under section 34 of ICTA;

"subordinate interest" means an interest in or right over the related agricultural land, whether granted by the former owner or anyone else.

(2) In section 389 and this section—

"capital consideration" means consideration which consists of a capital sum or would be a capital sum if it had consisted of a money payment, and

"rent" includes any consideration which is not capital consideration.

Amendments (Textual)

F2. Word in s. 390. (1) inserted (with effect in accordance with s. 883. (1) of the amending Act) by Income Tax (Trading and Other Income) Act 2005 (c. 5), Sch. 1 para. 557. (a) (with Sch. 2)

F3. S. 390. (1)(b) and word inserted (with effect in accordance with s. 883. (1) of the amending Act) by Income Tax (Trading and Other Income) Act 2005 (c. 5), Sch. 1 para. 557. (b) (with Sch. 2)

Chapter 6. Supplementary provisions

391 Trades

An allowance or charge to which a person is entitled or liable under this Part is to be given effect in calculating the profits of that person's trade, by treating—

(a) the allowance as an expense of the trade, and

(b) the charge as a receipt of the trade.

392[F4. UK property and Schedule A] businesses

(1) This section applies if a person who is entitled or liable to an allowance or charge for a chargeable period was not carrying on a trade in that period.

(2) If the person was carrying on [F5a UK property business, or a Schedule A business,] at any time in that period, the allowance or charge is to be given effect in calculating the profits of that business, by treating—

(a) the allowance as an expense of that business, and

(b) the charge as a receipt of that business.

[F6. (2. A) If the person is within the charge to income tax in respect of the allowance or charge and he was not carrying on a UK property business at any time in that period, the allowance or charge is to be given effect by treating him as if he had been carrying on such a business in that period and as if—

(a) the allowance were an expense of that business, and

(b) the charge were a receipt of that business.]

(3) If the person [F7is a company within the charge to corporation tax in respect of the allowance or charge and it] was not carrying on a Schedule A business at any time in that period, the allowance or charge is to be given effect by treating [F8the company] as if [F9it] had been carrying on such a business in that period and as if—

(a) the allowance were an expense of that business, and

(b) the charge were a receipt of that business.

Amendments (Textual)

F4. Words in s. 392 substituted (with effect in accordance with s. 883. (1) of the amending Act) by Income Tax (Trading and Other Income) Act 2005 (c. 5), Sch. 1 para. 558. (5) (with Sch. 2)

F5. Words in s. 392. (2) substituted (with effect in accordance with s. 883. (1) of the amending Act) by Income Tax (Trading and Other Income) Act 2005 (c. 5), Sch. 1 para. 558. (2) (with Sch. 2)

F6. S. 392. (2. A) inserted (with effect in accordance with s. 883. (1) of the amending Act) by Income Tax (Trading and Other Income) Act 2005 (c. 5), Sch. 1 para. 558. (3) (with Sch. 2)

F7. Words in s. 392. (3) inserted (with effect in accordance with s. 883. (1) of the amending Act) by Income Tax (Trading and Other Income) Act 2005 (c. 5), Sch. 1 para. 558. (4)(a) (with Sch. 2)

F8. Words in s. 392. (3) substituted (with effect in accordance with s. 883. (1) of the amending Act) by Income Tax (Trading and Other Income) Act 2005 (c. 5), Sch. 1 para. 558. (4)(b) (with Sch. 2)

F9. Word in s. 392. (3) substituted (with effect in accordance with s. 883. (1) of the amending Act) by Income Tax (Trading and Other Income) Act 2005 (c. 5), Sch. 1 para. 558. (4)(c) (with Sch. 2)

Meaning of "freehold interest", "lease" etc.

393 Meaning of "freehold interest", "lease", etc.

(1) In this Part "freehold interest in land" means—

  (a) the fee simple estate in the land, or

  (b) in relation to Scotland, the interest of the owner.

(2) In this Part "freehold interest in land" also includes—

  (a) an agreement to acquire the fee simple estate in the land, or

  (b) in relation to Scotland, an agreement to acquire the interest of the owner.

(3) In this Part "lease" includes—

  (a) an agreement for a lease if the term to be covered by the lease has begun, and

  (b) any tenancy,

but does not include a mortgage (and "lessee", "lessor" and "leasehold interest" are to be read accordingly).

(4) In the application of this Part to Scotland—

  (a) "leasehold interest" means the interest of a tenant in property subject to a lease, and

  (b) any reference to an interest which is reversionary on a leasehold interest or on a lease is to be read as a reference to the interest of the landlord in the property subject to the leasehold interest or lease.

Part 4A FLAT CONVERSION ALLOWANCES

[F1 Part 4. A FLAT CONVERSION ALLOWANCES

Amendments (Textual)

F1. Pt. 4. A (ss. 393. A-393. W) inserted (with effect as mentioned in s. 67 of the amending Act) by Finance Act 2001 (c. 9), s. 67, Sch. 19 Pt. 1

Modifications etc. (not altering text)

C1. Pt. 4. A modified (24.2.2003) by Proceeds of Crime Act 2002 (c. 29), s. 458. (1), Sch. 10 para. 22 (with Sch. 10 para. 25); S.I. 2003/120, art. 2, Sch. (with arts. 3 4) (as amended (20.2.2003) by S.I. 2003/333, art. 14)

C2 Pt. 4. A (ss. 393. A-393. W) modified (prosp.) by Proceeds of Crime Act 2002 (c. 29) , ss. 448 , 458. (1) , Sch. 10 para. 22 , 25

Chapter 1. INTRODUCTION

393. A Flat conversion allowances

(1) Allowances are available under this Part if a person incurs qualifying expenditure in respect of a flat.

(2) Allowances under this Part are made to the person who—

    (a) incurred the expenditure, and

    (b) has the relevant interest in the flat.

(3) In this Part " flat " means a dwelling which—

    (a) is a separate set of premises (whether or not on the same floor),

    (b) forms part of a building, and

    (c) is divided horizontally from another part of the building.

(4) In this Part " dwelling " means a building or part of a building occupied or intended to be occupied as a separate dwelling.

Chapter 2. QUALIFYING EXPENDITURE

393. B Meaning of "qualifying expenditure"

(1) In this Part " qualifying expenditure " means capital expenditure incurred on, or in connection with—

    (a) the conversion of part of a qualifying building into a qualifying flat,

    (b) the renovation of a flat in a qualifying building if the flat is, or will be, a qualifying flat, or

    (c) repairs to a qualifying building, to the extent that the repairs are incidental to expenditure within paragraph (a) or (b).

(2) Expenditure within subsection (1)(a) or (b) is not qualifying expenditure unless the part of the building, or the flat, in respect of which the expenditure is incurred—

    (a) was unused, or

    (b) was used only for storage,

throughout the period of one year ending immediately before the date on which the conversion or renovation work began.

(3) Expenditure is not qualifying expenditure if it is incurred on or in connection with—

    (a) the acquisition of land or rights in or over land,

    (b) the extension of a qualifying building (except to the extent required for the purpose of providing a means of getting to or from a qualifying flat),

    (c) the development of land adjoining or adjacent to a qualifying building, or

    (d) the provision of furnishings or chattels.

(4) For the purposes of this section, expenditure incurred on repairs to a building is to be treated as capital expenditure if it is not expenditure that would be allowed to be deducted in calculating the profits of a [F2. UK property business or] Schedule A business for tax purposes.

(5) Treasury regulations may make further provision as to expenditure which is, or is not, qualifying expenditure.

Amendments (Textual)

F2. Words in s. 393. B(4) inserted (with effect in accordance with s. 883. (1) of the amending Act) by Income Tax (Trading and Other Income) Act 2005 (c. 5), Sch. 1 para. 559 (with Sch. 2)

Chapter 3. QUALIFYING BUILDINGS AND QUALIFYING FLATS

393. C Meaning of "qualifying building"

(1) In this Part " qualifying building " means a building in respect of which the following

requirements are met—

(a) all or most of the ground floor of the building must be authorised for business use,

(b) it must appear that, when the building was constructed, the storeys above the ground floor were for use primarily as one or more dwellings,

(c) the building must not have more than 4 storeys above the ground floor, and

(d) the construction of the building must have been completed before 1st January 1980.

(2) In subsection (1)(a) " authorised for business use " means—

(a) in the case of a building in England or Wales, authorised for use within class A1, A2, A3, B1 or D1. (a) specified in the Schedule to the Town and Country Planning (Use Classes) Order 1987;

(b) in the case of a building in Scotland—

(i) authorised for use within class 1, 2, 3 or 4 specified in the Schedule to the Town and Country Planning (Use Classes) (Scotland) Order 1997,

(ii) authorised for a use specified in Article 3. (5)(j) of that Order, or

(iii) authorised for use for the provision of medical or health services other than from premises attached to the residence of the consultant or practitioner;

(c) in the case of a building in Northern Ireland—

(i) authorised for use within class 1, 2, 3, 4 or 15. (a) specified in the Schedule to the Planning (Use Classes) Order (Northern Ireland) 1989, or

(ii) authorised for a use specified in Article 3. (5)(b), (c) or (h) of that Order.

(3) The attic storey does not count for the purposes of subsection (1)(c) unless it is or has been in use as a dwelling or part of a dwelling.

(4) The requirement in subsection (1)(d) is met even if the building has been extended on or after 1st January 1980, provided any extension was completed on or before 31st December 2000.

(5) Treasury regulations may make further provision as to the circumstances in which a building is, or is not, a qualifying building.

393. D Meaning of "qualifying flat"

(1) In this Part " qualifying flat " means a flat in respect of which the following requirements are met—

(a) the flat must be in a qualifying building,

(b) the flat must be suitable for letting as a dwelling,

(c) the flat must be held for the purpose of short-term letting,

(d) it must be possible to gain access to the flat without using the part of the ground floor of the building that is authorised for business use (as defined in section 393. C(2)),

(e) the flat must not have more than 4 rooms,

(f) the flat must not be a high value flat,

(g) the flat must not be (or have been) created or renovated as part of a scheme involving the creation or renovation of one or more high value flats, and

(h) the flat must not be let to a person connected with the person who incurred the expenditure on its conversion or renovation.

(2) In subsection (1)(c) " short-term letting " means letting as a dwelling on a lease for a term (or, in Scotland, period) of not more than 5 years.

(3) For the purposes of subsection (1)(e), the following are ignored in determining the number of rooms in a flat—

(a) any kitchen or bathroom, and

(b) any closet, cloakroom or hallway not exceeding 5 square metres in area.

(4) For the purposes of this Part, if a flat is a qualifying flat immediately before a period when it is temporarily unsuitable for letting as a dwelling, it is to be treated as being a qualifying flat during that period.

(5) Treasury regulations may make further provision as to the circumstances in which a flat is, or

is not, a qualifying flat.

393. E High value flats

(1) For the purposes of section 393. D(1) a flat is a high value flat if the notional rent exceeds the relevant limit set out in the Table in subsection (5).

(2) The " notional rent " means the rent that could reasonably be expected for the flat on the relevant date, on the assumption that, on that date—

(a) the conversion or renovation has been completed,

(b) the flat is let furnished,

(c) the lease does not require the tenant to pay a premium or make any other payments to the landlord or a person connected with the landlord,

(d) the tenant is not connected with the person incurring the expenditure on the conversion or renovation of the flat, and

(e) in the case of a flat in England or Wales or Scotland, the flat is let on a shorthold tenancy.

(3) The " relevant date " means the date on which expenditure on—

(a) the conversion of part of the building into the flat, or

(b) (as the case may be) the renovation of the flat,

is first incurred.

(4) " Shorthold tenancy " means—

(a) in the case of a flat in England or Wales, an assured shorthold tenancy;

(b) in the case of a flat in Scotland, a short assured tenancy.

(5) The limit for the notional rent is as shown in the Table—

TABLE: NOTIONAL RENT LIMITS

Number of rooms in flat	Flats in Greater London	Flats elsewhere
1 or 2 rooms	£350 per week	£150 per week
3 rooms	£425 per week	£225 per week
4 rooms	£480 per week	£300 per week

(6) Treasury regulations may make provision amending the notional rent limits in the Table in subsection (5).

(7) Section 393. D(3) (determination of number of rooms in flat) applies for the purposes of this section.

Chapter 4. THE RELEVANT INTEREST IN THE FLAT

393. F General rule as to what is the relevant interest

(1) The relevant interest in a flat in relation to any qualifying expenditure is the interest in the flat to which the person who incurred the expenditure was entitled when it was incurred.

(2) Subsection (1) is subject to the following provisions of this Chapter and to section 393. V (provisions applying on termination of lease).

(3) If—

(a) the person who incurred the qualifying expenditure was entitled to more than one interest in the flat when the expenditure was incurred, and

(b) one of those interests was reversionary on all the others,

the reversionary interest is the relevant interest in the flat.

(4) An interest does not cease to be the relevant interest merely because of the creation of a lease or other interest to which that interest is subject.

(5) If—

(a) the relevant interest is a leasehold interest, and

(b) that interest is extinguished on the person entitled to it acquiring the interest which is reversionary on it,
the interest into which the leasehold interest merges becomes the relevant interest when the leasehold interest is extinguished.

393. G Interest acquired on completion of conversion

For the purposes of determining the relevant interest in a flat, a person who—
 (a) incurs expenditure on the conversion of part of a building into the flat, and
 (b) is entitled to an interest in the flat on or as a result of the completion of the conversion,
is treated as having had that interest when the expenditure was incurred.

Chapter 5. INITIAL ALLOWANCES

393. H Initial allowances

(1) A person who has incurred qualifying expenditure in respect of a flat is entitled to an initial allowance in respect of the expenditure.
(2) The amount of the initial allowance is 100% of the qualifying expenditure.
(3) A person claiming an initial allowance under this section may require the allowance to be reduced to a specified amount.
(4) The initial allowance is made for the chargeable period in which the qualifying expenditure is incurred.

393. I Flat not qualifying flat or relevant interest sold before flat first let

(1) No initial allowance is to be made under section 393. H if, at the relevant time, the flat is not a qualifying flat.
(2) An initial allowance which has been made in respect of a flat which is to be a qualifying flat is to be withdrawn if—
 (a) the flat is not a qualifying flat at the relevant time, or
 (b) the person to whom the allowance was made has sold the relevant interest in the flat before the relevant time.
(3) All such assessments and adjustments of assessments are to be made as are necessary to give effect to this section.
(4) In this section " the relevant time " means the time when the flat is first suitable for letting as a dwelling.

Chapter 6. WRITING-DOWN ALLOWANCES

393. J Entitlement to writing-down allowances

(1) A person is entitled to a writing-down allowance for a chargeable period if he has incurred qualifying expenditure in respect of a flat and, at the end of the chargeable period—
 (a) the person is entitled to the relevant interest in the flat,
 (b) the person has not granted a long lease of the flat out of the relevant interest in consideration of the payment of a capital sum, and

(c) the flat is a qualifying flat.

(2) In subsection (1)(b) " long lease " means a lease the duration of which exceeds 50 years.

(3) Whether the duration of a lease exceeds 50 years is to be determined—

(a) in accordance with section 38. (1) to (4) and (6) of ICTA, and

(b) without regard to section 393. V(3) (new lease granted as a result of the exercise of an option treated as continuation of old lease).

(4) A person claiming a writing-down allowance may require the allowance to be reduced to a specified amount.

393. K Amount of allowance

(1) The writing-down allowance for a chargeable period is 25% of the qualifying expenditure.

(2) The allowance is proportionately increased or reduced if the chargeable period is more or less than a year.

(3) The amount of the writing-down allowance for a chargeable period is limited to the residue of qualifying expenditure.

(4) For this purpose the residue is ascertained immediately before writing off the writing-down allowance at the end of the chargeable period.

393. L Meaning of "the residue of qualifying expenditure"

The residue of qualifying expenditure is the qualifying expenditure that has not yet been written off in accordance with Chapter 8.

Chapter 7. BALANCING ADJUSTMENTS

393. M When balancing adjustments are made

(1) A balancing adjustment is made if—

(a) qualifying expenditure has been incurred in respect of a flat, and

(b) a balancing event occurs.

(2) A balancing adjustment is either a balancing allowance or a balancing charge and is made for the chargeable period in which the balancing event occurs.

(3) A balancing allowance or balancing charge is made to or on the person who incurred the qualifying expenditure.

(4) No balancing adjustment is made if the balancing event occurs more than 7 years after the time when the flat was first suitable for letting as a dwelling.

(5) If more than one balancing event occurs, a balancing adjustment is made only on the first of them.

393. N Balancing events

(1) The following are balancing events for the purposes of this Part—

(a) the relevant interest in the flat is sold;

(b) a long lease of the flat is granted out of the relevant interest in consideration of the payment of a capital sum;

(c) if the relevant interest is a lease, the lease ends otherwise than on the person entitled to it acquiring the interest reversionary on it;

(d) the person who incurred the qualifying expenditure dies;

(e) the flat is demolished or destroyed;

(f) the flat ceases to be a qualifying flat (without being demolished or destroyed).

(2) Section 393. J(2) and (3) (meaning of " long lease ") apply for the purposes of subsection (1)(b).

393. O Proceeds from balancing events

(1) References in this Part to the proceeds from a balancing event are to the amounts received or receivable in connection with the event, as shown in the Table—

TABLE: BALANCING EVENTS AND PROCEEDS

1. Balancing event	2. Proceeds from event
1. The sale of the relevant interest.	The net proceeds of the sale.
2. The grant of a long lease out of the relevant interest.	If the capital sum paid in consideration of the grant is less than the commercial premium, the commercial premium.
	In any other case, the capital sum paid in consideration of the grant.
3. The coming to an end of a lease, where a person entitled to the lease and a person entitled to any superior interest are connected persons.	The market value of the relevant interest in the flat at the time of the event.
4. The death of the person who incurred the qualifying expenditure.	The residue of qualifying expenditure immediately before the death.
5. The demolition or destruction of the flat.	The net amount received for the remains of the flat, together with—
	(a) any insurance money received in respect of the demolition or destruction, and
	(b) any other compensation of any description so received, so far as it consists of capital sums.
6. The flat ceases to be a qualifying flat.	The market value of the relevant interest in the flat at the time of the event.

(2) The amounts referred to in column 2 of the Table are those received or receivable by the person who incurred the qualifying expenditure.

(3) In Item 2 of the Table " the commercial premium " means the premium that would have been given if the transaction had been at arm's length.

393. P Calculation of balancing adjustments

(1) A balancing allowance is made if—

(a) there are no proceeds from the balancing event, or

(b) the proceeds from the balancing event are less than the residue of qualifying expenditure immediately before the event.

(2) The amount of the balancing allowance is the amount of—

(a) the residue (if there are no proceeds);

(b) the difference (if the proceeds are less than the residue).

(3) A balancing charge is made if the proceeds from the balancing event are more than the residue, if any, of qualifying expenditure immediately before the event.

(4) The amount of the balancing charge is the amount of—

(a) the difference, or

(b) the proceeds (if the residue is nil).

(5) The amount of a balancing charge made on a person must not exceed the total amount of—

(a) any initial allowances made to the person in respect of the expenditure, and

(b) any writing-down allowances made to the person in respect of the expenditure for chargeable periods ending on or before the date of the balancing event giving rise to the balancing adjustment.

Chapter 8. WRITING OFF QUALIFYING EXPENDITURE

393. Q Introduction

For the purposes of this Part qualifying expenditure is written off to the extent and at the times specified in this Chapter.

393. R Writing off initial allowances and writing-down allowances

(1) If an initial allowance is made in respect of the qualifying expenditure, the amount of the allowance is written off at the time when the flat is first suitable for letting as a dwelling.
(2) If a writing-down allowance is made in respect of the qualifying expenditure, the amount of the allowance is written off at the end of the chargeable period for which the allowance is made.
(3) If a balancing event occurs at the end of the chargeable period referred to in subsection (2), the amount written off under that subsection is to be taken into account in calculating the residue of qualifying expenditure immediately before the event to determine what balancing adjustment (if any) is to be made.

393. S Treatment of demolition costs

(1) This section applies if—
    (a) a qualifying flat is demolished, and
    (b) the person who incurred the qualifying expenditure incurs the cost of the demolition.
(2) The net cost of the demolition is added to the residue of qualifying expenditure immediately before the demolition.
(3) " The net cost of the demolition " means the amount, if any, by which the cost of the demolition exceeds any money received for the remains of the flat.
(4) If this section applies, neither the cost of the demolition nor the net cost of the demolition is treated for the purposes of any Part of this Act as expenditure on any other property replacing the flat demolished.

Chapter 9. SUPPLEMENTARY PROVISIONS

393. T Giving effect to allowances and charges

(1) This section applies if a person is entitled or liable under this Part to an allowance or charge for a chargeable period.
(2) If the person's interest in the flat is an asset of [F3 a UK property business, or a Schedule A business,] carried on by him at any time in that period, the allowance or charge is to be given effect in calculating the profits of that business for that period, by treating—
    (a) the allowance as an expense of that business, and
    (b) the charge as a receipt of that business.
[F4. (2. A) If the person is within the charge to income tax in respect of the allowance or charge and his interest in the flat is not an asset of a UK property business carried on by him at any time in that period, the allowance or charge is to be given effect by treating him as if he had been carrying on a UK property business in that period and as if—
    (a) the allowance were an expense of that business, and
    (b) the charge were a receipt of that business.]
(3) If [F5the person is a company within the charge to corporation tax in respect of the allowance or charge and its] interest in the flat is not an asset of a Schedule A business carried on by [F6the

company] at any time in that period, the allowance or charge is to be given effect by treating [F6the company] as if [F7it] had been carrying on a Schedule A business in that period and as if—

(a) the allowance were an expense of that business, and

(b) the charge were a receipt of that business.

Amendments (Textual)

F3. Words in s. 393. T(2) substituted (with effect in accordance with s. 883. (1) of the amending Act) by Income Tax (Trading and Other Income) Act 2005 (c. 5), Sch. 1 para. 560. (2) (with Sch. 2)

F4. S. 393. T(2. A) inserted (with effect in accordance with s. 883. (1) of the amending Act) by Income Tax (Trading and Other Income) Act 2005 (c. 5), Sch. 1 para. 560. (3) (with Sch. 2)

F5. Words in s. 393. T(3) substituted (with effect in accordance with s. 883. (1) of the amending Act) by Income Tax (Trading and Other Income) Act 2005 (c. 5), Sch. 1 para. 560. (4)(a) (with Sch. 2)

F6. Words in s. 393. T(3) substituted (with effect in accordance with s. 883. (1) of the amending Act) by Income Tax (Trading and Other Income) Act 2005 (c. 5), Sch. 1 para. 560. (4)(b) (with Sch. 2)

F7. Word in s. 393. T(3) substituted (with effect in accordance with s. 883. (1) of the amending Act) by Income Tax (Trading and Other Income) Act 2005 (c. 5), Sch. 1 para. 560. (4)(c) (with Sch. 2)

393. U Apportionment of sums partly referable to non-qualifying assets

(1) If the sum paid for the sale of the relevant interest in a flat is attributable—

(a) partly to assets representing expenditure for which an allowance can be made under this Part, and

(b) partly to assets representing other expenditure,

only so much of the sum as on a just and reasonable apportionment is attributable to the assets referred to in paragraph (a) is to be taken into account for the purposes of this Part.

(2) Subsection (1) applies to other proceeds from a balancing event in respect of a flat as it applies to a sum given for the sale of the relevant interest in the flat.

(3) Subsection (1) does not affect any other provision of this Act requiring an apportionment of the proceeds of a balancing event.

393. V Provisions applying on termination of lease

(1) This section applies for the purposes of this Part if a lease is terminated.

(2) If, with the consent of the lessor, the lessee of a flat remains in possession of the flat after the termination without a new lease being granted to him the lease is treated as continuing so long as the lessee remains in possession.

(3) If on the termination a new lease is granted to the lessee as a result of the exercise of an option available to him under the terms of the first lease, the second lease is treated as a continuation of the first.

(4) If on the termination the lessor pays a sum to the lessee in respect of a flat comprised in the lease, the lease is treated as if it had come to an end by surrender in consideration of the payment.

(5) If on the termination—

(a) another lease is granted to a different lessee, and

(b) in connection with the transaction that lessee pays a sum to the person who was the lessee under the first lease,

the two leases are to be treated as if they were the same lease which had been assigned by the lessee under the first lease to the lessee under the second lease in consideration of the payment.

393. W Meaning of "lease" etc.

(1) In this Part " lease " includes—
    (a) an agreement for a lease if the term to be covered by the lease has begun, and
    (b) any tenancy,
 but does not include a mortgage (and " lessee ", " lessor " and " leasehold interest " are to be read accordingly).
(2) In the application of this Part to Scotland—
    (a) " leasehold interest " (or " leasehold estate ") means the interest of a tenant in property subject to a lease, and
    (b) any reference to an interest which is reversionary on a leasehold interest or on a lease is to be read as a reference to the interest of the landlord in the property subject to the leasehold interest or lease.]

Part 5. Mineral extraction allowances

Part 5. Mineral extraction allowances

Chapter 1. Introduction

394 Mineral extraction allowances

(1) Allowances are available under this Part if a person carries on a mineral extraction trade and incurs qualifying expenditure.
(2) In this Part "mineral extraction trade" means a trade which consists of, or includes, the working of a source of mineral deposits.
(3) In this Part "mineral deposits" includes any natural deposits capable of being lifted or extracted from the earth, and for this purpose geothermal energy is to be treated as a natural deposit.
(4) Any reference in this Part to mineral deposits is to mineral deposits of a wasting nature.
(5) In this Part "source of mineral deposits" includes a mine, an oil well and a source of geothermal energy.

395 Qualifying expenditure

(1) In this Part "qualifying expenditure" means—
    (a) expenditure on mineral exploration and access which is qualifying expenditure under Chapter 2,
    (b) expenditure on acquiring a mineral asset which is qualifying expenditure under Chapter 3,
    (c) expenditure which is treated as qualifying expenditure on mineral exploration and access under section 407. (5) or 408. (2), and
    (d) expenditure which is qualifying expenditure under Chapter 5 (expenditure on works likely to become valueless and post-trading restoration expenditure).
But this is subject to subsections (2) and (3).
(2) Expenditure is not qualifying expenditure if it is excluded from being qualifying expenditure by section 399.
(3) Chapter 4 contains provisions limiting in certain cases the amount of expenditure which is

qualifying expenditure.

396 Meaning of "mineral exploration and access"

(1) In this Part "mineral exploration and access" means—
    (a) searching for or discovering and testing the mineral deposits of a source, or
    (b) winning access to such deposits.
(2) Expenditure on seeking planning permission necessary to enable—
    (a) mineral exploration and access to be undertaken at any place, or
    (b) any mineral deposits to be worked,
is treated as expenditure on mineral exploration and access if planning permission is not granted.
(3) "Seeking planning permission" includes pursuing an appeal against a refusal to grant planning permission.

397 Meaning of "mineral asset"

In this Part "mineral asset" means—
    (a) any mineral deposits or land comprising mineral deposits, or
    (b) any interest in or right over such deposits or land.

398 Relationship between main types of qualifying expenditure

Subject to Chapter 4, expenditure on—
    (a) the acquisition of, or of rights over, the site of a source of mineral deposits, or
    (b) the acquisition of, or of rights over, mineral deposits,
is to be treated as expenditure on acquiring a mineral asset and not as expenditure on mineral exploration and access.

399 Expenditure excluded from being qualifying expenditure

(1) Expenditure on the provision of plant or machinery is not qualifying expenditure except as provided by section 402 (pre-trading expenditure on plant or machinery).
(2) Expenditure on works constructed wholly or mainly for subjecting the raw product of a source to any process is not qualifying expenditure, unless the process is designed for preparing the raw product for use as such.
(3) Expenditure on buildings or structures provided for occupation by, or for the welfare of, workers is not qualifying expenditure except as provided by section 415.
(4) Expenditure on a building is not qualifying expenditure if the whole of the building was constructed for use as an office.
(5) Subsection (6) applies if part of a building or structure has been constructed for use as an office.
(6) The expenditure on the office part is not qualifying expenditure if it was more than 10% of the capital expenditure incurred on the construction of the whole.

Chapter 2. Qualifying expenditure on mineral exploration and access

400 Qualifying expenditure on mineral exploration and access

(1) Expenditure on mineral exploration and access is qualifying expenditure if—

    (a) it is capital expenditure, and

    (b) it is incurred for the purposes of a mineral extraction trade.

(2) Expenditure on mineral exploration and access incurred by a person in connection with a mineral extraction trade which that person carries on then or subsequently is to be treated as incurred for the purposes of that trade.

(3) But pre-trading expenditure on mineral exploration and access is qualifying expenditure only to the extent provided by—

section 401 (pre-trading exploration expenditure), or

section 402 (pre-trading expenditure on plant or machinery).

(4) Any pre-trading expenditure that is qualifying expenditure under either of those sections is to be treated as incurred on the first day of trading.

(5) In this Chapter—

    (a) "pre-trading expenditure" means capital expenditure incurred before the day on which a person begins to carry on a mineral extraction trade, and

    (b) "the first day of trading", in relation to a person's pre-trading expenditure, means the day on which that person begins to carry on the mineral extraction trade.

401 Pre-trading exploration expenditure

(1) This section applies if—

    (a) a person incurs pre-trading expenditure on mineral exploration and access at a source, and

    (b) the expenditure is not incurred on the provision of plant or machinery.

(2) The amount of the expenditure ("pre-trading exploration expenditure") that is qualifying expenditure depends on whether mineral exploration and access is continuing at the source on the first day of trading.

(3) If it is, so much of the pre-trading exploration expenditure as exceeds any relevant receipts is qualifying expenditure.

(4) If it is not, only so much of the pre-trading exploration expenditure as—

    (a) was incurred within 6 years ending on the first day of trading, and

    (b) exceeds any relevant receipts,

is qualifying expenditure.

(5) "Relevant receipts" means capital sums received—

    (a) by the person incurring the pre-trading exploration expenditure referred to in subsection (3) or (4), and

    (b) before the first day of trading,

so far as they are reasonably attributable to that expenditure.

402 Pre-trading expenditure on plant or machinery

(1) This section applies if—

    (a) a person incurs pre-trading expenditure on the provision of plant or machinery for mineral exploration and access,

    (b) the plant or machinery was used in connection with mineral exploration and access at a source, and

    (c) before the first day of trading, the plant or machinery is sold, demolished, destroyed or abandoned.

(2) The amount of the expenditure ("pre-trading expenditure on plant or machinery") that is qualifying expenditure depends on whether mineral exploration and access is continuing at the source on the first day of trading.

(3) If it is, so much of the pre-trading expenditure on plant or machinery as exceeds any relevant receipts is qualifying expenditure.

(4) If it is not, only so much of the pre-trading expenditure on plant or machinery as—
    (a) was incurred within 6 years ending on the first day of trading, and
    (b) exceeds any relevant receipts,
is qualifying expenditure.

(5) "Relevant receipts" means—
    (a) if the plant or machinery is sold, the net proceeds to the person of the sale;
    (b) if the plant or machinery is demolished or destroyed, the net amount received by the person for the remains of the plant or machinery, together with—
(i) any insurance money received by him in respect of the demolition or destruction, and
(ii) any other compensation of any description so received, so far as it consists of capital sums;
    (c) if the plant or machinery is abandoned—
(i) any insurance money received by the person in respect of the abandonment, and
(ii) any other compensation of any description so received, so far as it consists of capital sums.

Chapter 3. Qualifying expenditure on acquiring a mineral asset

403 Qualifying expenditure on acquiring a mineral asset

(1) Expenditure on acquiring a mineral asset is qualifying expenditure if—
    (a) it is capital expenditure, and
    (b) it is incurred for the purposes of a mineral extraction trade.

(2) Subsection (1) is subject to—
section 404 (exclusion of undeveloped market value of land), and
section 406 (reduction where premium relief previously allowed).

(3) In this Chapter "the buyer", in relation to the acquisition of a mineral asset, means the person acquiring it.

404 Exclusion of undeveloped market value of land

(1) If the mineral asset is an interest in land, so much of the buyer's expenditure on acquiring the asset as is equal to the undeveloped market value of the interest is not qualifying expenditure.

(2) "The undeveloped market value of the interest" means the amount that, at the time of the acquisition, the interest might reasonably be expected to fetch on a sale in the open market on the assumptions in subsection (3).

(3) The assumptions are that—
    (a) there is no source of mineral deposits on or in the land, and
    (b) it will only ever be lawful to carry out existing permitted development.

(4) Development is existing permitted development if at the time of the acquisition—
    (a) it has been, or had begun to be, lawfully carried out, or
    (b) it could be lawfully carried out under planning permission granted by a general development order.

(5) In applying subsection (4) in relation to land outside the United Kingdom—
    (a) whether, at the time of the acquisition, development has been, or had begun to be, lawfully carried out is to be determined according to the law of the territory in which the land is situated, and
    (b) whether, at that time, development could be lawfully carried out under planning permission granted by a general development order is to be determined as if the land were in England.

(6) References in this section to the time of acquisition are not affected by section 434 (expenditure incurred before trade carried on).

(7) This section does not apply to the buyer's expenditure if an election under section 569

(election to treat sale as being for alternative amount) is made in relation to the acquisition.

405 Qualifying expenditure where buildings or structures cease to be used

(1) This section applies if—

(a) section 404 (exclusion of undeveloped market value of land) applies to limit the buyer's qualifying expenditure on acquiring the mineral asset,

(b) the undeveloped market value of the interest in land includes the value of any buildings or structures on the land, and

(c) at the time of the acquisition, or at any later time, the buildings or structures permanently cease to be used for any purpose.

(2) The buyer is to be treated—

(a) as having incurred qualifying expenditure, on acquiring a mineral asset, of an amount equal to the unrelieved value of the buildings or structures, and

(b) as having incurred it when the buildings or structures permanently cease to be used for any purpose.

(3) The unrelieved value of the buildings or structures is—

where—

V is the value of the buildings or structures at the date of the acquisition (disregarding any value properly attributable to the land on which they stand),

A is the amount of any allowances made to the buyer under the provisions of this Act other than Part 10 (assured tenancy allowances) in respect of—

(a) the buildings or structures, or

(b) assets in the buildings or structures, and

B is the amount of any balancing charges made on the buyer under those provisions in respect of those buildings or structures or assets in them.

(4) References in this section to the time of acquisition are not affected by section 434 (time when expenditure incurred).

406 Reduction where premium relief previously allowed

(1) This section applies if—

(a) the mineral asset is or includes an interest in land, and

(b) for chargeable periods previous to the chargeable period for which the buyer first becomes entitled to an allowance under this Part in respect of the expenditure on acquiring the mineral asset, deductions are made under [F1sections 60 to 67 of ITTOIA 2005 or under sections 87 and 87. A of ICTA] (deductions in calculating trading profits where premiums etc. taxable).

(2) The amount of the expenditure on the acquisition of the mineral asset that is qualifying expenditure is reduced by—

where—

D is the total of the deductions made under [F2sections 60 to 67 of ITTOIA 2005 or under sections 87 and 87. A of ICTA] in the earlier chargeable periods mentioned in subsection (1)(b),

E is the amount of the capital expenditure on the acquisition of the interest in land that would have been qualifying expenditure if the buyer had been entitled to allowances under this Part in those earlier periods, and

T is the total amount of the capital expenditure on the acquisition of the interest in land.

Amendments (Textual)

F1 Words in s. 406. (1) substituted (6.4.2005) by Income Tax (Trading and Other Income) Act 2005 (c. 5) , s. 883. (1) , Sch. 1 para. 561. (2) (with Sch. 2)

F2 Words in s. 406. (2) substituted (6.4.2005) by Income Tax (Trading and Other Income) Act

Chapter 4. Qualifying expenditure: second-hand assets

407 Acquisition of mineral asset owned by previous trader

(1) This section applies if—

(a) a person carrying on a mineral extraction trade ("the buyer") incurs capital expenditure on acquiring a mineral asset ("asset X") for the purposes of that trade, and

(b) the conditions in subsection (3) are met.

(2) In this section "the buyer's expenditure" means the expenditure referred to in subsection (1)(a), less any amount which, under section 404 (exclusion of undeveloped market value of land), is not qualifying expenditure on the acquisition of the mineral asset.

(3) The conditions are that—

(a) expenditure was previously incurred on acquiring asset X or bringing it into existence by—

(i) the person from whom the buyer acquired asset X, or

(ii) an earlier owner of asset X,

in connection with a mineral extraction trade carried on by the person incurring that expenditure,

(b) part of the value of asset X is properly attributable to expenditure ("E1") on mineral exploration and access by the previous trader, and

(c) it is just and reasonable to attribute part of the buyer's expenditure ("E2") to that part of the value of asset X.

(4) In arriving at E1, any expenditure that is or has been deducted in calculating, for tax purposes, the profits of a trade carried on by the previous trader must be excluded.

(5) If this section applies—

(a) so much of the buyer's expenditure as is equal to the lesser of E1 and E2 is to be treated as qualifying expenditure on mineral exploration and access, and

(b) the buyer's expenditure on acquiring the mineral asset is reduced by the same amount.

(6) "The previous trader" means—

(a) the person incurring the expenditure mentioned in subsection (3)(a), or

(b) if there has been more than one such person, the last before the buyer acquired asset X.

(7) In this section references to asset X include—

(a) two or more assets which together make up asset X, and

(b) one asset from which, or two or more assets from the combination of which, asset X is derived.

408 Acquisition of oil licence from non-trader

(1) This section applies if—

(a) a person carrying on a mineral extraction trade ("the buyer") incurs capital expenditure on acquiring an interest in an oil licence for the purposes of that trade,

(b) the person from whom the interest was acquired ("the seller") disposed of the interest without having carried on a mineral extraction trade,

(c) part of the value of the interest is attributable to expenditure ("E1") on mineral exploration and access by the seller, and

(d) it is just and reasonable to attribute part of the buyer's expenditure ("E2") to that part of the value of the interest.

(2) If this section applies—

(a) so much of the buyer's expenditure as is equal to the lesser of E1 and E2 is to be treated as qualifying expenditure on mineral exploration and access, and

(b) the buyer's expenditure on acquiring the interest in the oil licence is reduced by an amount equal to E2.

(3) In this section "oil licence" and "interest in an oil licence" have the same meaning as in Chapter 3 of Part 12.

409 Acquisition of other assets from non-traders

(1) This section applies if—

(a) a person carrying on a mineral extraction trade ("the buyer") incurs capital expenditure on acquiring any assets for the purposes of that trade,

(b) the person from whom the assets were acquired ("the seller") disposed of the assets without having carried on a mineral extraction trade,

(c) the assets represent expenditure on mineral exploration and access incurred by the seller, and

(d) section 408 (acquisition of oil licence from non-trader) does not apply in relation to the acquisition.

(2) If this section applies, the buyer's expenditure is qualifying expenditure only to the extent that it does not exceed the amount of the seller's expenditure on mineral exploration and access that is represented by the assets.

(3) The references in this section to assets representing expenditure on mineral exploration and access include any results obtained from any search, exploration or inquiry on which the expenditure was incurred.

Qualifying expenditure on assets limited by reference to historic costs

410 UK oil licence: limit is original licence payment

(1) This section applies if a person carrying on a mineral extraction trade ("the buyer") incurs capital expenditure on acquiring a mineral asset which is a UK oil licence, or an interest in such a licence, for the purposes of that trade.

(2) If this section applies, the buyer's expenditure is qualifying expenditure only to the extent that it does not exceed—

(a) the original licence payment, or

(b) if the mineral asset is an interest in a UK oil licence, such part of the original licence payment as it is just and reasonable to attribute to the interest.

(3) In this section "the original licence payment" means the amount paid to the relevant authority for the purpose of obtaining the licence by the person to whom the licence was granted.

(4) This section does not affect any expenditure that is treated as qualifying expenditure on mineral exploration and access under—

section 407. (5) (acquisition of mineral asset owned by previous trader), or

section 408. (2) (acquisition of oil licence from non-trader).

(5) In this section "UK oil licence" and "the relevant authority" have the same meaning as in Chapter 3 of Part 12.

411 Assets generally: limit is residue of previous trader's qualifying expenditure

(1) This section applies if—

(a) a person carrying on a mineral extraction trade ("the buyer") incurs capital expenditure on acquiring an asset ("asset X") for the purposes of that trade, and

(b) expenditure was previously incurred on acquiring asset X or bringing it into existence by—

(i) the person from whom the buyer acquired asset X, or

(ii) an earlier owner of asset X,

in connection with a mineral extraction trade carried on by the person incurring that expenditure.

(2) In this section "the buyer's expenditure" means the expenditure referred to in subsection (1)(a) less any amount which, under section 404 (exclusion of undeveloped market value of land), is not qualifying expenditure on the acquisition of the mineral asset.

(3) If this section applies, the buyer's expenditure is qualifying expenditure only to the extent that it does not exceed the residue of the previous trader's qualifying expenditure.

(4) The residue of the previous trader's qualifying expenditure is—

where—

QE is so much of the expenditure incurred by the previous trader on the acquisition or bringing into existence of asset X as constitutes qualifying expenditure for the purposes of this Part,

A is the total of any allowances made under this Part in respect of the previous trader's qualifying expenditure, and

B is the total of any balancing charges made under this Part in respect of the previous trader's qualifying expenditure.

(5) "The previous trader" means—

    (a) the person incurring the expenditure mentioned in subsection (1)(b), or

    (b) if there has been more than one such person, the last before the buyer acquired asset X.

(6) In this section references to asset X include—

    (a) two or more assets which together make up asset X, and

    (b) one asset from which, or two or more assets from the combination of which, asset X is derived.

(7) For the purposes of subsection (4), if the previous trader incurred expenditure on the acquisition or bringing into existence of one or more assets from which asset X is derived, QE is so much of that expenditure as—

    (a) was qualifying expenditure for the purposes of this Part, and

    (b) is just and reasonable to attribute to asset X;

and a similar apportionment is to be made to arrive at A and B.

(8) This section does not affect any expenditure that is treated as qualifying expenditure on mineral exploration and access under—

section 407. (5) (acquisition of mineral asset owned by previous trader), or

section 408. (2) (acquisition of oil licence from non-trader).

412 Transfers of mineral assets within group: limit is initial group expenditure

(1) Subject to section 413, this section applies if—

    (a) a company ("the buyer") incurs capital expenditure on acquiring a mineral asset ("asset X") from another company ("the seller"), and

    (b) the seller is a group company in relation to the buyer at the time of the acquisition.

(2) The buyer's expenditure on acquiring asset X is to be left out of account for the purposes of this Part to the extent that it exceeds—

    (a) the capital expenditure incurred by the seller on acquiring asset X, or

    (b) if asset X is an interest or right granted by the seller in a mineral asset acquired by the seller ("asset Y"), so much of the capital expenditure incurred by the seller on asset Y as on a just and reasonable apportionment is referable to asset X.

(3) If there is a sequence of acquisitions within subsection (1), apply subsection (2) in the same sequence (starting with the first acquisition in the sequence).

(4) Subsections (5) to (7) apply if—

    (a) the buyer is carrying on a mineral extraction trade, and

    (b) the asset is an interest in land.

(5) Section 404 (exclusion of undeveloped market value of land) applies to the buyer as if the time of the buyer's acquisition of the interest in land were—

    (a) the time of the seller's acquisition of the interest, or

    (b) if there is a sequence of acquisitions within subsection (1), the time when the interest was acquired by the company which is the seller in the first acquisition in the sequence.

(6) Subject to subsection (7), section 405 (qualifying expenditure where buildings or structures cease to be used) applies to the buyer as if the time of the buyer's acquisition of the interest in land were the time of the seller's acquisition of the interest.

(7) If there is a sequence of acquisitions within subsection (1), section 405 applies as if—

    (a) the time of the acquisition were the time when the interest was acquired by the company which is the seller in the first acquisition in the sequence, but

    (b) the allowances and balancing charges to be taken into account in calculating (under section 405. (3)) the unrelieved value of the buildings or structures included any allowances or charges made to or on any seller in the sequence.

413 Transfers of mineral assets within group: supplementary

(1) For the purposes of section 412, a company is a group company in relation to another company

if—

  (a) it controls, or is controlled by, the other company, or

  (b) both companies are under the control of another person.

(2) Section 412 does not apply if—

  (a) section 410 (UK oil licences: limit is original licence payment) applies to the acquisition, or

  (b) the acquisition is a sale in respect of which an election is made under section 569 (election to treat sale as being for an alternative amount).

(3) Section 412 applies regardless of section 568 (sales between connected persons etc., or to obtain tax advantage, treated as at market value).

(4) Section 412 does not affect any expenditure that is treated as qualifying expenditure on mineral exploration and access under—

section 407. (5) (acquisition of mineral asset owned by previous trader), or

section 408. (2) (acquisition of oil licence from non-trader).

Chapter 5. Other kinds of qualifying expenditure

414 Expenditure on works likely to become valueless

(1) Expenditure is qualifying expenditure if—

  (a) it is capital expenditure on constructing works in connection with the working of a source of mineral deposits,

  (b) it is incurred for the purposes of a mineral extraction trade, and

  (c) the works—

(i) are likely to be of little or no value, when the source is no longer worked, to the last person working the source, or

(ii) if the source is worked under a foreign concession, are likely to become valueless, when the concession ends, to the last person working the source under the concession.

(2) For the purposes of subsection (1), expenditure on constructing works does not include expenditure on acquiring the site of the works or any right in or over the site.

(3) In subsection (1)(c) "foreign concession" means a right or privilege granted by the government of, or any municipality or other authority in, a territory outside the United Kingdom.

415 Contribution to buildings or works for benefit of employees abroad

(1) Subject to subsection (3), expenditure is qualifying expenditure if—

  (a) it is incurred by a person carrying on a mineral extraction trade outside the United Kingdom and for the purposes of that trade,

  (b) it is a contribution consisting of a capital sum to the cost of buildings or works to which this section applies, and

  (c) the buildings or works are likely to be of little or no value, when the source is no longer worked, to the last person working the source.

(2) The buildings or works to which this section applies are—

  (a) buildings to be occupied by persons employed at or in connection with the working of a source outside the United Kingdom;

  (b) works for the supply of water, gas or electricity wholly or mainly to buildings occupied or to be occupied by persons so employed;

  (c) works to be used to provide other services or facilities wholly or mainly for the welfare of persons so employed or their dependants.

(3) Expenditure is not qualifying expenditure if the person making the contribution—

(a) acquires an asset as a result of the expenditure, or

(b) is entitled to an allowance for the expenditure under any other provision of the Tax Acts.

416 Expenditure on restoration within 3 years of ceasing to trade

(1) If—

(a) a person who has ceased to carry on a mineral extraction trade incurs expenditure on the restoration of a relevant site, and

(b) the expenditure is incurred within 3 years from the last day of trading and meets the further conditions in subsection (3),

the net cost of the restoration is qualifying expenditure.

(2) The qualifying expenditure is treated as incurred on the last day of trading.

(3) The further conditions are that the expenditure—

(a) has not been deducted in calculating for tax purposes the profits of any trade carried on by that person, and

(b) would have been—

(i) deductible in calculating the profits of the trade, or

(ii) capable of being qualifying expenditure under this Chapter,

if the expenditure had been incurred while the trade was being carried on.

(4) If any expenditure incurred by a person is qualifying expenditure under this section—

(a) the whole of the expenditure on the restoration (not just the net cost) is not deductible in calculating the person's income for any tax purposes, and

(b) none of the amounts subtracted to produce the net cost is to be treated as the person's income for any tax purposes.

(5) "Restoration" includes—

(a) landscaping,

(b) in relation to land in the United Kingdom, the carrying out of any works required as a condition of granting planning permission for development consisting of the winning and working of minerals, and

(c) in relation to land outside the United Kingdom, the carrying out of any works required by any equivalent condition imposed under the law of the territory in which the land is situated.

(6) A "relevant site" means—

(a) the site of a source to the working of which the mineral extraction trade related, or

(b) land used in connection with working such a source.

(7) "The net cost of the restoration" means the expenditure incurred on the restoration less any amounts—

(a) received within 3 years from the last day of trading, and

(b) attributable to the restoration of the relevant site (for instance, amounts for spoil or other assets removed from the site or for tipping rights).

(8) All such adjustments are to be made, by way of discharge or repayment of tax or otherwise, as are necessary to give effect to this section.

[F3. Chapter 5. AFirst-year qualifying expenditure

Amendments (Textual)

F3. Pt. 5 Ch. 5. A inserted (with effect as mentioned in s. 63 of the amending Act) by Finance Act 2002 (c. 23), s. 63, Sch. 21 para. 9

416. A First-year allowances available for certain types of qualifying expenditure

A first-year allowance is not available unless the qualifying expenditure is first-year qualifying expenditure under section 416. B (expenditure incurred wholly for purposes of a ring fence trade).

Types of expenditure which may qualify for first year allowances

416. B Expenditure incurred by company for purposes of a ring fence trade

(1) Expenditure is first-year qualifying expenditure if—

    (a) it is incurred on or after 17th April 2002,

    (b) it is incurred by a company,

    (c) it is incurred wholly for the purposes of a ring fence trade, and

    (d) it is not excluded by—

(i) subsection (2) (acquisition of mineral asset), or

(ii) subsection (3) (acquisition of asset representing expenditure of connected company).

(2) Expenditure is not first-year qualifying expenditure under this section if it is expenditure on acquiring a mineral asset.

(3) Expenditure is not first-year qualifying expenditure under this section if it is expenditure incurred by a company on the acquisition of an asset representing expenditure incurred by a company connected with that company.

(4) To the extent that references in this section to an asset representing expenditure incurred by a company include a reference to an asset representing expenditure on mineral exploration and access, they also include a reference to any results obtained from any search, exploration or inquiry on which any such expenditure was incurred.

(5) In this section " ring fence trade " means a ring fence trade in respect of which tax is chargeable under section 501. A of the Taxes Act 1988 (supplementary charge in respect of ring fence trades).

Supplementary

416. C Time when expenditure is incurred

(1) In determining whether expenditure is first-year qualifying expenditure under this Chapter, any effect of the provisions specified in subsection (2) on the time at which the expenditure is to be treated as incurred is to be disregarded.

(2) The provisions are—

    (a) section 400. (4) (which treats certain pre-trading expenditure as incurred on the first day of trading), and

    (b) section 434 (which treats certain other expenditure incurred for the purposes of a trade about to be carried on as incurred on that day).]

Chapter 6. Allowances and charges

Amendments (Textual)

F4. S. 416. D and preceding crossheading inserted (with effect as mentioned in s. 63. (3) of the amending Act) by Finance Act 2002 (c. 23), s. 63, Sch. 21 para. 10

416. D First-year allowances

(1) A person is entitled to a first-year allowance in respect of first-year qualifying expenditure if the expenditure is incurred in a chargeable period to which this Act applies.

(2) Any first-year allowance is made for the chargeable period in which the first-year qualifying expenditure is incurred.

(3) The amount of the allowance is a percentage of the first-year qualifying expenditure in respect of which the allowance is made, as shown in the Table—

Table

Amount of first-year allowances

Type of first-year qualifying expenditure | Amount |

Expenditure qualifying under section 416B (expenditure incurred wholly for the purposes of a ring fence trade) | 100% |

(4) A person who is entitled to a first-year allowance may claim the allowance in respect of the whole or a part of the first-year qualifying expenditure.

(5) This section is subject to section 416. E (artificially inflated claims for first-year allowances).

[F5416. E Artificially inflated claims for first-year allowances

(1) To the extent that a transaction is attributable to arrangements entered into wholly or mainly for a disqualifying purpose, it shall be disregarded in determining for a chargeable period the amount of any first-year allowance to which a person is entitled.

(2) For the purposes of this section, arrangements are entered into wholly or mainly for a " disqualifying purpose " if their main object, or one of their main objects, is to enable a person to obtain—

    (a) a first-year allowance to which he would not otherwise be entitled, or

    (b) a first-year allowance of a greater amount than that to which he would otherwise be entitled.

(3) In this section " arrangements " includes any scheme, agreement or understanding, whether or not legally enforceable.]]

Amendments (Textual)

F5. S. 416. E inserted (with effect as mentioned in s. 63. (3) of the amending Act) by Finance Act 2002 (c. 23), s. 63, Sch. 21 para. 11

Writing-down and balancing allowances and balancing charges

417 Determination of entitlement or liability

(1) Whether a person who has incurred qualifying expenditure is entitled to a writing-down allowance or a balancing allowance, or liable to a balancing charge, for a chargeable period depends on—

    (a) how much of the expenditure is unrelieved qualifying expenditure for that period ("UQE"), and

    (b) the total of any disposal receipts to be brought into account for that period ("TDR") by reference to the expenditure.

(2) If UQE exceeds TDR, the person is entitled to a writing-down allowance or a balancing allowance for the period.

(3) If TDR exceeds UQE, the person is liable to a balancing charge for the period.

(4) The entitlement under subsection (2) is to a writing-down allowance except in cases for which sections 426 to 431 provide for the entitlement to be to a balancing allowance.

418 Amount of allowances and charges

(1) The amount of the writing-down allowance to which a person is entitled for any chargeable period in respect of qualifying expenditure is—

    (a) in the case of qualifying expenditure on the acquisition of a mineral asset, 10% of the amount by which UQE exceeds TDR;

    (b) in the case of other qualifying expenditure, 25% of the amount by which UQE exceeds TDR.

(2) If the chargeable period is more or less than a year, the amount of the writing-down allowance is proportionately increased or reduced.

(3) If the mineral extraction trade has been carried on for part only of the chargeable period, the amount of the writing-down allowance is proportionately reduced.

(4) The amount of the balancing charge to which a person is liable for a chargeable period in respect of qualifying expenditure is—

    (a) the amount by which TDR exceeds UQE, or

    (b) if less, the allowances for earlier chargeable periods in respect of the expenditure less the total of any balancing charges for those periods in respect of the expenditure.

[F6. Where a person is liable to a balancing charge in respect of first-year qualifying expenditure for the chargeable period in which he incurred the expenditure, any first-year allowance made in respect of the expenditure shall be treated for the purposes of paragraph (b) as if it were an allowance for an earlier chargeable period.]

F6. (5)The amount of the balancing allowance to which a person is entitled for a chargeable period in respect of qualifying expenditure is the amount by which UQE exceeds TDR.

(6) A person claiming a writing-down allowance or a balancing allowance may require the allowance to be reduced to a specified amount.

Amendments (Textual)

F6. Words in s. 418. (4) inserted (with effect as mentioned in s. 63. (3) of the amending Act) by Finance Act 2002 (c. 23), s. 63, Sch. 21 para. 12

Unrelieved qualifying expenditure

419 Unrelieved qualifying expenditure

(1) A person's unrelieved qualifying expenditure for the chargeable period in which the qualifying expenditure is incurred is

[F7. (a)the whole of it, unless the expenditure is first-year qualifying expenditure, or

(b) if the expenditure is first-year qualifying expenditure, none of it,

but paragraph (b) is subject to subsections (3) to (5).]

(2) A person's unrelieved qualifying expenditure for a chargeable period after that in which the qualifying expenditure is incurred is the amount, if any, by which it exceeds the aggregate of—

(a) the allowances made in respect of the expenditure for earlier chargeable periods, and

(b) the total of any disposal receipts for earlier chargeable periods.

[F8. (3) If, in the case of expenditure which is first-year qualifying expenditure, a disposal receipt falls to be brought into account for the chargeable period in which the expenditure is incurred (" the initial period "), subsection (4) below applies.

(4) Where this subsection applies, the unrelieved balance of the expenditure shall be taken to be unrelieved qualifying expenditure for the initial period, but only for the purpose specified in subsection (5).

(5) The purpose is that of determining in accordance with sections 417 and 418—

(a) any question whether the person who incurred the expenditure—

(i) is entitled to a balancing allowance for the initial period, or

(ii) is liable to a balancing charge for that period, and

(b) if so, the amount of that balancing allowance or balancing charge.

(6) In this section " the unrelieved balance of the expenditure " means so much of the first-year qualifying expenditure in question as remains after deducting the amount of any first-year allowance given in respect of the whole or any part of that expenditure.]

Amendments (Textual)

F7. Words in s. 419. (1) substituted (with effect as mentioned in s. 63 of the amending Act) by Finance Act 2002 (c. 23), s. 63, Sch. 21 para. 13. (2)

F8. S. 419. (3)-(6) inserted (with effect as mentioned in s. 63 of the amending Act) by Finance Act 2002 (c. 23), s. 63, Sch. 21 para. 13. (3)

Disposal values

420 Meaning of "disposal receipt"

In sections 417 to 419 "disposal receipt" means a disposal value that a person is required to bring into account in accordance with—

(a) sections 421 to 425, or

(b) paragraph 11 of Schedule 12 to FA 1997 (finance lease or loan: receipt of major lump sum) or any other enactment.

421 Disposal of, or ceasing to use, asset

(1) This section applies if—

(a) a person has incurred qualifying expenditure on providing assets (including the construction of works), and

(b) any of those assets—

(i) is disposed of, or

(ii) permanently ceases to be used by him for the purposes of a mineral extraction trade (whether because of the discontinuance of the trade or for any other reason).

(2) The person is required to bring the disposal value of the asset into account for the chargeable period in which the disposal or cessation occurs.

422 Use of asset otherwise than for permitted development etc.

(1) This section applies if—

(a) a person has acquired a mineral asset,

(b) at any time after the acquisition, the asset begins to be used (by him or another person) in a way which constitutes development, and

(c) the development is not—

(i) existing permitted development, or

(ii) development for the purposes of a mineral extraction trade carried on by the person.

(2) The person is required to bring the disposal value of the mineral asset into account for the chargeable period in which the use begins.

(3) Development is existing permitted development if at the time of the acquisition—

(a) it has been, or had begun to be, lawfully carried out, or

(b) it could be lawfully carried out under planning permission granted by a general development order.

(4) In applying subsection (3) in relation to land outside the United Kingdom—

(a) whether, at the time of the acquisition, development has been, or had begun to be, lawfully carried out is to be determined according to the law of the territory in which the land is situated, and

(b) whether, at that time, development could be lawfully carried out under planning permission granted by a general development order is to be determined as if the land were in England.

423 Sections 421 and 422: amount of disposal value to be brought into account

(1) The disposal value to be brought into account under section 421 or 422 depends on the event requiring it to be brought into account, as shown in the Table—

Table

Disposal value for sections 421 and 422

1. Event | 2. Disposal value |

The net proceeds of the sale, together with—

(a) any insurance money received in respect of the asset as a result of an event affecting the price obtainable on the sale, and

(b) any other compensation of any description so received, so far as it consists of capital sums.

2. Sale of the asset where—

(a) the sale is at less than market value,

(b) there is no charge to tax under [F9. ITEPA 2003], and

(c) the condition in subsection (3) is met by the buyer.

The net amount received for the remains of the asset, together with—

(a) any insurance money received in respect of the demolition or destruction, and

(b) any other compensation of any description so received, so far as it consists of capital sums.

4. Permanent loss of the asset otherwise than as a result of its demolition or destruction. | Any insurance money received in respect of the loss and, so far as it consists of capital sums, any other compensation of any description so received. |

5. Permanent discontinuance of the trade followed by the occurrence of an event within any of items 1 to 4. | The disposal value for the item in question. |

6. Any event not falling within any of items 1 to 5. | The market value of the asset at the time of the event. |

(2) The amounts referred to in column 2 of the Table are those received by the person required to

bring the disposal value into account.

(3) The condition referred to in item 2 of the Table is met by the buyer if—

(a) the buyer's expenditure on the acquisition of the asset cannot be qualifying expenditure under Part 2 or 6 (plant and machinery and research and development allowances), or

(b) the buyer is a dual resident investing company which is connected with the seller.

Amendments (Textual)

F9 Words in s. 423. (1) substituted (with effect in accordance with s. 723. (1)(a)(b) of the amending Act) by Income Tax (Earnings and Pensions) Act 2003 (c. 1) , s. 723 , Sch. 6 para. 254 (with Sch. 7)

Modifications etc. (not altering text)

C2. S. 423 excluded (E.W.S.) (8.6.2005) by Railways Act 2005 (c. 14), s. 60. (2), Sch. 10 para. 14. (2)(a); S.I. 2005/1444, art. 2. (1), Sch. 1

424 Disposal value restricted in case of interest in land

(1) If the asset in relation to which a disposal value is required to be brought into account under section 421 or 422 is an interest in land, the disposal value is restricted by excluding the undeveloped market value of the interest.

(2) "The undeveloped market value of the interest" means the amount that, at the time of the disposal, the interest might reasonably be expected to fetch on a sale in the open market on the assumptions in subsection (3).

(3) The assumptions are that—

(a) there is no source of mineral deposits on or in the land, and

(b) it will only ever be lawful to carry out existing permitted development.

(4) Development is existing permitted development if at the time of the disposal—

(a) it has been, or had begun to be, lawfully carried out, or

(b) it could be lawfully carried out under planning permission granted by a general development order.

(5) In applying subsection (4) in relation to land outside the United Kingdom—

(a) whether, at the time of the disposal, development has been, or had begun to be, lawfully carried out is to be determined according to the law of the territory in which the land is situated, and

(b) whether, at that time, development could be lawfully carried out under planning permission granted by a general development order is to be determined as if the land were in England.

425 Receipt of capital sum

(1) This section applies if a person—

(a) has incurred qualifying expenditure, and

(b) receives a capital sum which, in whole or in part, it is reasonable to attribute to that expenditure.

(2) The person is required to bring into account as a disposal value for the chargeable period in which the capital sum is received so much of the capital sum as is reasonably attributable to the qualifying expenditure.

(3) This section does not apply if the capital sum falls to be brought into account under section 421 or 422.

Cases in which a person is entitled to a balancing allowance

426 Pre-trading expenditure

A person's entitlement to an allowance for a chargeable period is to a balancing allowance if—

(a) the expenditure is qualifying expenditure under—

(i) section 401. (4) (pre-trading exploration expenditure where exploration etc. has ceased before first day of trading), or

(ii) section 402 (pre-trading expenditure on plant or machinery), and

(b) the first day of trading occurs in that chargeable period.

427 Giving up exploration, search or inquiry

A person's entitlement to an allowance for a chargeable period is to a balancing allowance if—

(a) the qualifying expenditure is expenditure on mineral exploration and access,

(b) he gives up the exploration, search or inquiry to which the expenditure related in that chargeable period, and

(c) he does not then or later carry on a mineral extraction trade which consists of or includes the working of mineral deposits to which the expenditure related.

428 Ceasing to work mineral deposits

(1) A person's entitlement to an allowance for a chargeable period is to a balancing allowance if—

(a) in that chargeable period he permanently ceases to work particular mineral deposits, and

(b) the qualifying expenditure is expenditure incurred—

(i) on mineral exploration and access relating solely to those deposits, or

(ii) on acquiring a mineral asset consisting of those deposits or part of them.

(2) If the person carrying on the mineral extraction trade is entitled to two or more mineral assets which at any time were—

(a) comprised in a single mineral asset, or

(b) otherwise derived from a single mineral asset,

subsection (1) does not apply until such time as the person permanently ceases to work the deposits comprised in all the mineral assets concerned taken together.

(3) For the purposes of subsection (2), if a mineral asset relates to, but does not actually consist of, mineral deposits, the deposits to which the asset relates are to be treated as comprised in the asset.

429 Buildings etc. for benefit of employees abroad ceasing to be used

A person's entitlement to an allowance for a chargeable period is to a balancing allowance if—

(a) the expenditure is qualifying expenditure under section 415 (contributions to buildings or works for benefit of employees abroad), and

(b) in that chargeable period the buildings or works permanently cease to be used for the purposes of or in connection with the mineral extraction trade.

430 Disposal of asset, etc.

(1) A person's entitlement to an allowance for a chargeable period is to a balancing allowance if—

(a) the qualifying expenditure was incurred on the provision of any assets, and

(b) in that chargeable period any of those assets—

(i) is disposed of, or

(ii) otherwise permanently ceases to be used by him for the purposes of the mineral extraction trade.

(2) A person's entitlement to an allowance for a chargeable period is to a balancing allowance if any of the following events occurs in that chargeable period in relation to assets representing the qualifying expenditure—

(a) the person loses possession of the assets in circumstances where it is reasonable to assume that the loss is permanent;

(b) the assets cease to exist as such (as a result of destruction, dismantling or otherwise);

(c) the assets begin to be used wholly or partly for purposes other than those of the mineral extraction trade carried on by the person.

431 Discontinuance of trade

A person's entitlement to an allowance for a chargeable period is to a balancing allowance if in that chargeable period the mineral extraction trade is permanently discontinued.

Chapter 7. Supplementary provisions

432 Giving effect to allowances and charges

An allowance or charge to which a person is entitled or liable under this Part is to be given effect

in calculating the profits of that person's mineral extraction trade, by treating—
    (a) the allowance as an expense of the trade, and
    (b) the charge as a receipt of the trade.

433 Treatment of demolition costs

(1) The net cost to a person of demolishing an asset which represents qualifying expenditure is added to that qualifying expenditure in determining the amount of any balancing allowance or balancing charge for the chargeable period in which the demolition occurs.
(2) "The net cost of the demolition" means the amount, if any, by which the cost of the demolition exceeds any money received for the remains of the asset.
(3) If this section applies, the net cost of the demolition is not treated as expenditure incurred on any other asset which replaces the demolished asset.

434 Time when expenditure incurred

(1) For the purposes of this Part, expenditure incurred for the purposes of a mineral extraction trade by a person about to carry it on is treated as incurred by that person on the first day on which that person does carry it on.
(2) Subsection (1) does not apply to pre-trading expenditure on mineral exploration and access (for which specific provision is made by section 400. (4)).

435 Shares in assets

(1) This Part applies in relation to a share in an asset as it applies (under section 571) in relation to a part of an asset.
(2) For the purposes of those provisions, a share in an asset is treated as used for the purposes of a trade so long as, and only so long as, the asset is used for the purposes of the trade.

436 Meaning of "development" etc.

(1) In this Part—
"development"
"development order",
"general development order", and
"planning permission",
have the meaning given by the relevant planning enactment.
(2) "The relevant planning enactment" means—
    (a) in relation to land in England or Wales, section 336. (1) of the Town and Country Planning Act 1990 (c. 8);
    (b) in relation to land in Scotland, section 277. (1) of the Town and Country Planning (Scotland) Act 1997 (c. 8);
    (c) in relation to land in Northern Ireland, Article 2. (2) of the Planning (Northern Ireland) Order 1991 (S.I.1991/1220 (N.I.11)).

Part 6. Research and development allowances

Part 6. Research and development allowances

Chapter 1. Introduction

437 Research and development allowances

(1) Allowances are available under this Part if a person incurs qualifying expenditure on research and development.

[F1. (2)In this Part "research and development"—

(a) means activities that fall to be treated as research and development in accordance with generally accepted accounting practice, and

(b) includes oil and gas exploration and appraisal.

(3) But—

(a) activities that, as a result of regulations made under section 1006 of ITA 2007, are "research and development" for the purposes of that section are also "research and development" for the purposes of this Part, and

(b) activities that, as a result of any such regulations, are not "research and development" for the purposes of that section are also not "research and development" for the purposes of this Part.]

Amendments (Textual)

F1. S. 437. (2)(3) substituted for s. 437. (2) (6.4.2007) by Income Tax Act 2007 (c. 3), s. 1034. (1), Sch. 1 para. 407 (with Sch. 2)

438 Expenditure on research and development

(1) Expenditure on research and development includes all expenditure incurred for—

(a) carrying out research and development, or

(b) providing facilities for carrying out research and development.

(2) But it does not include expenditure incurred in the acquisition of—

(a) rights in research and development, or

(b) rights arising out of research and development.

(3) Nor does it include expenditure on the provision of a dwelling.

(4) But if—

(a) part of a building consists of a dwelling and the rest of the building is used for research and development, and

(b) no more than 25% of the capital expenditure referable to the construction or acquisition of the whole building is referable to the construction or acquisition of the dwelling,

the whole of the building is to be treated as used for research and development.

(5) For the purposes of subsection (4)(b), the expenditure referable to the construction or acquisition of the building is to be apportioned in a just and reasonable manner.

(6) Any additional VAT liability or rebate (as to which see Chapter 4) is to be disregarded in applying subsection (4)(b).

Chapter 2. Qualifying expenditure

439 Qualifying expenditure

(1) In this Part "qualifying expenditure" means capital expenditure incurred by a person on research and development directly undertaken by him or on his behalf if—

(a) he is carrying on a trade when the expenditure is incurred and the research and development relates to that trade, or

(b) after incurring the expenditure he sets up and commences a trade connected with the research and development.

(2) The same expenditure may not be taken into account as qualifying expenditure in relation to more than one trade.

(3) The trade by reference to which expenditure is qualifying expenditure is referred to in this Part as "the relevant trade" in relation to that expenditure.

(4) If capital expenditure is partly within subsection (1) and partly not, the expenditure is to be apportioned in a just and reasonable manner.

(5) References in this Chapter to research and development related to a trade include—

(a) research and development which may lead to or facilitate an extension of that trade, and

(b) research and development of a medical nature which has a special relation to the welfare of workers employed in that trade.

440 Excluded expenditure: land

(1) Expenditure on the acquisition of land, or rights in or over land, is not qualifying expenditure.

(2) But that does not prevent such expenditure from being qualifying expenditure so far as it is referable to the acquisition of—

(a) a building or structure already constructed on the land,

(b) rights in or over such a building or structure, or

(c) plant or machinery which forms part of such a building or structure.

(3) For the purposes of subsection (2), the expenditure is to be apportioned in a just and reasonable manner.

Chapter 3. Allowances and charges

441 Allowances

(1) A person who incurs qualifying expenditure is entitled to an allowance in respect of that expenditure for the relevant chargeable period equal to—

(a) the amount of the qualifying expenditure, or

(b) if a disposal value is required to be brought into account for that period in respect of that expenditure, the amount (if any) by which that expenditure exceeds the disposal value.

(2) The relevant chargeable period is—

(a) the chargeable period in which the expenditure is incurred, or

(b) if the expenditure was incurred before the chargeable period in which the relevant trade is set up and commenced, that chargeable period.

(3) A person claiming an allowance under this section may require the allowance to be reduced to a specified amount.

442 Balancing charges

(1) This section applies if—

(a) an allowance is made to a person for a chargeable period in respect of qualifying expenditure, and

(b) the person is required to bring a disposal value into account for a later chargeable period in respect of that expenditure.

(2) The person is liable to a balancing charge for the later chargeable period in respect of the qualifying expenditure.

(3) The amount of the balancing charge is—

(a) the amount (if any) by which the disposal value to be brought into account for the period exceeds any unclaimed allowance, or

(b) if less, the allowance made in respect of the qualifying expenditure.

(4) "Unclaimed allowance" means any part of the allowance to which the person was entitled in respect of the qualifying expenditure but which has not been claimed.

(5) This section is to be read with section 449 (effect on balancing charges of additional VAT rebates in earlier chargeable periods).

443 Disposal values and disposal events

(1) A person is required to bring a disposal value into account in respect of qualifying expenditure incurred by him if—

(a) he ceases to own an asset representing the expenditure, or

(b) an asset representing the expenditure is demolished or destroyed at a time when he owns the asset.

(2) Subsection (1) is to be read with section 555 (disposal of oil licence with exploitation value).

(3) But a person is not required to bring a disposal value into account under subsection (1) if the disposal event gives rise to a balancing charge under Part 2 or 3 (plant and machinery allowances and industrial buildings allowances).

(4) The disposal value to be brought into account under subsection (1) depends on the disposal event, as shown in the Table—

Table

Disposal values

1. Disposal event	2. Disposal value
1. Sale of the asset at not less than market value.	The net proceeds of the sale.
	The net amount received for the remains of the asset, together with— (a) any insurance money received in respect of the demolition or destruction, and (b) any other compensation of any description so received, so far as it consists of capital sums.
3. Any event not falling within item 1 or 2.	The market value of the asset at the time of the event.

(5) Subsection (4) is subject to—

section 445 (costs of demolition),

section 553 (nil value in case of disposal of oil licence relating to undeveloped area), and

section 555 (disposal of oil licence with exploitation value).

(6) A person is also required to bring a disposal value into account by section 448 (additional VAT rebate generates disposal value).

(7) In this Chapter "disposal event" means an event of a kind that requires a disposal value to be brought into account under subsection (1).

Modifications etc. (not altering text)

C2. S. 443. (4) excluded (24.2.2003) by Proceeds of Crime Act 2002 (c. 29), s. 458. (1), Sch. 10 para. 26 (with Sch. 10 para. 29); S.I. 2003/120, art. 2, Sch. (with arts. 3 4) (as amended (20.2.2003) by S.I. 2003/333, art. 14)

444 Disposal events: chargeable period for which disposal value is to be brought into account

(1) The chargeable period for which a disposal value is to be brought into account under section 443. (1) in respect of qualifying expenditure is given by this section.

(2) Subsection (3) applies if the disposal event occurs in or after the chargeable period for which the allowance in respect of the expenditure is made.

(3) The disposal value is to be brought into account for—

(a) the chargeable period in which the event occurs, or

(b) if the event occurs after the chargeable period in which the relevant trade is permanently discontinued, that chargeable period.

(4) If the disposal event occurs before the chargeable period for which the allowance in respect of the expenditure is made, the disposal value is to be brought into account for that chargeable period.

445 Costs of demolition

(1) This section applies if—

(a) an asset representing qualifying expenditure incurred by a person is demolished at a time when the person owns the asset, and

(b) the person incurred costs of demolition.

(2) The disposal value which the person is required to bring into account in respect of the qualifying expenditure is to be reduced by the cost to the person of the demolition.

(3) If the amount of the disposal value is reduced to nil (or less than nil) under subsection (2), the person is not required to bring a disposal value into account.

(4) If—

(a) the cost to the person of the demolition exceeds the disposal value, and

(b) before its demolition the asset had not begun to be used for purposes other than research and development related to the relevant trade,

the person is to be treated as incurring qualifying expenditure equal to the excess.

(5) That qualifying expenditure is to be treated as incurred—

(a) when the demolition occurs, or

(b) if that is on or after the date on which the relevant trade is permanently discontinued, immediately before the discontinuance.

(6) If this section applies, the cost to the person of the demolition is not to be treated for the purposes of this Act as expenditure on any property that replaces the demolished asset.

Chapter 4. Additional VAT liabilities and rebates

446 Introduction

For the purposes of this Chapter—

(a) "additional VAT liability" and "additional VAT rebate" have the meaning given by section 547,

(b) the time when—

(i) a person incurs an additional VAT liability, or

(ii) an additional VAT rebate is made to a person,

is given by section 548, and

(c) the chargeable period in which, and the time when, an additional VAT liability or an additional VAT rebate accrues are given by section 549.

447 Additional VAT liability treated as additional expenditure etc.

(1) If a person—

(a) has incurred qualifying expenditure ("the original expenditure"), and

(b) incurs an additional VAT liability in respect of that expenditure,

the liability is to be treated as capital expenditure incurred on the same research and development as the original expenditure.

(2) But subsection (1) does not apply if by the time the liability is incurred—

(a) the person who incurred the original expenditure has ceased to own the asset representing that expenditure, or

(b) that asset has been demolished or destroyed.

(3) Any allowance arising as a result of this section is available for—

(a) the chargeable period in which the liability accrues, or

(b) if the liability accrued before the chargeable period in which the relevant trade is set up and commenced, that chargeable period,

rather than for the relevant chargeable period specified in section 441. (2).

448 Additional VAT rebate generates disposal value

(1) This section applies if—

(a) a person has incurred qualifying expenditure, and

(b) an additional VAT rebate is made to the person in respect of that expenditure.

(2) But this section does not apply if by the time the rebate is made—

(a) the person has ceased to own the asset representing that expenditure, or

(b) that asset has been demolished or destroyed.

(3) And this section does not apply if the rebate falls to be brought into account for the purpose of making allowances and charges under Part 2 or 3 (plant and machinery allowances and industrial buildings allowances).

(4) The person must bring the amount of the rebate into account—

(a) as a disposal value in respect of the qualifying expenditure for the appropriate chargeable period, or

(b) if the person would have to bring a disposal value into account under section 443. (1) in respect of that expenditure for that chargeable period, as an addition to that disposal value.

(5) "Appropriate chargeable period" means—

(a) the chargeable period in which the rebate accrues, or

(b) if the rebate accrued before the chargeable period in which the relevant trade is set up and commenced, that chargeable period.

449 Effect on balancing charges of additional VAT rebates in earlier chargeable periods

(1) Section 442 (balancing charges) has effect subject to this section if—

(a) an allowance is made to a person for a chargeable period ("the original period") in respect of qualifying expenditure,

(b) the person is required to bring a disposal value into account for a later chargeable period in respect of that expenditure, and

(c) the person has been required by section 448. (4)(a) to bring one or more disposal values ("VAT disposal values") into account in respect of that expenditure for one or more chargeable periods after the original period but before the later chargeable period.

(2) In relation to the later chargeable period, subsection (3)(a) of section 442 applies as if the unclaimed allowance were reduced by—

where—

DV is the total amount of the VAT disposal values, and

BC is the total amount of any balancing charges to which the person is liable under that section as a result of bringing into account the VAT disposal values.

(3) In relation to the later chargeable period, subsection (3)(b) of section 442 applies as if the allowance made in respect of the qualifying expenditure were reduced by BC.

Chapter 5. Supplementary provisions

450 Giving effect to allowances and charges

An allowance or charge to which a person is entitled or liable under this Part for a chargeable period is to be given effect in calculating the profits of the relevant trade, by treating—
    (a) the allowance as an expense of the trade, and
    (b) the charge as a receipt of the trade.

451 Sales: time of cessation of ownership

Any reference in this Part to the time when a person ceases to own an asset is to be read, in the case of a sale, as a reference to whichever is the earlier of—
    (a) the time of completion, and
    (b) the time when possession is given.

Part 7. Know-how allowances

Part 7. Know-how allowances

Chapter 1. Introduction

452 Know-how allowances

(1) Allowances are available under this Part if a person incurs qualifying expenditure on the acquisition of know-how.
(2) In this Part "know-how" means any industrial information or techniques likely to assist in—
    (a) manufacturing or processing goods or materials,
    (b) working a source of mineral deposits (including searching for, discovering or testing mineral deposits or obtaining access to them), or
    (c) carrying out any agricultural, forestry or fishing operations.
(3) In subsection (2)(b)—
    (a) "mineral deposits" includes any natural deposits capable of being lifted or extracted from the earth and for this purpose geothermal energy is to be treated as a natural deposit, and
    (b) "source of mineral deposits" includes a mine, an oil well and a source of geothermal energy.

453 Know-how as property

(1) Know-how is to be treated as property for the purposes of this Act.
(2) References in this Act to the purchase or sale of property include the acquisition or disposal of know-how.

Chapter 2. Qualifying expenditure

454 Qualifying expenditure

(1) In this Part "qualifying expenditure" means, subject to section 455, capital expenditure incurred on the acquisition of know-how by a person if—

(a) the person is carrying on a trade at the time of the acquisition and the know-how is acquired for use in that trade,

(b) the person acquires the know-how and subsequently sets up and commences a trade in which it is used,

(c) the person acquires the know-how together with the trade or part of a trade in which it was used and the parties to the acquisition make an election under [F1section 194 of ITTOIA 2005 or under] section 531. (3)(a) of ICTA (consideration for know-how on disposal of trade to be treated as payment for goodwill unless parties otherwise elect), or

(d) the person acquires the know-how together with the trade or part of a trade in which it was used and the trade in question was, before the acquisition, carried on wholly outside the United Kingdom.

(2) The same expenditure may not be taken into account as qualifying expenditure in relation to more than one trade.

(3) Qualifying expenditure incurred before the setting up and commencement of the relevant trade is to be treated for the purposes of this Part as incurred when the trade is set up and commenced.

(4) "Relevant trade" means the trade by reference to which expenditure is qualifying expenditure.

Amendments (Textual)

F1 Words in s. 454. (1)(c) inserted (6.4.2005) by Income Tax (Trading and Other Income) Act 2005 (c. 5) , s. 883. (1) , Sch. 1 para. 562 (with Sch. 2)

455 Excluded expenditure

(1) Expenditure on the acquisition of know-how is not qualifying expenditure to the extent that it is otherwise deducted for tax purposes.

(2) Expenditure on the acquisition of know-how is not qualifying expenditure if—

(a) the buyer is a body of persons over whom the seller has control,

(b) the seller is a body of persons over whom the buyer has control, or

(c) the buyer and the seller are both bodies of persons and another person has control over both of them.

(3) In subsection (2) "body of persons" includes a partnership.

(4) Expenditure on the acquisition of know-how is not qualifying expenditure if it is treated as a payment for goodwill under [F2section 194. (3) of ITTOIA 2005 or under] section 531. (2) of ICTA (consideration for know-how on disposal of trade to be treated as payment for goodwill, unless parties otherwise elect etc.).

Amendments (Textual)

F2 Words in s. 455. (4) inserted (6.4.2005) by Income Tax (Trading and Other Income) Act 2005 (c. 5) , s. 883. (1) , Sch. 1 para. 563 (with Sch. 2)

Chapter 3. Allowances and charges

456 Pooling of expenditure

(1) Qualifying expenditure has to be pooled for the purpose of determining a person's entitlement to writing-down allowances and balancing allowances and liability to balancing charges.

(2) There is a separate pool for each trade in respect of which the person has qualifying

expenditure.

457 Determination of entitlement or liability

(1) Whether a person is entitled to a writing-down allowance or a balancing allowance, or liable to a balancing charge, for a chargeable period is determined separately for each pool of qualifying expenditure and depends on—

(a) the available qualifying expenditure in that pool for that period ("AQE"), and

(b) the total of any disposal values to be brought into account in that pool for that period ("TDV").

(2) If AQE exceeds TDV, the person is entitled to a writing-down allowance or a balancing allowance for the period.

(3) If TDV exceeds AQE, the person is liable to a balancing charge for the period.

(4) The entitlement under subsection (2) is to a writing-down allowance except for the final chargeable period when it is to a balancing allowance.

(5) The final chargeable period is the chargeable period in which the trade is permanently discontinued.

458 Amount of allowances and charges

(1) The amount of the writing-down allowance to which a person is entitled for a chargeable period is 25% of the amount by which AQE exceeds TDV.

(2) If the chargeable period is more or less than a year, the amount is proportionately increased or reduced.

(3) If the trade has been carried on for part only of the chargeable period, the amount is proportionately reduced.

(4) A person claiming a writing-down allowance may require the allowance to be reduced to a specified amount.

(5) The amount of the balancing charge to which a person is liable for a chargeable period is the amount by which TDV exceeds AQE.

(6) The amount of the balancing allowance to which a person is entitled for the final chargeable period is the amount by which AQE exceeds TDV.

459 Available qualifying expenditure

A person's available qualifying expenditure in a pool for a chargeable period consists of—

(a) any qualifying expenditure allocated to the pool for that period in accordance with section 460, and

(b) any unrelieved qualifying expenditure carried forward in the pool from the previous chargeable period under section 461.

460 Allocation of qualifying expenditure to pools

(1) The following rules apply to the allocation of a person's qualifying expenditure to a pool.

(2) An amount of qualifying expenditure is not to be allocated to the pool for a chargeable period if that amount has been taken into account in determining the person's available qualifying expenditure for an earlier chargeable period.

(3) Qualifying expenditure is not to be allocated to the pool for a chargeable period before that in which the expenditure is incurred.

461 Unrelieved qualifying expenditure

(1) A person has unrelieved qualifying expenditure to carry forward from a chargeable period if for that period AQE exceeds TDV.

(2) The amount of the unrelieved qualifying expenditure is—

    (a) the excess less the writing-down allowance made for the period, or

    (b) if no writing-down allowance is claimed for the period, the excess.

(3) No amount may be carried forward as unrelieved qualifying expenditure from the final chargeable period.

462 Disposal values

(1) A person is required to bring a disposal value into account for the chargeable period in which he sells know-how on which he has incurred qualifying expenditure.

(2) The disposal value to be brought into account is the net proceeds of the sale, so far as they consist of capital sums.

(3) But no disposal value need be brought into account if the consideration received for the sale is treated as a payment for goodwill under [F3section 194. (2) of ITTOIA 2005 or under] section 531. (2) of ICTA (consideration for know-how on disposal of trade to be treated as payment for goodwill, unless parties otherwise elect).

Amendments (Textual)

F3 Words in s. 462. (3) inserted (6.4.2005) by Income Tax (Trading and Other Income) Act 2005 (c. 5) , s. 883. (1) , Sch. 1 para. 564 (with Sch. 2)

463 Giving effect to allowances and charges

An allowance or charge to which a person is entitled or liable under this Part for a chargeable period is to be given effect in calculating the profits of the trade, by treating—

    (a) the allowance as an expense of the trade, and

    (b) the charge as a receipt of the trade.

Part 8. Patent allowances

Part 8. Patent allowances

Chapter 1. Introduction

464 Patent allowances

(1) Allowances are available under this Part if a person incurs qualifying expenditure on the purchase of patent rights.

(2) In this Part "patent rights" means the right to do or authorise the doing of anything which would, but for that right, be an infringement of a patent.

465 Future patent rights

(1) References in this Part to expenditure incurred on the purchase of patent rights include

expenditure incurred on obtaining a right to acquire future patent rights.

(2) If a person—

(a) incurs expenditure on obtaining a right to acquire future patent rights, and

(b) subsequently acquires those rights,

the expenditure is to be treated as having been expenditure on the purchase of those rights.

(3) "A right to acquire future patent rights" means a right to acquire in the future patent rights relating to an invention in respect of which the patent has not yet been granted.

(4) References in this Part to the proceeds of a sale of patent rights include a sum received from a person which is treated under this section as expenditure incurred by him on the purchase of patent rights.

466 Grant of licences

(1) The acquisition of a licence in respect of a patent is to be treated as the purchase of patent rights.

(2) The grant of a licence in respect of a patent is to be treated as a sale of part of patent rights.

(3) But the grant by a person entitled to patent rights of an exclusive licence is to be treated as a sale of the whole of those rights.

(4) "Exclusive licence" means a licence to exercise those rights to the exclusion of the grantor and all other persons for the period remaining until the rights come to an end.

Chapter 2. Qualifying expenditure

467 Qualifying expenditure

Expenditure is qualifying expenditure only if it is—

(a) qualifying trade expenditure, or

(b) qualifying non-trade expenditure.

468 Qualifying trade expenditure

(1) "Qualifying trade expenditure" means capital expenditure incurred by a person on the purchase of patent rights for the purposes of a trade within the charge to tax carried on by the person.

(2) The same expenditure may not be taken into account as qualifying trade expenditure in relation to more than one trade.

(3) Expenditure incurred for the purposes of a trade by a person about to carry on the trade is to be treated as if it had been incurred by him on the first day on which he carries on the trade.

(4) But subsection (3) does not apply if the person has before that day sold all the rights on the purchase of which the expenditure was incurred.

469 Qualifying non-trade expenditure

"Qualifying non-trade expenditure" means capital expenditure incurred by a person on the purchase of patent rights if—

(a) any income receivable by the person in respect of the rights would be liable to tax, and

(b) the expenditure is not qualifying trade expenditure.

Chapter 3. Allowances and charges

470 Pooling of expenditure

(1) Qualifying expenditure has to be pooled for the purpose of determining a person's entitlement to writing-down allowances and balancing allowances and liability to balancing charges.
(2) There is a separate pool—
    (a) for each trade in respect of which the person has qualifying trade expenditure, and
    (b) for all of the person's qualifying non-trade expenditure.

471 Determination of entitlement or liability

(1) Whether a person is entitled to a writing-down allowance or a balancing allowance, or liable to a balancing charge, for a chargeable period is determined separately for each pool of qualifying expenditure and depends on—
    (a) the available qualifying expenditure in that pool for that period ("AQE"), and
    (b) the total of any disposal receipts to be brought into account in that pool for that period ("TDR").
(2) If AQE exceeds TDR, the person is entitled to a writing-down allowance or a balancing allowance for the period.
(3) If TDR exceeds AQE, the person is liable to a balancing charge for the period.
(4) The entitlement under subsection (2) is to a writing-down allowance except for the final chargeable period when it is to a balancing allowance.
(5) The final chargeable period for a pool to which qualifying trade expenditure has been allocated is the chargeable period in which the trade is permanently discontinued.
(6) The final chargeable period for a pool to which qualifying non-trade expenditure has been allocated is the chargeable period in which the last of the patent rights on which the person has incurred qualifying non-trade expenditure—
    (a) comes to an end without any of those rights being revived, or
    (b) is wholly disposed of.

472 Amount of allowances and charges

(1) The amount of the writing-down allowance to which a person is entitled for a chargeable period is 25% of the amount by which AQE exceeds TDR.
(2) If the chargeable period is more or less than a year, the amount is proportionately increased or reduced.
(3) If in the case of qualifying trade expenditure the trade has been carried on for part only of the chargeable period, the amount is proportionately reduced.
(4) A person claiming a writing-down allowance may require the allowance to be reduced to a specified amount.
(5) The amount of the balancing charge to which a person is liable for a chargeable period is the amount by which TDR exceeds AQE.
(6) The amount of the balancing allowance to which a person is entitled for the final chargeable period is the amount by which AQE exceeds TDR.

473 Available qualifying expenditure

A person's available qualifying expenditure in a pool for a chargeable period consists of—
    (a) any qualifying expenditure allocated to the pool for that period in accordance with section 474, and
    (b) any unrelieved qualifying expenditure carried forward in the pool from the previous

chargeable period under section 475.

474 Allocation of qualifying expenditure to pools

(1) The following rules apply to the allocation of a person's qualifying expenditure to a pool.
(2) An amount of qualifying expenditure is not to be allocated to the pool for a chargeable period if that amount has been taken into account in determining the person's available qualifying expenditure for an earlier chargeable period.
(3) Qualifying expenditure is not to be allocated to the pool for a chargeable period before that in which the expenditure is incurred.
(4) Qualifying expenditure incurred on patent rights is not to be allocated to the pool for a chargeable period if in any earlier period those rights—
    (a) have come to an end without any of them having been revived, or
    (b) have been wholly disposed of.

475 Unrelieved qualifying expenditure

(1) A person has unrelieved qualifying expenditure to carry forward from a chargeable period if for that period AQE exceeds TDR.
(2) The amount of the unrelieved qualifying expenditure is—
    (a) the excess less the writing-down allowance made for the period, or
    (b) if no writing-down allowance is claimed for the period, the excess.
(3) No amount may be carried forward as unrelieved qualifying expenditure from the final chargeable period.

476 Disposal value of patent rights

(1) In this Chapter "disposal receipt" means a disposal value that a person is required to bring into account in accordance with—
    (a) this section, or
    (b) paragraph 11 of Schedule 12 to FA 1997 (finance lease or loan: receipt of major lump sum) or any other enactment.
(2) A person is required to bring a disposal value into account for the chargeable period in which he sells the whole or a part of any patent rights on which he has incurred qualifying expenditure.
(3) Subject to section 477, the disposal value to be brought into account is the net proceeds of the sale, so far as they consist of capital sums.

477 Limit on amount of disposal value

(1) The amount of any disposal value, or the total amount of any disposal values, required to be brought into account by a person—
    (a) on the sale of the whole of any patent rights, or
    (b) on one or more sales of part of any patent rights,
is limited to the capital expenditure incurred by the person on purchasing the rights.
(2) But subsection (3) applies if the person acquired the rights as a result of—
    (a) a transaction which was between connected persons, or
    (b) a series of transactions each of which was between connected persons.
(3) That amount, or total amount, is limited to the capital expenditure on purchasing the rights incurred by whichever party to the transaction, or to any of the transactions, incurred the greatest such expenditure.

Chapter 4. Giving effect to allowances and charges

478 Persons having qualifying trade expenditure

An allowance or charge to which a person is entitled or liable under this Part for a chargeable period in respect of qualifying trade expenditure is to be given effect in calculating the profits of the trade, by treating—
    (a) the allowance as an expense of the trade, and
    (b) the charge as a receipt of the trade.

479 Persons having qualifying non-trade expenditure: income tax

(1) This section applies for income tax purposes if a person is entitled or liable under this Part to an allowance or charge for a chargeable period ("the current tax year") in respect of qualifying non-trade expenditure.
(2) An allowance is to be given effect by deducting it from or setting it off against the person's income from patents for the current tax year.
[F1. (2. A)The allowance is given effect at Step 2 of the calculation in section 23 of ITA 2007.]
(3) If the amount to be deducted from or set off against the person's income from patents for that tax year exceeds the amount of that income, the excess must be deducted from or set off against the person's income from patents for the next tax year, and so on for subsequent tax years.
(4) A charge is to be given effect by treating the charge as income to be [F2assessed to income tax].
Amendments (Textual)
F1. S. 479. (2. A) inserted (6.4.2007) by Income Tax Act 2007 (c. 3), s. 1034. (1), Sch. 1 para. 408 (with Sch. 2)
F2 Words in s. 479. (4) substituted (6.4.2005) by Income Tax (Trading and Other Income) Act 2005 (c. 5) , s. 883. (1) , Sch. 1 para. 565 (with Sch. 2)

480 Persons having qualifying non-trade expenditure: corporation tax

(1) This section applies for corporation tax purposes if a company is entitled or liable under this Part to an allowance or charge for a chargeable period ("the current accounting period") in respect of qualifying non-trade expenditure.
(2) An allowance is to be given effect by deducting it from the company's income from patents for the current accounting period.
(3) If the amount to be deducted from the company's income from patents for that period exceeds the amount of that income, the excess must (if the company remains within the charge to tax) be deducted from its income from patents for the next accounting period, and so on for subsequent accounting periods.
(4) A charge is to be given effect by treating the charge as income of the company from patents.

Chapter 5. Supplementary provisions

481 Anti-avoidance: limit on qualifying expenditure

(1) In the two cases given below, the amount (if any) by which the capital expenditure incurred by

a person ("the buyer") on the purchase of patent rights exceeds the relevant limit is to be left out of account in determining the buyer's qualifying expenditure.

(2) The first case is where the buyer and the seller are connected with each other.

(3) The second case is where it appears that the sole or main benefit which (but for this section) might have been expected to accrue to the parties from—

(a) the sale, or

(b) transactions of which the sale is one,

was obtaining an allowance under this Part.

(4) If the seller is required to bring a disposal value into account under this Part because of the sale, the relevant limit is that disposal value.

(5) If subsection (4) does not apply but the seller—

(a) receives a capital sum on the sale, and

(b) is chargeable to tax in respect of that sum in accordance with section [F3 587 of ITTOIA 2005 or section] 524 of ICTA,

the relevant limit is that sum.

(6) If neither subsection (4) nor subsection (5) applies, the relevant limit is whichever of the following is the smallest—

(a) the market value of the rights;

(b) if the seller incurred capital expenditure on acquiring the rights, the amount of that expenditure;

(c) if a person connected with the seller incurred capital expenditure on acquiring the rights, the amount of that expenditure.

Amendments (Textual)

F3 Words in s. 481. (5)(b) inserted (6.4.2005) by Income Tax (Trading and Other Income) Act 2005 (c. 5) , s. 883. (1) , Sch. 1 para. 566 (with Sch. 2)

482 Sums paid for Crown use etc. treated as paid under licence

(1) This section applies if an invention which is the subject of a patent is used by or for the services of—

(a) the Crown under sections 55 to 59 of the Patents Act 1977 (c. 37), or

(b) the government of a country outside the United Kingdom under corresponding provisions of the law of that country.

(2) The use is to be treated as having taken place under a licence.

(3) Sums paid in respect of the use are to be treated as having been paid under a licence.

483 Meaning of "income from patents"

For the purposes of this Part a person's "income from patents" means—

(a) royalties or other sums paid in respect of the use of a patent,

(b) balancing charges to which the person is liable under this Part, and

(c) amounts on which tax is payable under [F4section 587, 593 or 594 of ITTOIA 2005 or under] section 524 or 525 of ICTA (taxation of receipts from sale of patent rights).

Amendments (Textual)

F4 Words in s. 483. (c) inserted (6.4.2005) by Income Tax (Trading and Other Income) Act 2005 (c. 5) , s. 883. (1) , Sch. 1 para. 567 (with Sch. 2)

Part 9. Dredging allowances

Part 9. Dredging allowances

484 Dredging allowances

(1) Allowances are available under this Part if a person carries on a qualifying trade and qualifying expenditure has been incurred on dredging.

(2) In this Part "qualifying trade" means a trade or undertaking the whole or part of which—

(a) consists of the maintenance or improvement of the navigation of a harbour, estuary or waterway, or

(b) is of a kind listed in Table A or B in section 274 (meaning of qualifying trade for purposes of industrial buildings allowances).

(3) "Dredging" does not include anything done otherwise than in the interests of navigation.

(4) Subject to subsection (3), "dredging" includes—

(a) the removal of anything forming part of, or projecting from the bed of, the sea or any inland water—

(i) by whatever means it is removed, and

(ii) even if, at the time of removal, it is wholly or partly above water, and

(b) the widening of an inland waterway.

485 Qualifying expenditure

(1) Expenditure on dredging is qualifying expenditure if—

(a) it is capital expenditure,

(b) it is incurred for the purposes of a qualifying trade by the person carrying on the trade, and

(c) if the person does not carry on a qualifying trade within section 484. (2)(a), the dredging is for the benefit of vessels coming to, leaving or using a dock or other premises occupied by the person for the purposes of the qualifying trade.

(2) If capital expenditure is incurred—

(a) partly for the purposes of a qualifying trade, and

(b) partly for other purposes,

the qualifying expenditure is the part of the capital expenditure that, on a just and reasonable apportionment, is referable to the purposes of the qualifying trade.

(3) If part only of a trade or undertaking is within section 484. (2), subsection (2) of this section applies as if—

(a) the part which is within section 484. (2), and

(b) the part which is not,

were separate trades.

486 Pre-trading expenditure of qualifying trades, etc.

(1) If a person incurs capital expenditure with a view to carrying on a trade or a part of a trade, this Part applies as if the expenditure were incurred by the person on the first day on which the trade or part of the trade is carried on.

(2) If a person incurs capital expenditure—

(a) in connection with a dock or other premises, and

(b) with a view to occupying the dock or premises for the purposes of a qualifying trade which is not a qualifying trade within section 484. (2)(a),

this Part applies as if the expenditure were incurred by the person when he first occupies the dock or premises for the purposes of the qualifying trade.

Writing-down and balancing allowances

487 Writing-down allowances

(1) A person is entitled to a writing-down allowance for a chargeable period if—

(a) qualifying expenditure has been incurred on dredging,

(b) at any time during the chargeable period, the person is carrying on the qualifying trade for the purposes of which the qualifying expenditure was incurred, and

(c) that time falls within the writing-down period.

(2) The writing-down period, in relation to qualifying expenditure incurred by a person, is 25 years beginning with the first day of the chargeable period of that person in which the qualifying expenditure was incurred.

(3) The amount of the writing-down allowance is 4% of the qualifying expenditure.

(4) The allowance is proportionately increased or reduced if the chargeable period is more or less than a year.

(5) The total amount of any writing-down allowances made in respect of any qualifying expenditure, whether to the same or different persons, must not exceed the amount of the expenditure.

(6) A person claiming a writing-down allowance may require the allowance to be reduced to a specified amount.

(7) A person is not entitled to a writing-down allowance for the chargeable period in which a balancing allowance is made to him in respect of the qualifying expenditure.

488 Balancing allowances

(1) A person is entitled to a balancing allowance for a chargeable period if—

(a) qualifying expenditure has been incurred on dredging,

(b) in that chargeable period, the qualifying trade for the purposes of which the expenditure was incurred has been—

(i) permanently discontinued, or

(ii) sold,

(c) the person is the last person carrying on the qualifying trade before its discontinuance or sale, and

(d) the amount of the expenditure exceeds the amount of the allowances previously made in respect of it, whether to the same or different persons.

(2) The amount of the balancing allowance is the amount of the difference.

(3) For the purposes of subsection (1)—

(a) the permanent discontinuance of a trade does not include an event treated as a permanent discontinuance under [F1 section 18 of ITTOIA 2005 or section 337. (1) of ICTA (effect of company ceasing to trade etc.)], and

(b) a sale does not include a sale which is within subsection (4) or (5).

(4) A sale is within this subsection if any of the following conditions is met—

(a) the buyer is a body of persons over whom the seller has control;

(b) the seller is a body of persons over whom the buyer has control;

(c) both the seller and the buyer are bodies of persons and another person has control over both of them;

(d) the seller and the buyer are connected persons.

In this subsection "body of persons" includes a partnership.

(5) A sale is within this subsection if it appears that the sole or main benefit which might be expected to accrue to the parties, or any of them, from—

(a) the sale, or

(b) transactions of which the sale is one,

is the obtaining of a tax advantage under any of the provisions of this Act apart from Part 2 (plant and machinery allowances).
Amendments (Textual)
F1 Words in s. 488. (3)(a) substituted (6.4.2005) by Income Tax (Trading and Other Income) Act 2005 (c. 5) , s. 883. (1) , Sch. 1 para. 568 (with Sch. 2)

Giving effect to allowances

489 Giving effect to allowances

An allowance to which a person is entitled under this Part is to be given effect in calculating the profits of that person's trade, by treating the allowance as an expense of the trade.

Part 10. Assured tenancy allowances

Part 10. Assured tenancy allowances

Chapter 1. Introduction

490 Assured tenancy allowances

(1) Allowances are available under this Part if qualifying expenditure has been incurred on a building which consists of or includes a qualifying dwelling-house.
(2) A dwelling house is not a qualifying dwelling-house unless—
    (a) it is let on a tenancy which is for the time being an assured tenancy, or
    (b) it has been let on an assured tenancy and the conditions in subsection (4) are met.
(3) "Assured tenancy" means—
    (a) an assured tenancy within the meaning of section 56 of the Housing Act 1980 (c. 51), or
    (b) an assured tenancy (but not an assured shorthold tenancy) for the purposes of the Housing Act 1988 (c. 50).
(4) The conditions referred to in subsection (2)(b) are that—
    (a) the dwelling-house is for the time being subject to a regulated tenancy or a housing association tenancy, and
    (b) the landlord under the tenancy is an approved body or was an approved body but has ceased to be such for any reason.
(5) In subsection (4) "regulated tenancy" and "housing association tenancy" have the same meaning as in the Rent Act 1977 (c. 42).
(6) Further requirements that have to be met for a dwelling-house to be a qualifying dwelling-house are given in sections 504 and 505; and subsection (2) is subject to section 506. (2)(b) (temporary disuse of dwelling-house ignored).

491 Allowances available in relation to old expenditure only

(1) Allowances under this Part are not available unless—
    (a) the qualifying expenditure was incurred after 9th March 1982 and before 1st April 1992, and

(b) if the tenancy is an assured tenancy for the purposes of the Housing Act 1988, expenditure has been incurred which is within subsection (2) or (3).

(2) Expenditure is within this subsection if it was incurred by—

(a) a company which was an approved body on 15th March 1988, or

(b) a person who sold the relevant interest in the building, before any of the dwelling-houses comprised in it were used, to a company which was an approved body on 15th March 1988, and either it was incurred before 15th March 1988 or it consists of the payment of sums under a contract entered into before that date.

(3) Expenditure is within this subsection if it was incurred by a company which—

(a) was an approved body on 15th March 1988, and

(b) bought or contracted to buy the relevant interest in the building before that date.

492 Meaning of "approved body"

In this Part "approved body" has the meaning given in section 56. (4) of the Housing Act 1980 (c. 51).

493 Expenditure on the construction of a building

(1) For the purposes of this Part, expenditure on the construction of a building does not include expenditure on the acquisition of land or rights in or over land.

(2) This Part has effect in relation to capital expenditure incurred by a person on repairs to a part of a building as if it were capital expenditure on the construction of that part of the building for the first time.

Chapter 2. The relevant interest

494 Introduction

This Chapter identifies, in a case where a person has incurred expenditure on the construction of a building which is to be or include a qualifying dwelling-house—

(a) the relevant interest in the building, and

(b) the relevant interest in a dwelling-house comprised in the building.

The relevant interest in the building

495 General rule as to what is the relevant interest in the building

(1) The relevant interest in the building is the interest in the building to which the person who incurred the expenditure on the construction of the building was entitled when the expenditure was incurred.

(2) Subsection (1) is subject to the following provisions of this Chapter.

(3) If—

(a) the person who incurred the expenditure on the construction of the building was entitled to more than one interest in the building when the expenditure was incurred, and

(b) one of those interests was reversionary on all the others,

the reversionary interest is the relevant interest.

496 Interest acquired on completion of construction

For the purpose of determining the relevant interest, a person who—

(a) incurs expenditure on the construction of a building, and

(b) is entitled to an interest in the building on or as a result of the completion of the construction,

is treated as having had that interest when the expenditure was incurred.

497 Effect of creation of subordinate interest

An interest does not cease to be the relevant interest merely because of the creation of a lease or other interest to which that interest is subject.

498 Merger of leasehold interest

If the relevant interest is a leasehold interest which is extinguished on—

(a) being surrendered, or

(b) the person entitled to it acquiring the interest which is reversionary on it,

the interest into which the leasehold interest merges becomes the relevant interest when the leasehold interest is extinguished.

499 Provisions applying on termination of lease

(1) This section applies if the relevant interest in relation to expenditure on the construction of a building is a lease.

(2) If, with the consent of the lessor, the lessee of a building remains in possession after the termination of the lease without a new lease being granted to him, the lease is treated as continuing as long as the lessee remains in possession.

(3) If on the termination of the lease a new lease is granted to the lessee as a result of the exercise of an option available to him under the terms of the first lease, the second lease is treated as a continuation of the first.

(4) If on the termination of the lease the lessor pays a sum to the lessee in respect of a building comprised in the lease, the lease is treated as if it had come to an end by surrender in consideration of the payment.

(5) If on the termination of the lease—

(a) a new lease is granted to a different lessee, and

(b) in connection with the transaction that lessee makes a payment to the former lessee,

the two leases are treated as if they were the same lease which had been assigned by the former lessee to the new lessee in consideration of the payment.

The relevant interest in the dwelling-house

500 The relevant interest in the dwelling-house

The relevant interest in a dwelling-house comprised in a building is the relevant interest in the building, to the extent that it subsists in the dwelling-house.

Chapter 3. Qualifying expenditure

501 Capital expenditure on construction

If—

(a) capital expenditure has been incurred on the construction of a building which was to be or include a qualifying dwelling-house, and

(b) the relevant interest in the building has not been sold or, if it has been sold, it has been sold only after the first use of the building,

the capital expenditure is qualifying expenditure.

502 Purchase of unused dwelling-house where developer not involved

(1) This section applies if—

(a) expenditure has been incurred on the construction of a building which was to be or include a qualifying dwelling-house,

(b) the relevant interest was sold before the first use of any dwelling-house comprised in the building,

    (c) a capital sum was paid by the purchaser for the relevant interest, and

    (d) section 503 (purchase of dwelling-house sold unused by developer) does not apply.

(2) The lesser of—

    (a) the capital sum paid by the purchaser for the relevant interest, and

    (b) the expenditure incurred on the construction of the building,

is qualifying expenditure.

(3) The qualifying expenditure is to be treated as having been incurred when the capital sum became payable.

(4) If the relevant interest was sold more than once before the first use of any dwelling-house comprised in the building, subsection (2) has effect only in relation to the last of those sales.

503 Purchase of dwelling-house sold unused by developer

(1) This section applies if—

    (a) expenditure has been incurred by a developer on the construction of a building which was to be or include a qualifying dwelling-house, and

    (b) the relevant interest was sold by the developer in the course of the development trade before the first use of any dwelling-house comprised in the building.

(2) If—

    (a) the sale of the relevant interest by the developer was the only sale of that interest before the first use of any dwelling-house comprised in the building, and

    (b) a capital sum was paid by the purchaser for the relevant interest,

the capital sum is qualifying expenditure.

(3) If—

    (a) the sale by the developer was not the only sale before the first use of any dwelling-house comprised in the building, and

    (b) a capital sum was paid by the purchaser for the relevant interest on the last sale,

the lesser of that capital sum and the price paid for the relevant interest on its sale by the developer is qualifying expenditure.

(4) The qualifying expenditure is treated as having been incurred when the capital sum referred to in subsection (2)(b) or (3)(b) became payable.

(5) For the purposes of this section—

    (a) a developer is a person who carries on a trade which consists in whole or in part in the construction of buildings with a view to their sale, and

    (b) an interest in a building is sold by the developer in the course of the development trade if the developer sells it in the course of the trade or (as the case may be) that part of the trade that consists in the construction of buildings with a view to their sale.

Chapter 4. Qualifying dwelling-houses

504 Requirements relating to the landlord

(1) A dwelling-house is a qualifying dwelling-house only if the landlord is—

    (a) a company, and

    (b) the person who—

(i) incurred the qualifying expenditure on the building in which the dwelling-house is comprised, or

(ii) is for the time being entitled to the relevant interest in the dwelling-house.

(2) The requirement that the landlord must be a company does not apply in relation to expenditure incurred—

    (a) before 5th May 1983, or

    (b) on or after that date pursuant to a contract entered into before that date,

unless a person other than a company became entitled to the relevant interest on or after that date.

505 Qualifying dwelling-houses: exclusions

(1) A dwelling-house is not a qualifying dwelling-house if any of the exclusions given below apply.

Exclusion 1

The landlord under the tenancy is—

    (a) a housing association which is approved for the purposes of section 488 of ICTA, or

    (b) a self-build society within the meaning of the Housing Associations Act 1985 (c. 69).

Exclusion 2

The landlord and the tenant are connected persons.

Exclusion 3

The tenant is a director of a company which is or is connected with the landlord.

Exclusion 4

The landlord is a close company and the tenant is, for the purposes of Part XI of ICTA—

    (a) a participator in that company, or

    (b) an associate of such a participator.

Exclusion 5

The tenancy is entered into as part of a mutual arrangement for avoidance.

(2) In exclusion 5, a "mutual arrangement for avoidance" means an arrangement—

    (a) between the landlords (or owners) of different dwelling-houses, and

    (b) under which one landlord takes a person as a tenant in circumstances in which, if that person was the tenant of a dwelling-house let by the other landlord, that dwelling-house would not be a qualifying dwelling-house because of exclusion 2, 3 or 4.

506 Dwelling-house ceasing to be qualifying dwelling-house

(1) If a dwelling-house ceases to be a qualifying dwelling-house otherwise than on a sale of the relevant interest in the dwelling-house, this Part has effect as if—

    (a) the relevant interest in the dwelling-house had been sold at that time, and

    (b) the net proceeds of the sale were equal to the market value of that interest at that time.

(2) For the purposes of this Part—

    (a) a dwelling-house is not to be regarded as ceasing altogether to be used merely because it falls temporarily out of use, and

    (b) if, immediately before any period of temporary disuse, a dwelling-house is a qualifying dwelling-house, it is to be regarded as continuing to be a qualifying dwelling-house during the period of temporary disuse.

Chapter 5. Writing-down allowances

507 Entitlement to writing-down allowance

(1) A person is entitled to a writing-down allowance for a chargeable period if—

    (a) qualifying expenditure has been incurred on a building,

    (b) that person is or has been an approved body,

    (c) at the end of that chargeable period the person is entitled to the relevant interest in the building, and

(d) at the end of that chargeable period, the building is or includes a qualifying dwelling-house or two or more qualifying dwelling-houses.

(2) A person claiming a writing-down allowance may require the allowance to be reduced to a specified amount.

508 Basic rule for calculating amount of allowance

(1) The basic rule is that the writing-down allowance for a chargeable period is 4% of the qualifying expenditure attributable to the dwelling-house or (as the case may be) each dwelling-house falling within section 507. (1)(d).

(2) The allowance is proportionately increased or reduced if the chargeable period is more or less than a year.

(3) The basic rule does not apply if section 509 applies.

509 Calculation of allowance after sale of relevant interest

(1) This section applies if—

    (a) the relevant interest in a qualifying dwelling-house is sold, and

    (b) a balancing adjustment falls to be made under section 513 as a result of the sale.

(2) If this section applies, the writing-down allowance for any chargeable period ending after the sale is—

where—

RQE is the amount of the residue of qualifying expenditure attributable to the dwelling-house immediately after the sale,

A is the length of the chargeable period, and

B is the length of the period from the date of the sale to the end of the period of 25 years beginning with the day on which the dwelling-house was first used.

(3) On any later such sale, the writing-down allowance is further adjusted in accordance with this section.

510 Allowance limited to residue of qualifying expenditure attributable to dwelling-house

(1) The amount of the writing-down allowance for a chargeable period in respect of a dwelling-house is limited to the residue of qualifying expenditure attributable to it.

(2) For this purpose the residue is ascertained immediately before writing off the writing-down allowance at the end of the chargeable period.

Interpretation

511 Qualifying expenditure attributable to dwelling-house

(1) If the building concerned consists of a single qualifying dwelling-house, then, subject to the relevant limit, the whole of the qualifying expenditure is attributable to the dwelling-house.

(2) If the qualifying dwelling-house forms part of a building, the qualifying expenditure attributable to the dwelling-house is, subject to the relevant limit, the total of—

    (a) the part of the qualifying expenditure properly attributable to that dwelling-house, and

    (b) if there are common parts of the building, such part of the qualifying expenditure on those common parts—

(i) as it is just and reasonable to attribute to that dwelling-house, and

(ii) as does not exceed 10% of the part referred to in paragraph (a).

(3) In this section "the relevant limit" means—

    (a) £60,000, if the dwelling-house is in Greater London, and

    (b) £40,000, if the dwelling-house is elsewhere.

(4) In subsection (2) "common parts", in relation to a building, means common parts of the building which—

    (a) are not intended to be in separate occupation (whether for domestic, commercial or other purposes), but

    (b) are intended to be of benefit to some or all of the qualifying dwelling-houses included in the building.

(5) For the purposes of subsection (2), the qualifying expenditure on any common parts of a building is so much of the expenditure on the construction of the building as it is just and reasonable to attribute to those parts.

512 Residue of qualifying expenditure attributable to dwelling-house

(1) The residue of qualifying expenditure attributable to a dwelling-house is the qualifying expenditure attributable to that dwelling-house that has not yet been written off in accordance with Chapter 7.

(2) Subsection (1) is subject to section 528 (treatment of demolition costs).

Chapter 6. Balancing adjustments

513 When balancing adjustments are made

(1) A balancing adjustment is made if—

    (a) qualifying expenditure has been incurred on a building, and

    (b) a balancing event occurs in relation to a dwelling-house comprised in the building while it is a qualifying dwelling-house.

(2) A balancing adjustment is either a balancing allowance or a balancing charge and is made for the chargeable period in which the balancing event occurs.

(3) A balancing allowance or balancing charge is made to or on the person entitled to the relevant interest in the dwelling-house immediately before the balancing event.

(4) No balancing adjustment is made if the balancing event occurs more than 25 years after the dwelling-house was first used.

514 Balancing events

The following are balancing events in relation to a qualifying dwelling-house—

    (a) the relevant interest in the dwelling-house is sold;

    (b) if the relevant interest in the dwelling-house is a lease, the lease ends otherwise than on the person entitled to it acquiring the interest reversionary on it;

    (c) the dwelling-house is demolished or destroyed;

    (d) the dwelling-house ceases altogether to be used (without being demolished or destroyed).

515 Proceeds from balancing events

(1) References in this Part to the proceeds from a balancing event are to the amounts received or receivable in connection with the event, as shown in the Table—

Table

Balancing events and proceeds

1. Balancing event	2. Proceeds from event
1. The sale of the relevant interest.	The net proceeds of the sale.

The net amount received for the remains of the dwelling-house, together with—

(a) any insurance money received in respect of the demolition or destruction, and

(b) any other compensation of any description so received, so far as it consists of capital sums.

3. The dwelling-house ceases altogether to be used. | Any compensation of any description received in respect of the event, so far as it consists of capital sums. |

(2) The amounts referred to in column 2 of the Table are those received or receivable by the person whose entitlement to a balancing allowance or liability to a balancing charge is in question.

Calculation of balancing adjustments

516 Dwelling-house a qualifying dwelling-house throughout

(1) This section provides for balancing adjustments in cases where the dwelling-house was a qualifying dwelling-house for the whole of the relevant period of ownership.

(2) A balancing allowance is made if—

    (a) there are no proceeds from the balancing event, or

    (b) the proceeds from the balancing event are less than the residue of qualifying expenditure attributable to the dwelling-house immediately before the event.

(3) The amount of the balancing allowance is the amount of—

(a) the residue (if there are no proceeds);

(b) the difference (if the proceeds are less than the residue).

(4) A balancing charge is made if the proceeds from the balancing event are more than the residue of qualifying expenditure attributable to the dwelling-house immediately before the event.

(5) The amount of the balancing charge is the amount of the difference.

517 Dwelling-house not a qualifying dwelling-house throughout

(1) This section provides for balancing adjustments where the building was not a qualifying dwelling-house for a part of the relevant period of ownership.

(2) A balancing allowance is made if—

(a) the proceeds from the balancing event are less than the starting expenditure attributable to the dwelling-house, and

(b) the total amount of the relevant allowances in respect of that expenditure is less than the adjusted net cost of the dwelling-house.

(3) The amount of the balancing allowance is the amount of the difference between the adjusted net cost of the dwelling-house and the total amount of the relevant allowances.

(4) A balancing charge is made if the proceeds from the balancing event are equal to or more than the starting expenditure attributable to the dwelling-house.

(5) The amount of the balancing charge is equal to the total amount of the relevant allowances.

(6) A balancing charge is also made if—

(a) the proceeds from the balancing event are less than the starting expenditure attributable to the dwelling-house, and

(b) the total amount of the relevant allowances in respect of that expenditure is more than the adjusted net cost in relation to the dwelling-house.

(7) The amount of the balancing charge is the amount of the difference between the total amount of those allowances and the adjusted net cost.

(8) "The relevant allowances" means—

(a) any initial allowance under paragraph 1 of Schedule 12 to FA 1982, and

(b) any writing-down allowance made for a chargeable period ending on or before the date of the balancing event in question.

518 Overall limit on balancing charge

(1) The amount of a balancing charge made on a person in respect of any qualifying expenditure attributable to a dwelling-house must not exceed the total amount of the relevant allowances made to that person.

(2) "The relevant allowances" has the meaning given by section 517. (8).

519 Recovery of old initial allowances made on incorrect assumptions

(1) This section applies if—

(a) an initial allowance has been made under paragraph 1 of Schedule 12 to FA 1982 in respect of expenditure relating to a dwelling-house, and

(b) when the dwelling-house comes to be used, it is not a qualifying dwelling-house.

(2) All such assessments and adjustments of assessments are to be made as are necessary to secure that, despite the repeal of Schedule 12 to FA 1982, effect is given to the prohibition in paragraph 1. (3) of that Schedule (on the making of initial allowances in respect of dwelling-houses which are not qualifying dwelling-houses).

Meaning of "the relevant period of ownership" etc.

520 The relevant period of ownership

The relevant period of ownership is the period beginning—

(a) with the day on which the dwelling-house was first used for any purpose, or

(b) if the relevant interest in the dwelling-house has been sold after that day, with the day following that on which the sale (or the last such sale) occurred,

and ending with the day on which the balancing event occurs.

521 Starting expenditure

(1) This section gives the starting expenditure attributable to a dwelling-house for the purposes of section 517.

(2) If the person to or on whom the balancing allowance or balancing charge falls to be made is the person who incurred the qualifying expenditure attributable to the dwelling-house, that expenditure is the starting expenditure.

(3) Otherwise, the starting expenditure is the residue of qualifying expenditure attributable to the dwelling-house at the beginning of the relevant period of ownership.

(4) If section 528 (treatment of demolition costs) applies, the starting expenditure is increased by an amount equal to the net cost of the demolition.

522 Adjusted net cost

The amount of the adjusted net cost in relation to a dwelling-house is—

where—

S is the starting expenditure attributable to the dwelling-house,

P is the amount of any proceeds from the balancing event,

I is the number of days in the relevant period of ownership on which the dwelling-house was a qualifying dwelling-house, and

R is the number of days in the whole of the relevant period of ownership.

Chapter 7. Writing off qualifying expenditure attributable to dwelling-house

523 Introduction

For the purposes of this Part qualifying expenditure attributable to a dwelling-house is written off to the extent and at the times specified in this Chapter.

524 Writing off initial allowances

If an initial allowance was made under paragraph 1 of Schedule 12 to FA 1982 in respect of a qualifying dwelling-house, the amount of the allowance is written off at the time of the first use of the dwelling-house.

525 Writing off writing-down allowances

(1) If a writing-down allowance is made in respect of qualifying expenditure attributable to a dwelling-house, the amount of the allowance is written off at the end of the chargeable period for which the allowance is made.

(2) If a balancing event occurs at the end of a chargeable period, the amount written off under subsection (1) is to be taken into account in calculating the residue of qualifying expenditure immediately before the event to determine what balancing adjustment (if any) is to be made.

526 Writing off expenditure for periods when building not used as qualifying dwelling-house

(1) This section applies if for any period or periods between—

    (a) the time when the whole or a part of the building was first used for any purpose, and

(b) the time when the residue of qualifying expenditure attributable to a dwelling-house falls to be ascertained,

the building or part has not been a qualifying dwelling-house.

(2) An amount equal to the notional writing-down allowances for the period or periods is written off at the time when the residue falls to be ascertained.

(3) The notional writing-down allowances are the allowances that would have been made for the period or periods in question (if the building or part had remained a qualifying dwelling-house), at such rate or rates as would have been appropriate, having regard to any relevant sale.

(4) In subsection (3) "relevant sale" means a sale of the relevant interest as a result of which a balancing adjustment falls to be made under section 513.

527 Writing off or increase of expenditure where balancing adjustment made

(1) This section applies if the relevant interest in the dwelling-house is sold.

(2) If a balancing allowance is made, the amount by which the residue of qualifying expenditure attributable to the dwelling-house before the balancing event exceeds the net proceeds from the event is written off at the time of the event.

(3) If a balancing charge is made, the amount of the residue of qualifying expenditure attributable to the dwelling-house is increased at the time of the balancing event by the amount of the charge.

(4) But if the balancing charge is made under section 517. (6) (difference between relevant allowances and adjusted net cost), the residue of qualifying expenditure attributable to the dwelling-house immediately after the balancing event is limited to the net proceeds from the event.

528 Treatment of demolition costs

(1) This section applies if—

    (a) a dwelling-house is demolished, and

    (b) the person to or on whom any balancing allowance or balancing charge is or might be made is the person incurring the cost of the demolition.

(2) The net cost of the demolition is added to the residue of qualifying expenditure attributable to the qualifying dwelling-house immediately before the demolition.

(3) "The net cost of the demolition" means the amount, if any, by which the cost of the demolition exceeds any money received for the remains of the property.

(4) If this section applies, the net cost of the demolition is not treated for the purposes of this Part as expenditure on any other property replacing the property demolished.

Chapter 8. Supplementary provisions

529 Giving effect to allowances and charges

(1) If a person who is entitled or liable to an allowance or charge for a chargeable period was carrying on [F1a UK property business, or a Schedule A business,] at any time in that period, the allowance or charge is to be given effect in calculating the profits of that business, by treating—

    (a) the allowance as an expense of that business, and

    (b) the charge as a receipt of that business.

[F2. (1. A) If the person entitled or liable to an allowance or charge for a chargeable period is within the charge to income tax in respect of the allowance or charge and he was not carrying on a UK property business at any time in that period, the allowance or charge is to be given effect by

251

treating him as if he had been carrying on such a business in that period and as if—

(a) the allowance were an expense of that business, and

(b) the charge were a receipt of that business.]

(2) [F3. If the person entitled or liable to an allowance or charge for a chargeable period is a company within the charge to corporation tax in respect of the allowance or charge and it] was not carrying on a Schedule A business at any time in that period, the allowance or charge is to be given effect by treating [F4the company] as if [F5it] had been carrying on such a business in that period and as if—

(a) the allowance were an expense of that business, and

(b) the charge were a receipt of that business.

Amendments (Textual)

F1. Words in s. 529. (1) substituted (with effect in accordance with s. 883. (1) of the amending Act) by Income Tax (Trading and Other Income) Act 2005 (c. 5), Sch. 1 para. 569. (2) (with Sch. 2)

F2. S. 529. (1. A) inserted (with effect in accordance with s. 883. (1) of the amending Act) by Income Tax (Trading and Other Income) Act 2005 (c. 5), Sch. 1 para. 569. (3) (with Sch. 2)

F3. Words in s. 529. (2) substituted (with effect in accordance with s. 883. (1) of the amending Act) by Income Tax (Trading and Other Income) Act 2005 (c. 5), Sch. 1 para. 569. (4)(a) (with Sch. 2)

F4. Words in s. 529. (2) substituted (with effect in accordance with s. 883. (1) of the amending Act) by Income Tax (Trading and Other Income) Act 2005 (c. 5), Sch. 1 para. 569. (4)(b) (with Sch. 2)

F5. Word in s. 529. (2) substituted (with effect in accordance with s. 883. (1) of the amending Act) by Income Tax (Trading and Other Income) Act 2005 (c. 5), Sch. 1 para. 569. (4)(c) (with Sch. 2)

530 Apportionment of sums partly referable to non-qualifying assets

(1) If the sum paid for the sale of the relevant interest in a building is attributable—

(a) partly to assets representing expenditure for which an allowance can be made under this Part, and

(b) partly to assets representing other expenditure,

only so much of the sum paid as on a just and reasonable apportionment is attributable to the assets referred to in paragraph (a) is to be taken into account for the purposes of this Part.

(2) Subsection (1) applies to other proceeds from a balancing event in respect of a building as it applies to a sum given for the sale of the relevant interest in the building.

(3) Subsection (1) does not affect any other provision of this Part requiring an apportionment of the proceeds of a balancing event.

531 Meaning of "dwelling-house", "lease" etc.

(1) In this Part "dwelling-house" has the same meaning as in the Rent Act 1977 (c. 42).

(2) In this Part "lease" includes—

(a) an agreement for a lease if the term to be covered by the lease has begun, and

(b) any tenancy,

but does not include a mortgage (and "lessee", "lessor" and "leasehold interest" are to be read accordingly).

(3) In the application of this Part to Scotland—

(a) "leasehold interest" means the interest of a tenant in property subject to a lease, and

(b) any reference to an interest which is reversionary on a leasehold interest or on a lease is to be read as a reference to the interest of the landlord in the property subject to the leasehold interest or lease.

Part 11. Contributions

Part 11. Contributions

Chapter 1. Exclusion of expenditure met by contributions

532 The general rule excluding contributions
(1) For the purposes of this Act, the general rule is that a person ("R") is to be regarded as not having incurred expenditure to the extent that it has been, or is to be, met (directly or indirectly) by—
  (a) a public body, or
  (b) a person other than R.
(2) In this Chapter "public body" means the Crown or any government or public or local authority (whether in the United Kingdom or elsewhere).
(3) The general rule does not apply for the purposes of Part 9 (dredging allowances).
(4) The general rule is subject to the exceptions in sections 534 to 536.
533 Exclusion of contributions to dredging
(1) For the purposes of Part 9, a person ("D") who has incurred expenditure is to be regarded as not having incurred it for the purposes of a trade carried on or to be carried on by D to the extent that it has been, or is to be, met (directly or indirectly) by—
  (a) a public body, or
  (b) capital sums contributed by another person for purposes other than those of D's trade.
(2) Subsection (1) is not subject to the exceptions in sections 534 to 536.

Exceptions to the general rule excluding contributions

534 Northern Ireland regional development grants
(1) A person is to be regarded as having incurred expenditure (despite section 532. (1)) to the extent that it is met (directly or indirectly) by a grant—
  (a) made under Northern Ireland legislation, and
  (b) declared by the Treasury by order to correspond to a grant under Part II of the Industrial Development Act 1982 (c. 52).
(2) Subject to subsection (3), the grant is to be treated as not falling within subsection (1) if, by virtue of paragraph 8 of Schedule 3 to OTA 1975, expenditure which has been or is to be met by the grant is not to be regarded for any of the purposes of Part I of OTA 1975 as having been incurred by any person.
(3) If only a proportion of the expenditure which has been or is to be met by the grant is expenditure which, if it were not so met, would be allowable under section 3 or 4 of OTA 1975, only a corresponding proportion of the grant is to be treated as not falling within subsection (1).
535 Insurance or compensation money
A person is to be regarded as having incurred expenditure (despite section 532. (1)) to the extent that it is met (directly or indirectly) by—
  (a) insurance money, or
  (b) other compensation money,
payable in respect of an asset which has been destroyed, demolished or put out of use.
536 Contributions not made by public bodies and not eligible for tax relief
(1) A person ("R") is to be regarded as having incurred expenditure (despite section 532. (1)) to

the extent that the requirements in subsections (2) and (3) are satisfied in relation to the expenditure.

(2) The first requirement is that the person meeting R's expenditure ("C") is not a public body.

(3) The second requirement is that—

(a) no allowance can be made under Chapter 2 in respect of C's expenditure, and

(b) the expenditure is not allowed to be deducted in calculating the profits of a trade or relevant activity carried on by C.

(4) When determining for the purposes of subsection (3)(a) whether an allowance can be made under Chapter 2, assume that C is within the charge to tax.

(5) In subsection (3)(b) "relevant activity" means—

(a) for the purposes of Part 2—

(i) an ordinary [F1property] business;

(ii) a furnished holiday lettings business;

(iii) an overseas property business;

(iv) a profession or vocation;

(v) any concern listed in [F2section 12. (4) of ITTOIA 2005 or] section 55. (2) of ICTA (mines, transport undertakings etc.);

(vi) the management of an investment company;

(b) for other purposes, a profession or vocation.

Amendments (Textual)

F1 Word in s. 536. (5)(a)(i) substituted (6.4.2005) by Income Tax (Trading and Other Income) Act 2005 (c. 5) , s. 883. (1) , Sch. 1 para. 570. (a) (with Sch. 2)

F2 Words in s. 536. (5)(a)(v) inserted (6.4.2005) by Income Tax (Trading and Other Income) Act 2005 (c. 5) , s. 883. (1) , Sch. 1 para. 570. (b) (with Sch. 2)

Chapter 2. Contribution allowances

Amendments (Textual)

F3. Words in s. 537. (1) cross-heading substituted (with effect in accordance with s. 92 of the amending Act) by Finance Act 2005 (c. 7), Sch. 6 para. 5; S.I. 2007/949, art. 2

537 Conditions for contribution allowances under [F4. Parts 2, 3, 4 and 5]

(1) This section gives general conditions for making contribution allowances under [F5. Parts 2, 3, 4 and 5].

(2) The general conditions are that—

(a) a person ("C") has contributed a capital sum to expenditure on the provision of an asset,

(b) the expenditure would (ignoring section 532. (1))—

(i) have been regarded as wholly incurred by another person ("R"), and

(ii) if R is not a public body, have entitled R to allowances under Part 2, 3, 4 or 5 or to allocate the expenditure to a pool under Part 2, and

(c) C and R are not connected persons.

(3) In this section "public body" means the Crown or any public or local authority in the United Kingdom.

(4) In this Chapter "relevant activity" has the meaning given by section 536. (5).

Amendments (Textual)

F4. Words in s. 537. (1) sidenote substituted (with effect in accordance with s. 92 of the amending Act) by Finance Act 2005 (c. 7), Sch. 6 para. 5; S.I. 2007/949, art. 2

F5. Words in s. 537. (1) substituted (with effect in accordance with s. 92 of the amending Act) by Finance Act 2005 (c. 7), Sch. 6 para. 5; S.I. 2007/949, art. 2

538 Plant and machinery

(1) This section is about contribution allowances under Part 2 and applies if—

(a) the general conditions for contribution allowances are met, and

(b) C's contribution is made for the purposes of a trade or relevant activity carried on, or to be carried on, by C.

(2) C is to be treated for the purposes of allowances under Part 2 as if—

(a) the contribution were expenditure incurred by C on the provision, for the purposes of C's trade or relevant activity, of the asset provided by means of C's contribution,

(b) C owned the asset as a result of incurring that expenditure at any time when R owns it or is treated under Part 2 as owning it, and

(c) the asset were at all material times in use for the purposes of C's trade or relevant activity.

(3) Expenditure treated as incurred under subsection (2)(a), if allocated to any pool, must be allocated to a single asset pool.

(4) Subsections (5) and (6) apply for the purposes of contribution allowances under Part 2 if the whole or a part of the trade or relevant activity for the purposes of which C's contribution was made is transferred.

(5) If the whole of the trade or relevant activity is transferred, writing-down allowances for chargeable periods ending after the date of the transfer are to be made to the transferee instead of to the transferor.

(6) If a part of the trade or relevant activity is transferred, writing-down allowances for chargeable periods ending after the date of the transfer are to be made to the transferee instead of to the transferor to the extent that they are properly referable to the part transferred.

539 Industrial buildings

(1) This section is about contribution allowances under Part 3 and applies if—

(a) the general conditions for contribution allowances are met, and

(b) C's contribution is made for the purposes of a trade or relevant activity carried on, or to be carried on—

(i) by C, or

(ii) by a tenant of land in which C has an interest.

(2) C is to be treated for the purposes of allowances under Part 3 as if—

(a) the contribution were expenditure incurred by C on the provision, for the purposes of the trade or relevant activity, of an asset similar to that provided by means of C's contribution, and

(b) the asset were at all material times in use for the purposes of the trade or relevant activity.

(3) Subsection (4) applies if—

(a) C's contribution was made for the purposes of a trade or relevant activity carried on, or to be carried on, by a tenant of land in which C had an interest, and

(b) C was entitled to allowances as a result of subsection (2).

(4) A person is entitled to a writing-down allowance for a chargeable period if at the end of the period the person is entitled to the interest held by C when the contribution was made.

(5) For the purposes of subsection (4), the provisions of Part 3 relating to the relevant interest apply (with any necessary modifications) in relation to the contribution made for the purposes of the trade or relevant activity carried on, or to be carried on, by the tenant as they apply in relation to expenditure incurred on the construction of an industrial building.

(6) Section 311 (calculation of writing-down allowance after sale of relevant interest) does not apply in relation to writing-down allowances to be made in respect of contributions.

540 Agricultural buildings

(1) This section is about contribution allowances under Part 4 and applies if—

(a) the general conditions for contribution allowances are met, and

(b) C's contribution is made for the purposes of a trade or relevant activity carried on, or to be carried on—

(i) by C, or

(ii) by a tenant of land in which C has a interest.

(2) C is to be treated for the purposes of allowances under Part 4 as if—

(a) the contribution were expenditure incurred by C on the provision, for the purposes of the trade or relevant activity, of an asset similar to that provided by means of C's contribution, and

(b) the asset were at all material times in use for the purposes of the trade or relevant activity.

(3) Subsection (4) applies if—

(a) C's contribution was made for the purposes of a trade or relevant activity carried on, or to be carried on, by a tenant of land in which C had an interest, and

(b) C was entitled to allowances as a result of subsection (2).

(4) A person is entitled to a writing-down allowance for a chargeable period if at the end of the period the person is entitled to the interest held by C when the contribution was made.

(5) For the purposes of subsection (4), the provisions of Part 4 relating to the relevant interest apply (with any necessary modifications) in relation to the contribution made for the purposes of the trade or relevant activity carried on, or to be carried on, by the tenant as they apply in relation to expenditure incurred on the construction of an agricultural building.

541 Mineral extraction

(1) This section is about contribution allowances under Part 5 and applies if—

(a) the general conditions for contribution allowances are met, and

(b) C's contribution is made for the purposes of a trade carried on, or to be carried on, by C.

(2) C is to be treated for the purposes of allowances under Part 5 as if—

(a) the contribution were expenditure incurred by C on the provision, for the purposes of C's trade, of an asset similar to that provided by means of C's contribution, and

(b) the asset were at all material times in use for the purposes of C's trade.

Effect of transfers of C's trade on contribution allowances under Parts 3, 4 and 5.

542 Transfer of C's trade or relevant activity

(1) Subsections (2) and (3) apply for the purposes of contribution allowances under [F6. Parts 3, 4 and 5] if—

(a) C's contribution was made for the purposes of C's trade or relevant activity, and

(b) the whole or a part of the trade or relevant activity is subsequently transferred.

(2) If the whole of the trade or relevant activity is transferred, writing-down allowances for chargeable periods ending after the date of the transfer are to be made to the transferee instead of to the transferor.

(3) If a part of the trade or relevant activity is transferred, writing-down allowances for chargeable periods ending after the date of the transfer are to be made to the transferee instead of to the transferor to the extent that they are properly referable to the part transferred.

Amendments (Textual)

F6. Words in s. 542. (1) substituted (with effect as mentioned in s. 67 of the amending Act) by Finance Act 2001 (c. 9), s. 67, Sch. 19 Pt. 2 para. 4

Contribution allowances under Part 9.

543 Contribution allowances under Part 9.

A person who contributes a capital sum to expenditure incurred by another person on dredging is to be regarded for the purposes of Part 9 as incurring capital expenditure on that dredging.

Contribution allowances under Part 9

543 Contribution allowances under Part 9.

A person who contributes a capital sum to expenditure incurred by another person on dredging is to be regarded for the purposes of Part 9 as incurring capital expenditure on that dredging.

Contribution allowances under Part 9

543 Contribution allowances under Part 9.

A person who contributes a capital sum to expenditure incurred by another person on dredging is to be regarded for the purposes of Part 9 as incurring capital expenditure on that dredging.

Part 12. Supplementary provisions

Part 12. Supplementary provisions

Chapter 1. Life assurance business

544 Management assets

(1) No allowances are to be given or charges imposed in respect of management assets of any life assurance business carried on by a company except under Part 2 (plant and machinery allowances).

(2) An asset is a management asset of any life assurance business carried on by a company if it is provided for use, or used, for the management of that business of that company.

[F1. (3) The management of any life assurance business consists of pursuing those purposes expenditure on which falls to be regarded as expenses payable for the purposes of section 76 of ICTA .]

F2. (5). . . . .

Amendments (Textual)

F1. S. 544. (3) substituted for s. 544. (3)(4) (with effect in accordance with art. 1. (2) of the amending S.I.) by Finance Act 2004, Sections 38 to 40 and 45 and Schedule 6 (Consequential Amendments of Enactments) Order 2004 (S.I. 2004/2310), art. 1. (2), Sch. para. 57. (2)

F2. S. 544. (5) repealed (with effect in accordance with Sch. 10 para. 17. (2) of the amending Act) by Finance Act 2007 (c. 11), Sch. 10 para. 14. (8)(b), Sch. 27 Pt. 2. (10)

545 Investment assets

(1) This section applies if a company which is carrying on any life assurance business holds an asset for purposes other than the management of that business.

(2) "Investment asset" means an asset that is within subsection (1).

[F3. (3)Any allowance under this Act in respect of an investment asset shall be treated as referable to the category or categories of business to which income arising from the asset is or would be referable.

If income so arising is or would be referable to more than one category of business, the allowance shall be apportioned in accordance with [F4section 432. A] of ICTA in the same way as the income.]

(4) If the company is charged to tax in respect of its life assurance business under Case I of Schedule D, no allowance in respect of an investment asset is to be taken into account in calculating the company's profits from that business.

(5) If the company is charged to tax [F5under section 436. A of ICTA (gross roll-up business), no allowance] in respect of an investment asset is to be taken into account in calculating the company's profits from [F6gross roll-up business].

Amendments (Textual)

F3 S. 545. (3) substituted (retrospective to 6.4.2001) by Finance Act 2001 (c. 9) , s. 76 , Sch. 25

para. 7

F4. Words in s. 545. (3) substituted (with effect in accordance with s. 38. (2) of the amending Act) by Finance Act 2007 (c. 11), Sch. 7 para. 71. (2) (with Sch. 7 Pt. 2)

F5. Words in s. 545. (5) substituted (with effect in accordance with s. 38. (2) of the amending Act) by Finance Act 2007 (c. 11), Sch. 7 para. 71. (3)(a) (with Sch. 7 Pt. 2)

F6. Words in s. 545. (5) substituted (with effect in accordance with s. 38. (2) of the amending Act) by Finance Act 2007 (c. 11), Sch. 7 para. 71. (3)(b) (with Sch. 7 Pt. 2)

Chapter 2. Additional VAT liabilities and rebates: interpretation, etc.

546 Introduction

This Chapter has effect for the interpretation of, and for otherwise supplementing—
    (a) Chapter 18 of Part 2 (plant and machinery allowances: additional VAT liabilities and rebates),
    (b) Chapter 10 of Part 3 (industrial buildings allowances: additional VAT liabilities and rebates), and
    [F7. (ba) Chapter 10 of Part 3. A (business premises renovation allowances: additional VAT liabilities and rebates),]
    (c) Chapter 4 of Part 6 (research and development allowances: additional VAT liabilities and rebates).
Amendments (Textual)
F7. S. 546. (ba) inserted (with effect in accordance with s. 92 of the amending Act) by Finance Act 2005 (c. 7), Sch. 6 para. 6; S.I. 2007/949, art. 2

547 "Additional VAT liability" and "additional VAT rebate"

(1) "Additional VAT liability" means an amount which a person becomes liable to pay by way of adjustment under the VAT capital items legislation in respect of input tax.
(2) "Additional VAT rebate" means an amount which a person becomes entitled to deduct by way of adjustment under the VAT capital items legislation in respect of input tax.

548 Time when additional VAT liability or rebate is incurred or made

(1) The time when a person incurs an additional VAT liability or an additional VAT rebate is made to a person is the last day of the period—
    (a) which is one of the periods making up the VAT period of adjustment applicable to the asset in question under the VAT capital items legislation, and
    (b) in which the increase or decrease in use giving rise to the liability or rebate occurs.
(2) "VAT period of adjustment" means a period specified under the VAT capital items legislation by reference to which adjustments are made in respect of input tax.

549 Chargeable period in which, and time when, additional VAT liability or rebate accrues

(1) The chargeable period in which, and the time when, an additional VAT liability or additional

VAT rebate accrues is set out in the Table.

Table

Accrual of VAT liabilities and rebates

Circumstances	Chargeable period	Time of accrual
The liability or rebate is accounted for in a VAT return.	The chargeable period which includes the last day of the period to which the VAT return relates.	The last day of the period to which the VAT return relates.
The Commissioners of Customs and Excise assess the liability or rebate as due before a VAT return is made.	The chargeable period which includes the day on which the assessment is made.	The day on which the assessment is made.
The relevant activity is permanently discontinued before the liability or rebate is accounted for in a VAT return or assessed by the Commissioners.	The chargeable period in which the relevant activity is permanently discontinued.	The last day of the chargeable period in which the relevant activity is permanently discontinued.

(2) In the Table—

   (a) "VAT return" means a return made to the Commissioners of Customs and Excise for the purposes of value added tax, and

   (b) "the relevant activity" means the trade or, in relation to Part 2, the qualifying activity to which the additional VAT liability or additional VAT rebate relates.

550 Apportionment of additional VAT liabilities and rebates

(1) This section applies if—

   (a) any provision of this Act requires an allowance or charge to which a person is entitled or liable in respect of any qualifying expenditure to be determined by reference to—

(i) a proportion only of that expenditure, or

(ii) a proportion only of what that allowance or charge would have been apart from that provision, and

   (b) the person incurs an additional VAT liability or an additional VAT rebate is made to the person in respect of that expenditure.

(2) The additional VAT liability or rebate is subject to the same apportionment as the original expenditure, allowance or charge.

551 Supplementary

(1) In this Chapter, "the VAT capital items legislation" means any Act or instrument (whenever passed or made) providing for the proportion of input tax on an asset of a specified description which may be deducted by a person from his output tax to be adjusted from time to time as a result of—

   (a) an increase, or

   (b) a decrease,

in the extent to which the asset is used by him for making taxable supplies (or taxable supplies of a specified class or description) during a specified period.

(2) In this Chapter "the VAT capital items legislation" also includes any other Act or instrument (whenever passed or made) which provides for Article 20. (2) to (4) of the Sixth VAT Directive to be given effect.

(3) "The Sixth VAT Directive" means the Sixth Directive (77/388/EEC) of the Council of the European Communities on Value Added Tax, dated 17th May 1977.

(4) In this Chapter "input tax", "output tax" and "taxable supply" have the same meaning as in VATA 1994.

Chapter 3. Disposals of oil licences: provisions relating to Parts 5 and 6

552 Meaning of "oil licence" and "interest in an oil licence"

(1) In this Chapter "oil licence" means a UK oil licence or a foreign oil concession.

(2) In this Chapter "UK oil licence" means a licence under—

(a) Part I of the Petroleum Act 1998 (c. 17) ("the 1998 Act"), or

(b) the Petroleum (Production) Act (Northern Ireland) 1964 (c. 28 (N.I.)) ("the 1964 Act"),

authorising the winning of oil.

(3) In this Chapter "foreign oil concession" means any right which—

(a) is a right to search for or win oil that exists in its natural condition in a place to which neither the 1998 Act nor the 1964 Act applies, and

(b) is conferred or exercisable (whether or not under a licence) in relation to a particular area.

(4) In this Chapter "interest in an oil licence" includes, if there is an agreement which—

(a) relates to oil from the whole or a part of the licensed area, and

(b) was made before the extraction of the oil to which it relates,

any entitlement under the agreement to, or to a share of, that oil or the proceeds of its sale.

Oil licences relating to undeveloped areas

553 Consideration to be treated as nil

(1) This section applies if—

(a) there is a material disposal of an oil licence which, at the time of the disposal, relates to an undeveloped area, and

(b) any of the consideration for the disposal consists of—

(i) another oil licence, or an interest in another oil licence, which at that time relates to an undeveloped area, or

(ii) an obligation to undertake exploration work or appraisal work in an area which is or forms part of the licensed area in relation to the licence disposed of.

(2) The value of the consideration within subsection (1)(b) is to be treated as nil for the purposes of—

(a) Part 5 (mineral extraction allowances),

(b) Part 6 (research and development allowances), and

(c) section 555 (disposal of oil licence with exploitation value).

(3) A "material disposal" of an oil licence means any disposal (including a part disposal and a disposal of an interest in an oil licence) other than a disposal in relation to which section 568 or 569 (sales treated as being for alternative amount) has effect.

(4) If—

(a) the material disposal is part of a larger transaction under which one party makes to another material disposals of two or more licences, and

(b) at the time of disposal, each of those licences relates to an undeveloped area,

the licensed area for the purposes of subsection (1)(b) is the totality of the licensed areas in relation to those licences.

(5) In relation to a material disposal of a licence under which the buyer acquires an interest in the licence only so far as it relates to part of the licensed area, any reference in this section and section 554 to the licensed area is to be read as a reference only to that part of the licensed area to which the buyer's acquisition relates.

(6) In subsection (1)(b)—

"exploration work", in relation to an area, means work carried out for the purpose of searching for oil anywhere in that area, and

"appraisal work", in relation to an area, means work carried out for the purpose of ascertaining—

- the extent or characteristics of any oil-bearing area the whole or part of which lies in that area, or

- what the reserves of oil of any such oil-bearing area are.

554 Circumstances in which oil licence relates to undeveloped area

(1) A UK oil licence relates to an undeveloped area if—

(a) no consent for development has been granted to the licensee for any part of the licensed area by the relevant authority, and

(b) no programme of development has been served on the licensee or approved for any part of the licensed area by the relevant authority.

(2) A foreign oil concession relates to an undeveloped area if—

(a) no development has actually taken place in any part of the licensed area, and

(b) no condition for the carrying out of development anywhere in that area has been satisfied—

(i) by the grant of any consent by the authorities of a country or territory exercising jurisdiction in relation to the area, or

(ii) by the approval or service on the licensee, by any such authorities, of any programme of development.

(3) Subsections (4) and (5) of section 36 of FA 1983 (meaning of development) apply for the purposes of subsections (1) and (2).

(4) In subsection (1) "licensee" means—

(a) the person entitled to the benefit of the licence or, if two or more persons are entitled to the benefit, each of those persons, and

(b) a person who has rights under an agreement which is—

(i) approved by [F8the Commissioners for Her Majesty's Revenue and Customs], and

(ii) certified by the relevant authority to confer on that person rights which are the same as, or similar to, those conferred by a licence.

(5) In subsection (2) "licensee" means the person with the concession or any person having an interest in it.

Amendments (Textual)

F8. Words in Act substituted (18.4.2005) by Commissioners for Revenue and Customs Act 2005 (c. 11), s. 53. (1), Sch. 4 para. 83. (1); S.I. 2005/1126, art. 2. (2)(h)

Disposal of oil licence with exploitation value

555 Disposal of oil licence with exploitation value

(1) This section applies if—

(a) a person ("the seller") disposes of an interest in an oil licence to another ("the buyer"), and

(b) part of the value of the interest is attributable to allowable exploration expenditure incurred by the seller.

(2) For the purposes of Part 6 (research and development allowances) the disposal is to be treated as a disposal by which the seller ceases to own an asset representing the allowable exploration expenditure to which that part of the value of the interest is attributable.

(3) Part 6 applies as if the disposal value to be brought into account were equal to so much of the buyer's expenditure on acquiring the interest as it is just and reasonable to attribute to that part of the value of the interest.

(4) In this section "allowable exploration expenditure" means expenditure which—

(a) is incurred on mineral exploration and access within the meaning of Part 5 (mineral extraction allowances), and

(b) is qualifying expenditure for the purposes of Part 6.

Minor definitions

556 Minor definitions

(1) In this Chapter "licensed area" means (subject to section 553. (4) and (5))—

(a) in relation to a UK oil licence, the area to which the licence applies, and

(b) in relation to a foreign oil concession, the area in relation to which the right to search for or win oil is conferred or exercisable under the concession.

(2) In this Chapter "the relevant authority", in relation to a UK oil licence means—

(a) in the case of a licence under Part I of the 1998 Act, the Secretary of State, and

(b) in the case of a licence under the 1964 Act, the Department of Enterprise, Trade and Investment in Northern Ireland.

(3) In this Chapter "oil"—

(a) in relation to a UK oil licence, means any substance won or capable of being won under the authority of a licence granted under Part I of the 1998 Act or the 1964 Act, other than methane gas won in the course of operations for making and keeping mines safe, and

(b) in relation to a foreign oil concession, means any petroleum (as defined by section 1 of the 1998 Act).

Chapter 4. Partnerships, successions and transfers

557 Application of sections 558 and 559.

Sections 558 (effect of partnership changes) and 559 (effect of successions) apply for the purposes of this Act other than—

(a) Part 2 (plant and machinery allowances),

(b) Part 6 (research and development allowances), and

(c) Part 10 (assured tenancy allowances).

558 Effect of partnership changes

(1) This section applies if—

(a) a relevant activity has been set up and is at any time carried on in partnership,

(b) there has been a change in the persons engaged in carrying on the relevant activity, and

[F9. (c) the change does not [F10—

(i) involve all of the persons carrying on the relevant activity before the change permanently ceasing to carry it on, or

(ii) result in the relevant activity being treated under section 18 or 362 of ITTOIA 2005 as permanently ceasing to be carried on by a company or treated as discontinued under section 337.

(1) of ICTA (companies beginning or ceasing to carry on trade etc.).]]

(2) In this section—

" the present partners " means the person or persons for the time being carrying on the relevant activity, and

" predecessors ", in relation to the present partners, means their predecessors in carrying on the relevant activity.

(3) Any allowance or charge is to be made to or on the present partners.

(4) The amount of any allowance or charge arising under subsection (3) is to be calculated as if—

(a) the present partners had at all times been carrying on the relevant activity, and

(b) everything done to or by their predecessors in carrying on the relevant activity had been done to or by the present partners.

(5) In this section " relevant activity " means a trade, property business, profession or vocation.

Amendments (Textual)

F9. S. 558. (1)(c) substituted (with effect as mentioned in s. 69. (2) of the amending Act) by Finance Act 2001 (c. 9), s. 69. (1), Sch. 21 para. 4. (2)

F10 S. 558. (1)(c)(i) (ii) substituted for words in para. (c) (with effect in accordance with s. 883. (1) of the amending Act) by Income Tax (Trading and Other Income) Act 2005 (c. 5) , Sch. 1 para. 571 (with Sch. 2)

559 Effect of successions

(1) This section applies if—

(a) a person ("the successor") succeeds to a relevant activity which until that time was carried on by another person ("the predecessor"), and

[F11. (b)the following condition is met.]

[F12. (1. A)The condition is that—

(a) all of the persons carrying on the relevant activity before the succession permanently cease to carry it on, or

(b) the relevant activity is treated under section 18 or 362 of ITTOIA 2005 as permanently ceasing to be carried on by a company or treated as discontinued under section 337. (1) of ICTA (companies beginning or ceasing to carry on trade etc.).]

(2) The property in question is to be treated as if—

(a) it had been sold to the successor when the succession takes place, and

(b) the net proceeds of the sale were the market value of the property.

(3) The property in question is any property which—

(a) immediately before the succession, was in use for the purposes of the discontinued relevant activity, and

(b) immediately after the succession, and without being sold, is in use for the purposes of the new relevant activity.

(4) No entitlement to an initial allowance arises under this section.

(5) In this section "relevant activity" means a trade, property business, profession or vocation.

Amendments (Textual)

F11. S. 559. (1)(b) substituted (with effect in accordance with s. 883. (1) of the amending Act) by Income Tax (Trading and Other Income) Act 2005 (c. 5), Sch. 1 para. 572. (2) (with Sch. 2)

F12. S. 559. (1. A) inserted (with effect in accordance with s. 883. (1) of the amending Act) by Income Tax (Trading and Other Income) Act 2005 (c. 5), Sch. 1 para. 572. (3) (with Sch. 2)

560 Transfer of insurance company business

(1) This section applies if—

(a) assets are transferred as part of, or in connection with, the transfer of the whole or part of the business of an insurance company to another company,

(b) the transfer is—

(i) in accordance with [F13 an insurance business transfer scheme to transfer business which consists of the effecting or carrying out of contracts of long-term insurance, or]

(ii) a qualifying overseas transfer within the meaning of paragraph 4. A of Schedule 19. AC to ICTA (overseas life insurance companies).

(2) But this section does not apply in relation to any asset transferred to a non-resident company unless the asset will fall to be treated, immediately after the transfer, as an asset which is held for the purposes of the whole or a part of so much of any business carried on by the non-resident company as is carried on through a [F14permanent establishment] in the United Kingdom.

(3) This section also does not apply if section 561 applies (transfer of a UK trade to a company in another member State).

(4) If this section applies—

(a) any allowances and charges that would have been made to or on the transferor are to be made instead to or on the transferee, and

(b) the amount of any such allowance or charge is to be calculated as if everything done to or by the transferor had been done to or by the transferee,

but no sale or transfer of assets made to the transferee by the transferor is to be treated as giving rise to any such allowance or charge.

(5) In this section—

F15. (a). . . . .

F16. (b). . . . .

F17. (c). . . . .

[F18. (d) "non-resident company" means a company resident outside the United Kingdom.]

Amendments (Textual)

F13. Words in s. 560. (1)(b)(i) substituted (1.12.2001) by The Financial Services and Markets Act 2000 (Consequential Amendments) (Taxes) Order 2001 (S.I. 2001/3629), art. 108. (2)(4)

F14. Words in s. 560. (2) substituted (with effect in accordance with s. 153. (4) of the amending Act) by Finance Act 2003 (c. 14), s. 153. (1)(d)

F15. S. 560. (5)(a) repealed (with effect in accordance with Sch. 10 para. 17. (2) of the amending Act) by Finance Act 2007 (c. 11), Sch. 10 para. 14. (8)(c), Sch. 27 Pt. 2. (10)

F16. S. 560. (5)(b) repealed (with effect in accordance with Sch. 9 para. 17. (1) of the amending Act) by Finance Act 2007 (c. 11), Sch. 9 para. 1. (2)(f), Sch. 27 Pt. 2. (9)

F17. S. 560. (5)(c) repealed (with effect in accordance with Sch. 10 para. 17. (2) of the amending Act) by Finance Act 2007 (c. 11), Sch. 10 para. 14. (8)(c), Sch. 27 Pt. 2. (10)

F18. S. 560. (5)(b)-(d) substituted (1.12.2001) for s. 560. (5)(b) by The Financial Services and Markets Act 2000 (Consequential Amendments) (Taxes) Order 2001 (S.I. 2001/3629), art. 108. (3)(b)(4)

Modifications etc. (not altering text)

C1. S. 560 modified (1.1.2002) by S.I. 1997/473, reg. 53. D (as inserted by S.I. 2001/3975, reg. 8)

C2 S. 560 amendment to earlier affecting provision SI 1997/473 (8.4.2004) by The Friendly Societies (Modification of the Corporation Tax Acts) (Amendment) Regulations 2004 (S.I. 2004/822) , regs. 1 , 40

561 [F19. Transfer or division of UK business]

[F20. (1)This section applies if and in so far as—

(a) a qualifying company resident in one member State ("the transferor") transfers the whole or part of a business carried on by it in the United Kingdom to one or more qualifying companies resident in one or more other member States ("the transferee" or "the transferees"),

(b) section 140. A of TCGA 1992 (transfer of assets treated as no-gain no-loss disposal) applies in relation to the transfer, and

(c) immediately after the transfer the transferee (or one or more of the transferees)—

(i) is resident in the United Kingdom, or

(ii) carries on in the United Kingdom through a permanent establishment a business which consists of, or includes, the business or part of the business transferred.]

(2) If this section applies—

(a) the transfer itself does not give rise to any allowances or charges under this Act, and

(b) in relation to assets included in the transfer, anything done to or by [F21the transferor] before the transfer is to be treated after the transfer as having been done to or by [F22the transferee (or each transferee)].

(3) If, for the purposes of subsection (2)(b), expenditure falls to be apportioned between assets included in the transfer and other assets, the apportionment is to be made in a just and reasonable manner.

(4) In this section " qualifying company " means a body incorporated under the law of a member State.

(5) If this section applies, section 343. (2) of ICTA does not apply (effect of company reconstruction without change of ownership).

Amendments (Textual)

F19. S. 561 heading substituted (with effect in accordance with reg. 3. (1) of the amending S.I.) by The Corporation Tax (Implementation of the Mergers Directive) Regulations 2007 (S.I. 2007/3186), reg. 1. (2), Sch. 1 para. 25. (4) (as modified by S.I. 2008/1579, regs. 1. (2), 4. (1))

F20. S. 561. (1) substituted (with effect in accordance with reg. 3. (1) of the amending S.I.) by The Corporation Tax (Implementation of the Mergers Directive) Regulations 2007 (S.I. 2007/3186), reg. 1. (2), Sch. 1 para. 25. (2) (as modified by S.I. 2008/1579, regs. 1. (2), 4. (1))

F21. Words in s. 561. (2)(b) substituted (with effect in accordance with reg. 3. (1) of the amending S.I.) by The Corporation Tax (Implementation of the Mergers Directive) Regulations 2007 (S.I. 2007/3186), reg. 1. (2), Sch. 1 para. 25. (3)(a) (as modified by S.I. 2008/1579, regs. 1. (2), 4. (1))

F22. Words in s. 561. (2)(b) substituted (with effect in accordance with reg. 3. (1) of the amending S.I.) by The Corporation Tax (Implementation of the Mergers Directive) Regulations 2007 (S.I. 2007/3186), reg. 1. (2), Sch. 1 para. 25. (3)(b) (as modified by S.I. 2008/1579, regs. 1. (2), 4. (1))

[F23561. A Transfer of asset by reason of cross-border merger

(1) This section applies to the transfer of a qualifying asset as part of the process of a merger to which section 140. E of TCGA 1992 (mergers: assets within UK tax charge) applies (or would apply but for section 140. E(2)(c)).

(2) Where this section applies to a transfer—

(a) the transfer does not give rise to any allowance or charge under this Act,

(b) anything done to or by the transferor in relation to assets transferred is to be treated after the transfer as having been done to or by the transferee (with any necessary apportionment of expenditure being made in a reasonable manner), and

(c) section 343 of ICTA (company reconstruction without change of ownership) shall not apply.

(3) For the purposes of subsection (1) an asset is a "qualifying asset" if—

(a) it is transferred to the transferee as part of the process of the merger, and

(b) subsections (4) and (5) are satisfied in respect of it.

(4) This subsection is satisfied in respect of an asset if—

(a) the transferor is resident in the United Kingdom at the time of the transfer, or

(b) the asset is an asset of a permanent establishment in the United Kingdom of the transferor.

(5) This subsection is satisfied in respect of an asset if—

(a) the transferee is resident in the United Kingdom at the time of the transfer, or

(b) the asset is an asset of a permanent establishment of the transferee in the United Kingdom immediately following the transfer.]

Amendments (Textual)

F23. S. 561. A substituted (with effect in accordance with reg. 3. (2) of the amending S.I.) by The Corporation Tax (Implementation of the Mergers Directive) Regulations 2007 (S.I. 2007/3186), reg. 1. (2), Sch. 2 para. 14

Chapter 5. Miscellaneous

562 Apportionment where property sold together

(1) Any reference in this Act to the sale of property includes the sale of that property together with any other property.

(2) For the purposes of subsection (1), all property sold as a result of one bargain is to be treated as sold together even though—

(a) separate prices are, or purport to be, agreed for separate items of that property, or

(b) there are, or purport to be, separate sales of separate items of that property.

(3) If an item of property is sold together with other property, then, for the purposes of this Act—

(a) the net proceeds of the sale of that item are to be treated as being so much of the net proceeds of sale of all the property as, on a just and reasonable apportionment, is attributable to that item, and

(b) the expenditure incurred on the provision or purchase of that item is to be treated as being so much of the consideration given for all the property as, on a just and reasonable apportionment, is attributable to that item.

(4) This section applies, with the necessary modifications, to other proceeds (consisting of insurance money or other compensation) as it applies in relation to the net proceeds of a sale.

(5) This section applies in relation to Part 5 as if expenditure on the provision or purchase of an item of property included expenditure on the acquisition of—

(a) a mineral asset (as defined by section 397), or

(b) land outside the United Kingdom.

Procedure for determining certain questions

563 Procedure for determining certain questions affecting two or more persons

(1) This section applies in relation to the determination of a question if—

(a) at the time when the question falls to be determined, it appears that the determination is material to the liability to tax (for whatever period) of two or more persons, and

(b) section 564 provides for this section to apply.

(2)The Commissioners who are to determine the question, for the purposes of the tax of all the persons concerned, are given in subsections (3) to (5).

(3)If—

(a) the same body of General Commissioners has jurisdiction with respect to all the persons concerned, and

(b) those persons do not agree that the determination is to be made by the Special Commissioners,

the determination is to be made by that body of General Commissioners.

(4)If—

(a) different bodies of General Commissioners have jurisdiction with respect to the persons concerned, and

(b) those persons do not agree that the determination is to be made by the Special Commissioners,

the determination is to be made by such of those bodies of General Commissioners as the [F8the Commissioners for Her Majesty's Revenue and Customs] may direct.

(5)In any other case, the determination is to be made by the Special Commissioners.

(6)The Commissioners must determine the question in the same way as an appeal, but all the persons concerned are entitled—

(a) to appear before and be heard by the Commissioners, or

(b) to make representations to them in writing.

Amendments (Textual)

F8. Words in Act substituted (18.4.2005) by Commissioners for Revenue and Customs Act 2005 (c. 11), s. 53. (1), Sch. 4 para. 83. (1); S.I. 2005/1126, art. 2. (2)(h)

Modifications etc. (not altering text)

C3. S. 563. (2)-(6) applied (with effect in accordance with s. 883. (1) of the amending Act) by Income Tax (Trading and Other Income) Act 2005 (c. 5), ss. 607, (with Sch. 2)

564 Questions to which procedure in section 563 applies

(1) Section 563 applies in relation to the determination for the purposes of any of Parts 3 to 11 or this Part of any question about the way in which a sum is to be apportioned.

(2) Section 563 applies in relation to any determination of the market value of property for the purposes of—

(a) any provision of Part 2 (plant and machinery allowances),

(b) section 423 (mineral extraction allowances: amount of disposal value to be brought into account),

(c) section 559 (effect of successions),

(d) section 568 or 569 (sales treated as being for alternative amount), or

(e) section 573 (transfers treated as sales).

(3) Section 563 applies in relation to any determination of the amount of any sums paid or proceeds for the purposes of section 357 (industrial buildings allowances: arrangements having an artificial effect on pricing).

(4) If section 561 (transfer of a UK trade to a company in another member State) applies, section 563 applies—

(a) for the purposes of the tax of both company A and company B referred to in that section, and

(b) in relation to the determination of any question of apportionment of expenditure under section 561. (3).

Tax agreements for income tax purposes

565 Tax agreements for income tax purposes

(1) This section applies if—

(a) a person is entitled to an allowance for income tax purposes,

(b) that person enters into a tax agreement with [F8an officer of Revenue and Customs] for the tax year in which the allowance would be given effect, and

(c) no assessment giving effect to the allowance is made for that tax year.

(2) In this section " tax agreement " means an agreement in writing as to the extent to which the allowance in question is to be given effect for the tax year in question.

(3) If this section applies, the allowance is to be treated as if it had been given effect under an assessment—

(a) for the tax year for which the tax agreement is made, and

(b) to the extent set out in the tax agreement.

(4) A tax agreement may relate to any method by which allowances are given effect under this Act.

Amendments (Textual)

F8. Words in Act substituted (18.4.2005) by Commissioners for Revenue and Customs Act 2005 (c. 11), s. 53. (1), Sch. 4 para. 83. (1); S.I. 2005/1126, art. 2. (2)(h)

Companies not resident in the United Kingdom

566 Companies not resident in the United Kingdom

(1) This section applies if a company not resident in the United Kingdom is—

(a) within the charge to corporation tax in respect of one source of income, and

(b) within the charge to income tax in respect of another source.

(2) Allowances related to any source of income are to be given effect against income chargeable to the same tax as is chargeable on income from that source.

Sales treated as being for alternative amount

567 Sales treated as being for alternative amount: introductory

(1) Sections 568 to 570 apply for the purposes of Parts 3, [F243. A,] 4, [F254. A,] 5, 6 and 10.

(2) For the purposes of sections 568 to 570, the control test is met if—

(a) the buyer is a body of persons over whom the seller has control,

(b) the seller is a body of persons over whom the buyer has control,

(c) both the seller and the buyer are bodies of persons and another person has control over both of them, or

(d) the seller and the buyer are connected persons.

(3) In subsection (2) " body of persons " includes a partnership.

(4) For the purposes of sections 568 to 570, the tax advantage test is met if it appears that the sole or main benefit which might be expected to accrue from—

(a) the sale, or

(b) transactions of which the sale is one,

is the obtaining of a tax advantage by all or any of the parties under any provision of this Act except Part 2.

(5) Sections 568 to 570 do not apply if section 561 applies (transfer of a UK trade to a company in another member State).

Amendments (Textual)

F24. Word in s. 567. (1) inserted (with effect in accordance with s. 92 of the amending Act) by Finance Act 2005 (c. 7), Sch. 6 para. 7; S.I. 2007/949, art. 2

F25. Words in s. 567. (1) inserted (with effect as mentioned in s. 67 of the amending Act) by Finance Act 2001 (c. 9), s. 67, Sch. 19 Pt. 2 para. 5

Modifications etc. (not altering text)

C4. Ss. 567-570 excluded (E.W.S.) (8.6.2005) by Railways Act 2005 (c. 14), s. 60. (2), Sch. 10 para. 4. (4); S.I. 2005/1444, art. 2. (1), Sch. 1

C5. Ss. 567-570 excluded (E.W.S.) (24.7.2005) by Railways Act 2005 (c. 14), s. 60. (2), Sch. 10 para. 24. (4); S.I. 2005/1909, art. 2, Sch.

568 Sales treated as being at market value

(1) A sale of property that is not at market value is treated as being at market value if—

(a) the control test is met, or

(b) the tax advantage test is met.

(2) This section is subject to any election under section 569.

Modifications etc. (not altering text)

C4. Ss. 567-570 excluded (E.W.S.) (8.6.2005) by Railways Act 2005 (c. 14), s. 60. (2), Sch. 10 para. 4. (4); S.I. 2005/1444, art. 2. (1), Sch. 1

C5. Ss. 567-570 excluded (E.W.S.) (24.7.2005) by Railways Act 2005 (c. 14), s. 60. (2), Sch. 10 para. 24. (4); S.I. 2005/1909, art. 2, Sch.

569 Election to treat sale as being for alternative amount

(1) The parties to a sale of property that is not for the alternative amount may elect for the sale to be treated as being for the alternative amount if—

(a) the control test is met or section 573 applies (transfers treated as sales), and

(b) the tax advantage test is not met.

(2) Subsection (1) is subject to section 570.

(3) The alternative amount is the lower of market value and—

(a) if the sale is relevant for the purposes of Part 3 or 10, the residue of the qualifying expenditure immediately before the sale;

(b) if the sale is relevant for the purposes of Part 5, the unrelieved qualifying expenditure immediately before the sale;

(c) if the sale is relevant for the purposes of Part 6—

(i) in a case where an allowance under Part 6 is given for the expenditure represented by the asset sold, nil;

(ii) in any other case, the qualifying expenditure represented by the asset sold.

(4) In subsection (3) " residue of qualifying expenditure ", " unrelieved qualifying expenditure " and " qualifying expenditure " have the same meaning as in the Part for the purposes of which the sale is relevant.

(5) If the sale—

(a) is relevant for the purposes of Part 3 or 10, and

(b) is treated as being for the residue of the qualifying expenditure immediately before the sale,

no balancing adjustment is to be made as a result of the sale under section 319 (building not an industrial building, etc. throughout) or 517 (building not a qualifying dwelling-house throughout).

(6) If, after the date of the sale, an event occurs as a result of which a balancing charge would have

fallen to be made on the seller if—

(a) he had continued to own the property, and

(b) he had done all such things, and been allowed all such allowances, as were done by or allowed to the buyer,

the balancing charge is to be made on the buyer.

(7) All such assessments and adjustments of assessments are to be made as are necessary to give effect to the election.

(8) For the purposes of this section and section 570, a sale is relevant for the purposes of a Part if it is of property of a kind that is relevant for deciding whether an allowance or charge is made under that Part.

Modifications etc. (not altering text)

C4. Ss. 567-570 excluded (E.W.S.) (8.6.2005) by Railways Act 2005 (c. 14), s. 60. (2), Sch. 10 para. 4. (4); S.I. 2005/1444, art. 2. (1), Sch. 1

C5. Ss. 567-570 excluded (E.W.S.) (24.7.2005) by Railways Act 2005 (c. 14), s. 60. (2), Sch. 10 para. 24. (4); S.I. 2005/1909, art. 2, Sch.

570 Elections: supplementary

(1) Section 569. (1) does not apply to a sale that is relevant for the purposes of Part [F263. A,] 4 [F27or 4. A].

(2) No election under section 569 may be made if—

(a) the circumstances of the sale or the parties to it mean that a relevant allowance or charge will not be capable of falling to be made, or

(b) the buyer is a dual resident investing company.

(3) In subsection (2)(a) " relevant allowance or charge " means an allowance or charge under Part 3, 5, 6, 9 or 10 which (ignoring the circumstances mentioned in subsection (2)(a)) would or might fall to be made, as a result of the sale, to or on any of the parties to it.

(4) If the sale is relevant for the purposes of Part 10, no election under section 569 may be made unless, at the time of the sale or any earlier time, both the seller and the buyer are or have been approved bodies (as defined in section 492).

(5) An election under section 569 must be made by notice to [F8an officer of Revenue and Customs] not later than 2 years after the sale.

Amendments (Textual)

F8. Words in Act substituted (18.4.2005) by Commissioners for Revenue and Customs Act 2005 (c. 11), s. 53. (1), Sch. 4 para. 83. (1); S.I. 2005/1126, art. 2. (2)(h)

F26. Word in s. 570. (1) inserted (with effect in accordance with s. 92 of the amending Act) by Finance Act 2005 (c. 7), Sch. 6 para. 8; S.I. 2007/949, art. 2

F27. Words in s. 570. (1) inserted (with effect as mentioned in s. 67 of the amending Act) by Finance Act 2001 (c. 9), s. 67, Sch. 19 Pt. 2 para. 6

Modifications etc. (not altering text)

C4. Ss. 567-570 excluded (E.W.S.) (8.6.2005) by Railways Act 2005 (c. 14), s. 60. (2), Sch. 10 para. 4. (4); S.I. 2005/1444, art. 2. (1), Sch. 1

C5. Ss. 567-570 excluded (E.W.S.) (24.7.2005) by Railways Act 2005 (c. 14), s. 60. (2), Sch. 10 para. 24. (4); S.I. 2005/1909, art. 2, Sch.

[F28. Anti-avoidance

Amendments (Textual)

F28 S. 570. A and cross-heading inserted (10.7.2003) by Finance Act 2003 (c. 14) , s. 164. (1) (with s. 164. (2))

570. AAvoidance affecting proceeds of balancing event

(1) This section applies where an event occurs in relation to an asset (a " balancing event ") as a result of which a balancing allowance would (but for this section) fall to be made to a person ("the taxpayer") under Part 3, [F29. 3. A] 4, 4. A, 5 or 10.

(2) The taxpayer is not entitled to any balancing allowance if, as a result of a tax avoidance scheme, the amount to be brought into account as the proceeds from the event is less than it would otherwise have been.

(3) In subsection (2) a " tax avoidance scheme " means a scheme or arrangement the main purpose, or one of the main purposes, of which is the obtaining of a tax advantage by the taxpayer.

(4) Where this section applies to deny a balancing allowance, the residue of qualifying expenditure immediately after the balancing event is nevertheless calculated as if the balancing allowance had been made.

(5) In this section as it applies for the purposes of Part 5 (mineral extraction allowances)—

(a) the references to the proceeds from the balancing event that are to be brought into account shall be read as references to the disposal value to be brought into account, and

(b) the reference to the residue of qualifying expenditure shall be read as a reference to the unrelieved qualifying expenditure.]

Amendments (Textual)

F29. Word in s. 570. A(1) inserted (with effect in accordance with s. 92 of the amending Act) by Finance Act 2005 (c. 7), Sch. 6 para. 9; S.I. 2007/949, art. 2

Chapter 6. Final provisions

Amendments (Textual)

F30. S. 570. B and cross-heading inserted (6.4.2007) by Income Tax Act 2007 (c. 3), s. 1034. (1), Sch. 1 para. 409 (with Sch. 2)

570. BOrders and regulations made by Treasury or Commissioners

(1) Any orders or regulations made by the Treasury or the Commissioners for Her Majesty's Revenue and Customs under this Act must be made by statutory instrument.

(2) Any orders or regulations made by the Treasury or the Commissioners under this Act are subject to annulment in pursuance of a resolution of the House of Commons.

(3) Subsection (2) does not apply to any regulations made under section 70. YJ or any order made under section 82. (4)(d).]

General interpretation

571 Application of Act to parts of assets

(1) In this Act references to an asset of any kind (including a building or structure, plant or machinery or works) include a part of an asset.

(2) But subsection (1) does not apply if the context otherwise requires.

572 References to sale of property and time of sale

(1) In this Act references to the sale of property include—

(a) the exchange of property, and

(b) the surrender for valuable consideration of a leasehold interest (or, in Scotland, the interest of the tenant in property subject to a lease).

(2) For the purposes of subsection (1), any provision of this Act referring to a sale has effect with the necessary modifications, including, in particular, those in subsection (3).

(3) The modifications are that—

(a) references to the net proceeds of sale and to the price include the consideration for the exchange or surrender, and

(b) references to capital sums included in the net proceeds of sale or paid on a sale include so much of the consideration for the exchange or surrender as would have been a capital sum if it had been a money payment.

(4) Any reference in this Act (except in Part 6) to the time of any sale is to be read as a reference to whichever is the earlier of—

(a) the time of completion, and

(b) the time when possession is given.

573 Transfers treated as sales

(1) This section applies for the purposes of Parts 3, [F31 3. A,] 4 [F32 , 4. A] and 10 and other provisions of this Act relevant to those Parts if—

(a) there is a transfer of the interest which is the relevant interest for the purposes of the Part in question, and

(b) the transfer is not a sale.

(2) The transfer is treated as a sale of the relevant interest.

(3) The sale is treated as being at market value, subject to any election under section 569 (election to treat sale as being for alternative amount).

(4) This section does not apply if section 561 applies (transfer of a UK trade to a company resident in another member State).

Amendments (Textual)

F31. Word in s. 573. (1) inserted (with effect in accordance with s. 92 of the amending Act) by Finance Act 2005 (c. 7), Sch. 6 para. 10; S.I. 2007/949, art. 2

F32. Words in s. 573. (1) inserted (with effect as mentioned in s. 67 of the amending Act) by Finance Act 2001 (c. 9), s. 67, Sch. 19 Pt. 2 para. 7

Modifications etc. (not altering text)

C6. S. 573 excluded (E.W.S.) (8.6.2005) by Railways Act 2005 (c. 14), s. 60. (2), Sch. 10 para. 15. (2); S.I. 2005/1444, art. 2. (1), Sch. 1

574 Meaning of "control"

(1) In this Act " control " is used in the sense given in this section [F33. (but, for the purposes of section 575, this definition applies only where expressly indicated)].

(2) In relation to a body corporate (" company A "), " control " means the power of a person (" P ") to secure—

(a) by means of the holding of shares or the possession of voting power in relation to that or any other body corporate, or

(b) as a result of any powers conferred by the articles of association or other document regulating that or any other body corporate,

that the affairs of company A are conducted in accordance with P's wishes.

(3) In relation to a partnership, " control " means the right to a share of more than half of the assets, or of more than one half of the income, of the partnership.

Amendments (Textual)

F33. Words in s. 574. (1) inserted (6.4.2007) by Income Tax Act 2007 (c. 3), s. 1034. (1), Sch. 1 para. 410 (with Sch. 2)

[F34575. Meaning of "connected" persons

(1) For the purposes of this Act whether a person is connected with another is determined in accordance with this section unless otherwise indicated.

(2) An individual ("A") is connected with another individual ("B") if—

(a) A is B's spouse or civil partner,

(b) A is a relative of B,

(c) A is the spouse or civil partner of a relative of B,

(d) A is a relative of B's spouse or civil partner, or

(e) A is the spouse or civil partner of a relative of B's spouse or civil partner.

(3) A person, in the capacity as trustee of a settlement, is connected with—

(a) any individual who is a settlor in relation to the settlement,

(b) any person connected with such an individual,

(c) any close company whose participators include the trustees of the settlement,

(d) any non-UK resident company which, if it were UK resident, would be a close company whose participators include the trustees of the settlement,

(e) any body corporate controlled (within the meaning of section 574) by a company within paragraph or ,

(f) if the settlement is the principal settlement in relation to one or more sub-fund settlements, a person in the capacity as trustee of such a sub-fund settlement, and

(g) if the settlement is a sub-fund settlement in relation to a principal settlement, a person in the capacity as trustee of any other sub-fund settlements in relation to the principal settlement.

(4) A person who is a partner in a partnership is connected with—

(a) any partner in the partnership,

(b) the spouse or civil partner of any individual who is a partner in the partnership, and

(c) a relative of any individual who is a partner in the partnership.

But this subsection does not apply in relation to acquisitions or disposals of assets of the partnership pursuant to genuine commercial arrangements.

(5) A company is connected with another company if—

(a) the same person has control of both companies,

(b) a person ("A") has control of one company and persons connected with A have control of the other company,

(c) A has control of one company and A together with persons connected with A have control of the other company, or

(d) a group of two or more persons has control of both companies and the groups either consist of the same persons or could be so regarded if (in one or more cases) a member of either group were replaced by a person with whom the member is connected.

(6) A company is connected with another person ("A") if—

(a) A has control of the company, or

(b) A together with persons connected with A have control of the company.

(7) In relation to a company, any two or more persons acting together to secure or exercise control of the company are connected with—

(a) one another, and

(b) any person acting on the directions of any of them to secure or exercise control of the company.

Amendments (Textual)

F34. Ss. 575, 575. A substituted for s. 575 (6.4.2007) by Income Tax Act 2007 (c. 3), s. 1034. (1), Sch. 1 para. 411 (with Sch. 2)

575. ASection 575: supplementary

(1) In section 575 and this section—

"company" includes any body corporate or unincorporated association, but does not include a partnership (and see also subsection (2)),

"control" is to be read in accordance with section 416 of ICTA (except where otherwise indicated),

"principal settlement" has the meaning given by paragraph 1 of Schedule 4. ZA to TCGA 1992,

"relative" means brother, sister, ancestor or lineal descendant,

"settlement" has the same meaning as in Chapter 5 of Part 5 of ITTOIA 2005 (see section 620 of that Act), and

"sub-fund settlement" has the meaning given by paragraph 1 of Schedule 4. ZA to TCGA 1992.

(2) For the purposes of section 575—

(a) a unit trust scheme is treated as if it were a company, and

(b) the rights of the unit holders are treated as if they were shares in the company.

(3) For the purposes of section 575 "trustee", in the case of a settlement in relation to which there would be no trustees apart from this subsection, means any person—

(a) in whom the property comprised in the settlement is for the time being vested, or

(b) in whom the management of that property is for the time being vested.

Section 466. (4) of ITA 2007 does not apply for the purposes of this subsection.

(4) If any provision of section 575 provides that a person ("A") is connected with another person ("B"), it also follows that B is connected with A.]

Amendments (Textual)

F34. Ss. 575, 575. A substituted for s. 575 (6.4.2007) by Income Tax Act 2007 (c. 3), s. 1034. (1), Sch. 1 para. 411 (with Sch. 2)

F35 576 Meaning of "the Inland Revenue" etc.

. . . .

Amendments (Textual)

F35. S. 576 repealed (18.4.2005) by Commissioners for Revenue and Customs Act 2005 (c. 11), s. 53. (1), Sch. 4 para. 85, Sch. 5; S.I. 2005/1126, art. 2. (2)(h)(i)

577 Other definitions

(1) In this Act—

"dual resident investing company" has the same meaning as in section 404 of ICTA (limitation of group relief in relation to certain dual resident companies);

"market value", in relation to any asset, means the price the asset would fetch in the open market;

"the normal time limit for amending a tax return", in relation to a tax year, means the first anniversary of the 31st January following the tax year;

"notice" means a notice in writing;

"property business" means [F36a UK property business,] a Schedule A business or an overseas property business;

" tax return " has the meaning given by section 3. (3);

F37. . . . .

F38. . . . .

(2) Any reference to the setting up, commencement or permanent discontinuance of—

    (a) a trade,

    (b) a property business,

    (c) a profession, or

    (d) a vocation,

includes, except where the contrary is expressly provided, the occurring of an event which, under any provision of the Income Tax Acts or Corporation Tax Acts, is to be treated as equivalent to the setting up, commencement or permanent discontinuance of a trade, property business, profession or vocation.

(3) Any reference in this Act to an allowance made includes an allowance which would be made but for an insufficiency of profits, or other income, against which to make it.

(4) For the purposes of this Act a person obtains a tax advantage if he—

    (a) obtains an allowance or a greater allowance, or

    (b) avoids a charge or secures the reduction of a charge.

(5) In Schedule 1—

    (a) Part 1 gives the meaning of abbreviated references in this Act to Acts about tax, and

    (b) Part 2 lists where expressions used in this Act are defined or otherwise explained.

Amendments (Textual)

F36. Words in s. 577. (1) inserted (6.4.2005) by Income Tax (Trading and Other Income) Act 2005 (c. 5), s. 883. (1), Sch. 1 para. 573 (with Sch. 2)

F37. Words in s. 577. (1) repealed (6.4.2007) by Income Tax Act 2007 (c. 3), s. 1034. (1), Sch. 1 para. 412. (a), Sch. 3 Pt. 1 (with Sch. 2)

F38. Words in s. 577. (1) repealed (6.4.2007) by Income Tax Act 2007 (c. 3), s. 1034. (1), Sch. 1 para. 412. (b), Sch. 3 Pt. 1 (with Sch. 2)

Amendments, repeals, citation etc.

578 Consequential amendments

Schedule 2 contains consequential amendments.

579 Commencement and transitional provisions and savings

(1) This Act has effect—

    (a) for income tax purposes, as respects allowances and charges falling to be made for chargeable periods ending on or after 6th April 2001, and

    (b) for corporation tax purposes, as respects allowances and charges falling to be made for chargeable periods ending on or after 1st April 2001.

(2) References in this Act to a chargeable period to which this Act applies are to the chargeable periods given in subsection (1).

(3) Subsection (1) is subject to Schedule 3, which contains transitional provisions and savings.

580 Repeals

Schedule 4 contains repeals.

581 Citation

This Act may be cited as the Capital Allowances Act 2001.

Schedules

Schedule 1. Abbreviations and defined expressions

Section 577

Part 1. Abbreviations

FA 1937 | The Finance Act 1937 (c. 54) |
FA 1941 | The Finance Act 1941 (c. 30) |
FA 1956 | The Finance Act 1956 (c. 54) |
FA 1965 | The Finance Act 1965 (c. 25) |
CAA 1968 | The Capital Allowances Act 1968 (c. 3) |
TMA 1970 | The Taxes Management Act 1970 (c. 9) |
FA 1971 | The Finance Act 1971 (c. 68) |
OTA 1975 | The Oil Taxation Act 1975 (c. 22) |
FA 1976 | The Finance Act 1976 (c. 40) |
FA 1982 | The Finance Act 1982 (c. 39) |
FA 1983 | The Finance Act 1983 (c. 28) |
FA 1986 | The Finance Act 1986 (c. 41) |
ICTA | The Income and Corporation Taxes Act 1988 (c. 1) |
FA 1989 | The Finance Act 1989 (c. 26) |
CAA 1990 | The Capital Allowances Act 1990 (c. 1) |
TCGA 1992 | The Taxation of Chargeable Gains Act 1992 (c. 12) |
F(No.2)A 1992 | The Finance (No. 2) Act 1992 (c. 48) |
VATA 1994 | The Value Added Tax Act 1994 (c. 23) |
FA 1995 | The Finance Act 1995 (c. 4) |
FA 1997 | The Finance Act 1997 (c. 16) |
FA 1998 | The Finance Act 1998 (c. 36) |
[F1ITEPA 2003 | The Income Tax (Earnings and Pensions) Act 2003] |
[F2ITTOIA 2005 | The Income Tax (Trading and Other Income) Act 2005] |
 [F3FA 2004 | The Finance Act 2004 (c. 12)] |
 [F4FA 2006 | The Finance Act 2006 (c. 25)] |
 [F5ITA 2007 | The Income Tax Act 2007.] |

Amendments (Textual)

F1. Words in Sch. 1 Pt. 1 inserted (with effect in accordance with s. 723. (1)(a)(b) of the amending Act) by Income Tax (Earnings and Pensions) Act 2003 (c. 1), s. 723, Sch. 6 para. 255 (with Sch. 7)

F2. Words in Sch. 1 Pt. 1 inserted (6.4.2005) by Income Tax (Trading and Other Income) Act 2005 (c. 5), s. 883. (1), Sch. 1 para. 574. (2) (with Sch. 2)

F3. Words in Sch. 1 Pt. 1 inserted (6.4.2006) by Finance Act 2004 (c. 12), s. 284. (1), Sch. 35 para. 49 (with Sch. 36)
F4. Words in Sch. 1 Pt. 1 inserted (with effect in accordance with s. 84. (5)(6) of the amending Act) by Finance Act 2006 (c. 25), s. 84. (4)
F5. Words in Sch. 1 Pt. 1 inserted (6.4.2007) by Income Tax Act 2007 (c. 3), s. 1034. (1), Sch. 1 para. 413. (2) (with Sch. 2)

Part 2. Defined expressions

accounting period | section 12 of ICTA |
additional VAT liability | section 547(1) |
additional VAT rebate | section 547(2) |
adjusted net cost (in Chapter 7 of Part 3) | section 323 |
adjusted net cost (in Chapter 6 of Part 10) | section 522 |
agricultural building | section 361(2)(a) |
approved body (in Part 10) | section 492 |
assured tenancy | section 490(3) |
available qualifying expenditure (in Part 2) | section 57 |
available qualifying expenditure (in Part 7) | section 459 |
available qualifying expenditure (in Part 8) | section 473 |
balancing adjustment (in Part 3) | section 314 |
[F6balancing adjustment (in Part 3A) | section 360M] |
balancing adjustment (in Part 4) | section 380 |
[F7balancing adjustment (in Part 4A) | section 393M] |
balancing adjustment (in Part 10) | section 513 |
balancing event (in Part 3) | section 315 |
[F6balancing event (in Part 3A) | section 360N] |
[F8balancing event (in Part 4A) | section 393N] |
balancing event (in Part 10) | section 514 |
body of persons | [F9section 989 of ITA 2007 and] section 832(1) of ICTA |
F10. . . | F10. . . |
building (in Part 3—includes structure) | section 271(1) |
section 4 and (in Chapter 2 of Part 1)
section 10. (1)
capital sum | section 4 |
car (in Part 2) | section 81 |
chargeable period | section 6 |
commercial building (in Part 3, in relation to qualifying enterprise zone expenditure) | section 281 |
connected persons (general meaning) | [F11section 575] |
connected persons (special extended meaning for certain purposes) | sections 156, 232, 246(2) and 266(5) |
control | section 574 |
the Corporation Tax Acts | section 831(1) of ICTA |
developer, carrying on a trade as (in Chapter 4 of Part 3) | section 293 |
development and development order (in Part 5) | section 436 |
disposal event (in Part 2) | section 60(2) |
disposal event (in Chapter 3 of Part 6) | section 443(7) |
disposal receipt (in Part 2) | section 60 |
disposal receipt (in Part 5) | section 420 |
disposal receipt (in Chapter 3 of Part 8) | section 476(1) |
dredging | section 484(3), (4) |

dual resident investing company | section 577(1) and section 404 of ICTA |
dwelling-house | section 531(1) |
[F12dwelling (in Part 4A) | section 393A(4)] |
enterprise zone (in Part 3) | section 298(3) |
expenditure on the construction of a building (in Part 3) | section 272 |
expenditure on the construction of a building (in Part 4) | section 363 |
expenditure on the construction of a building (in Part 10) | section 493 |
final chargeable period (in Part 2) | section 65 |
final chargeable period (in Part 7) | section 457(5) |
final chargeable period (in Part 8) | section 471(5) and (6) |
first-year qualifying expenditure | Chapter 4 of Part 2 |
fixture (in Part 2) | section 173(1) |
[F13flat (in Part 4A) | section 393A(3)] |
four-year cut-off (in Chapter 9 of Part 2) | section 86(3) |
furnished holiday lettings business (in Part 2) | section 17 |
general development order (in Part 5) | section 436 |
highway concession (in Chapter 9 of Part 3) | section 341(4) |
husbandry (in Part 4) | section 362 |
income from patents (in Part 8) | section 483 and paragraph 101(5) of Schedule 3 |
industrial building | section 271(2) and Chapter 2 of Part 3 |
F14. . . | F14. . . |
interest in an oil licence (in Chapter 3 of Part 12) | section 552(4) |
investment company | section 130 of ICTA |
investment asset (in relation to life assurance business) | section 545(2) |
know-how (in Part 7) | section 452(2) |
lease and related expressions (in Part 3) | section 360 |
[F6lease and related expressions (in Part 3A) | section 360Z4] |
lease and related expressions (in Part 4) | section 393 |
[F15lease and related expressions (in Part 4A) | section 393W] |
lease and related expressions (in Part 10) | section 531 |
life assurance business | section 544(5) and section 431(2) of ICTA |
long-life asset (in Chapter 10 of Part 2) | section 91 |
long-life asset expenditure (in F16... Part 2) | section 90 |
market value | section 577(1) |
mineral asset (in Part 5) | section 397 |
mineral exploration and access (in Part 5) | section 396 |
mineral extraction trade (in Part 5) | section 394(2) |
mineral deposits (in Part 5) | section 394(3) |
normal time limit for amending a tax return | section 577(1) |
notice | section 577(1) |
[F17offshore installation (except in Chapter 13 of Part 2) | [F18sections 1001 and 1002 of ITA 2007 and] section 837C of ICTA] |
oil (in Chapter 3 of Part 12) | section 556(3) |
oil licence (in Chapter 3 of Part 12) | section 552(1) |
ordinary [F19property] business | section 16 |
overseas property business | sections [F2070A(4) and 832(1) of ICTA and Chapter 2 of Part 3 of ITTOIA 2005] [F21(as applied by section 989 of ITA 2007)] |
partial depreciation subsidy | section 209 |
patent rights (in Part 8) | section 464(2) |
planning permission (in Part 5) | section 436 |
proceeds from a balancing event (in Part 3) | section 316 |
[F6proceeds from a balancing event (in Part 3A) | section 360O] |
proceeds from a balancing event (in Part 4) | section 383 |

[F22proceeds from a balancing event (in Part 4A) | section 393O] |
proceeds from a balancing event (in Part 10) | section 515 |
property business | section 577(1) |
public body (in Chapter 1 of Part 11) | section 532(2) |
qualifying activity (in Part 2) | Chapter 2 of Part 2 |
[F6qualifying building (in Part 3A) | section 360C] |
[F23qualifying building (in Part 4A) | section 393C] |
[F6qualifying business premises (in Part 3A) | section 360D] |
qualifying dwelling-house (in Part 10) | section 490(2) and Chapter 4 of Part 10 |
qualifying enterprise zone expenditure (in Part 3) | sections 299 to 304 |
[F6qualifying expenditure (in Part 3A) | section 360B] |
qualifying expenditure attributable to a dwelling-house (in Part 10) | section 511 |
[F24qualifying flat (in Part 4A) | section 393D] |
qualifying hire car (in Part 2) | section 82 |
qualifying hotel (in Part 3) | section 279 |
qualifying non-trade expenditure (in Part 8) | section 469 |
qualifying trade expenditure (in Part 8) | section 468 |
qualifying trade (in Part 3) | section 274 |
qualifying trade (in Part 9) | section 484(2) |
related agricultural land (in Part 4) | section 361(2)(b) |
relevant interest (in Part 3) | Chapter 3 of Part 3 |
[F6relevant interest (in Part 3A) | Chapter 4 of Part 3A] |
relevant interest (in Part 4) | Chapter 2 of Part 4 |
[F25relevant interest (in Part 4A) | Chapter 4 of Part 4A] |
relevant interest (in Part 10) | Chapter 2 of Part 10 |
relevant trade (in Part 6) | section 439(3) |
research and development | section [F26437(2) and (3)] |
residue of qualifying expenditure (in Part 3) | section 313 |
[F6residue of qualifying expenditure (in Part 3A) | section 360K] |
residue of qualifying expenditure (in Part 4) | section 386 |
[F27residue of qualifying expenditure (in Part 4A) | section 393L] |
residue of qualifying expenditure attributable to a dwelling-house (in Part 10) | section 512 |
ring fence trade (in Chapter 13 of Part 2) | section 162(2) |
sale | section 572(1) to (3) |
sale, time of | section 572(4) |
sale, transfers under Parts 3[F28, 3A], 4[F29, 4A] and 10 treated as | section 573 |
sale, treated as occurring on successions, for purposes of Parts other than Parts 2, 6 and 10 |
section 559 |
Schedule A business | [F30section 989 of ITA 2007 and] section 832(1) of ICTA |
short-life asset (in Part 2) | section 83 |
source of mineral deposits (in Part 5) | section 394(5) |
special leasing (in Part 2) | section 19 |
tax | section 832(3) of ICTA |
the Tax Acts | Schedule 1 to the Interpretation Act 1978 and section 831 of ICTA |
tax advantage | section 577(4) |
tax return | section 3(3) |
tax year | [F31section 4(2) of ITA 2007 (as applied by section 989 of that Act)] |
UK oil licence | section 552(2) |
[F32UK property business | F33...Chapter 2 of Part 3 of ITTOIA 2005] [F34(as applied by section 989 of ITA 2007)] |
United Kingdom | [F35section 1013 of ITA 2007 and section 830(1) of ICTA] |
unrelieved qualifying expenditure (in Part 2) | section 59 |
unrelieved qualifying expenditure (in Part 5) | section 419 |

unrelieved qualifying expenditure (in Part 7) | section 461 |

unrelieved qualifying expenditure (in Part 8) | section 475 |

within the charge to tax | [F36section 1009 of ITA 2007 and] section 832(1) of ICTA |

writing-down period (in Part 4) | section 372(2) |

writing-down period (in Part 9) | section 487(2) |

Amendments (Textual)

F6. Sch. 1 Pt. 2 entries inserted (with effect in accordance with s. 92 of the amending Act) by Finance Act 2005 (c. 7), Sch. 6 para. 11; S.I. 2007/949, art. 2

F7. Sch. 1 Pt. 2: entries inserted (with effect as mentioned in s. 67) by Finance Act 2001 (c. 9), s. 67, Sch. 19 Pt. 2 para. 8. (2)

F8. Sch. 1 Pt. 2: entries inserted (with effect as mentioned in s. 67) by Finance Act 2001 (c. 9), s. 67, Sch. 19 Pt. 2 para. 8. (2)

F9. Words in Sch. 1 Pt. 2 inserted (6.4.2007) by Income Tax Act 2007 (c. 3), s. 1034. (1), Sch. 1 para. 413. (3)(a) (with Sch. 2)

F10. Words in Sch. 1 Pt. 2 repealed (18.4.2005) by Commissioners for Revenue and Customs Act 2005 (c. 11), s. 53. (1), Sch. 4 para. 86. (a), 5; S.I. 2005/1126, art. 2. (2)(h)(i)

F11. Words in Sch. 1 Pt. 2 substituted (6.4.2007) by Income Tax Act 2007 (c. 3), s. 1034. (1), Sch. 1 para. 413. (3)(b) (with Sch. 2)

F12. Sch. 1 Pt. 2: entries inserted (with effect as mentioned in s. 67 of the amending Act) by Finance Act 2001 (c. 9), s. 67, Sch. 19 Pt. 2 para. 8. (2)

F13. Sch. 1 Pt. 2: entries inserted (with effect as mentioned in s. 67 of the amending Act) by Finance Act 2001 (c. 9), s. 67, Sch. 19 Pt. 2 para. 8. (2)

F14. Words in Sch. 1 Pt. 2 repealed (18.4.2005) by Commissioners for Revenue and Customs Act 2005 (c. 11), s. 53. (1), Sch. 4 para. 86. (b), 5; S.I. 2005/1126, art. 2. (2)(h)(i)

F15. Sch. 1 Pt. 2: entries inserted (with effect as mentioned in s. 67 of the amending Act) by Finance Act 2001 (c. 9), s. 67, Sch. 19 Pt. 2 para. 8. (2)

F16. Words in Sch. 1 Pt. 2 repealed (with effect in accordance with s. 167 of the amending Act) by Finance Act 2003 (c. 14), Sch. 43 Pt. 3. (9)

F17. Words in Sch. 1 Pt. 2 inserted (with effect in accordance with Sch. 27 para. 11 of the amending Act) by Finance Act 2004 (c. 12), Sch. 27 para. 10

F18. Words in Sch. 1 Pt. 2 inserted (6.4.2007) by Income Tax Act 2007 (c. 3), s. 1034. (1), Sch. 1 para. 413. (3)(c) (with Sch. 2)

F19. Word in Sch. 1 Pt. 2 substituted (6.4.2005) by Income Tax (Trading and Other Income) Act 2005 (c. 5), s. 883. (1), Sch. 1 para. 574. (3)(a) (with Sch. 2)

F20. Words in Sch. 1 Pt. 2 substituted (6.4.2005) by Income Tax (Trading and Other Income) Act 2005 (c. 5), s. 883. (1), Sch. 1 para. 574. (3)(b) (with Sch. 2)

F21. Words in Sch. 1 Pt. 2 inserted (6.4.2007) by Income Tax Act 2007 (c. 3), s. 1034. (1), Sch. 1 para. 413. (3)(d) (with Sch. 2)

F22. Sch. 1 Pt. 2: entries inserted (with effect as mentioned in s. 67 of the amending Act) by Finance Act 2001 (c. 9), s. 67, Sch. 19 Pt. 2 para. 8. (2)

F23. Sch. 1 Pt. 2: entries inserted (with effect as mentioned in s. 67 of the amending Act) by Finance Act 2001 (c. 9), s. 67, Sch. 19 Pt. 2 para. 8. (2)

F24. Sch. 1 Pt. 2: entries inserted (with effect as mentioned in s. 67 of the amending Act) by Finance Act 2001 (c. 9), s. 67, Sch. 19 Pt. 2 para. 8. (2)

F25. Sch. 1 Pt. 2: entries inserted (with effect as mentioned in s. 67 of the amending Act) by Finance Act 2001 (c. 9), s. 67, Sch. 19 Pt. 2 para. 8. (2)

F26. Words in Sch. 1 Pt. 2 substituted (6.4.2007) by Income Tax Act 2007 (c. 3), s. 1034. (1), Sch. 1 para. 413. (3)(e) (with Sch. 2)

F27. Sch. 1 Pt. 2: entries inserted (with effect as mentioned in s. 67 of the amending Act) by Finance Act 2001 (c. 9), s. 67, Sch. 19 Pt. 2 para. 8. (2)

F28. Word in Sch. 1 Pt. 2 inserted (with effect in accordance with s. 92 of the amending Act) by Finance Act 2005 (c. 7), Sch. 6 para. 11; S.I. 2007/949, art. 2

F29. Sch. 1 Pt. 2: words in entry inserted (with effect as mentioned in s. 67 of the amending Act) by Finance Act 2001 (c. 9), s. 67, Sch. 19 Pt. 2 para. 8. (3)

F30. Words in Sch. 1 Pt. 2 inserted (6.4.2007) by Income Tax Act 2007 (c. 3), s. 1034. (1), Sch. 1 para. 413. (3)(f) (with Sch. 2)

F31. Words in Sch. 1 Pt. 2 substituted (6.4.2007) by Income Tax Act 2007 (c. 3), s. 1034. (1), Sch. 1 para. 413. (3)(g) (with Sch. 2)

F32. Words in Sch. 1 Pt. 2 inserted (6.4.2005) by Income Tax (Trading and Other Income) Act 2005 (c. 5), s. 883. (1), Sch. 1 para. 574. (3)(c) (with Sch. 2)

F33. Words in Sch. 1 Pt. 2 repealed (6.4.2007) by Income Tax Act 2007 (c. 3), s. 1034. (1), Sch. 1 para. 413. (3)(h), Sch. 3 Pt. 1 (with Sch. 2)

F34. Words in Sch. 1 Pt. 2 inserted (6.4.2007) by Income Tax Act 2007 (c. 3), s. 1034. (1), Sch. 1 para. 413. (3)(h) (with Sch. 2)

F35. Words in Sch. 1 Pt. 2 substituted (6.4.2007) by Income Tax Act 2007 (c. 3), s. 1034. (1), Sch. 1 para. 413. (3)(i) (with Sch. 2)

F36. Words in Sch. 1 Pt. 2 inserted (6.4.2007) by Income Tax Act 2007 (c. 3), s. 1034. (1), Sch. 1 para. 413. (3)(j) (with Sch. 2)

Schedule 2. Consequential amendments

Section 578

The Taxes Management Act 1970 (c. 9)

Section 42 (procedure for making claims etc.)

1. In subsection (7), for paragraphs (c) and (d) substitute—
   "(c)sections 3, 83, 89, 129, 131, 135, 177, 183, 266, 268, 290, 355, 381 and 569 of the Capital Allowances Act; and
   (d) sections 40. B(5), 40. D, 41 and 42 of the Finance (No. 2) Act 1992."

Section 57 (regulations about appeals)

2. For subsection (3)(b) substitute—
   "(b)provisions corresponding to section 563 of the Capital Allowances Act (determination of apportionment affecting tax liability of two or more persons), and".

Section 58 (proceedings in tax cases in Northern Ireland)

3. In subsection (3)(b), for "section 151 of the Capital Allowances Act 1990 (proceedings to which more than one taxpayer is a party)" substitute " section 563 of the Capital Allowances Act (determination of apportionment affecting tax liability of two or more persons) ".

Section 98 (special returns, etc.)

4. (1)In the Table, in column 1, omit "Sections 23. (4) and 49. (4) of the Capital Allowances Act 1990".
(2) In the Table, in column 2, for "Sections 22. B(4), 23. (2), 33. F(5), 48, 49. (2), 51. (6. A) and 53. (1. H) of the Capital Allowances Act 1990" substitute " Sections 43. (5) and (6), 118 to 120, 145. (2) and (3) and 203 of the Capital Allowances Act ".

Schedule 3 (rules for assigning proceedings to General Commissioners)

5. In paragraph 10, for "section 151 of the Capital Allowances Act 1990" substitute " section 563 of the Capital Allowances Act ".

The Finance Act 1982 (c. 39)

Section 137 (expenditure met by regional development plans to be disregarded for certain purposes)

6. Omit subsections (2), (3), (6) and (7).

The London Regional Transport Act 1984 (c. 32)

Schedule 5 (transitional provisions and savings)

7. In paragraph 5, omit paragraph (b) and the word "and" before it.

The Films Act 1985 (c. 21)

Section 6 (certification of films as British films)

8. In subsection (1), for "section 68 of the Capital Allowances Act 1990 (expenditure on production and acquisition of films etc.)" substitute " section 40. D of the Finance (No. 2) Act 1992 (election relating to tax treatment of films expenditure) ".

Schedule 1 (certification of films as British films)

9. (1)In paragraph 2. (1), for "section 68 of the Capital Allowances Act 1990" substitute " section 40. D of the Finance (No. 2) Act 1992 ".
(2) In paragraph 3. (1), for "section 68 of the Capital Allowances Act 1990" substitute " section 40. D of the Finance (No. 2) Act 1992 ".

The Trustee Savings Banks Act 1985 (c. 58)

Schedule 2 (taxation)

10. In paragraph 1—
(a) in sub-paragraph (1), for "the Capital Allowances Act 1990" substitute " the Capital Allowances Act 2001 ", and
(b) in sub-paragraph (2), for "those Acts" substitute " that Act ".

The Income and Corporation Taxes Act 1988 (c. 1)

F1**11**. . . . .
Amendments (Textual)
F1. Sch. 2 para. 11 repealed (with effect in accordance with Sch. 26 Pt. 3. (12) Note of the amending Act) by Finance Act 2006 (c. 25), Sch. 26 Pt. 3. (12)

F2**12**. . . . .
Amendments (Textual)
F2. Sch. 2 para. 12 repealed (with effect in accordance with Sch. 26 Pt. 3. (12) Note of the amending Act) by Finance Act 2006 (c. 25), Sch. 26 Pt. 3. (12)

Section 65. A (Case V income from land outside UK: income tax)

13. In subsection (7), omit "and section 29 of the 1990 Act (provisions relating to furnished holiday accommodation)".

Section 70. A (Case V income from land outside UK: corporation tax)

14. In subsection (6), omit "and section 29 of the 1990 Act (provisions relating to furnished holiday accommodation)".

Section 75 (expenses of management: investment companies)

F3**15**. . . . .
Amendments (Textual)
F3. Sch. 2 para. 15 repealed (with effect in accordance with s. 42 of the amending Act) by Finance Act 2004 (c. 12), Sch. 42 Pt. 2. (3)

Section 83. A (gifts in kind to charities, etc.)

16. (1)In subsection (2), omit paragraph (b) and the word "or" before it.
(2) In subsection (3), omit paragraph (b) and the word "and" before it.
(3) In subsection (4)(a) after "subsection (3) above" insert " or section 63. (2) of the Capital Allowances Act ".

Section 84 (gifts to educational establishments)

17. (1)In subsection (1)—
(a) in paragraph (a), for "machinery or plant" substitute " plant or machinery ", and
(b) omit paragraph (b) and the word "or" before it.
(2) In subsection (2)—
(a) for "qualifies as machinery or plant" substitute " qualifies as plant or machinery ", and
(b) for "Part II of the 1990 Act as machinery or plant" substitute " Part 2 of the Capital

Allowances Act as plant or machinery ".

(3) In subsection (3), omit paragraph (b) and the word "and" before it.

(4) In subsection (4)(a), after "subsection (3) above" insert " or section 63. (2) of the Capital Allowances Act ".

Section 87 (taxable premiums etc.)

18. In subsection (7), for "Part IV of the 1990 Act in respect of expenditure falling within section 105. (1)(b) of that Act (mineral depletion)" substitute " Part 5 of the Capital Allowances Act in respect of expenditure falling within section 403 (mineral asset expenditure) ".

Section 91 (cemeteries)

19. For subsection (9) substitute—

"(9)Section 532 of the Capital Allowances Act (general rule excluding contributions) shall apply for the purposes of this section as it applies for the purposes of that Act."

Section 91. C (mineral exploration and access)

20. In paragraph (a), for "section 121. (1) of the Capital Allowances Act 1990" substitute " section 396. (1) of the Capital Allowances Act ".

Section 116 (arrangements for transferring relief)

21. In subsection (4), for paragraph (b) substitute—

"(b)any allowance to be given effect under Part 2 of the Capital Allowances Act in respect of a special leasing of plant or machinery were an allowance to be given effect in calculating the profits of that trade."

F422. . . . .
Amendments (Textual)
F4. Sch. 2 para. 22 repealed (6.4.2007) by Income Tax Act 2007 (c. 3), s. 1034. (1), Sch. 3 Pt. 1 (with Sch. 2)

Section 118 (restriction on relief: companies)

23. (1)In subsection (1), omit—

(a) "or allowed" (in each place),

(b) "or section 145 of the 1990 Act", and

(c) paragraph (b) and the word "or" before it.

(2) In subsection (2), in the definition of "the aggregate amount", omit—

(a) "or allowed",

(b) "or section 145 of the 1990 Act", and

(c) paragraph (b) and the word "or" before it.

(3) In relation to any chargeable period to which this Act applies, the repeals made by sub-paragraph (2) are not to exclude from a company's aggregate amount for the purposes of section 118 of ICTA any amounts included in the company's aggregate amount at any time before the chargeable periods to which this Act applies.

Section 197. C (definition of mileage profit)

F524...............................
Amendments (Textual)
F5. Sch. 2 para. 25 repealed (6.4.2003) by Income Tax (Earnings and Pensions) Act 2003 (c. 1), s. 723, Sch. 8 Pt. 1 (with Sch. 7)

Section 198 (relief for necessary expenses)

F525...............................
Amendments (Textual)
F5. Sch. 2 para. 25 repealed (6.4.2003) by Income Tax (Earnings and Pensions) Act 2003 (c. 1), s. 723, Sch. 8 Pt. 1 (with Sch. 7)

Section 343 (company reconstructions without a change of ownership)

26. In subsection (2), for "the Capital Allowances Acts" substitute " the Capital Allowances Act (including enactments which under this Act are to be treated as contained in that Act) ".

F627...............................
Amendments (Textual)
F6. Sch. 2 para. 27 repealed (6.4.2007) by Income Tax Act 2007 (c. 3), s. 1034. (1), Sch. 3 Pt. 1 (with Sch. 2)

F728...............................
Amendments (Textual)
F7. Sch. 2 para. 28 repealed (6.4.2007) by Income Tax Act 2007 (c. 3), s. 1034. (1), Sch. 3 Pt. 1 (with Sch. 2)

Section 384 (restrictions on right of set-off)

29. F8. (1)...............................
(2) In subsection (10), omit the words following paragraph (b) F9...
Amendments (Textual)
F8. Sch. 2 para. 29. (1) repealed (6.4.2007) by Income Tax Act 2007 (c. 3), s. 1034. (1), Sch. 3 Pt. 1 (with Sch. 2)
F9. Words in Sch. 2 para. 29. (2) repealed (6.4.2007) by Income Tax Act 2007 (c. 3), s. 1034. (1), Sch. 3 Pt. 1 (with Sch. 2)

F1030...............................
Amendments (Textual)
F10. Sch. 2 para. 30 repealed (6.4.2007) by Income Tax Act 2007 (c. 3), s. 1034. (1), Sch. 3 Pt. 1 (with Sch. 2)

F1131. . . . .

Amendments (Textual)

F11. Sch. 2 para. 31 repealed (6.4.2007) by Income Tax Act 2007 (c. 3), s. 1034. (1), Sch. 3 Pt. 1 (with Sch. 2)

Section 393. A (losses: set off against profits of the same, or an earlier, accounting period)

32. (1)In subsection (2. C)(b), for "section 62. A of the 1990 Act (demolition costs relating to offshore machinery or plant)" substitute " section 164 of the Capital Allowances Act (abandonment expenditure incurred before cessation of ring fence trade) ".
(2) Omit subsections (5) and (6).
(3) In subsection (11)—
(a) in paragraph (a), for "section 62. B of the 1990 Act (post-cessation abandonment expenditure related to offshore machinery or plant)" substitute " section 165 of the Capital Allowances Act (abandonment expenditure within 3 years of ceasing ring fence trade) ", and
(b) in paragraph (b), for "section 109 of that Act (restoration expenditure incurred after cessation of trade of mineral extraction)" substitute " section 416 of that Act (expenditure on restoration within 3 years of ceasing to trade) " and for "the last day on which it carried on the trade" substitute " the last day of trading ".
(4) In subsection (12), for "section 62. A of the 1990 Act" substitute " section 162 of the Capital Allowances Act ".

Section 395 (leasing contracts and company reconstructions)

33. In subsection (1)—
(a) in paragraph (a), for "machinery or plant" substitute " plant or machinery ", and
(b) in paragraph (c), for "within the meaning of Part II of the 1990 Act" substitute " within the meaning of Part 2 of the Capital Allowances Act ".

Section 397 (restriction of relief in case of farming and market gardening)

34. (1)In subsection (5)—
(a) omit the definition of "basis year", and
(b) in the definition of "chargeable period" omit the words from "or any basis period" to the end of the definition.
(2) Omit subsection (6).
(3) In subsection (7), for the words from "but so that" to the end of the subsection substitute "but disregarding—
   (a) any allowance or charge under the Capital Allowances Act (including enactments which under this Act are to be treated as contained in that Act); and
   (b) any provision of that Act requiring allowances and charges to be treated as expenses and receipts of the trade".

Section 400 (write-off of government investment)

35. (1)In subsection (2)(c), for "section 145. (2) of the 1990 Act" substitute " section 260. (2) of

the Capital Allowances Act ".

(2) In subsection (4), for "section 145. (3) of the 1990 Act" substitute " section 260. (3) of the Capital Allowances Act ".

(3) In subsection (6), for "section 153 of the 1990 Act" substitute " section 532 or 536 of the Capital Allowances Act ".

Section 403. ZB (amounts eligible for group relief: excess capital allowances)

36. In subsection (1), for the words from "the surrender period" to the end of the subsection substitute " for the surrender period to the extent that they are to be given effect under section 260 of the Capital Allowances Act (special leasing: excess allowance). "

Section 407 (relationship between group relief and other relief)

37. (1)In subsection (1)(b), for "section 145. (3) of the 1990 Act" substitute " section 260. (3) of the Capital Allowances Act ".

(2) In subsection (2)(b), for "section 145. (3) of the 1990 Act" substitute " section 260. (3) of the Capital Allowances Act ".

Section 411 (exclusion of double allowance)

38. In subsection (10)—

(a) omit "Without prejudice to the provisions of section 161. (5) of the 1990 Act", and

(b) for "that Act, except Parts III and VII" substitute " the Capital Allowances Act, except Parts 6 and 10 ".

Sections 434. D and 434. E (capital allowances: management assets; investment assets)

39. Omit sections 434. D and 434. E.

Section 487 (credit unions)

40. In subsection (4), for "section 306 of the 1970 Act (capital allowances)" substitute " Part 2 of the Capital Allowances Act (plant and machinery allowances) ".

Section 492 (treatment of oil extraction activities etc. for tax purposes)

41. (1)In subsection (5), for "section 141 of the 1990 Act" substitute " section 258 of the Capital Allowances Act ".

(2) In subsection (6), for "section 145 of the 1990 Act" substitute " section 259 or 260 of the Capital Allowances Act ".

(3) In subsection (7), for "section 145. (1) of the 1990 Act" substitute " section 259 of the Capital Allowances Act ".

Section 495 (regional development grants)

42. (1)In subsection (1), for "Part I, II or VII of the 1990 Act (capital allowances relating to industrial buildings, machinery or plant and research and development)" substitute " Part 2, 3 or 6 of the Capital Allowances Act (capital allowances relating to plant and machinery, industrial buildings or research and development) ".

(2) In subsection (3), for "Part I, II or VII of the 1990 Act" substitute " Part 2, 3 or 6 of the Capital Allowances Act ".

(3) In subsection (7), in the definition of "regional development grant" for the words from "means" to the end substitute " means a grant falling within section 534. (1) of the Capital Allowances Act ".

Section 518 (harbour reorganisation schemes)

43. In subsection (4), for "the provisions of the Capital Allowances Acts" substitute " the Capital Allowances Act (including enactments which under this Act are to be treated as contained in that Act) ".

Sections 520 to 523 (patents)

44. Omit sections 520 to 523.

Section 525 (capital sums: death, winding up or partnership change)

45. In subsection (3), for "section 152 of the 1990 Act (succession to trades)" substitute " section 559 of the Capital Allowances Act (effect of successions) ".

Section 528 (patents: manner of making allowances and charges)

46. (1)Omit subsection (1).

(2) In subsections (2) and (3), for "section 520, 522, 523 or 526 as those provisions apply" (in each place) substitute " section 526 as that provision applies ".

(3) After subsection (3) insert—

"(3. A)In this section references to a person's or a company's income from patents are references to that income after any allowance has been deducted from or set off against it under section 479 or 480 of the Capital Allowances Act."

(4) Omit subsection (4).

Section 530 (disposal of know-how)

47. Omit section 530.

Section 531 (disposal of know-how: supplementary provisions)

48. (1)In subsection (1), for "as disposal value under section 530. (5)" substitute " as a disposal value under section 462 of the Capital Allowances Act ".

(2) In subsection (3), omit the words following paragraph (b).

(3) In subsection (4), for "as disposal value under section 530. (5)" substitute " as a disposal value under section 462 of the Capital Allowances Act ".

(4) In subsection (7), omit "and section 530. (1) and (6)".

Section 532 (application of 1990 Act)

49. For section 532 substitute—
"532 Application of Capital Allowances Act
The Tax Acts have effect as if sections 524 to 529 and 531, this section and section 533 were contained in the Capital Allowances Act."

Section 533 (interpretation of sections 520 to 532)

50. (1)In each of subsections (1) to (5), for "sections 520 to 532" substitute " sections 524 to 529 ".
(2) In subsection (1)—
(a) in paragraph (b) of the definition of "income from patents", omit "520. (6), 523. (3)," and after "525" insert " or section 472. (5) of, or paragraph 100 of Schedule 3 to, the Capital Allowances Act ", and
(b) omit the definition of "the commencement of the patent".
(3) In subsection (7), for "sections 530 and 531" substitute " section 531 ".

Section 577 (business entertaining expenses)

51. F12. (1). . . . .
(2) In subsection (7)(a), omit ", or to the use of an asset for," (in both places).
(3) In subsection (10), omit ", or any claim for capital allowances in respect of the use of an asset for,".
Amendments (Textual)
F12. Sch. 2 para. 51. (1) repealed (with effect in accordance with s. 723. (1)(a)(b) of the amending Act) by Income Tax (Earnings and Pensions) Act 2003 (c. 1), s. 723, Sch. 8 Pt. 1 (with Sch. 7)

New sections 578. A and 578. B (expenditure on car hire)

52. After section 578 insert—
"578. A Expenditure on car hire
(1) This section provides for a reduction in the amounts—
    (a) allowable as deductions in computing profits chargeable to tax under Case I or II of Schedule D,
    (b) which can be included as expenses of management of an investment company (as defined by section 130), or
    (c) allowable as deductions from emoluments chargeable to tax under Schedule E,
for expenditure on the hiring of a car to which this section applies.
(2) This section applies to the hiring of a car—
    (a) which is not a qualifying hire car, and
    (b) the retail price of which when new exceeds £12,000.
"Car" and "qualifying hire car" are defined by section 578. B.
(3) The amount which would, apart from this section, be allowable or capable of being included must be reduced by multiplying it by the fraction—
where P is the retail price of the car when new.
(4) If an amount has been reduced under subsection (3) and subsequently—
    (a) there is a rebate (however described) of the rentals, or
    (b) there occurs in connection with the rentals a transaction that falls within section 94 (debts deducted and subsequently released),
the amount otherwise taxable in respect of the rebate or transaction must be reduced by

multiplying it by the fraction in subsection (3) above.

578. B Expenditure on car hire: supplementary

(1) In section 578. A "car" means a mechanically propelled road vehicle other than one—

(a) of a construction primarily suited for the conveyance of goods or burden of any description, or

(b) of a type not commonly used as a private vehicle and unsuitable for such use.

References to a car accordingly include a motor cycle.

(2) For the purposes of section 578. A, a car is a qualifying hire car if—

(a) it is hired under a hire-purchase agreement (within the meaning of section 784. (6)) under which there is an option to purchase exercisable on the payment of a sum equal to not more than 1 per cent. of the retail price of the car when new, or

(b) it is a qualifying hire car for the purposes of Part 2 of the Capital Allowances Act (under section 82 of that Act).

(3) In section 578. A and this section "new" means unused and not second-hand.

(4) The power under section 74. (4) of the Capital Allowances Act to increase or further increase the sums of money specified in Chapter 8 of Part 2 of that Act includes the power to increase or further increase the sum of money specified in section 578. A(2)(b) or (3)."

Section 623 (retirement annuities: relevant earnings)

F1353. . . . .

Amendments (Textual)

F13. Sch. 2 para. 53 repealed (6.4.2006) by Finance Act 2004 (c. 12), Sch. 42 Pt. 3. (with Sch. 36)

Section 646 (meaning of "net relevant earnings")

F1454. . . . .

Amendments (Textual)

F14. Sch. 2 para. 54 repealed (6.4.2006) by Finance Act 2004 (c. 12), Sch. 42 Pt. 3 (with Sch. 36)

Section 768 (change in ownership of company: disallowance of trading losses)

55. In subsection (6), for "section 161. (6) of the 1990 Act" substitute " section 577. (3) of the Capital Allowances Act ".

Section 768. B (change in ownership of investment company: deductions generally)

56. In subsection (8), for "section 28 of the 1990 Act" substitute " section 253 of the Capital Allowances Act ".

Section 781 (assets leased to traders and others)

57. In subsection (9), for "section 60. (2) of the 1990 Act" substitute " section 68 of the Capital Allowances Act ".

F1558. . . . .

F15. Sch. 2 para. 58 repealed (6.4.2007) by Income Tax Act 2007 (c. 3), s. 1034. (1), Sch. 3 Pt. 1 (with Sch. 2)

Section 831 (interpretation of Act)

59. Section 831. (3) continues to have effect with the addition of the definition of "the 1990 Act" (an amendment originally made by paragraph 8. (35) of Schedule 1 to the Capital Allowances Act 1990 (c. 1)).

Section 832 (interpretation of the Tax Acts)

60. In subsection (1)—
(a) in the definition of "capital allowance", for "the Capital Allowances Acts" substitute " the Capital Allowances Act (including enactments which under this Act are to be treated as contained in that Act) ", and
(b) for the definition of "the Capital Allowances Acts" substitute—
""the Capital Allowances Act" means the Capital Allowances Act 2001;".

Section 834 (interpretation of the Corporation Tax Acts)

61. In subsection (2), omit "and also for sections 144 and 145 of the 1990 Act".

F1662. . . . .
Amendments (Textual)
F16. Sch. 2 para. 62 repealed (6.4.2007) by Income Tax Act 2007 (c. 3), s. 1034. (1), Sch. 3 Pt. 1 (with Sch. 2)

Schedule 18 (group relief)

63. In paragraph 1. (6)—
(a) in paragraph (b)(i) and (ii), for "Part II of the 1990 Act" substitute " Part 2 of the Capital Allowances Act " and for "machinery or plant" substitute " plant or machinery ", and
(b) in paragraph (b)(iii), for "section 137 of the 1990 Act" substitute " Chapter 3 of Part 6 of the Capital Allowances Act " and for "Part VII" substitute " Part 6 ".

Schedule 19. AC (modification of Act in relation to overseas life insurance companies)

64. (1)Omit paragraph 9. C (application of section 434. D(4) in relation to overseas life insurance company).
F17. (2). . . . .
Amendments (Textual)
F17. Sch. 2 para. 64. (2) repealed (with effect in accordance with reg. 1 of the amending S.I.) by The Overseas Life Insurance Companies Regulations 2006 (S.I. 2006/3271), reg. 1, Sch. Pt. 1

Schedule 21 (tax relief in connection with schemes for

rationalising industry and other redundancy schemes)

65. In paragraph 6. (1)(a), for "Part I or II of the 1990 Act in taxing the trade" substitute " Part 2 or 3 of the Capital Allowances Act in calculating the profits of a trade ".

Schedule 24 (assumptions for calculating chargeable profits, creditable tax and corresponding United Kingdom tax of foreign companies)

66. (1)In paragraph 10. (1)—
(a) for "machinery or plant for the purposes of its trade, that machinery or plant shall be assumed, for the purposes of Part II of the 1990 Act" substitute " plant or machinery for the purposes of its trade, that plant or machinery shall be assumed, for the purposes of Part 2 of the Capital Allowances Act ", and
(b) for "section 81 of that Act (expenditure treated as equivalent to market value at the time the machinery or plant is brought into use)" substitute " section 13 of that Act (use for qualifying activity of plant or machinery provided for other purposes) ".
(2) In paragraph 10. (2), for "Part II of the 1990 Act" substitute " Part 2 of the Capital Allowances Act ".
F18. (3). . . . .
Amendments (Textual)
F18. Sch. 2 para. 66. (3) repealed (7.4.2005) by Finance Act 2005 (c. 7), Sch. 11 Pt. 2. (6)

Schedule 28. A (change in ownership of investment company: deductions)

67. (1)In paragraph 6. (d), for "section 28 of the 1990 Act" substitute " section 253 of the Capital Allowances Act ".
(2) In paragraph 13. (1)(e), for "section 28 of the 1990 Act" substitute " section 253 of the Capital Allowances Act ".

Schedule 28. AA (provision not at arms' length)

68. In paragraph 13. (a), for "the 1990 Act" substitute " the Capital Allowances Act ".

The Finance Act 1988 (c. 39)

Schedule 12 (building societies: change of status)

69. In paragraph 3. (1), for "the Capital Allowances Act 1990 (capital allowances)" substitute " the Capital Allowances Act 2001 ".

The Finance Act 1989 (c. 26)

Section 86 (spreading of relief for acquisition expenses)

F1970. . . . .
Amendments (Textual)
F19. Sch. 2 para. 70 repealed (with effect in accordance with s. 42 of the amending Act) by
Finance Act 2004 (c. 12), Sch. 42 Pt. 2. (3)

The Electricity Act 1989 (c. 29)

Schedule 11 (taxation provisions)

71. (1)For paragraph 5. (3) substitute—
"(3)Section 291. (1) of the Capital Allowances Act 2001 (supplementary provisions with respect
to elections) shall not prevent the application of section 290 of that Act (election to treat grant of
lease exceeding 50 years as sale) where the lease is a lease to which this sub-paragraph applies."
(2) In paragraph 5. (4)(a), for "section 44 of the Finance Act 1971 or section 24 of the 1990 Act"
substitute " Chapter 5 of Part 2 of the Capital Allowances Act 2001 ".
(3) In paragraph 5. (4)(b), for the words from "section 44" to "Chapter VI of Part II of the 1990
Act" substitute " Chapters 5 and 14 of Part 2 of the Capital Allowances Act 2001 ".
(4) For paragraph 5. (5) substitute—
"(5)In sub-paragraph (4) above "the transferor" means the transferor under the transfer scheme in
question and expressions which are used in Chapter 14 of Part 2 of the Capital Allowances Act
2001 have the same meanings as in that Chapter; and in construing that sub-paragraph section 511.
(2) of the 1988 Act shall be disregarded."

The Finance Act 1990 (c. 29)

Section 126 (pools payments for football ground improvements)

72. In subsection (4), for "Section 153 of the Capital Allowances Act 1990" substitute " Section
532 of the Capital Allowances Act 2001 ".

The Finance Act 1991 (c. 31)

Section 65 (reimbursement by defaulter in respect of certain abandonment expenditure)

73. In subsection (8), for "section 153 of the Capital Allowances Act 1990 (subsidies,
contributions, etc.)" substitute " section 532 of the Capital Allowances Act (the general rule
excluding contributions) ".

Section 78 (sharing of transmission facilities)

74. (1)In subsection (4)—
(a) for "Capital Allowances Act 1990" substitute " Capital Allowances Act ";
(b) for "machinery or plant" (in each place) substitute " plant or machinery "; and
(c) for "section 24 of that Act" substitute " section 60 of that Act ".
(2) In subsection (5) for "machinery or plant" (in both places) substitute " plant or machinery ".

The Social Security Contributions and Benefits Act 1992 (c. 4)

Schedule 2 (levy of Class 4 contributions with income tax)

75. (1)In paragraph 1, omit paragraph (b).

(2) In paragraph 2, omit the words from "subject to deduction" to the end.

The Social Security Contributions and Benefits (Northern Ireland) Act 1992 (c. 7)

Schedule 2 (levy of Class 4 contributions with income tax)

76. (1)In paragraph 1, omit paragraph (b).

(2) In paragraph 2, omit the words from "subject to deduction" to the end.

The Taxation of Chargeable Gains Act 1992 (c. 12)

Section 37 (consideration chargeable to tax on income)

77. In subsection (2), for paragraphs (a) and (b) substitute—

"(a)taken into account in the making of a balancing charge under the Capital Allowances Act but excluding Part 10 of that Act,

(b) brought into account as the disposal value of plant or machinery under Part 2 of that Act, or

(c) brought into account as the disposal value of an asset representing qualifying expenditure under Part 6 of that Act."

Section 41 (restriction of losses by reference to capital allowances etc.)

78. (1)In subsection (3), for paragraphs (a) and (b) substitute—

"(a)by a transfer by way of sale in relation to which an election under section 569 of the Capital Allowances Act was made, or

(b) by a transfer to which section 268 of that Act applies,".

(2) In subsection (4), for paragraph (a) substitute—

"(a)any allowance under the Capital Allowances Act,".

(3) In subsection (7)—

(a) for "machinery or plant" (in each place) substitute " plant or machinery ",

(b) for "Part II of the 1990 Act, and neither section 79 (assets used only partly for trade purposes) nor section 80 (wear and tear subsidies) of that Act" substitute " Part 2 of the Capital Allowances Act, and neither Chapter 15 (assets provided or used only partly for qualifying activity) nor Chapter 16 (partial depreciation subsidies) of that Part ", and

(c) for "capital expenditure" substitute " qualifying expenditure ".

Section 195 (allowance of certain drilling expenditure)

79. (1)In subsection (2), for paragraphs (b) and (c) substitute—

"(b)either it is expenditure in respect of which the person was entitled to an allowance under section 441 of the Capital Allowances Act (research and development allowances) for a relevant chargeable period which began before the date of the disposal or it would have been such expenditure if the trading condition had been fulfilled, and

(c) on the disposal, section 443 of that Act (disposal values) applies in relation to the expenditure or would apply if the trading condition had been fulfilled (and the expenditure had accordingly been qualifying expenditure under Part 6 of that Act)."

(2) In subsection (3)—

(a) for "section 137 of the 1990 Act" substitute " section 441 of the Capital Allowances Act ", and

(b) omit the definition of "basis year" and the word "and" before it.

(3) In subsection (4), for "trading receipt" substitute " disposal value " and for paragraphs (a) and (b) substitute—

"(a)is required to be brought into account under section 443 of the Capital Allowances Act; or

(b) would be required to be so brought into account if the trading condition had been fulfilled (and the expenditure had accordingly been qualifying expenditure under Part 6 of that Act)."

(4) Omit subsection (5).

(5) In subsection (6)—

(a) for "which had not in fact been allowed or become allowable" substitute " in respect of which the person had not in fact been entitled to an allowance ",

(b) for "section 137 of the 1990 Act" substitute " section 441 of the Capital Allowances Act ", and

(c) omit paragraph (b) and the word "and" before it.

(6) In subsection (8), for "Part VII of the Capital Allowances Act 1990 (allowances for research and development expenditure)" substitute " Part 6 of the Capital Allowances Act (research and development allowances) ".

Section 288 (interpretation)

80. In subsection (1), omit the definition of "the 1990 Act" and after the definition of "building society" insert—

""the Capital Allowances Act" means the Capital Allowances Act 2001;".

Schedule 3 (assets held on 31st March 1982)

81. In paragraph 7. (8), for "section 121 of the 1990 Act" substitute " section 394 of the Capital Allowances Act ".

The Finance (No. 2) Act 1992 (c. 48)

New sections 40. A to 40. D (films)

82. Before section 41 insert—

"40. A Revenue nature of expenditure on master versions of films

(1) Expenditure incurred on the production or acquisition of a master version of a film is to be regarded for the purposes of the Tax Acts as expenditure of a revenue nature unless an election under section 40. D below has effect with respect to it.

(2) If expenditure on the master version of a film is regarded as expenditure of a revenue nature under subsection (1) above, sums received from the disposal of the master version are to be regarded for the purposes of the Tax Acts as receipts of a revenue nature (if they would not be so regarded apart from this subsection).

(3) For the purposes of subsection (2) above sums received from the disposal of a master version of a film include—

(a) sums received from the disposal of any interest or right in or over the master version, including an interest or right created by the disposal, and

(b) insurance, compensation or similar money derived from the master version.

(4) In this section—

(a) "expenditure of a revenue nature" means expenditure which, if it were incurred in the course of a trade the profits of which are chargeable to tax under Case I of Schedule D, would be taken into account for the purpose of computing the profits or losses of the trade, and

(b) "receipts of a revenue nature" means receipts which, if they were receipts of such a trade, would be taken into account for that purpose.

(5) For the purposes of this section and sections 40. B to 40. D below, a "master version" of a film means a master negative, master tape or master audio disc of the film and includes any rights in the film (or its soundtrack) that are held or acquired with the master negative, master tape or master audio disc.

40. B Allocation of expenditure to periods

(1) In computing the profits or gains accruing to any person from a trade or business which consists of or includes the exploitation of master versions of films, expenditure which is—

(a) incurred on the production or acquisition of a master version of a film, and

(b) expenditure of a revenue nature (whether as a result of section 40. A above or otherwise), must be allocated to relevant periods in accordance with this section.

(2) Subsection (1) above does not apply if an election under section 40. D below has effect with respect to the expenditure.

(3) In this section "relevant period" means—

(a) a period for which the accounts of the trade or business concerned are made up, or

(b) if no accounts of the trade or business concerned are made up for a period—

(i) if the profits or gains accrue to a company within the charge to corporation tax, the accounting period of the company;

(ii) in any other case, the period the profits or gains of which are taken into account in assessing the income of the trade or business for a year of assessment.

(4) The amount of expenditure falling within subsection (1) above which falls to be allocated to any relevant period is so much as is just and reasonable, having regard to—

(a) the amount of that expenditure which remains unallocated at the beginning of that period,

(b) the proportion which the estimated value of the master version of the film which is realised in that period (whether by way of income or otherwise) bears to the aggregate of the value so realised and the estimated remaining value of the master version at the end of that period, and

(c) the need to bring the whole of the expenditure falling within subsection (1) above into account over the time during which the value of the master version is expected to be realised.

(5) In addition to any expenditure which is allocated to a relevant period in accordance with subsection (4) above, if a claim is made, there must also be allocated to that period so much of the unallocated expenditure as is specified in the claim and does not exceed the difference between—

(a) the amount allocated to that period in accordance with subsection (4) above, and

(b) the value of the master version of the film which is realised in that period (whether by way of income or otherwise).

(6) A claim under subsection (5) above must be made—

(a) for the purposes of income tax, on or before the first anniversary of the 31st January next following the year of assessment in which ends the relevant period mentioned in that subsection;

(b) for the purposes of corporation tax, not later than two years after the end of the relevant period to which the claim relates.

(7) In subsection (5) above "the unallocated expenditure", in relation to a relevant period, is any expenditure falling within subsection (1) above—

(a) which does not fall to be allocated to that period in accordance with subsection (4) above, and

(b) which has not been allocated to any earlier relevant period in accordance with subsection (4) or (5) above.

40. C Cases where section 40. B does not apply

(1) To the extent that a deduction has been made in respect of any expenditure for a relevant period under section 42 below—

(a) that expenditure must not be allocated under section 40. B above, and

(b) no other expenditure incurred on the production or acquisition of the master version of the film is to be allocated under section 40. B above to the relevant period.

(2) Section 40. B above does not apply to the profits of a trade in which the master version of the film constitutes trading stock, as defined by section 100. (2) of the Taxes Act 1988.

40. D Election for sections 40. A and 40. B not to apply

(1) Sections 40. A and 40. B above do not apply to expenditure—

(a) in relation to which an election is made under this section, and

(b) which meets the conditions in subsection (2) below.

(2) The conditions are that—

(a) the expenditure is incurred—

(i) by a person who carries on a trade or business which consists of or includes the exploitation of master versions of films, and

(ii) on the production or acquisition of a master version of a film,

(b) the master version is certified by the Secretary of State under paragraph 3 of Schedule 1 to the Films Act 1985 as a qualifying film, tape or disc for the purposes of this section, and

(c) the value of the master version is expected to be realisable over a period of not less than two years.

(3) An election under this section—

(a) must relate to all expenditure incurred (or to be incurred) on the production or acquisition of the master version in question,

(b) must be made by giving notice to [F20an officer of Revenue and Customs], in such form as the Board of Inland Revenue may determine, and

(c) is irrevocable.

(4) Notice under subsection (3)(b) above must be given—

(a) for the purposes of income tax, on or before the first anniversary of the 31st January next following the year of assessment in which ends the relevant period in which the master version of the film is completed;

(b) for the purposes of corporation tax, not later than two years after the end of the relevant period in which the master version of the film is completed.

(5) In subsection (4) above "relevant period" has the same meaning as in section 40. B above.

(6) For the purposes of subsection (4) above, the master version of a film is completed—

(a) at the time when it is first in a form in which it can reasonably be regarded as ready for copies of it to be made and distributed for presentation to the public, or

(b) if the expenditure in question was incurred on the acquisition of the master version and it was acquired after the time mentioned in paragraph (a) above, at the time it was acquired.

(7) An election may not be made under this section in relation to expenditure on a master version of a film if a claim has been made in respect of any of that expenditure under section 41 or 42 below."

Amendments (Textual)

F20. Words in Act substituted (18.4.2005) by Commissioners for Revenue and Customs Act 2005 (c. 11), s. 53. (1), Sch. 4 para. 83. (1); S.I. 2005/1126, art. 2. (2)(h)

Section 41 (relief for preliminary expenditure)

83. In subsection (1)(c), for "section 68. (9) of the 1990 Act" substitute " section 40. D above ".

Section 42 (relief for production or acquisition expenditure)

84. (1)In subsection (1)(b)—

(a) for "subsections (3) to (6) of section 68 of the 1990 Act" substitute " section 40. B above ", and

(b) for "subsection (9) of that section" substitute " section 40. D above ".

(2) In subsection (4)(c), for "section 68. (3) to (6) of the 1990 Act, section" substitute " section 40. B or ".

(3) In subsection (7), for "section 68. (3) to (6) of the 1990 Act" substitute " section 40. B above ".

Section 43 (interpretation of sections 41 and 42)

85. In subsection (1)—

(a) for "41 and 42" substitute " 40. A to 42 ",

(b) for "section 68. (10) of the 1990 Act" substitute " section 40. A(4) above ",

(c) for "section 68 of the 1990 Act", in each place where it occurs, substitute " section 40. D above ",

(d) for "section 68. (3) of the 1990 Act" substitute " section 40. B(3) above ", and

(e) omit the definition of "the 1990 Act".

Schedule 10 (furnished accommodation)

F2186. . . . .

Amendments (Textual)

F21. Sch. 2 para. 86 repealed (6.4.2005) by Income Tax (Trading and Other Income) Act 2005 (c. 5), s. 883. (1), Sch. 3 (with Sch. 2)

Schedule 17 (Northern Ireland electricity)

87. (1)In paragraph 5. (4)—

(a) for "section 11 of the Capital Allowances Act 1990 (long leases)" substitute " section 290 of the Capital Allowances Act 2001 (election to treat grant of lease exceeding 50 years as sale) ",

(b) for "long lease within the meaning" substitute " lease which satisfies the condition in subsection (1)(c) ",

(c) in paragraph (a), for "section 8" substitute " Chapter 8 of Part 3 ",

(d) in paragraph (b), for "section 11. (6)(a)" substitute " section 291. (1) ",

(e) for "sections 157 and 158" substitute " sections 567 to 570 ", and

(f) for "section 11" substitute " section 290 ".

(2) In paragraph 5. (5)—

(a) for "paragraphs (a) and (b) of subsection (1) of section 55 of the Capital Allowances Act 1990 (expenditure incurred by incoming lessee: transfer of allowances)" substitute " section 183. (1)(a) and (b) of the Capital Allowances Act (incoming lessee where lessor entitled to allowances) ",

(b) in paragraph (a) for "Part II of that Act" substitute " Part 2 of that Act ",

(c) after that paragraph insert " and ", and

(d) omit paragraph (c) and the word "and" before it.

(3) In paragraph 6. (1), for "section 11 of the Capital Allowances Act 1990" substitute " section 290 of the Capital Allowances Act 2001 ".

(4) In paragraph 6. (4), for "section 55 of the Capital Allowances Act 1990" substitute " section 183 of the Capital Allowances Act 2001 ".

The Finance Act 1993 (c. 34)

Section 92 (the basic rule: sterling to be used)

88. In subsection (2)—
(a) for "section 28 or 61. (1) of the Capital Allowances Act 1990", substitute " section 19 or 253 of the Capital Allowances Act ", and
(b) for "section 28 or 61. (1) of that Act" substitute " section 19 or 253 of that Act ".

Section 93 (use of currency other than sterling)

89. In subsection (5), for "section 22. B, 34, 35, 38. C, 38. D or 79. A of the Capital Allowances Act 1990" substitute " section 578. A(2) or (3) of the Taxes Act 1988 or section 43. (3), 74. (2), 75. (1), 76. (2), (3) or (4), 99. (1), (2) or (3) or 208. (1) of the Capital Allowances Act ".

The Agriculture Act 1993 (c. 37)

Schedule 2 (provisions relating to carrying out approved schemes or reorganisation)

90. In paragraph 19. (4) and (5)(b), for "the Capital Allowances Act 1990" substitute " the Capital Allowances Act 2001 ".

The Finance Act 1994 (c. 9)

Schedule 24 (provisions relating to the Railways Act 1993)

91. (1)In paragraph 1. (1)—
(a) omit the definition of "the Allowances Act",
(b) after the definition of "the Board" insert—
""the Capital Allowances Act" means the Capital Allowances Act 2001 and includes, where the context admits, enactments which under the Taxes Act 1988 are to be treated as contained in the Capital Allowances Act 2001;",
 and
(c) in the definition of "fixture", for "Chapter VI of Part II of the Allowances Act" substitute " Chapter 14 of Part 2 of the Capital Allowances Act ".
(2) In paragraph 1. (4)(c), for "the Capital Allowances Acts" substitute " the Capital Allowances Act ".
(3) In paragraph 20. (1) and (2)(a), for "the Capital Allowances Acts" substitute " the Capital Allowances Act ".
(4) In paragraph 20. (8), for "section 77 of the Allowances Act (successions to trades: connected persons)" substitute " sections 266 and 267 of the Capital Allowances Act (election where predecessor and successor are connected persons) ".
(5) In paragraph 21. (1), for "the Capital Allowances Acts" substitute " the Capital Allowances Act ".
(6) In paragraph 21. (2)—
(a) in paragraph (a), for "subsection (6) of section 21 of the Allowances Act (transfer of industrial buildings or structures to be deemed to be sale at market price)" substitute " section 573 of the

Capital Allowances Act (transfers treated as sales) as it applies for the purposes of Part 3 of that Act ",

(b) in paragraph (b), for "that subsection" substitute " that section " and for "the Capital Allowances Acts" substitute " that Act ", and

(c) for "by virtue of that subsection or any other provision of those Acts), sections 157 and 158 of the Allowances Act" substitute " under that section or any other provision of the Capital Allowances Act), sections 567 to 570 of that Act ".

(7) In paragraph 21. (3)—

(a) for "the Capital Allowances Acts" substitute " the Capital Allowances Act ",

(b) for "those Acts" substitute " that Act ",

(c) in paragraph (a), for "section 26. (1) or 59 of the Allowances Act" substitute " section 61. (2) to (4), 72. (3) to (5), 171, 196 or 423 of the Capital Allowances Act ", and

(d) in paragraph (c), for "section 54" substitute " sections 181. (1) and 182. (1) ".

(8) In paragraph 22. (2)—

(a) for "building or structure" (in both places) substitute " building ",

(b) for "Part I of the Allowances Act" substitute " Part 3 of the Capital Allowances Act ", and

(c) for "sections 157 and 158" substitute " sections 567 to 570 ".

(9) In paragraph 22. (3)—

(a) for "machinery or plant" (in the first and second places) substitute " plant or machinery ",

(b) for "section 24 of the Allowances Act (balancing adjustments) shall, subject to section 26. (2) and (3) of that Act (disposal value of machinery or plant not to exceed capital expenditure incurred on its provision)" substitute " section 55 of the Capital Allowances Act (determination of entitlement or liability) shall, subject to section 62 of that Act (general limit on amount of disposal value) ", and

(c) for "the Capital Allowances Acts" substitute " the Capital Allowances Act ".

(10) In paragraph 22. (4)—

(a) for "section 57. (2) of the Allowances Act" substitute " section 188 of the Capital Allowances Act ",

(b) for "section 24 of that Act shall, subject to section 26. (2) and (3)" substitute " section 55 of that Act shall, subject to section 62 ",

(c) in paragraph (a), for "Part II" substitute " Part 2 ", and

(d) for "the Capital Allowances Acts" substitute " the Capital Allowances Act ".

Schedule 25 (Northern Ireland Airports Limited)

92. (1)In paragraph 5. (2), for "the 1990 Act" (in both places) substitute " the Capital Allowances Act 2001 ".

(2) In paragraph 5. (3)—

(a) omit the definition of "the 1990 Act",

(b) for "section 4 of the 1990 Act" substitute " Chapter 7 of Part 3 of the Capital Allowances Act 2001 ", and

(c) for "section 20 of the 1990 Act" substitute " Chapter 3 of Part 3 of the Capital Allowances Act 2001 ".

The Coal Industry Act 1994 (c. 21)

Schedule 4 (taxation provisions)

93. (1)In paragraph 1. (2)—

(a) after the definition of "the 1988 Act" insert—

""the Capital Allowances Act" includes, where the context admits, enactments which under the 1988 Act are to be treated as contained in the Capital Allowances Act,",
and

(b) in the definition of "fixture", for "Chapter VI of Part II of the 1990 Act" substitute " Chapter 14 of Part 2 of the Capital Allowances Act ".

(2) In paragraph 19. (1) and (2), for "the Capital Allowances Acts" substitute " the Capital Allowances Act ".

(3) In paragraph 19. (3)(b) and (4)(b), for "section 145. (2) of the 1990 Act" substitute " section 260 of the Capital Allowances Act ".

(4) In paragraph 20. (1), for "the Capital Allowances Acts" substitute " the Capital Allowances Act ".

(5) In paragraph 20. (2)—

(a) in paragraph (a), for "subsection (6) of section 21 of the 1990 Act (transfer of industrial buildings or structures to be deemed to be sale at market price)" substitute " section 573 of the Capital Allowances Act (transfers treated as sales) as it applies for the purposes of Part 3 of that Act ",

(b) in paragraph (b), for "that subsection (6)" substitute " that section " and for "the Capital Allowances Acts" substitute " that Act ",

(c) for "that subsection" substitute " that section ", and

(d) for "those Acts), sections 157 and 158 of the 1990 Act" substitute " that Act), sections 567 to 570 of that Act ".

(6) In paragraph 20. (3)—

(a) for "the Capital Allowances Acts" substitute " the Capital Allowances Act ",

(b) for "those Acts" substitute " that Act ",

(c) in paragraph (a), for "section 26. (1) or 59 of the 1990 Act" substitute " section 61. (2) to (4), 72. (3) to (5), 171, 196 or 423 of the Capital Allowances Act ", and

(d) in paragraph (c), for "section 54" substitute " sections 181. (1) and 182. (1) ".

(7) In paragraph 20. (4), for "under section 99 of the 1990 Act (disposal receipts in relation to mineral extraction allowances)" substitute " in accordance with sections 421 to 425 of the Capital Allowances Act (mineral extraction allowances: disposal receipts) ".

(8) In paragraph 20. (5)—

(a) in paragraph (a), for "Part V of the 1990 Act (agricultural buildings etc.)" substitute " Part 4 of the Capital Allowances Act (agricultural buildings allowances) " and for "section 129. (2)" substitute " section 382 ",

(b) in paragraph (b), for "the Capital Allowances Acts" substitute " that Act ", and

(c) for "section 128. (2) of that Act (calculation of balancing allowance or charge)" substitute " section 385 of the Capital Allowances Act (calculation of balancing adjustment) ".

(9) In paragraph 20. (6)—

(a) in paragraph (a), for "relevant event for the purposes of section 138 of the 1990 Act (assets representing allowable scientific research expenditure ceasing to belong to traders)" substitute " disposal event for the purposes of Chapter 3 of Part 6 of the Capital Allowances Act (research and development allowances: allowances and charges) ",

(b) in paragraph (b), for "subsection (2) of that section" substitute " that Chapter ", and

(c) for "that section" substitute " that Chapter ".

(10) In paragraph 20. (7)—

(a) for "the 1990 Act" substitute " the Capital Allowances Act ", and

(b) for "section 157. (1)(a)" substitute " section 568. (1)(a) ".

(11) In paragraph 21. (2), for "the Capital Allowances Acts" substitute " the Capital Allowances Act ".

(12) In paragraph 21. (3)—

(a) for "Chapter VI of Part II of the 1990 Act" substitute " Chapter 14 of Part 2 of the Capital Allowances Act ",

(b) for "the Capital Allowances Acts" substitute " the Capital Allowances Act ",

(c) for "they did" substitute " it did ", and

(d) for "those Acts" substitute " that Act ".

(13) In paragraph 21. (4)—

(a) for "section 61 of the 1990 Act" substitute " section 70 of the Capital Allowances Act ",

(b) for "the Capital Allowances Acts" substitute " the Capital Allowances Act ",

(c) for "machinery or plant" (in each place) substitute " plant or machinery ".

(14) In paragraph 22, for "Part II of the 1990 Act" substitute " Part 2 of the Capital Allowances Act ".

The Atomic Energy Authority Act 1995 (c. 37)

Schedule 3 (taxation provisions)

94. (1)In paragraph 14. (1), for the definition of "the Capital Allowances Acts" substitute—
""the Capital Allowances Act" means the Capital Allowances Act 2001 and includes, where the context admits, enactments which under the 1988 Act are to be treated as contained in the Capital Allowances Act 2001."

(2) In paragraph 14. (3), for "Capital Allowances Acts" substitute " Capital Allowances Act ".

(3) For paragraph 15 substitute—
"15 Industrial buildings
Where any transfer effected by a transfer scheme is a relevant event for the purposes of section 311 of the Capital Allowances Act, the Secretary of State may for the purposes of that section by order make provision specifying the values to be assigned to RQE and B in relation to that event."

(4) In paragraph 16—

(a) for the heading substitute " Plant and machinery ", and

(b) for "Part II of the Capital Allowances Act 1990 (capital allowances in respect of machinery and plant)" substitute " Part 2 of the Capital Allowances Act (plant and machinery allowances) ".

(5) For paragraph 17 substitute—
"17 Research and development

(1) For the purposes of Part 6 of the Capital Allowances Act (research and development allowances) a successor company in which an asset representing allowable research and development expenditure is vested in accordance with a transfer scheme shall be treated as having incurred, on the date on which the transfer scheme comes into force, capital expenditure of the prescribed amount on the research and development in question; and that research and development shall be taken to have been directly undertaken by the successor company or on its behalf.

(2) In sub-paragraph (1) above "allowable research and development expenditure" means capital expenditure incurred by the Authority on research and development directly undertaken by the Authority or on their behalf.

(3) In this paragraph—
"asset" includes part of an asset;
"research and development" has the same meaning as in Part 6 of the Capital Allowances Act; and references to expenditure incurred on research and development shall be construed in accordance with section 438 of that Act."

(6) In paragraph 18. (1), for "section 520 of the 1988 Act (allowances for expenditure on purchase of patent rights)" substitute " section 468 of the Capital Allowances Act (qualifying trade expenditure) ".

(7) In paragraph 18. (2), for "section 533 of the 1988 Act" substitute " section 464. (2) of the Capital Allowances Act ".

(8) In paragraph 19. (1), for "section 530 of the 1988 Act (disposal of know-how)" substitute " section 454 of the Capital Allowances Act (qualifying expenditure) ".

(9) In paragraph 19. (2), after "Subsections (2) and (7) of section 531 of the 1988 Act (provisions supplementary to section 530)" insert " and subsections (2) and (3) of section 455 of the Capital Allowances Act (excluded expenditure) ".

(10) In paragraph 19. (3), for "section 533. (7) of the 1988 Act" substitute " section 452. (2) of the Capital Allowances Act ".

(11) In paragraph 20, for "Part II of the Capital Allowances Act 1990 (machinery and plant)" substitute " Parts 2, 7 and 8 of the Capital Allowances Act (plant and machinery, know-how and patents) ".

(12) In paragraph 22, for "Capital Allowances Acts" substitute " Capital Allowances Act ".

The Finance Act 1996 (c. 8)

Section 151 (benefits under pilot schemes)

95. In subsection (2), for "section 153 of the Capital Allowances Act 1990 (subsidies etc.)" substitute " section 532 of the Capital Allowances Act (exclusion of expenditure met by contributions) ".

Schedule 8 (loan relationships)

96. In paragraph 3. (6)(c)(i), for "section 28 of the Capital Allowances Act 1990 (machinery and plant of investment companies)" substitute " Part 2 of the Capital Allowances Act (plant and machinery allowances) ".

The Broadcasting Act 1996 (c. 55)

Schedule 7 (transfer schemes relating to BBC transmission network: taxation provisions)

97. (1)in paragraph 1. (1), omit the definition of "the Allowances Act" and for the definition of "the Capital Allowances Acts" substitute—

""the Capital Allowances Act" means the Capital Allowances Act 2001 and includes, where the context admits, enactments which under the Taxes Act 1988 are to be treated as contained in the Capital Allowances Act 2001."

(2) In paragraph 1. (3)(b), for "the Capital Allowances Acts" substitute " the Capital Allowances Act ".

(3) In paragraph 12. (3)—

(a) for "the Capital Allowances Acts" substitute " the Capital Allowances Act ", and

(b) for "those Acts" substitute " that Act ".

(4) In paragraph 13. (1)—

(a) in the heading, omit "and structures", and

(b) for "Part I of the Allowances Act (industrial buildings and structures)" substitute " Part 3 of the Capital Allowances Act (industrial buildings allowances) ".

(5) In paragraph 13. (2), for "Part I of the Allowances Act" substitute " Part 3 of the Capital Allowances Act ".

(6) In paragraph 14. (1)—

(a) in the heading, for "machinery and plant" substitute " plant and machinery ", and

(b) for "Part II of the Allowances Act (capital allowances in respect of machinery and plant)" substitute " Part 2 of the Capital Allowances Act (plant and machinery allowances) ".

(7) In paragraph 15. (2)—

(a) for "paragraphs (a) and (b) of subsection (1) of section 55 of the Allowances Act (expenditure incurred by incoming lessee: transfer of allowances)" substitute " section 183. (1)(a) and (b) of the Capital Allowances Act (incoming lessee where lessor entitled to allowances) ",

(b) for "Part II" substitute " Part 2 ", and

(c) for "subsection (4)(a)" substitute " subsection (1)(d) ".

(8) In paragraph 15. (3)—

(a) for "paragraphs (a), (c) and (d) of section 56 of the Allowances Act (expenditure incurred by incoming lessee: lessor not entitled to allowances)" substitute " section 184. (1)(a) to (c) of the Capital Allowances Act (incoming lessee where lessor not entitled to allowances) ", and

(b) for "Part II" substitute " Part 2 ".

(9) In paragraph 16, for "Part II of the Allowances Act (machinery and plant)" substitute " Part 2 of the Capital Allowances Act (plant and machinery allowances) ".

(10) For paragraph 17 substitute—

"17 Capital allowances: agricultural buildings allowances

(1) This paragraph applies where there is a relevant transfer of property which is the relevant interest in relation to any expenditure for which the BBC would be entitled to an allowance (other than a balancing allowance) under Part 4 of the Capital Allowances Act (agricultural buildings allowances).

(2) Where this paragraph applies, then, as respects the transferee—

(a) his acquisition of the relevant interest shall be treated for the purposes of Part 4 of the Capital Allowances Act as a balancing event within subsection (2)(a) of section 381 (regardless of the lack of any election); and

(b) section 376. (2) shall apply as if—

(i) the value to be assigned to RQE (residue of qualifying expenditure immediately after event) were the prescribed amount; and

(ii) the value to be assigned to B (remaining writing-down period) were such as the Secretary of state may by order specify.

(3) This paragraph shall not have effect in relation to any property if paragraph 12. (3) has effect in relation to it."

The Finance Act 1997 (c. 16)

Schedule 12 (leasing arrangements: finance leases and loans)

98. (1)For paragraph 11. (3)(a) to (c) substitute—

"(a)Part 2 of the Capital Allowances Act (plant and machinery allowances),

(b) Part 5 of that Act (mineral extraction allowances), or

(c) Part 8 of that Act (patent allowances)".

(2) In paragraph 11. (8), for "the Capital Allowances Acts" substitute " the Capital Allowances Act " and omit "or its basis period".

(3) For paragraph 11. (9)(a) and (b) substitute " section 40. B(1) or 42 of the Finance (No. 2) Act 1992 (expenditure in connection with films etc.), ".

(4) In paragraph 11. (10), for "under section 68. (8) of the Capital Allowances Act 1990" substitute " under section 40. A(2) of the Finance (No. 2) Act 1992 ".

(5) In paragraph 11. (13), for "section 154 of the Capital Allowances Act 1990" substitute " sections 537 to 542 of the Capital Allowances Act ".

(6) For paragraph 11. (14) substitute—

"(14)In sub-paragraph (8) above—

"the Capital Allowances Act" includes enactments which under the Taxes Act 1988 are to be treated as contained in the Capital Allowances Act;

"chargeable period" has the meaning given by section 6 of the Capital Allowances Act.".

(7) Omit paragraph 11. (15).

The Finance (No. 2) Act 1997 (c. 58)

Section 48 (films: relief for production or acquisition expenditure)

99. (1)In subsection (1), for "section 68. (3) to (6) of the 1990 Act, section" substitute " section 40. B or ".

(2) For subsection (9) substitute—

"(9)Subsections (1) to (5) of section 5 of the Capital Allowances Act 2001 (when capital expenditure is incurred) apply for determining when for the purposes of this section any expenditure is incurred as they apply for determining when for the purposes of that Act any capital expenditure is incurred, but as if, in subsection (6) of that section, "at an earlier time" were substituted for "in an earlier chargeable period"."

The Finance Act 1998 (c. 36)

Section 117 (company tax returns, assessments and related matters)

100. (1)In subsection (1), at the end of paragraph (b), insert " and ".

(2) For subsection (1)(d) and the word "and" before it substitute—

"and also make provision in relation to claims for allowances under the Capital Allowances Act."

Section 118 (claims for income tax purposes)

101. In subsection (5)(b), for "the Capital Allowances Act 1990" substitute " the Capital Allowances Act ".

Schedule 6 (adjustment on change of accounting basis)

F22102. . . . .

Amendments (Textual)

F22. Sch. 2 para. 102 repealed (with effect as mentioned in s. 64. (6), Sch. 22 paras 16, 17 of the amending Act) by Finance Act 2002 (c. 23), s. 141, (Sch. 40 Pt. 3. (8) Note 2)

Schedule 18 (company tax returns, assessments and related matters)

103. (1)For paragraph 78 (application of Part IX of the Schedule) substitute—

"78. This Part of this Schedule applies to claims for allowances under the Capital Allowances Act which—

(a) are made for corporation tax purposes, and

(b) are required under section 3 of that Act to be included in a tax return."

(2) For paragraph 79. (1) (claim to be included in company tax return) substitute—
"79. (1)A claim for capital allowances must be included in the claimant company's company tax return for the accounting period for which the claim is made."

The Finance Act 1999 (c. 16)

Schedule 6 (tax treatment of receipts by way of reverse premium)

104. In paragraph 5, for "section 153 of the Capital Allowances Act 1990 (subsidies, contributions, etc.)" substitute " section 532 of the Capital Allowances Act (the general rule excluding contributions) ".

The Greater London Authority Act 1999 (c. 29)

Schedule 33 (taxation)

105. (1)In paragraph 4. (3), for "the Capital Allowances Acts" substitute " the Capital Allowances Act 2001 ".
(2) In paragraph 4. (8), for "section 77 of the Capital Allowances Act 1990 (successions to trades: connected persons)" substitute " section 266 of the Capital Allowances Act 2001 (election where predecessor and successor are connected persons) ".
(3) For paragraph 4. (9) substitute—
"(9)Except as provided by this paragraph, a qualifying transfer in relation to which this paragraph applies shall be taken for the purposes of the Capital Allowances Act 2001 not to give rise to—
    (a) any writing-down allowances, balancing allowances or balancing charges under Chapter 5 of Part 2 of that Act (plant and machinery allowances and charges),
    (b) any disposal value being treated as received for the purposes of that Chapter,
    (c) any qualifying expenditure being treated as incurred for the purposes of that Chapter, or
    (d) any writing-down allowances, balancing allowances or balancing charges under Part 3 of that Act (industrial buildings allowances).
(10) In this paragraph and paragraph 10 below "the Capital Allowances Act 2001" includes, where the context admits, enactments which under the Taxes Act 1988 are to be treated as contained in the Capital Allowances Act 2001."
(4) In paragraph 10. (3), for "the Capital Allowances Acts" substitute " the Capital Allowances Act 2001 ".
(5) In paragraph 10. (9), for "section 77 of the Capital Allowances Act 1990 (successions to trades: connected persons)" substitute " section 266 of the Capital Allowances Act 2001 (election where predecessor and successor are connected persons) ".
(6) For paragraph 10. (10) substitute—
"(10)Except as provided by this paragraph, a relevant transfer in relation to which this paragraph applies shall be taken for the purposes of the Capital Allowances Act 2001 not to give rise to—
    (a) any writing-down allowances, balancing allowances or balancing charges under Chapter 5 of Part 2 of that Act (plant and machinery allowances and charges),
    (b) any disposal value being treated as received for the purposes of that Chapter,
    (c) any qualifying expenditure being treated as incurred for the purposes of that Chapter, or
    (d) any writing-down allowances, balancing allowances or balancing charges under Part 3 of that Act (industrial buildings allowances)."
(7) In paragraph 11. (2)—
(a) for "Part I of the Capital Allowances Act 1990" substitute " Part 3 of the Capital Allowances

Act 2001 ”, and

(b) for “Chapter VI of Part II” substitute “ Chapter 14 of Part 2 ”.

(8) In paragraph 11. (4)—

(a) for “Part I of the Capital Allowances Act 1990” substitute “ Part 3 of the Capital Allowances Act 2001 ”,

(b) for “Chapter VI of Part II of the Capital Allowances Act 1990” substitute “ Chapter 14 of Part 2 of the Capital Allowances Act 2001 ”, and

(c) for “section 51. (3)” substitute “ section 175. (1) ”.

(9) In paragraph 12. (1)—

(a) omit paragraph (a),

(b) for “section 52. (2)” substitute “ section 176. (2) or (3) ”, and

(c) for “section 60” substitute “ sections 67 and 68. ”

(10) In paragraph 12. (2)—

(a) for “Part II of the Capital Allowances Act 1990” substitute “ Part 2 of the Capital Allowances Act 2001 ”, and

(b) for “section 26. (1)(f)” substitute “ item 7 in the Table in section 61. (2) ”.

The Finance Act 2000 (c. 17)

Section 105 (corporation tax: use of currencies other than sterling)

106. In subsection (3), for “any of the items referred to in section 25. (1) of the Capital Allowances Act 1990 which fall to be taken into account” substitute “ any amount falls to be taken into account under Chapter 5 of Part 2 of the Capital Allowances Act as available qualifying expenditure ”.

Schedule 12 (provision of services through an intermediary)

F23 107. . . . .

Amendments (Textual)

F23. Sch. 2 para. 107 repealed (with effect in accordance with s. 723. (1)(a)(b) of the amending Act) by Income Tax (Earnings and Pensions) Act 2003 (c. 1), s. 723, Sch. 8 Pt. 1 (with Sch. 7)

Schedule 22 (tonnage tax)

108. (1)In paragraph 41. (4), for “section 82. A of the Capital Allowances Act 1990” substitute “ section 219 of the Capital Allowances Act 2001 ”.

(2) For paragraph 69. (2) substitute—

“(2)In this paragraph “unrelieved qualifying expenditure” has the same meaning as in Chapter 5 of Part 2 of the Capital Allowances Act 2001.”

(3) In paragraph 69. (4), for paragraphs (a) and (b) substitute “ section 130 of the Capital Allowances Act 2001 (notice postponing first-year or writing-down allowance) ”.

(4) For paragraph 70. (2) substitute—

“(2)Sections 61. (1)(e), 206. (3) and 207 of the Capital Allowances Act 2001 (effect of use partly for qualifying activity and partly for other purposes) apply as follows—

(a) references to a qualifying activity shall be read as not including references to the tonnage tax trade, and

(b) references to purposes other than those of a qualifying activity shall be read as including references to the purposes of the tonnage tax trade.”

(5) In paragraph 72. (1), for "sections 33. A to 33. F of the Capital Allowances Act 1990" substitute " sections 135 to 156 of the Capital Allowances Act 2001 ".

(6) For paragraph 73. (2) substitute—

"(2)Sections 206. (1), (2) and (4) and 207 of the Capital Allowances Act 2001 (operation of single asset pool for mixed use assets) apply as follows—

(a) references to a qualifying activity shall be read as not including references to the tonnage tax trade, and

(b) references to purposes other than those of a qualifying activity shall be read as including references to the purposes of the tonnage tax trade."

(7) For paragraph 75. (2) and (3) substitute—

"(2)If the asset was acquired before entry into tonnage tax, section 61. (1)(e) of the Capital Allowances Act 2001 applies (disposal event if plant or machinery begins to be used wholly or partly for purposes other than those of the qualifying activity), but reading the reference in that provision to the qualifying activity as a reference to the tonnage tax trade.

(3) If the asset was acquired after entry into tonnage tax and begins to be used wholly or partly for the purposes of a qualifying activity carried on by the company, section 13 of the Capital Allowances Act 2001 (use for qualifying activity of plant or machinery provided for other purposes) applies as follows—

(a) references to purposes which were not those of any qualifying activity shall be read as including references to the purposes of the tonnage tax trade, and

(b) references to the qualifying activity carried on by him shall be read as not including references to the tonnage tax trade."

(8) For paragraph 76. (2) substitute—

"(2)Sections 61. (1)(e), 206. (3) and 207 of the Capital Allowances Act 2001 (effect of use partly for qualifying activity and partly for other purposes) apply as follows—

(a) references to a qualifying activity shall be read as not including references to the tonnage tax trade, and

(b) references to purposes other than those of a qualifying activity shall be read as including references to the purposes of the tonnage tax trade."

(9) In paragraph 77. (2), for "Part II of the Capital Allowances Act 1990" substitute " Part 2 of the Capital Allowances Act 2001 "and for "references in that Part of that Act to a trade" substitute " references in that Part of that Act to a qualifying activity ".

(10) In paragraph 80. (2), for "section 24. (6)(c)(i) to (iii) of the Capital Allowances Act 1990" substitute " section 61. (1)(a) to (d) of the Capital Allowances Act 2001 ".

(11) In paragraph 80. (4), for "Sections 33. A to 33. F of the Capital Allowances Act 1990" substitute " Sections 135 to 156 of the Capital Allowances Act 2001 ".

(12) For paragraph 82 substitute—

"82. If any identifiable part of a building or structure is used for the purposes of a company's tonnage tax trade, that part is treated for the purposes of Part 3 of the Capital Allowances Act 2001 as used otherwise than as an industrial building."

(13) In paragraph 83. (1), for "disposal event occurs in relation to an industrial building or structure" substitute " balancing event occurs in relation to an industrial building ".

(14) For the first sentence of paragraph 83. (2) substitute—

"(2)A "balancing event" means an event by reason of which the company is required by Part 3 of the Capital Allowances Act 2001 to bring into account any proceeds."

(15) For paragraph 83. (3)(a) substitute—

"(a)the proceeds to be brought into account in respect of the industrial building are limited to the market value of the relevant interest when the company entered tonnage tax; and".

(16) In paragraph 84. (1), omit "or structure".

(17) In paragraph 84. (2), for "The provisions of section 8. (1) to (12) of the Capital Allowances Act 1990 (writing off of expenditure and meaning of "residue of expenditure")" substitute " Section 313 and Chapter 8 of Part 3 of the Capital Allowances Act 2001 (meaning of "residue of qualifying expenditure" and writing off qualifying expenditure) ".

(18) In paragraph 85. (1), for "Part II of the Capital Allowances Act 1990 (plant and machinery)" substitute " Part 2 of the Capital Allowances Act 2001 (plant and machinery allowances) ".

(19) In paragraph 86. (1), for "Part I of the Capital Allowances Act 1990 (industrial buildings)" substitute " Part 3 of the Capital Allowances Act 2001 (industrial buildings allowances) ".

(20) For paragraph 87. (1)(b) substitute—

"(b)the expenditure shall be disregarded for the purposes of calculating the person's entitlement to a writing-down allowance or balancing allowance or liability to a balancing charge."

(21) In paragraph 88. (1), for the definitions of "capital allowance" and "qualifying activity" substitute—

""capital allowance" means any allowance under the Capital Allowances Act 2001;

"qualifying activity" means any activity in respect of which a person may be entitled to a capital allowance;".

(22) For paragraph 88. (2) and (3) substitute—

"(2)In this Part of this Schedule any reference to pooling or to single asset pools, class pools or the main pool shall be construed in accordance with sections 53 and 54 of the Capital Allowances Act 2001."

(23) In paragraph 88. (4), for "the Capital Allowances Act 1990" substitute " the Capital Allowances Act 2001 ".

(24) In paragraph 89. (1), for "Part II of the Capital Allowances Act 1990" substitute " Part 2 of the Capital Allowances Act 2001 ".

(25) In paragraph 89. (2), for "section 82. A of the 1990 Act" substitute " section 219 of that Act ".

(26) In paragraph 92. (4), for "belonging to him for the purposes of Part II of the Capital Allowances Act 1990" substitute " owned by him for the purposes of Part 2 of the Capital Allowances Act 2001 ".

(27) In paragraph 94. (4), for "Part II of the Capital Allowances Act 1990" substitute " Part 2 of the Capital Allowances Act 2001 ".

(28) In paragraph 96. (2), for "the Capital Allowances Act 1990" substitute " the Capital Allowances Act 2001 ".

(29) In paragraph 100. (2)(b)(ii), for "section 30. (1)(a) or (c) of the Capital Allowances Act 1990" substitute " section 130 of the Capital Allowances Act 2001 ".

(30) In paragraph 100. (3), for "the balance that would otherwise have been carried forward under Part II of the Capital Allowances Act 1990" substitute " the unrelieved qualifying expenditure that would otherwise have been carried forward under Chapter 5 of Part 2 of the Capital Allowances Act 2001 ".

(31) In paragraph 110. (2), for "the provisions of Part II of the Capital Allowances Act 1990 apply" substitute " Part 2 of the Capital Allowances Act 2001 applies ".

(32) In paragraph 110. (4)—

(a) for "Part II of the Capital Allowances Act 1990" substitute " Part 2 of the Capital Allowances Act 2001 ", and

(b) for "section 24. (6)(c)" substitute " section 61. (1) ".

(33) For paragraph 112. (3) substitute—

"(3)In this paragraph "unrelieved qualifying expenditure" means the unrelieved qualifying expenditure that would otherwise have been carried forward under Chapter 5 of Part 2 of the Capital Allowances Act 2001."

(34) In paragraph 112. (5), for paragraphs (a) and (b) substitute " section 130 of the Capital Allowances Act 2001 (notice postponing first-year or writing-down allowance) ".

(35) In paragraph 113. (2), for "Part II of the Capital Allowances Act 1990" substitute " Part 2 of the Capital Allowances Act 2001 ".

(36) In paragraph 135—

(a) for "Part II of the Capital Allowances Act 1990 (plant and machinery)" substitute " Part 2 of the Capital Allowances Act 2001 (plant and machinery allowances) ", and

(b) for "unrelieved qualifying expenditure under Part I of that Act (industrial buildings)" substitute " the residue of qualifying expenditure under Part 3 of that Act (industrial buildings allowances) ".

The Transport Act 2000 (c. 38)

Schedule 26 (transfers: tax)

109. (1)In paragraph 1. (1)—

(a) omit the definition of "the 1990 Act",

(b) for the definition of "the Capital Allowances Acts" substitute—

""the Capital Allowances Act" means the Capital Allowances Act 2001 and includes, where the context admits, enactments which under the 1988 Act are to be treated as contained in the Capital Allowances Act 2001,",

and

(c) in the definition of "fixture", for "Chapter VI of Part II of the 1990 Act" substitute " Chapter 14 of Part 2 of the Capital Allowances Act ".

(2) In paragraph 1. (3), for "the Capital Allowances Acts" substitute " the Capital Allowances Act ".

(3) In paragraph 5. (1)(b), for "the Capital Allowances Acts" substitute " the Capital Allowances Act " and for "Part II of the 1990 Act" substitute " Part 2 of that Act ".

(4) In paragraph 5. (1)(c), for "those Acts" substitute " that Act ".

(5) In paragraph 5. (2)—

(a) for "those Acts" substitute " the Capital Allowances Act ", and

(b) for "section 54 of the 1990 Act" substitute " sections 181. (1) and 182. (1) of that Act ".

(6) In paragraph 6, for "Part II of the 1990 Act" substitute " Part 2 of the Capital Allowances Act ".

(7) In paragraph 13. (1) and (2)(a), for "the Capital Allowances Acts" substitute " the Capital Allowances Act ".

(8) In paragraph 14. (1)(c), for "the Capital Allowances Acts" substitute " the Capital Allowances Act ".

(9) In paragraph 14. (1)(d), for "those Acts" substitute " that Act ".

(10) In paragraph 14. (2)—

(a) for "those Acts" substitute " the Capital Allowances Act ",

(b) in paragraph (a), for "section 26. (1) or 59 of the 1990 Act" substitute " section 61. (2) to (4), 72. (3) to (5), 171, 196 or 423 of that Act ", and

(c) in paragraph (d), for "section 54 of the 1990 Act" substitute " sections 181. (1) and 182. (1) of that Act ".

(11) In paragraph 15, for "Part II of the 1990 Act" substitute " Part 2 of the Capital Allowances Act ".

(12) In paragraph 21. (1), for "Part I of the 1990 Act" substitute " Part 3 of the Capital Allowances Act ".

(13) In paragraph 21. (4), for "Sections 157 and 158 of that Act (sales between connected persons or without change of control)" substitute " Sections 567 to 570 of that Act (sales treated as being for alternative amount) ".

(14) In paragraph 21. (5)—

(a) for "machinery or plant" (in both places) substitute " plant or machinery ",

(b) for "the Capital Allowances Acts" substitute " the Capital Allowances Act ", and

(c) for "section 24 of the 1990 Act (balancing adjustments)" substitute " section 60 of that Act (meaning of "disposal value" and "disposal event") ".

(15) In paragraph 21. (6), for "section 26. (2) and (3) of that Act (disposal value of machinery or plant not to exceed capital expenditure incurred on its provision)" substitute " section 62 of that Act (general limit on amount of disposal value) ".

(16) In paragraph 21. (7), for "a fixture is treated by section 57. (2) of the 1990 Act as ceasing to

belong to a person" substitute " a person is treated by section 188 of the Capital Allowances Act as ceasing to own a fixture ".

(17) In paragraph 21. (8)—

(a) for "section 24 of that Act is, subject to section 26. (2) and (3) of that Act" substitute " section 60 of the Capital Allowances Act is, subject to section 62 of that Act ", and

(b) for "Part II of that Act" substitute " Part 2 of that Act ".

(18) In paragraph 21. (9), for "the Capital Allowances Acts" substitute " the Capital Allowances Act ".

(19) In paragraph 27. (1), for "Part I of the 1990 Act" substitute " Part 3 of the Capital Allowances Act ".

(20) In paragraph 27. (4), for "Sections 157 and 158 of that Act (sales between connected persons or without change of control)" substitute " Sections 567 to 570 of that Act (sales treated as being for alternative amount) ".

(21) In paragraph 27. (5)—

(a) for "machinery or plant", in both places where it occurs, substitute " plant or machinery ",

(b) for "the Capital Allowances Acts" substitute " the Capital Allowances Act ", and

(c) for "section 24 of the 1990 Act (balancing adjustments)" substitute " section 60 of that Act (meaning of "disposal value" and "disposal event") ".

(22) In paragraph 27. (6), for "section 26. (2) and (3) of that Act (disposal value of machinery or plant not to exceed capital expenditure incurred on its provision)" substitute " section 62 of that Act (general limit on amount of disposal value) ".

(23) In paragraph 27. (7), for "a fixture is treated by section 57. (2) of the 1990 Act as ceasing to belong to a person" substitute " a person is treated by section 188 of the Capital Allowances Act as ceasing to own a fixture ".

(24) In paragraph 27. (8)—

(a) for "section 24 of that Act is, subject to section 26. (2) and (3) of that Act" substitute " section 60 of the Capital Allowances Act is, subject to section 62 of that Act ", and

(b) for "Part II of that Act" substitute " Part 2 of that Act "

(25) In paragraph 27. (9), for "the Capital Allowances Acts" substitute " the Capital Allowances Act ".

(26) In paragraph 34. (1), for "Part I of the 1990 Act" substitute " Part 3 of the Capital Allowances Act ".

(27) In paragraph 34. (5), for "Sections 157 and 158 of that Act (sales between connected persons or without change of control)" substitute " Sections 567 to 570 of that Act (sales treated as being for alternative amount) ".

(28) In paragraph 34. (6)—

(a) for "machinery or plant" (in both places) substitute " plant or machinery ",

(b) for "the Capital Allowances Acts" substitute " the Capital Allowances Act ", and

(c) for "section 24 of the 1990 Act (balancing adjustments)" substitute " sections 60 of that Act (meaning of "disposal value" and "disposal event") ".

(29) In paragraph 34. (7), for "section 26. (2) and (3) of that Act (disposal value of machinery or plant not to exceed capital expenditure incurred on its provision)" substitute " section 62 of that Act (general limit on amount of disposal value) ".

(30) In paragraph 34. (8), for "a fixture is treated by section 57. (2) of the 1990 Act as ceasing to belong to a person" substitute " a person is treated by section 188 of the Capital Allowances Act as ceasing to own a fixture ".

(31) In paragraph 34. (9)—

(a) for "section 24 of that Act is, subject to section 26. (2) and (3) of that Act" substitute " section 60 of the Capital Allowances Act is, subject to section 62 of that Act ", and

(b) for "Part II of that Act" substitute " Part 2 of that Act ".

(32) In paragraph 34. (10), for "the Capital Allowances Acts" substitute " the Capital Allowances Act ".

Schedule 3. Transitionals and savings

Section 579

Part 1. Continuity of the law

1. The repeal of provisions and their enactment in a rewritten form in this Act does not affect the continuity of the law.
2. Paragraph 1—
(a) does not apply to any change in the law effected by this Act, and
(b) is subject to paragraph 8.
3. Any subordinate legislation or other thing which—
(a) has been made or done, or has effect as if made or done, under or for the purposes of a repealed provision, and
(b) is in force or effective immediately before the commencement of the corresponding rewritten provision,
has effect after that commencement as if made or done under or for the purposes of the rewritten provision.
4. Any reference (express or implied) in any enactment, instrument or document to—
(a) a rewritten provision, or
(b) things done or falling to be done under or for the purposes of a rewritten provision,
is to be read as including, in relation to times, circumstances or purposes in relation to which any corresponding repealed provision had effect, a reference to the repealed provision or (as the case may be) things done or falling to be done under or for the purposes of the repealed provision.
5. Any reference (express or implied) in any enactment, instrument or document to—
(a) a repealed provision, or
(b) things done or falling to be done under or for the purposes of a repealed provision,
is to be read as including, in relation to times, circumstances or purposes in relation to which any corresponding rewritten provision has effect, a reference to the rewritten provision or (as the case may be) things done or falling to be done under or for the purposes of the rewritten provision.
6. Paragraphs 1 to 5 have effect instead of section 17. (2) of the Interpretation Act 1978 (but are without prejudice to any other provision of that Act).
7. Paragraphs 4 and 5 apply only in so far as the context permits.

Part 2. Changes in the law

8. (1)This paragraph applies where, in the case of any person—
(a) a thing is done or an event occurs before the relevant date, and
(b) by reason of a change in the law effected by this Act, the tax consequences of that thing or event for a relevant chargeable period are different from what they would otherwise have been.
(2) If that person so elects, this Act has effect in relation to that period with such modifications as may be necessary to secure that those consequences are the same as they would have been without the change in the law.
(3) If this paragraph applies in the case of two or more persons in relation to the same thing or event, an election made under sub-paragraph (2) by any one of those persons is of no effect unless a corresponding election is made by the other or each of the others.
(4) An election under sub-paragraph (2) must be made by notice given to [F1an officer of Revenue and Customs]—
(a) for income tax purposes, within the normal time limit for amending a tax return for the tax year in which the chargeable period ends;

(b) for corporation tax purposes, no later than 2 years after the end of the chargeable period.

(5) In this paragraph—

"relevant chargeable period" means—

   - in relation to a change effected by section 536. (5)(a) or 537. (4), the earliest chargeable period for which the tax consequences of the thing or event are different from what they would otherwise have been;

   - in relation to any other change, a chargeable period which begins before and ends on or after the relevant date;

"the relevant date" means 6th April 2001 for income tax purposes and 1st April 2001 for corporation tax purposes.

Amendments (Textual)

F1. Words in Act substituted (18.4.2005) by Commissioners for Revenue and Customs Act 2005 (c. 11), s. 53. (1), Sch. 4 para. 83. (1); S.I. 2005/1126, art. 2. (2)(h)

Part 3. General

Capital expenditure

9. Subsections (2) and (3) of section 4 apply with the omission of the words "or property business" in relation to expenditure incurred or sums paid or received before 26th November 1996.

Exclusion of double relief

10. Section 9 does not apply in relation to expenditure incurred before 24th July 1996.

Part 4. Plant and machinery allowances

Introduction

Use for qualifying activity of plant or machinery provided for other purposes

11. Subsections (4) and (5) of section 13 do not apply if the plant or machinery was brought into use before 21st March 2000.

Use for qualifying activity of plant or machinery which is a gift

12. Section 14 applies with the insertion after subsection (1) of—

"(1. A)This section does not apply unless the donor was required by section 24. (6) of CAA 1990 to bring into account for the purposes there mentioned a disposal value equal to the price which the plant or machinery would have fetched if sold in the open market at the time of the gift.",

if the plant or machinery was brought into use before 27th July 1989.

Qualifying expenditure

Buildings, structures and land

13. Sections 21 to 24 do not apply in relation to expenditure—

(a) incurred before 30th November 1993;

(b) incurred before 6th April 1996 in pursuance of a contract entered into before 30th November 1993; or

(c) incurred before 6th April 1996 in pursuance of a contract entered into on or after 30th November 1993 for the purpose of securing that obligations under a contract entered into before

30th November 1993 are complied with.

First-year qualifying expenditure

ICT expenditure incurred by small companies
14. Section 45 does not apply in relation to expenditure incurred before 1st April 2000.

Hire-purchase and similar contracts

Plant or machinery acquired under hire purchase etc.
15. Section 67. (2) applies with the omission of the words in brackets if the contract under which the expenditure was incurred was entered into before 27th July 1989.
Plant or machinery on hire purchase etc.: fixtures
16. Section 69. (2) does not apply if the plant or machinery became a fixture before 28th July 2000.
Plant or machinery provided by lessee
17. In section 70. (1), paragraphs (c) and (d) do not apply if the lease was entered into before 12th July 1984, or on or after that date under an agreement made before that date.

Computer software

Software and rights to software
18. Section 71 does not apply to expenditure incurred before 10th March 1992.

Cars, etc.

Cars above the cost threshold
19. In relation to expenditure incurred or treated as incurred before 11th March 1992, or incurred under a contract entered into before that date—
(a) sections 74. (2) and 76. (3) apply with the substitution of " £8,000 " for "£12,000"; and
(b) sections 75. (1) and 76. (2) and (4) apply with the substitution of " £2,000 " for "£3,000".

Long-life assets

Long-life asset expenditure
20. (1)Chapter 10 of Part 2 does not apply to any expenditure incurred—
(a) before 26th November 1996, or
(b) before 1st January 2001 in pursuance of a contract entered into before 26th November 1996.
(2) Chapter 10 of Part 2 does not apply to expenditure incurred by any person ("the purchaser") on the acquisition of a long-life asset from another ("the seller") if—
(a) the seller has made a Part 2 claim in respect of expenditure incurred on the provision of the asset ("the seller's expenditure"),
(b) the claim is one which the seller was entitled to make,
(c) the seller's expenditure did not fall to be treated as long-life asset expenditure for the purposes of the claim, and
(d) the seller's expenditure would have been so treated if one or more of the assumptions specified in sub-paragraph (3) were made.
(3) The assumptions are that—
(a) expenditure falling within sub-paragraph (1) is not prevented by that sub-paragraph from being long-life asset expenditure,
(b) the seller's expenditure was not prevented by sub-paragraph (2) from being long-life asset

expenditure, and

(c) Chapter 10 of Part 2 or any provision corresponding to it applied for chargeable periods ending before 26th November 1996.

(4) The reference in sub-paragraph (1) to expenditure incurred in pursuance of a contract entered into before 26th November 1996 does not, in the case of a contract varied at any time on or after that date, include a reference to any expenditure incurred under the contract that exceeds the expenditure that would have been incurred if the contract had not been varied.

(5) Expressions used in this paragraph and in Chapter 10 of Part 2 have the same meaning in this paragraph as in that Chapter; and in particular references in this paragraph to a "Part 2 claim" are to be read in accordance with section 103. (3).

Overseas leasing

Meaning of "overseas leasing"

21. Section 105. (2) applies with the substitution for paragraph (b) of—

"(b)does not use the plant or machinery for the purposes of a qualifying activity carried on there or for earning profits chargeable to tax by virtue of section 830. (4) of ICTA,",

in relation to the use of plant or machinery for leasing under a lease entered into before 16th March 1993.

Recovery of first-year allowances in case of joint lessees

22. (1)Sub-paragraphs (2) and (3) apply if—

(a) expenditure has been incurred on the provision of plant or machinery which is leased as described in section 116. (1), and

(b) the whole or a part of the expenditure has qualified for a first-year allowance under—

(i) section 43. (4) of CAA 1990, or

(ii) paragraph 47. (7).

(2) Section 117. (1) applies as if the reference in paragraph (b) to expenditure qualifying for a normal writing-down allowance under section 116. (3) included a reference to expenditure qualifying for the first-year allowance.

(3) Subsections (3) to (5) of section 117 apply as if the reference in section 117. (3)(b) to expenditure qualifying for a normal writing-down allowance under section 116. (3) included a reference to expenditure qualifying for the first-year allowance.

Letting ships or aircraft to obtain old first-year allowance not a qualifying purpose

23. Subsections (1) and (2) of section 123 do not apply if the main object, or one of the main objects—

(a) of the letting of the ship or aircraft on charter,

(b) of a series of transactions of which the letting of the ship or aircraft on charter was one, or

(c) of any of the transactions in such a series,

was to obtain a first-year allowance in respect of expenditure which was first-year qualifying expenditure under paragraph 47 and was incurred by any person on the provision of the ship or aircraft.

Ships: deferments etc.

Further registration requirement

24. Section 154 does not apply in the case of a ship that was brought into use before 20th July 1994 for the purposes of a qualifying activity carried on by the person incurring the expenditure on the provision of the ship or a person connected with him.

Mining and oil industries

Pre-trading expenditure on mineral exploration and access

25. Section 161 does not apply if—

(a) the person incurred the pre-trading expenditure before 1st April 1986; and

(b) before the first day of trading, the mineral exploration and access at the source in question had ceased.

Abandonment expenditure incurred before cessation of ring fence trade

26. Section 164 does not apply if the chargeable period in which the abandonment expenditure was incurred ended before 1st July 1991.

Abandonment expenditure incurred after cessation of ring fence trade

27. Section 165 does not apply if the abandonment expenditure was incurred before 1st July 1991.

Oil production sharing contracts

28. Sections 167 to 171 do not apply if —

(a) the expenditure was incurred before 21st March 2000; or

(b) the expenditure is treated as incurred by virtue of section 13 and the conditions mentioned in subsection (1) of that section were fulfilled before that date.

Fixtures

Meaning of "interest in land" for purposes of Chapter 14 of Part 2 (fixtures)

29. (1)Sub-paragraph (2) applies if paragraph 51 of Schedule 12 to the Abolition of Feudal Tenure etc. (Scotland) Act 2000 has not come into force before the commencement of section 175.

(2) Section 175. (1) has effect until the appointed day as if for paragraph (b) there were substituted—

"(b)in Scotland, the estate or interest of the proprietor of the dominium utile (or, in the case of property other than feudal property, of the owner) and any agreement to acquire such an estate or interest,".

(3) In sub-paragraph (2) "the appointed day" means such day as may be appointed by the Scottish Ministers under section 71 of the Abolition of Feudal Tenure etc. (Scotland) Act 2000 for the coming into force of the Act.

Equipment lessors

30. Section 177. (1)(a)(i) does not apply if the agreement for the lease of the plant or machinery was entered into before 19th March 1997.

Equipment lessee has qualifying activity etc.

31. Section 178 applies—

(a) if the agreement for the lease of the plant or machinery was entered into before 19th March 1997, with the omission of the words "which is or is to be" in paragraph (a) and the addition of the word " and " at the end of that paragraph; and

(b) if that expenditure was incurred before 24th July 1996, with the omission of paragraph (c) and the substitution for paragraph (b) of—

"(b)if the equipment lessee had incurred the capital expenditure incurred by the equipment lessor on the provision of the plant or machinery, he would, by virtue of section 176, be treated as the owner of the fixture as a result of incurring the expenditure".

Equipment lessor has right to sever fixture that is not part of building

32. Section 179. (1) does not apply if the agreement for the lease of the plant or machinery was entered into before 19th March 1997 and applies with—

(a) the addition at the end of paragraph (e) of the word " and ", and

(b) the omission of paragraph (g) and the word "and" immediately before it,

if the expenditure of the equipment lessor was incurred before 24th July 1996.

Equipment lease is part of affordable warmth programme

33. Section 180 does not apply if the expenditure of the equipment lessor was incurred before 28th July 2000.

Purchaser of land giving consideration for fixture

34. Section 181 applies with—

(a) the omission of the word "and" at the end of paragraph (b) of subsection (1); and

(b) the insertion after that paragraph of—

"(bb)at the time of the purchasers' acquisition of the interest, either no person has previously become entitled to an allowance in respect of any capital expenditure incurred on the provision of the fixture or, if any person has become so entitled, that person has been or is required to bring the disposal value of the fixture into account under Chapter 5, and",

if the purchaser acquired the interest in the relevant land before 24th July 1996.

Purchaser of land discharging obligations of equipment lessee

35. Section 182 applies with—

(a) the omission of the word "and" at the end of paragraph (c) of subsection (1); and

(b) the insertion after that paragraph of—

"(cc)at the time of the purchasers' acquisition of the interest, either no person has previously become entitled to an allowance in respect of any capital expenditure incurred on the provision of the fixture or, if any person has become so entitled, that person has been or is required to bring the disposal value of the fixture into account under Chapter 5, and",

if the purchaser acquired the interest in the relevant land before 24th July 1996.

Incoming lessee where lessor entitled to allowances

36. Section 183 applies with the insertion after subsection (2) of—

"(3)No election may be made under this section if it appears that the sole or main benefit that may be expected to accrue to the lessor from the grant of the lease and the making of an election is the obtaining of an allowance or deduction or a greater allowance or deduction or the avoidance or reduction of a charge under this Part.",

if the person who had the interest in the relevant land granted the lease before 24th July 1996.

Incoming lessee where lessor not entitled to allowances

37. Section 184 applies with—

(a) the omission of the word "and" at the end of paragraph (c) of subsection (1); and

(b) the insertion after that paragraph of—

"(cc)at the time of the grant of the lease, no person has previously become entitled to an allowance in respect of any capital expenditure incurred on the provision of the fixture, and",

if the person who had the interest in the relevant land granted the lease before 24th July 1996.

Fixture on which a plant and machinery allowance has been claimed

38. Section 185 does not apply if the disposal event which required the disposal value to be brought into account as mentioned in subsection (1)(d) occurred before 24th July 1996.

Fixture on which industrial buildings allowance has been made

39. Section 186 does not apply if the time mentioned in subsection (1)(c)(ii) is before 24th July 1996.

Fixture on which research and development allowance has been made

40. Section 187 does not apply if the time mentioned in subsection (1)(d)(ii) is before 24th July 1996.

Disposal value in relation to fixtures: general

41. In relation to a fixture which a person is treated as ceasing to own before 24th July 1996, section 196 applies with the substitution for subsection (6) of—

"(6)If—

(a) a person ("the former owner") is treated by virtue of section 188, 190 or 191 as ceasing to own a fixture,

(b) another person incurs expenditure on the provision of the fixture, and

(c) the former owner brings a disposal value into account under Chapter 5,

there is to be disregarded for the purposes of this Part so much (if any) of that expenditure as exceeds that disposal value.

(7) In relation to expenditure incurred before 27th July 1989, subsection (6) has effect with the substitution for the words following "the fixture" in paragraph (b) of the words "there is to be disregarded for the purposes of this Part so much (if any) of that expenditure as exceeds the

disposal value which the former owner is required to bring into account under Chapter 5"".

Assets provided or used only partly for qualifying activity

Effect of significant reduction in use for purposes of qualifying activity
42. Section 208 does not apply if the change of circumstances referred to in subsection (1)(b) of that section occurs before 21st March 2000.

Anti-avoidance

Relevant transactions: sale, hire-purchase (etc.) and assignment
43. Section 213. (3) does not apply if the plant or machinery was brought into use before 27th July 1989.
Hire purchase etc. and finance leases
44. Sections 220 and 229 do not apply in relation to expenditure incurred before 2nd July 1997, or in the 12 months beginning with that date in pursuance of a contract entered into before that date.
Sale and finance leasebacks
45. Sections 221, 222 and 224 to 226 do not apply in relation to expenditure incurred before 2nd July 1998 if the relevant transaction—
(a) is a purchase under a contract entered into before 2nd July 1997;
(b) is itself a contract entered into before that date; or
(c) is an assignment made before that date, or in pursuance of a contract entered into before that date.

Additional VAT liabilities and rebates

Expenditure which is first-year qualifying expenditure: general
46. (1)For the purposes of section 236. (1)(a) (entitlement to first-year allowance in respect of additional VAT liability where original expenditure was first-year qualifying expenditure), first-year qualifying expenditure includes expenditure which is first-year qualifying expenditure under paragraph 47 or 48.
(2) A first-year allowance under this paragraph is made for the chargeable period in which the additional VAT liability accrues.
(3) The amount of such an allowance is a percentage of the additional VAT liability in respect of which the allowance is made, as shown in the Table—
Table
Amount of first-year allowances (pre-commencement original expenditure)

Type of original first-year qualifying expenditure	Amount
Expenditure qualifying under paragraph 47 (expenditure incurred 1992-93).	40%
Expenditure qualifying under paragraph 48 (expenditure incurred 1997-98 by small or medium-sized enterprises) which is not long-life asset expenditure.	50%
Expenditure qualifying under paragraph 48 (expenditure incurred 1997-98 by small or medium-sized enterprises) which is long-life asset expenditure.	12%

Expenditure incurred 1992-93.
47. (1)Expenditure is first-year qualifying expenditure under this paragraph if—
(a) it was incurred in the period beginning with 1st November 1992 and ending with 31st October 1993, and
(b) it is not excluded by sub-paragraphs (3) to (8).
(2) In determining whether expenditure is first-year qualifying expenditure under this paragraph, any effect of section 12 on the time at which it is to be treated as incurred is to be disregarded.
(3) Expenditure is not first-year qualifying expenditure under this paragraph if it was incurred—

(a) in the chargeable period in which there was a permanent discontinuance of the qualifying activity, or

(b) on the provision of a car other than a qualifying hire car (as defined by section 82).

(4) Expenditure on the provision of plant or machinery for leasing is not first-year qualifying expenditure under this paragraph if it appears that the expenditure is of the kind described in section 109. (2) or 110. (2) (expenditure on plant or machinery which is used for overseas leasing etc.).

(5) Expenditure on the provision of plant or machinery for leasing is not first-year qualifying expenditure under this paragraph if—

(a) the expenditure was incurred on or after 14th April 1993,

(b) the person to whom the plant or machinery is to be or is leased, or a person who is connected with that person, used the plant or machinery for any purpose at any time before its provision for leasing, and

(c) the expenditure does not fall within any of the categories of expenditure on plant or machinery for leasing given in sub-paragraph (6).

(6) The categories referred to in sub-paragraph (5)(c) are as follows.

Category 1. Expenditure on leasing qualifying by reference to Chapter 11 of Part 2 (overseas leasing)

It appears that the plant or machinery—

(a) will be used for a qualifying purpose (as defined by sections 122 to 125) in the designated period (as defined by section 106), and

(b) will not be used for any other purpose at any time in that period.

Category 2. Enterprise zones

The circumstances of the incurring of the expenditure are that—

(a) the expenditure is incurred on the provision of plant or machinery which is to be an integral part of a building or structure, and

(b) expenditure incurred at that time on the construction of the building or structure would be qualifying enterprise zone expenditure to which Chapter 5 of Part 3 (initial allowances for qualifying enterprise zone expenditure) would apply.

Category 3. Fixtures

The circumstances of the incurring of the expenditure are that—

(a) expenditure is incurred on the provision of plant or machinery which is fixed to land or a building,

(b) the person who incurs it is the lessor of the land or building, and

(c) a transfer of the person's interest in the land or building would operate to transfer that person's interest in the plant or machinery.

Category 4. Cars hired out to the disabled etc.

The expenditure is incurred on the provision of a car which is within section 82. (4) (cars hired out to persons receiving disability allowances etc.).

(7) Sub-paragraph (4) does not prevent expenditure being first-year qualifying expenditure, if it appears that—

(a) the plant or machinery will be leased as described in section 116. (1), and

(b) the circumstances are such that section 116. (3) will require the whole or any part of the expenditure to be treated as not subject to section 107, 109 or 110.

(8) Any first-year allowance under sub-paragraph (7) (when read with section 236) is to be made on the same basis and subject to the same apportionments (if any) as would be applicable in the case of a writing-down allowance under section 116. (5).

Expenditure by small or medium-sized enterprises, 1997-98.

48. (1)Expenditure is first-year qualifying expenditure under this paragraph if—

(a) it was incurred in the period beginning with 2nd July 1997 and ending with 1st July 1998;

(b) it was incurred by a small or medium-sized enterprise; and

(c) it is not excluded by sub-paragraph (3).

(2) In determining whether expenditure is first-year qualifying expenditure under this paragraph,

any effect of section 12 on the time at which it is to be treated as incurred is to be disregarded.

(3) Expenditure is not first-year qualifying expenditure under this paragraph if it is within any of the general exclusions given in section 46. (2).

(4) In this paragraph, "small or medium-sized enterprise" is to be read in accordance with sections 47 to 49, read with paragraph 50.

Whether a company is a member of large or medium-sized group

49. (1)This paragraph applies in relation to any expenditure incurred before 12th May 1998, and for the purpose of determining—

(a) whether expenditure incurred under a contract entered into before that date is first-year qualifying expenditure under section 44, or

(b) whether expenditure is first-year qualifying expenditure under paragraph 46 or 48.

(2) Section 49 applies with the substitution in subsection (2) of " parent company " for "parent undertaking" and the omission of the words in brackets in subsection (5).

(3) In section 49 as it so applies "parent company"—

(a) except in the case of a company formed and registered in Northern Ireland, has the same meaning as in Part VII of the Companies Act 1985 (c. 6);

(b) in the case of such a company, has the same meaning as in Part VIII of the Companies (Northern Ireland) Order 1986 (S.I.1986/1032 (N.I.6)).

Expenditure which is not first-year qualifying expenditure

50. For the purposes of section 236. (1)(a)—

(a) section 40 (expenditure for Northern Ireland purposes by small or medium-sized enterprises) does not apply if the expenditure was incurred before 12th May 1998;

(b) section 44 (expenditure by small or medium-sized enterprises) does not apply if the expenditure was incurred before 2nd July 1998;

(c) section 45 (ICT expenditure by small enterprises) does not apply if the expenditure was incurred before 1st April 2000.

Anti-avoidance

51. Sections 243. (7) and 244 do not apply in relation to expenditure incurred before 2nd July 1998 if the relevant transaction—

(a) is a purchase under a contract entered into before 2nd July 1997;

(b) is itself a contract entered into before that date; or

(c) is an assignment made before that date, or in pursuance of a contract entered into before that date.

Supplementary provisions

Successions by beneficiaries

52. Section 266. (7) does not apply if the succession occurred before 27th July 1989.

53. Subsections (6) and (7) of section 268 do not apply if the election under that section was made before 6th April 1990.

General

Vehicles provided by employees in 1990-91.

54. (1)This paragraph applies if—

(a) at the beginning of the tax year 1990-91 machinery consisting of a mechanically propelled road vehicle was provided by a person for use in the performance of the duties of an office or employment held by him, and

(b) the machinery was also provided by him at the end of the tax year 1989-90 for use in the performance of the duties of that office or employment but without that provision being necessary.

(2) Part 2 of this Act has effect as if the person had incurred capital expenditure on the provision of the machinery for the purposes of the office or employment in the tax year 1990-91—

(a) the amount of that expenditure being taken as the price which the machinery would have fetched if sold in the open market on 6th April 1990, and

(b) the person being treated as owning the machinery as a result of his having incurred that expenditure.

Certain expenditure incurred before 6th April 1976.

55. Part 2 of this Act does not apply to capital expenditure—

(a) which was not eligible expenditure within the meaning of section 39 of FA 1976 (which brought expenditure previously not within Chapter I of Part III of FA 1971 within that Chapter but with certain exceptions), and

(b) which was incurred in a chargeable period ending before 6th April 1976.

Part 5. Industrial buildings allowances

Industrial buildings

Bridge undertakings

56. In section 274, item 8 of Table B (bridge undertakings) does not apply if the expenditure was treated as incurred before the end of the tax year 1956-57.

Building used by more than one licensee

57. Section 278 does not apply if the licence was granted before 10th March 1982.

Qualifying hotels

58. (1)Section 279 does not apply if the expenditure on the construction of the building was incurred before 12th April 1978.

(2) Expenditure is not to be treated for the purposes of sub-paragraph (1) as having been incurred after the date on which it was in fact incurred by reason only of section 10. (1) of CAA 1990.

Non-industrial part of building disregarded

59. Section 283. (2) applies with the substitution of " 10% " for "25%" if the expenditure was incurred before 16th March 1983.

Qualifying expenditure

Purchase of used building from developer

60. Section 297 does not apply if the purchase price on the sale by the developer mentioned in subsection (1)(b) of that section became payable before 27th July 1989.

Qualifying enterprise zone expenditure

61. Sections 300 and 302 do not apply if—

(a) the purchase price payable on the sale of the relevant interest in the building before it was used, or

(b) if there was more than one such sale before the building was used, the purchase price payable on the last of those sales,

became payable before 16th December 1991.

62. Sections 301, 303 and 304 do not apply in relation to buildings first used before 16th December 1991.

63. If—

(a) the relevant interest in a building was sold on a date falling after the end of the period of two years beginning with the date on which the building or structure was first used; and

(b) that period ended, and the date on which the relevant interest was transferred fell, within the period beginning with 13th January 1994 and ending with 31st August 1994,

paragraphs (c) and (d) of sections 301. (1) and 303. (1) apply as if the period there referred to were the period beginning with the date on which the building or structure was first used and ending with 31st August 1994.

Initial allowances

Building occupied by qualifying licensee
64. Section 305. (1)(b) does not apply if the licence was granted before 10th March 1982.
Grants affecting entitlement to initial allowances
65. Section 308. (2)(c) applies as if the reference to a grant under section 101 of the Greater London Authority Act 1999 (c. 29) included a reference to a grant under section 12 of the London Regional Transport Act 1984 (c. 32) or section 3 of the Transport (London) Act 1969 (c. 35).

Writing-down allowances

Basic rule for calculating amount of allowance
66. Section 310. (1)(b) applies with the substitution of " 2% " for "4%" in the case of expenditure incurred before 6th November 1962.
Calculation of amount after relevant event
67. Section 311. (1) applies with the substitution (in the definition of "B") of " 50 years " for "25 years" in the case of expenditure incurred before 6th November 1962.

Balancing adjustments

When balancing adjustments are made
68. Section 314. (4) applies with the substitution of " 50 years " for "25 years" if the qualifying expenditure was incurred before 6th November 1962.
Net allowance given
69. (1)Section 324 applies in relation to a mills, factories or exceptional depreciation allowance as it applies in relation to an allowance of any kind mentioned in that section.
(2) In sub-paragraph (1) "mills, factories or exceptional depreciation allowance", in relation to any building or structure, means—
(a) any allowance granted for a tax year under section 15 of FA 1937 in respect of it or premises of which it forms part, including any amount which under that section was to be allowed as a deduction in computing profits or gains for that year, and
(b) any allowance granted under section 19 of FA 1941 in respect of it or premises of which it forms part.
(3) Where such an allowance as is mentioned in sub-paragraph (2) was granted in respect of premises which include several buildings or structures—
(a) the whole amount of the allowance is to be apportioned between the buildings and structures, and
(b) only that part of the allowance which is apportioned to the building or structure in question is to be taken into account.
70. For the purposes of section 324 an allowance is treated as having been made to a woman in relation to any qualifying expenditure if—
(a) it was made to her husband for a chargeable period ending before 6th April 1990 in respect of an interest of hers which was the relevant interest in relation to that expenditure,
(b) a balancing event occurs on or after that date, and
(c) she is entitled to all or part of the proceeds from that balancing event.
Balancing adjustment on realisation of capital value
71. Sections 328 to 331 do not apply if the capital expenditure referred to in section 327 was incurred under a contract which—
(a) was entered into before 13th January 1994, and

(b) was not a conditional contract which became unconditional on or after 26th February 1994.

Writing off qualifying expenditure

Writing off qualifying expenditure when building not an industrial building
72. For the purposes of section 336 a building is not treated as having been an industrial building—
(a) under item 5. (b) or (c) or 6 of Table A in section 274 (working foreign plantations or fishing) for any tax year before 1953-54, or
(b) under item 7 of Table B in section 274 (tunnel undertakings) for any tax year before 1952-53.
Crown or other person not within the charge to tax entitled to the relevant interest
73. Section 339 does not apply by virtue of subsection (1)(b) if the interest was sold before 29th July 1988.

Highway undertakings

Special provisions relating to highway concessions
74. Sections 341. (4)(a), 343 and 344 do not apply in relation to expenditure incurred before 6th April 1995.

Additional VAT liabilities and rebates

Additional VAT liabilities and initial allowances: 1992-93 cases
75. (1)This paragraph applies if—
(a) a person was entitled to an initial allowance in respect of 1992-93 qualifying expenditure,
(b) the person entitled to the relevant interest in relation to that expenditure incurs an additional VAT liability in respect of that expenditure, and
(c) the additional VAT liability is incurred at a time when the building is, or is to be, an industrial building—
(i) occupied for the purposes of a trade carried on by the person entitled to the relevant interest or a qualifying lessee, or
(ii) used for the purposes of trade carried on by a qualifying licensee.
(2) If this paragraph applies, the person entitled to the relevant interest is entitled to an initial allowance on the amount of the additional VAT liability.
(3) The amount of the initial allowance is 20% of the additional VAT liability.
(4) The allowance is made for the chargeable period in which the additional VAT liability accrues.
(5) The persons mentioned in sub-paragraph (1)(a) and (b) need not be the same.
(6) In this paragraph "qualifying lessee" and "qualifying licensee" have the same meaning as in section 305.
Additional VAT liabilities and initial allowances: further case
76. (1)This paragraph applies if—
(a) a person was entitled to an initial allowance in respect of qualifying enterprise zone expenditure, and
(b) the person entitled to the relevant interest in relation to that expenditure incurs an additional VAT liability in respect of that expenditure,
but there is no entitlement to an initial allowance under section 346 because the condition in subsection (1)(d) of that section is not met.
(2) If in such a case—
(a) the conditions in paragraph 74. (1) are met except for the condition that the original entitlement to an initial allowance was in respect of 1992-93 qualifying expenditure, and
(b) some or all of the qualifying enterprise zone expenditure would have been 1992-93 qualifying

expenditure but for paragraph 76. (2),

the person entitled to the relevant interest is entitled to an initial allowance under paragraph 74. (3) on the appropriate part or on all of the additional VAT liability (as the case may be).

(3) The allowance is made for the chargeable period in which the additional VAT liability accrues.

1992-93 qualifying expenditure

77. (1)"1992-93 qualifying expenditure" means expenditure which is—

(a) qualifying expenditure which is within section 294 and is 1992-93 construction expenditure, or

(b) the 1992-93 element of qualifying expenditure which is within section 295 or 296.

(2) Qualifying enterprise zone expenditure is not to be taken into account as 1992-93 qualifying expenditure for the purposes of sub-paragraph (1).

(3) Expenditure is 1992-93 construction expenditure if it was incurred on the construction of a building under a contract which was entered into—

(a) in the period beginning with 1st November 1992 and ending with 31st October 1993, or

(b) for the purpose of securing compliance with obligations under a contract entered into in that period,

and which was not entered into for the purpose of securing compliance with obligations under a contract entered into before 1st November 1992.

(4) The 1992-93 element of qualifying expenditure within section 295 or 296 is—

where—

QE is the amount of qualifying expenditure,

E is the amount of 1992-93 construction expenditure, and

T is the amount of expenditure on the construction of the building.

(5) If the expenditure on the construction of the building was incurred by a person carrying on a trade as a developer who—

(a) was entitled to the relevant interest in the building before 1st November 1992, and

(b) sold that interest in the course of that trade under a contract entered into in the period beginning with 1st November 1992 and ending with 31st October 1993,

the 1992-93 construction expenditure for the purposes of sub-paragraph (4) includes any expenditure on the construction of the building incurred under a contract entered into before 1st November 1993 or for the purpose of securing compliance with obligations under such a contract.

Supplementary provisions

Arrangements having an artificial effect on pricing

78. Section 357 does not apply if the sale price fixed as mentioned in subsections (1) and (2)—

(a) became payable before 29th November 1994; or

(b) was fixed by a contract entered into before 29th November 1994 and became payable before 6th April 1995.

General

Expenditure on preparatory work on land where building used before 6th April 1956.

79. (1)Sub-paragraph (2) applies where section 21. (9) of CAA 1990 (expenditure on preparatory work on land where building used before 6th April 1956) applied to any expenditure immediately before the commencement of Part 3 of this Act, so that Part I of that Act (industrial buildings and structures) except for section 1 (initial allowances) applied to part of the expenditure separately from the remainder.

(2) Where this sub-paragraph applies, Part 3 of this Act, except for Chapter 5, similarly applies to the part of the expenditure separately from the remainder.

Part 6. Agricultural buildings allowances

Overall limit on balancing charge

80. For the purposes of section 387 an allowance is treated as having been made to a woman in relation to any qualifying expenditure if—
(a) it was made to her husband for a chargeable period ending before 6th April 1990 in respect of an interest of hers which was the relevant interest in relation to that expenditure,
(b) a balancing event occurs on or after that date, and
(c) she is entitled to all or part of the proceeds from that balancing event.

Meaning of "freehold interest in land" for purposes of Part 4.

81. (1)Sub-paragraphs (2) and (3) apply if paragraph 51 of Schedule 12 to the Abolition of Feudal Tenure etc. (Scotland) Act 2000 has not come into force before the commencement of Part 4 of this Act.
(2) Section 393. (1) has effect until the appointed day as if for paragraph (b) there were substituted—
    "(b)in relation to Scotland, the estate or interest of the proprietor of the dominium utile (or, in the case of property other than feudal property, of the owner);".
(3) Section 393. (2) has effect until the appointed day as if for paragraph (b) there were substituted—
    "(b)in relation to Scotland, an agreement to acquire the estate or interest mentioned in subsection (1)(b);".
(4) In sub-paragraphs (2) and (3) "the appointed day" means such day as may be appointed by the Scottish Ministers under section 71 of the Abolition of Feudal Tenure etc. (Scotland) Act 2000 for the coming into force of the Act.

Exclusion of expenditure incurred before 1st April 1986.

82. References in Part 4 of this Act to qualifying expenditure do not include—
(a) expenditure incurred before 1st April 1986; or
(b) payments made before 1st April 1987 under a contract entered into before 14th March 1984.

The writing-down period

83. (1)This paragraph applies where it is provided under Part 4 that writing-down allowances are to be made in respect of any expenditure during a writing-down period of any specified length.
(2) If allowances were made under paragraph 27. (2) of Schedule 14 to FA 1965—
(a) for income tax purposes, for either of the tax years 1964-65 and 1965-66, and
(b) for accounting periods of a company falling wholly or partly within either of those years,
the periods for which allowances were made are added together in calculating the writing-down period, even though (according to the calendar) the same time is counted twice.

Part 7. Mineral extraction allowances

Qualifying expenditure on acquiring a mineral asset

Qualifying expenditure where buildings or structures cease to be used

84. In section 405. (3) "A" does not include, in cases where the buildings or structures have permanently ceased to be used for any purpose before 27th July 1989, the amount of any agricultural buildings allowances.

Qualifying expenditure: second-hand assets

Claims before 26th November 1996 in respect of acquisition of mineral asset owned by previous trader

85. Section 407. (4) does not apply in relation to claims made before 26th November 1996.
Acquisition of oil licence from non-trader before 13th September 1995.

86. Section 408 does not apply to acquisitions occurring before 13th September 1995.
Restrictions on qualifying expenditure in case of UK oil licence and certain other assets inapplicable for expenditure pre-16th July 1985.

87. (1)The sections listed in sub-paragraph (2) do not apply if—

(a) asset X is a mineral asset situated in the United Kingdom, and

(b) the capital expenditure incurred by the buyer consists of the payment of sums under a contract entered into by him before 16th July 1985.

(2) The sections are—

(a) section 407 (acquisition of mineral asset owned by previous trader),

(b) section 410 (UK oil licence: qualifying expenditure limited by reference to original licence payment), and

(c) section 411 (assets generally: qualifying expenditure limited by reference to previous trader's unrelieved qualifying expenditure).

(3) Sections 407 and 411 apply, in relation to a case where asset X is a mineral asset situated in the United Kingdom, as if the references to an earlier owner of the asset did not include a person who has not owned the asset at any time after 31st March 1986.

(4) In the case of a mineral asset which consists of or includes an interest in or right over mineral deposits or land, the asset is not to be regarded for the purposes of this paragraph as situated in the United Kingdom unless the deposits or land are or is so situated.

(5) Expressions used in this paragraph and Chapter 4 of Part 5 have the same meaning in this paragraph as they have in that Chapter.
Expenditure incurred pre-1st April 1986.

88. (1)Part 5 of this Act does not apply in relation to expenditure incurred before 1st April 1986 ("old expenditure") except as provided by the following provisions of this paragraph.

(2) Sections 401 and 402 apply to old expenditure if—

(a) that expenditure was incurred on mineral exploration and access,

(b) immediately before 1st April 1986, no allowance had been made under Chapter III of Part I of CAA 1968 in respect of it, and

(c) after that day and before mineral exploration and access ceases at the source in question, the person by whom the expenditure was incurred began or begins to carry on a trade of mineral extraction.

In this sub-paragraph "source" has the same meaning as it had in Schedule 14 to FA 1986.

(3) For the purposes of Part 5—

(a) expenditure which by virtue of any provision of section 119 of CAA 1990 (read with any provision of Schedule 14 to FA 1986) was treated immediately before the coming into force of this Act as expenditure incurred on 1st April 1986 for any purpose or purposes is to continue to be so treated;

(b) any allowances treated as having been made under Schedule 13 to FA 1986 is to continue to be so treated;

(c) any amount treated as qualifying expenditure for the purposes of that Schedule is to continue to be so treated; and

(d) in relation to any expenditure to which paragraph 6. (4)(a) of Schedule 14 to FA 1986 applied, section 424 does not apply (so that no deduction is to be made from the amount of any disposal receipt by reference to the undeveloped market value of the land in question).

(4) In the case of expenditure incurred in the acquisition of a mineral asset, nothing in sub-paragraph (3)(c) affects the time as at which under section 404 the undeveloped market value of an interest is to be determined.

(5) In a case where—

(a) by virtue of any provision of this paragraph, the whole or any part of the outstanding balance (within the meaning of paragraph 1 of Schedule 14 to FA 1986) of an item of old expenditure is treated for the purposes of Part 5 as qualifying expenditure, and

(b) a balancing charge falls to be made under Chapter 6 of that Part in respect of the expenditure, then, in determining the amount on which that charge falls to be made, subsection (4) of section 418 has effect (subject to sub-paragraph (6)) as if paragraph (b) of that subsection included a reference to allowances made in respect of the item under Chapter III of Part I of CAA 1968.

(6) Where the qualifying expenditure in respect of which a balancing charge falls to be made represents part only of the outstanding balance of an item of old expenditure, the reference in sub-paragraph (5) to allowances made in respect of that item is to be construed as a reference to such part of those allowances as it is just and reasonable to apportion to that part of the balance (having regard to any apportionment made under paragraph 3. (2) of Schedule 14 to FA 1986).

Part 8. Research and development allowances

Expenditure incurred partly on research and development

89. Section 439. (4) does not apply to expenditure incurred before 27th July 1989.

References to research and development in relation to new trades

90. (1)Where—

(a) a trade is set up and commenced in the year of assessment 1999-00, and

(b) its first period of account ends after 6th April 2001,

Part 6 of this Act has effect in relation to that year as if references to research and development were references to scientific research.

(2) In this paragraph "scientific research" means any activities in the fields of natural or applied science for the extension of knowledge.

Disposal of oil licences

91. (1)Sub-paragraphs (2) and (3) apply where—

(a) a person ("the transferor") disposes of any interest in an oil licence to another ("the transferee") during the transitional period,

(b) part of the value of the interest is attributable to allowable exploration expenditure incurred by the transferor, and

(c) an election is made in accordance with this paragraph specifying an amount as the amount to be treated as so attributable.

(2) Chapter 3 of Part 6 has effect in relation to the disposal as if—

(a) the disposal were a disposal by which an asset representing the allowable exploration expenditure ceases to belong to the transferor, and

(b) the disposal value of that asset were an amount equal to the amount specified in the election.

(3) For the purposes of Part 5 of this Act, the amount of any expenditure incurred—

(a) by the transferee in acquiring the interest from the transferor, or

(b) by any person subsequently acquiring the interest (or an interest deriving from the interest), which is taken to be attributable to expenditure incurred, before the disposal to the transferee, on mineral exploration and access is the lesser of the amount specified in the election and the amount which, apart from this sub-paragraph, would be taken to be so attributable.

(4) An election—

(a) must be made by notice to [F2the Commissioners for Her Majesty's Revenue and Customs] given by the transferor, and

(b) subject to sub-paragraph (5), does not have effect unless a copy of it is served on the transferee and the transferee consents to it.

(5) If the Special Commissioners are satisfied—

(a) that the disposal was made under or in pursuance of an agreement entered into by the transferor and the transferee on the mutual understanding that a quantified (or quantifiable) part of the value of the interest disposed of was attributable to allowable exploration expenditure, and

(b) that the part quantified in accordance with that understanding and the amount specified in the election are the same,

they may dispense with the need for the transferee to consent to the election.

(6) Any question falling to be determined by the Special Commissioners under sub-paragraph (5) is to be determined by them in the same way as an appeal; but both the transferor and the transferee are entitled to appear and be heard by those Commissioners or to make representations to them in writing.

(7) Subject to sub-paragraph (8), an election may specify any amount, including a nil amount, as the amount to be treated as mentioned in sub-paragraph (1)(c).

(8) Where—

(a) a return has been made for a chargeable period of the transferor, and

(b) the return includes, at the time when it is made, an amount which, disregarding the provisions of this paragraph, would be treated under Chapter 3 of Part 6 as a trading receipt accruing in that period,

the election must not specify an amount less than the amount included in the return unless [F2the Commissioners for Her Majesty's Revenue and Customs] agrees the lesser amount in question.

(9) An election made in accordance with this paragraph—

(a) is irrevocable, and

(b) may not be varied after it is made.

(10) For the purposes of this paragraph a disposal is a disposal made during the transitional period if it is one made—

(a) before 13th September 1995, or

(b) on or after that date in pursuance of any obligation to make the disposal which, immediately before that date, was an unconditional obligation.

(11) For the purposes of sub-paragraph (10), the fact that a third party who is not connected with the transferor or the transferee may, by exercising any right or withholding any permission, prevent the fulfilment of an obligation does not prevent the obligation from being treated as unconditional.

(12) In sub-paragraph (11) the reference to a third party is a reference to any person, body, government or public authority, whether within or outside the United Kingdom.

(13) In this paragraph—

"allowable exploration expenditure" has the same meaning as in section 555;

"mineral exploration and access" has the same meaning as in Part 5.

(14) All such assessments and adjustments of assessments are to be made as are necessary to give effect to this paragraph.

Amendments (Textual)

F2. Words in Act substituted (18.4.2005) by Commissioners for Revenue and Customs Act 2005 (c. 11), s. 53. (1), Sch. 4 para. 83. (2); S.I. 2005/1126, art. 2. (2)(h)

Part 9. Patent allowances

Expenditure incurred before 1st April 1986.

Scope of paragraphs 93 to 101.

92. (1)Paragraphs 93 to 101 apply to capital expenditure incurred by a person before 1st April 1986 on the purchase of patent rights.

(2) Chapters 2 to 4 of Part 8 do not apply to such expenditure, except for certain provisions which are specifically applied by paragraph 101.

Qualifying expenditure and unrelieved qualifying expenditure

93. (1)In this paragraph and paragraphs 94 to 101, "qualifying expenditure" means capital expenditure incurred before 1st April 1986 on the purchase of patent rights.

(2) The result of Steps 1 to 3 is the unrelieved qualifying expenditure for a chargeable period.

Step 1

Take an item of qualifying expenditure.

Step 2

Subtract any writing-down allowances made in respect of that expenditure for earlier chargeable periods.

Step 3

If the person who incurred the expenditure sold any part of the patent rights before the beginning of the chargeable period, subtract the net proceeds of sale (so far as they consist of capital sums).

Entitlement to writing-down allowances

94. (1)A writing-down allowance is made for a chargeable period in respect of an item of qualifying expenditure if—

(a) the chargeable period falls wholly or partly within the writing-down period for that expenditure (as determined in accordance with paragraph 95),

(b) paragraph 97 does not prohibit writing-down allowances for that period, and

(c) either—

(i) the trade use condition is met for that period, or

(ii) any income receivable by that person in respect of the patent rights in that period would be liable to tax.

(2) The trade use condition is that—

(a) the person is carrying on in the chargeable period a trade which is within the charge to tax, and

(b) at any time in the chargeable period the patent rights, or other rights out of which they were granted, were, or were to be, used for the purposes of the trade.

(3) The total writing-down allowances made in respect of an item of qualifying expenditure (whether to the same or to different persons) must not exceed the amount of that expenditure.

The writing-down period

95. (1)The writing-down period for an item of qualifying expenditure—

(a) begins at the beginning of the chargeable period in respect of which the expenditure is incurred, and

(b) is of a length determined in accordance with the Table, which shows the basic rule, and the rules which apply instead of the basic rule in the cases described in items 2 and 3.

Table

Length of writing-down periods for qualifying expenditure

Rule	Length of writing-down period
1. Basic rule.	17 years.

Whichever is shorter—

(a) 17 years;

(b) the number of years comprised within the specified period.

3. Patent rights begin one complete year or more after the commencement of the patent, and item 2

does not apply. | 17 years, less the number of complete years which, when the rights began, have elapsed since the commencement of the patent; or if 17 complete years have so elapsed, one year. |

(2) For the purpose of determining the writing-down period, expenditure incurred for the purposes of a trade by a person about to carry on the trade is treated as if incurred on the first day on which that person carries on that trade, unless that person has by then sold all the rights on which the expenditure was incurred.

(3) "The commencement of the patent", means, in relation to a patent, the date as from which the patent rights become effective.

Calculation of writing-down allowances

96. (1)The basic rule for calculating a writing-down allowance for an item of qualifying expenditure is—

where —

E is the amount of the qualifying expenditure;

C is the length of the part of the chargeable period falling within the writing-down period;

W is the length of the writing-down period.

(2) The basic rule is subject to the rules about—

(a) cessation of writing-down allowances (paragraph 97), and

(b) reduced writing-down allowances (paragraph 98).

End of writing-down allowances

97. (1)No writing-down allowance is to be made to a person for a chargeable period in respect of qualifying expenditure incurred on the purchase of patent rights if any of the following occur in that period—

(a) the patent rights come to an end without being subsequently revived,

(b) the person sells all of those rights, or so much of them as that person still owned at the beginning of the chargeable period, or

(c) the person sells part of those rights, and the net proceeds of sale for that period (so far as they consist of capital sums) are not less than the amount of the unrelieved qualifying expenditure for that period.

(2) If a writing-down allowance in respect of qualifying expenditure is prohibited by sub-paragraph (1) for a chargeable period, no writing-down allowance is to be made in respect of that expenditure for any subsequent chargeable period.

Reduced writing-down allowance

98. (1)If a person sells part of any patent rights in a chargeable period, and for that period U is greater than N, the writing-down allowance for that period is—

where—

U is the unrelieved qualifying expenditure for the chargeable period,

N is the net proceeds of any sales of the patent rights which take place in the chargeable period (so far as those proceeds consist of capital sums), and

Y is the number of complete years of the writing-down period remaining at the beginning of the chargeable period.

(2) If an amount is calculated under sub-paragraph (1) for a chargeable period, that amount is also the amount of the writing-down allowance for subsequent chargeable periods until another sale in a period for which U is greater than N causes a fresh calculation to be made under sub-paragraph (1).

(3) If a chargeable period is more or less than a year, an allowance calculated under sub-paragraph (1) or (2) is proportionately increased or reduced.

Balancing allowance on sale or expiry of patent rights

99. (1)A person is entitled to a balancing allowance for a chargeable period in respect of qualifying expenditure if there is unrelieved qualifying expenditure for that period and any of the following occur in that period—

(a) the patent rights come to an end without subsequently being revived, or

(b) the person sells all of those rights, or so much of them as that person still owned at the beginning of the period.

This is subject to sub-paragraph (2).

(2) The person is not entitled to a balancing allowance unless—

(a) a writing-down allowance has been given in respect of the expenditure, or

(b) a writing-down allowance could, but for the rights coming to an end or being sold, have been given in respect of the expenditure.

(3) The amount of the balancing allowance is—

(a) in the case of a sale, equal to the unrelieved qualifying expenditure for the chargeable period, less the net proceeds of sales taking place in the chargeable period (so far as they consist of capital sums), and

(b) in any other case, equal to the unrelieved qualifying expenditure for the chargeable period.

Balancing charges

100. (1)A balancing charge is made on a person for a chargeable period in respect of qualifying expenditure if in that period—

(a) the person sells some or all of the patent rights, and

(b) the net proceeds of sale (so far as they consist of capital sums) from the sales in that period exceed any unrelieved qualifying expenditure for that period.

The charge is calculated in accordance with sub-paragraphs (2) to (5).

(2) If there is no unrelieved qualifying expenditure, the amount of the balancing charge is equal to the net proceeds of sale (so far as they consist of capital sums).

This is subject to sub-paragraphs (4) and (5).

(3) If there is some unrelieved qualifying expenditure, the amount of the balancing charge is equal to the amount by which the net proceeds of sale (so far as they consist of capital sums) exceed the unrelieved qualifying expenditure.

This is subject to sub-paragraphs (4) and (5).

(4) The total amount of the first balancing charge must not exceed the total writing-down allowances actually given in respect of the expenditure.

(5) The total amount on which a second or further balancing charge is made must not exceed the total writing-down allowances actually made in respect of the expenditure, less the amount of any earlier charge.

Giving effect to allowances and charges

101. (1)Sub-paragraph (2) applies if—

(a) a person is entitled to a writing-down allowance or a balancing allowance or liable to a balancing charge in respect of qualifying expenditure, and

(b) the trade use condition is met.

(2) The allowance or charge is to be given effect in calculating the profits of that person's trade, by treating—

(a) the allowance as an expense of the trade, and

(b) the charge as a receipt of the trade.

(3) Sub-paragraph (4) applies if—

(a) a person is entitled to a writing-down allowance or a balancing allowance or liable to a balancing charge in respect of qualifying expenditure, and

(b) the trade use condition is not met.

(4) Sections 479 and 480 apply in relation to giving effect to the allowance or charge referred to in sub-paragraph (3) as they apply in relation to giving effect to an allowance or charge under Chapter 3 of Part 8 in respect of qualifying non-trade expenditure.

(5) For the purposes of Part 8 a person's "income from patents" includes balancing charges to which the person is liable in respect of qualifying expenditure.

Supplementary provisions

Limit on qualifying expenditure

102. Section 481 does not apply to expenditure incurred before 1st April 1986, and subsections (5)

and (6) of that section do not apply to expenditure incurred before 27th July 1989.

Part 10. Dredging allowances

Writing-down allowances

103. (1)Section 487. (2) applies with the substitution of " 50 years " for "25 years" in the case of expenditure incurred before 6th November 1962.
(2) Section 487. (3) applies with the substitution of " 2% " for "4%" in the case of expenditure incurred before 6th November 1962.

Balancing allowances

104. The reference in section 488. (1)(d) to allowances previously made in respect of the expenditure—
(a) includes any initial allowance made in respect of it under section 17 of FA 1956 or section 67 of CAA 1968, and
(b) except in relation to initial allowances, is to be construed as if section 17 of FA 1956 had always had effect (instead of having effect only for chargeable periods after the year 1955-56).

The writing-down period

105. (1)This paragraph applies where it is provided under Part 9 that writing-down allowances are to be made in respect of any expenditure during a writing-down period of any specified length.
(2) If allowances were made under paragraph 27. (2) of Schedule 14 to the Finance Act 1965—
(a) for income tax purposes, for either of the tax years 1964-65 and 1965-66, and
(b) for accounting periods of a company falling wholly or partly within either of those years,
the periods for which allowances were made are added together in calculating the writing-down period, even though (according to the calendar) the same time is counted twice.

Part 11. Contributions

Regional development grants

106. (1)Section 534. (1) applies as if a grant falling within that subsection included—
(a) a grant made under Part II of the Industrial Development Act 1982 (c. 52) on an application made before 1st April 1988;
(b) a grant made under Part I of the Industry Act 1972 (c. 63), or a grant made under Northern Ireland legislation and declared by the Treasury to correspond to a grant under that Part.
(2) Section 534. (2) does not apply if the expenditure was incurred, or the grant was paid, before 10th March 1982.

Contributions not made by public bodies and not eligible for tax relief

107. Section 536 applies with the omission of subsection (3)(b) in relation to contributions made before 27th July 1989.

Conditions for allowances

108. In section 536. (5), as it applies for the purposes of section 537. (2), paragraphs (a)(iv) and (b) do not apply in relation to contributions made before 27th July 1989.

Agricultural buildings

109. Section 538. (2)(b)(ii) applies in relation to contributions made before 6th April 1990 with the omission of "or to allocate the expenditure to a pool under Part 2".
110. Sections 368, 375 and 379 apply with the necessary modifications, instead of section 542, in relation to contributions made before 27th July 1989.

Part 12. Supplemental

Transfer of insurance company business

111. Section 560 applies with—
(a) the substitution for subsection (1) of—
"(1)This section applies if assets are transferred as part of, or in connection with, a transfer of the whole or part of the long term business of an insurance company to another company in accordance with a scheme sanctioned by a court under section 49 of the Insurance Companies Act 1982.";
 and
(b) the omission of subsection (2),
in relation to transfers sanctioned or authorised before 1st July 1994.

Election regarding sale consideration

112. (1)In relation to a transfer to which this paragraph applies, section 569. (3) applies with the substitution for paragraph (a) of—
   "(a)any of the parties is not resident in the United Kingdom at the time of the transfer and the circumstances are not at that time such that a relevant allowance or charge falls or might fall to be made to or on that party as a result of the transfer;".
(2) This paragraph applies to—
(a) a transfer before 16th March 1993;
(b) a transfer in pursuance of a contract entered into before that date; and
(c) a transfer in pursuance of a contract entered into for the purpose of securing that obligations under a contract entered into before that date are complied with.

Part 13. Other enactments

113. (1)Subsections (2) and (3) of section 578. A of ICTA (expenditure on car hire) apply with the substitution of " £8,000 " for "£12,000" in relation to expenditure incurred under a contract entered into before 11th March 1992.
(2) Subsection (4) of that section does not apply in relation to rebates made or transactions occurring before 29th April 1996.
F3114. . . . .
Amendments (Textual)

F3. Sch. 3 para. 114 repealed (6.4.2005) by Income Tax (Trading and Other Income) Act 2005 (c. 5), s. 883. (1), Sch. 3 (with Sch. 2)

115. The repeals made by CAA 1990 do not have effect in relation to capital expenditure—

(a) which was not eligible expenditure within the meaning of section 39 of FA 1976 (which brought expenditure previously not within Chapter I of Part III of FA 1971 within that Chapter but with certain exceptions), and

(b) which was incurred in a chargeable period ending before 6th April 1976.

116. (1)Sections 40. A to 40. D of F(No.2)A 1992 (films) apply with the necessary modifications in relation to—

(a) expenditure on the production of a film—

(i) completed before 21st March 2000, or

(ii) completed on or after that date, if the first day of principal photography is before that date, unless the person incurring the expenditure elects that those modifications should not apply;

(b) expenditure on the acquisition of a film, tape or disc incurred before 6th April 2000.

(2) The necessary modifications are—

(a) the substitution for section 40. A(1) of—

"(1)Expenditure which—

   (a) is incurred on the production or acquisition of a film, tape or disc, and

   (b) would, apart from this subsection, constitute capital expenditure on the provision of plant or machinery for the purposes of Part 2 of the Capital Allowances Act,

is to be regarded for the purposes of the Tax Acts as expenditure of a revenue nature unless an election under section 40. D below has effect with respect to it.";

(b) in section 40. A(2), the substitution of " the production or acquisition of a film, tape or disc " for "the [F4original master] version of a film" and of " of the film, tape or disc " for "of the [F4original master] version";

(c) in section 40. A(3), the substitution of " [F5a film,] tape or disc " for "[F6the original master] version of a film" and of " the film, tape or disc " for "the [F7original master] version" (in both places);

(d) the [F8insertion after section 40. A(4)] of—

"(5)In this section and sections 40. B to 40. D below—

   (a) any reference to a film is a reference to an original master negative of the film and its soundtrack, if any;

   (b) any reference to a tape is a reference to an original master film tape or original master audio tape; and

   (c) any reference to a disc is a reference to an original master film disc or original master audio disc;

and any reference to the acquisition of a film, tape or disc includes a a reference to the acquisition of any description of rights in a film, tape or disc.";

(e) in section 40. B(1), the substitution of " films, tapes or discs " for "[F9original master] versions of films" and of " [F10a film,] tape or disc " for "[F11the original master] version of a film";

(f) in section 40. B(4), the substitution of " film, tape or disc " for "[F12original master] version of the film" and of " film, tape or disc " for "[F12original master] version";

(g) in section 40. B(5), the substitution of " film, tape or disc " for "[F12original master] version of the film";

(h) in section 40. C(1), the substitution of " film, tape or disc " for "[F12original master] version of the film";

(i) in section 40. C(2), the substitution of " film, tape or disc " for "[F12original master] version of the film";

(j) in section 40. D(2), the substitution of " films, tapes or discs " [F13for "original master versions of films", of a " film, tape or disc " for "the original master version of a film" and of " film, tape or disc " for "original master version" (in both places);"]

(k) in section 40. D(3), the substitution of " film, tape or disc " for "[F14original master] version";

(l) in section 40. D(4), the substitution of " film, tape or disc " for "[F14original master] version of the film" (in both places);

(m) in section 40. D(6), the substitution of " a film, tape or disc " for "the [F14original master] version of a film" and of " of the film, tape or disc " for "of the [F14original master] version"; and

(n) in section 40. D(7), the substitution of "[F15a film,] tape or disc " for "[F16the original master] version of a film".

(3) An election under sub-paragraph (1)(a) is irrevocable.

(4) For the purposes of sub-paragraph (1)(a) a film is completed at the time when it is first in a form in which it can reasonably be regarded as ready for copies of it to be made and distributed for presentation to the general public.

(5) In sub-paragraph (1)(b)—

(a) "film" means an original master negative of the film and its soundtrack, if any;

(b) "tape" means an original master film tape or original master audio tape; and

(c) "disc" means an original master film disc or original master audio disc;

and the acquisition of a film, tape or disc includes the acquisition of any description of rights in a film, tape or disc.

Amendments (Textual)

F4. Words in Sch. 3 para. 116. (2)(b) substituted (2.12.2004 retrospective) by Finance Act 2005 (c. 7), Sch. 3 paras. 27. (2), 31. (3)

F5. Words in Sch. 3 para. 116. (2)(c) substituted (2.12.2004 retrospective) by Finance Act 2005 (c. 7), Sch. 3 paras. 27. (3)(a), 31. (3)

F6. Words in Sch. 3 para. 116. (2)(c) substituted (2.12.2004 retrospective) by Finance Act 2005 (c. 7), Sch. 3 paras. 27. (3)(b), 31. (3)

F7. Words in Sch. 3 para. 116. (2)(c) substituted (2.12.2004 retrospective) by Finance Act 2005 (c. 7), Sch. 3 paras. 27. (3)(c), 31. (3)

F8. Words in Sch. 3 para. 116. (2)(d) substituted (2.12.2004 retrospective) by Finance Act 2005 (c. 7), Sch. 3 paras. 27. (4), 31. (3)

F9. Words in Sch. 3 para. 116. (2)(e) substituted (2.12.2004 retrospective) by Finance Act 2005 (c. 7), Sch. 3 paras. 27. (5)(a), 31. (3)

F10. Words in Sch. 3 para. 116. (2)(e) substituted (2.12.2004 retrospective) by Finance Act 2005 (c. 7), Sch. 3 paras. 27. (5)(b), 31. (3)

F11. Words in Sch. 3 para. 116. (2)(e) substituted (2.12.2004 retrospective) by Finance Act 2005 (c. 7), Sch. 3 paras. 27. (5)(c), 31. (3)

F12. Words in Sch. 3 para. 116. (2)(f)-(i) substituted (2.12.2004 retrospective) by Finance Act 2005 (c. 7), Sch. 3 paras. 27. (6), 31. (3)

F13. Words in Sch. 3 para. 116. (2)(j) substituted (2.12.2004 retrospective) by Finance Act 2005 (c. 7), Sch. 3 paras. 27. (7), 31. (3)

F14. Words in Sch. 3 para. 116. (2)(k)-(m) substituted (2.12.2004 retrospective) by Finance Act 2005 (c. 7), Sch. 3 paras. 27. (8), 31. (3)

F15. Words in Sch. 3 para. 116. (2)(n) substituted (2.12.2004 retrospective) by Finance Act 2005 (c. 7), Sch. 3 paras. 27. (9)(a), 31. (3)

F16. Words in Sch. 3 para. 116. (2)(n) substituted (2.12.2004 retrospective) by Finance Act 2005 (c. 7), Sch. 3 paras. 27. (9)(b), 31. (3)

117. Section 40. D of F(No.2)A 1992 (election relating to tax treatment of films expenditure) applies with the omission of—

(a) paragraph (a) of subsection (1); and

(b) subsections (3) to (7),

if the film, tape or disc of the film was completed before 10th March 1992.

Schedule 4. Repeals

Section 580

Taxes Management Act 1970 (c. 9)	In section 98 in column 1 of the Table the words "Sections 23(4) and 49(4) of the Capital Allowances Act 1990".
Finance Act 1982 (c. 39)	Section 137(2), (3), (6) and (7).
London Regional Transport Act 1984 (c. 32)	In Schedule 5, paragraph 5(b) and the word "and" before it.
Income and Corporation Taxes Act 1988 (c. 1)	In sections 65A(7) and 70A(6) the words "and section 29 of the 1990 Act (provisions relating to furnished holiday accommodation)".
	In section 83A, in subsection (2), paragraph (b) and the word "or" before it and in subsection (3), paragraph (b) and the word "and" before it.
	In section 84, in subsection (1), paragraph (b) and the word "or" before it and in subsection (3), paragraph (b) and the word "and" before it.
	In section 117, in subsection (1), the words "or allowed" (in each place), "or section 141 of the 1990 Act", paragraph (b) and the word "or" before it, and, in subsection (2), in the definition of "the aggregate amount", the words "or allowed", "or section 141 of the 1990 Act", paragraph (b) and the word "or" before it.
	In section 118, in subsection (1) the words "or allowed" (in each place), "or section 145 of the 1990 Act", paragraph (b) and the word "or" before it, and, in subsection (2), in the definition of "the aggregate amount", the words "or allowed", "or section 145 of the 1990 Act", and paragraph (b) and the word "or" before it.
	In section 198(2), the words "and Part II of the 1990 Act (capital allowances in respect of machinery and plant)".
	In section 384(10), the words following paragraph (b).
	Section 393A(5) and (6).
	In section 397, in subsection (5), the definition of "basis year" and, in the definition of "chargeable period", the words from "or any basis period" to the end of the definition; and subsection (6).
	In section 411(10) the words "Without prejudice to the provisions of section 161(5) of the 1990 Act".
	Sections 434D and 434E.
	Sections 520 to 523.
Income and Corporation Taxes Act 1988 (c. 1) —cont.	Section 528(1) and (4).
	Section 530.
	In section 531, in subsection (3), the words following paragraph (b) and in subsection (7) the words "and section 530(1) and (6)".
	In section 533(1), in paragraph (b) of the definition of "income from patents", the words "520(6), 523(3)," and the definition of "the commencement of the patent".
	In section 577, in subsection (1), paragraph (c) and the word "and" before it, in subsection (7)(a) the words ", or to the use of an asset for," (in both places) and in subsection (10) the words ", or any claim for capital allowances in respect of the use of an asset for,".
	In section 834(2), the words "and also for sections 144 and 145 of the 1990 Act".
	In Schedule 19AC, paragraph 9C.
Finance Act 1989 (c. 26)	Section 121.
	In Schedule 13, paragraph 27.
Capital Allowances Act 1990 (c. 1)	The whole Act.
Finance Act 1990 (c. 29)	Sections 60, 87 and 103.
	In Schedule 7, paragraph 9.
	In Schedule 9, paragraph 5.
	In Schedule 13, paragraphs 1 to 6.
	Schedule 17.
Finance Act 1991 (c. 31)	Sections 59 to 61.
	Schedule 14.
	In Schedule 15, paragraph 28.
Disability Living Allowance and Disability Working Allowance Act 1991 (c. 21)	In Schedule 2,

paragraphs 20 and 21. |

Water (Consolidation) (Consequential Provisions) Act 1991 (c. 60) | In Schedule 1, paragraph 53. |

Social Security Contributions and Benefits Act 1992 (c. 4) | In Schedule 2, paragraph 1(b) and, in paragraph 2, the words from "subject to deduction" to the end. |

Social Security (Consequential Provisions) Act 1992 (c. 6) | In Schedule 2, paragraph 109. |

Social Security Contributions and Benefits (Northern Ireland) Act 1992 (c. 7) | In Schedule 2, paragraph 1(b) and, in paragraph 2, the words from "subject to deduction" to the end. |

Social Security (Consequential Provisions) (Northern Ireland) Act 1992 (c. 9) | In Schedule 2, paragraph 38. |

Taxation of Chargeable Gains Act 1992 (c. 12) | In section 195, in subsection (3), the words from "and "basis year"" to the end, subsection (5) and in subsection (6), paragraph (b) and the word "and" before it. |

| In section 288(1), the definition of "the 1990 Act". |

| In Schedule 10, paragraph 21. |

Finance (No. 2) Act 1992 (c. 48) | In section 43(1), the definition of "the 1990 Act". |

| Sections 67 to 71. |

| Schedule 13. |

| In Schedule 17, in paragraph 5(5), paragraph (c) and the word "and" before it. |

Finance Act 1993 (c. 34) | Sections 113 to 117. |

| Schedules 12 and 13. |

Finance Act 1994 (c. 9) | Sections 117, 118(6)(a), 119(1), 120 and 121. |

| Sections 211(1) and 212 to 213. |

| Section 214(4) to (6). |

| In Schedule 24, in paragraph 1(1), the definition of "the Allowances Act". |

| In Schedule 25, in paragraph 5(3), the definition of "the 1990 Act". |

Value Added Tax Act 1994 (c. 23) | In Schedule 14, paragraph 11. |

Finance Act 1995 (c. 4) | Sections 94 to 101. |

| In Schedule 8, paragraphs 23(1) and 24. |

| In Schedule 9, paragraph 3. |

Finance Act 1996 (c. 8) | Sections 135(3) to (5), 179 and 180. |

| In Schedule 20, paragraph 44. |

| In Schedule 21, paragraphs 26 to 34. |

| Schedule 35. |

| In Schedule 39, paragraph 1(1), (3) and (4). |

Broadcasting Act 1996 (c. 55) | In Schedule 7, in paragraph 1(1), the definition of "the Allowances Act" and in paragraph 13(1), in the heading the words "and structures". |

Planning (Consequential Provisions) (Scotland) Act 1997 (c. 11) | In Schedule 2, paragraph 45. |

Finance Act 1997 (c. 16) | Sections 66(2) and (5), 84 and 86. |

| In Schedule 12, in paragraph 11, in sub-paragraph (8) the words "or its basis period" and sub-paragraph (15). |

| Schedule 14. |

| In Schedule 15, paragraphs 3, 4, 5(3), 7, 8 and (9)(2). |

| Schedule 16. |

Finance (No. 2) Act 1997 (c. 58) | Sections 42 to 47. |

Social Security Act 1998 (c. 14) | Section 59(2). |

Petroleum Act 1998 (c. 17) | In Schedule 4, paragraph 27. |

Finance Act 1998 (c. 36) | Sections 83 to 85. |

Finance Act 1998 (c. 36)—cont. | In Schedule 5, paragraphs 40 and 47 to 61. |

| In Schedule 7, in paragraph 1 the word "528(1)(a)" and paragraph 4. |

Finance Act 1999 (c. 16) | Sections 50(2), 77 and 78. |

| In Schedule 5, paragraph 2(3). |

| In Schedule 11, paragraphs 4 to 8. |

Greater London Authority Act 1999 (c. 29) | In Schedule 33, paragraph 12(1)(a). |

Finance Act 2000 (c. 17) | Sections 70 to 72. |
| Section 75(1) to (3), (5) and (6)(b) and (c). |
| Section 76(1). |
| Section 77. |
| Section 79. |
| Sections 80 and 81. |
| Section 113. |
| In Schedule 19, paragraphs 7 to 11. |
| In Schedule 22, in paragraph 84(1) the words "or structure". |
Transport Act 2000 (c. 38) | In Schedule 26, in paragraph 1(1), the definition of "the 1990 Act". |

Open Government Licence v3.0

Printed in Great Britain
by Amazon

20865454R00194